STEALING OBEDIENCE: NARRATIVES OF AGENCY AND IDENTITY IN LATER ANGLO-SAXON ENGLAND

Narratives of monastic life in Anglo-Saxon England depict individuals as responsible agents in the assumption and performance of religious identities. To modern eyes, however, many of the 'choices' they make would actually appear to be compulsory. *Stealing Obedience* explores how a Christian notion of agent action – where freedom incurs responsibility – was a component of identity in the last hundred years of Anglo-Saxon England, and investigates where agency (in the modern sense) might be sought in these narratives.

Katherine O'Brien O'Keeffe looks at Benedictine monasticism through the writings of Ælfric, Anselm, Osbern of Canterbury, and Goscelin of Saint-Bertin, as well as liturgy, canon and civil law, chronicle, dialogue, and hagiography, to analyse the practice of obedience in the monastic context. *Stealing Obedience* brings a highly original approach to the study of Anglo-Saxon narratives of obedience in the adoption of religious identity.

(Toronto Anglo-Saxon Series)

KATHERINE O'BRIEN O'KEEFFE is a professor in the Department of English and the director of the Medieval Studies Program at the University of California, Berkeley.

KATHERINE O'BRIEN O'KEEFFE

Stealing Obedience:

Narratives of Agency and Identity in Later Anglo-Saxon England

UNIVERSITY OF TORONTO PRESS
Toronto Buffalo London

Toronto Buffalo London
www.utppublishing.com

Reprinted in paperback 2016

ISBN 978-0-8020-9707-1 (cloth)
ISBN 978-1-4875-2062-5 (paper)

Library and Archives Canada Cataloguing in Publication

O'Keeffe, Katherine O'Brien
Stealing obedience : narratives of agency and identity in later Anglo-Saxon England / Katherine O'Brien O'Keeffe.

(Toronto Anglo-Saxon series)
Includes bibliographical references and index.
ISBN 978-0-8020-9707-1 (hardcover). – ISBN 978-1-4875-2062-5 (paperback)

1. Wulfstan, of Winchester, fl. 1000. Life of St. Aethelwold. 2. English literature – Old English, ca. 450-1100 – History and criticism. 3. Obedience in literature. 4. Agent (Philosophy) in literature. 5. Identity (Philosophical concept) in literature. I. Title. II. Series: Toronto Anglo-Saxon series

PR173.O34 2012 829'.09 C2011-907912-7

University of Toronto Press gratefully acknowledges the financial assistance of the Centre for Medieval Studies, University of Toronto in the publication of this book.

University of Toronto Press acknowledges the financial assistance to its publishing program of the Canada Council for the Arts and the Ontario Arts Council, an agency of the Government of Ontario.

Canada Council for the Arts Conseil des Arts du Canada

ONTARIO ARTS COUNCIL
CONSEIL DES ARTS DE L'ONTARIO
an Ontario government agency
un organisme du gouvernement de l'Ontario

Government of Canada gouvernement du Canada Canada

To my family:
You know who you are

Contents

Acknowledgments

It is a pleasure to record my thanks to individuals and institutions that have in so many ways made possible the years of research and writing underlying this book. Work on the book was materially supported by a fellowship from the John Simon Guggenheim Memorial Foundation, which made possible sustained reading in manuscript collections in England and provided vital time for writing and thinking. A research leave at the University of Notre Dame and discretionary funds from the Timothy O'Meara Chair in English, which I was honoured to hold there, made possible necessary access in this country and abroad to major research libraries and provided support for travel and books. I am grateful to the College of Letters and Science at the University of California, Berkeley, for a research leave in fall 2009 to complete the writing of the book and a COR grant to prepare the manuscript.

I am deeply indebted to a number of libraries in the United States and in the United Kingdom for their kindness in permitting me access to their collections. In the United States: the University of California, Berkeley, Library; the Flora Lamson Hewlett Library of the Graduate Theological Union, Berkeley; the Widener Library of Harvard University, and the Theodore Hesburgh Library at the University of Notre Dame. In Cambridge, England: the University Library, the Parker Library of Corpus Christi College, and the Wren Library of Trinity College. In London, the British Library. For many years the Library of the Medieval Institute at the University of Notre Dame supported my work with its dedicated librarians and its superb collection for Medieval Studies. That support is visible in every page of this book.

During the process of constructing the arguments in the individual chapters, I was fortunate to have audiences and interlocutors at different universities to which I was invited to present my work. I should like to thank the Anglo-Saxon Studies Colloquium at Columbia University, the Harvard University Graduate Colloquium, the Dartmouth Medieval Colloquium, and the Department of Anglo-Saxon, Norse and Celtic at the University of Cambridge for inviting me to present different parts of the book in progress. The conversations generated in these colloquia and lectures allowed me to refine my thinking and strengthen my arguments. I should also like to record my thanks to the two anonymous readers at the University of Toronto Press for their helpful comments.

An earlier version of chapter 3, 'Edith's Choice,' appeared in *Latin Learning and English Lore: Studies in Anglo-Saxon Literature for Michael Lapidge*, edited by Katherine O'Brien O'Keeffe and Andy Orchard, 2 vols. (Toronto: University of Toronto Press, 2005), II: 253–74. It appears here by permission of the University of Toronto Press. An earlier version of chapter 4 appeared as 'Leaving Wilton: Gunhild and the Phantoms of Agency' in *JEGP* 106 (2007): 203–23, and appears here with their permission. I presented portions of the arguments in the Introduction and chapters 1 and 2 in my 2008 Chadwick Lecture, 'Stealing Obedience: Narratives of Agency in Later Anglo-Saxon England.' This was printed by the Department of Anglo-Saxon Norse and Celtic, University of Cambridge as H.M. Chadwick Memorial Lectures 19. For permission to publish plate 1 and the cover art I should like to acknowledge the kindness of the British Library Board. I am grateful to the Centre for Medieval Studies, University of Toronto, for financial assistance in the publication of this book.

Without the support of friends and colleagues this book could not have been written. Julia Crick, Patricia Dailey, Thomas N. Hill, Nicholas Howe, Christopher A. (Drew) Jones, Peter Jackson, Rachel Koopmans, Elizabeth C. Teviodale, and Emily V. Thornbury have read arguments, answered queries, and offered helpful suggestions. Benjamin Saltzman expertly prepared the bibliography and the index for the book. I am grateful to Vincent Gillespie, Nicholas Watson, and Robert E. O'Brien S.J. for memorable and thought-provoking conversations about topics in the book. Rosalind C. Love generously made available to me her searchable text of the *Liber confortatorius* and sped my work in following Goscelin and Eve. I am grateful to Daniel Donoghue for his kindness in arranging access to the Widener Library during my research semester in Cambridge, MA. Over the years of writing this book, Michael Lapidge has shown me such intellectual generosity, not least in making available some of his unpublished work, that I am lost for words. I am grateful for his help and advice on two continents. Miranda Wilcox has been a faithful interlocutor for the central arguments of this book, taking precious time from her own work to read mine and help me think through my premises. Graham Hammill has heard more about the book than perhaps he cared to; he has always listened and always offered good advice. Maura Nolan has been there from the beginning, as reader, prodder, and coach. I couldn't ask for a better reader or a greater inspiration. And to my husband, Paul E. Szarmach, I owe everything.

Abbreviations

Acta SS	*Acta Sanctorum*, ed. J. Bolland et al. (Antwerp and Brussels, 1643–)
AB	*Analecta Bollandiana*
ALL I	Michael Lapidge, *Anglo-Latin Literature 600–899* (London: Hambledon Press, 1996)
ALL II	Michael Lapidge, *Anglo-Latin Literature 900–1066* (London: Hambledon Press, 1993)
ANS	*Anglo-Norman Studies*
ASE	*Anglo-Saxon England*
ASPR	G.P. Krapp and E.V.K. Dobbie, eds., The Anglo-Saxon Poetic Records, 6 vols. (New York: Columbia University Press, 1931–42)
BHL	*Bibliotheca Hagiographica Latina*
BL	British Library
BT	Joseph Bosworth, *An Anglo-Saxon Dictionary*, ed. and enlarged by T. Northcote Toller (1898; Oxford: Oxford University Press, 1973)
CCCM	Corpus Christianorum, Continuatio Mediaevalis
CCM	Corpus Consuetudinum Monasticarum
CCSL	Corpus Christianorum, Series Latina
CH I	Peter Clemoes, ed., *Ælfric's Catholic Homilies: The First Series, Text*, EETS s.s. 17 (Oxford: Oxford University Press, 1997)
CH II	Malcolm Godden, ed., *Ælfric's Catholic Homilies: The Second Series, Text*, EETS s.s. 5 (Oxford: Oxford University Press, 1979)

CH III	Malcolm Godden, ed., *Ælfric's Catholic Homilies: Introduction, Commentary and Gloss*, EETS s.s. 18 (Oxford: Oxford University Press, 2000)
CPG	*Clavis Patrum Graecorum*, ed. M. Geerard, 5 vols. with suppl. (Turnhout: Brepols, 1983–98)
CSEL	Corpus Scriptorum Ecclesiasticorum Latinorum
DOE	Dictionary of Old English
EETS	Early English Text Society
Gneuss, *Handlist*	Helmut Gneuss, *Handlist of Anglo-Saxon Manuscripts: A List of Manuscripts and Manuscript Fragments Written or Owned in England up to 1100* (Tempe: ACMRS, 2001)
JEGP	*Journal of English and Germanic Philology*
JML	*Journal of Medieval Latin*
Ker, *Catalogue*	N.R. Ker, *Catalogue of Manuscripts Containing Anglo-Saxon* (Oxford, 1957; reissued Oxford: Clarendon Press, 1990)
LC	*Liber confortatorius*
Lewis and Short	Charleton T. Lewis and Charles Short, *A Latin Dictionary* (1879; Oxford: Clarendon Press, 1989)
LS	Ælfric, *Lives of Saints*
MGH	Monumenta Germaniae Historica
AA	Auctores Antiquissimi
SRG	Scriptores rerum Germanicarum
SRM	Scriptores rerum Merovingicarum
OE	Old English
OMT	Oxford Medieval Texts
PBA	*Proceedings of the British Academy*
PG	Patrologia Graeca, ed. J.P. Migne, 161 vols. (Paris, 1857–66)
PL	Patrologia Latina, ed. J.P. Migne, 221 vols. (Paris, 1844–64)
PRG	Pontificale Romano-Germanicum
RS	Rolls Series
RSB	*Regula S. Benedicti*
SC	Sources chrétiennes
TCBS	*Transactions of the Cambridge Bibliographical Society*

STEALING OBEDIENCE:
NARRATIVES OF AGENCY AND IDENTITY IN LATER ANGLO-SAXON ENGLAND

Plate 1. (c) The British Library Board. London, British Library, Arundel 155, fol. 133r.

Introduction: On Stealing Obedience

'Hanc oboedientiam mihi furatus es.'
(Wulfstan, *Vita Sancti Æthelwoldi*, cap. 14)

In an episode of Wulfstan of Winchester's *uita* of St Æthelwold, designed to show the saint's prudent action as abbot, Æthelwold is remembered in testing one Ælfstan, a member of the monastic *familia* of Abingdon. As Wulfstan, and later Ælfric of Eynsham, narrate the story, Æthelwold reveals sanctity in the double valence of lion and lamb by exacting a monastic discipline whose contours were defined by obedience at once humble and immediate. Ælfstan had been ordered by Æthelwold to see to food for the monastery's craftsmen ('praeuidere cibaria artificum monasterii').[1] Wulfstan records that Ælfstan carried out this order sedulously, cooking the meals for the workmen every day, lighting the fire, carrying water, and cleaning the pans.[2] The monk's efforts were so diligent that when the abbot visited the kitchen, he thought that Ælfstan must have had the help of a second man in his labours ('cum solatio et iuuamine alterius

1 Michael Lapidge and Michael Winterbottom, eds., *Wulfstan of Winchester, The Life of St Æthelwold* (Oxford: Clarendon Press, 1991), cap. 14, p. 26. The author is Wulfstan ('Cantor'), precentor at the Old Minster, Winchester. For what is known of the life of Wulfstan see Michael Lapidge, *The Cult of St Swithun*, Winchester Studies 4.ii (Oxford: Clarendon Press, 2003), 337–41. The account in Ælfric's *uita* of Æthelwold, cap. 10 (their Appendix A, p. 74), is almost identical.

2 '[C]ui seruitio ipse deuotissime se subdens coxit carnes cotidie et operariis sedulus ministrabat, focum accendens et aquam adportans et uasa denuo emundans.' Lapidge and Winterbottom, *Life of St Æthelwold*, cap. 14, p. 26.

ministri').[3] But Ælfstan's industry elicited not approval from Æthelwold but a reproof:

> Accidit namque quadam die, dum abbas more solito peragraret monasterium, ut aspiceret illum fratrem stantem iuxta feruens caldarium, in quo uictualia praeparabat artificibus, et intrans uidit omnia uasa mundissima ac pauimentum scopatum; dixitque ad eum hilari uultu: 'O mi frater Ælfstane, hanc oboedientiam mihi furatus es, quam me ignorante exerces. Sed si talis miles Christi es qualem te ostendis, mitte manum tuam in bullientem aquam et unum frustum de imis mihi impiger adtrahe.'[4]
>
> [It happened on a certain day when the abbot was walking through the monastery, as was his custom, that he saw that brother standing near a boiling cauldron, in which he was preparing food for the craftsmen, and entering he saw all the kitchen implements perfectly clean and the floor swept; and he said to him with a cheerful face: My brother Ælfstan, you have stolen this obedience from me, in which you employ yourself without my knowledge. But if you are such a soldier of Christ as you show yourself to be, put your hand into the boiling water and quick, take out a morsel for me from the bottom.][5]

Immediately ('statim sine mora'), Ælfstan plunges his hand into the boiling cauldron. Not feeling the heat and completely unharmed, he retrieves the morsel for Æthelwold. Later in his life, Wulfstan reports, Ælfstan was ordained an abbot and went on to become bishop of Ramsbury.[6]

If Ælfstan was, as the chapter describes him, a man of great obedience ('magnae oboedientiae uir'), what in his behaviour provoked Æthelwold to test that virtue so dramatically by ordering him to plunge his hand into the boiling cauldron?[7] Throughout his *uita* of St Æthelwold, Wulfstan took pains to demonstrate how Æthelwold's famous severity to malefactors was balanced by his gentle treatment of the humble and obedient ('humilibus uero et oboedientibus'), that is, those practising the cardinal virtues of Benedictine monasticism.[8] Yet for all Wulfstan's efforts to show

---

3 Ibid.

4 Lapidge and Winterbottom, *Life of St Æthelwold*, cap. 14, pp. 26–8.

5 All translations are my own, unless otherwise indicated.

6 This Ælfstan later became abbot of the Old Minster (after 964) and then bishop of Ramsbury. See Lapidge, *The Cult of St Swithun*, 284–5, n. 158.

7 Lapidge and Winterbottom, *Life of St Æthelwold*, cap. 14, pp. 26–8.

8 Ibid., cap. 28, p. 44.

that Æthelwold's exactions were not from cruelty but love, what stands out in his account is the abbot's 'zelus rectitudinis' [zeal for right], which pressed him to impose the yoke of discipline on the monks in his charge.[9] However benign the abbot may have been to the humble and the obedient, the narrative of Æthelwold's testing of Ælfstan gives a striking account of the ways monastic obedience ordered relations between an abbot and his subject and mediated the exercise of the subject's will.

While this episode of the *uita* seeks to achieve its end by treating obedience as an untroubled category of monastic behaviour – that is, as the given by which Æthelwold's character as abbot is illustrated – the narrative offers a number of puzzles. Which inmate of Abingdon is the hero of this account – the *pastor* charged with overseeing the salvation of his subject, or the subject who proves himself a man of great obedience? Phrasing the question in this way, as it suggests a struggle or even a competition between the two men, is only partially helpful. Clearly, narrative convention in a *uita* points to the saint as the hero of the account. But the preoccupation of the narrative is actually the relation between the two men, and if there is a struggle (or a competition) between them, that tension can only take on meaning in terms of the ideal relation between abbot and subject to which the *uita* appeals. And the key to the relation between them in the narrative is obedience, the pre-eminent virtue of Benedictine monasticism. But the narrative's appeal to obedience produces further puzzles: given Æthelwold's initial order (to see to food for the monastery's craftsmen), Ælfstan's strenuous efforts in the kitchen would appear to be an act of obedience. Yet Æthelwold reacts severely to Ælfstan's labours. And what of Æthelwold's second command: how does his order that Ælfstan plunge his hand into boiling liquid (an act redolent of judicial ordeal) address the proper relation between the two men?

Æthelwold's accusation, 'you have stolen this obedience from me,' charges that Ælfstan has somehow taken for himself the abbot's function.[10]

9 Ibid. Alan Thacker, 'Æthelwold and Abingdon,' in *Bishop Æthelwold: His Career and Influence*, ed. Barbara Yorke (Woodbridge: The Boydell Press, 1988), 43–64 at 56, observe 'the story emphasises rigour and discipline and is very unlike the stories told of, say, Cuthbert.'

10 Michel Foucault, 'About the Beginning of the Hermeneutics of the Self,' in *Religion and Culture by Michel Foucault*, ed. Jeremy R. Carrette (Manchester: Manchester University Press, 1999), 158–81 at 174 observes: 'Obedience in the monastic institutions must bear on all the aspects of life; there is an adage, very well known in the monastic literature, which says, "everything that one does not do on order of one's director, or everything that one does without his permission, constitutes a theft."' Unfortunately, he provides

In naming Ælfstan's activity 'theft,' his accusation identifies it as a transgression whose result was the undoing of monastic identity by putting in doubt the very relation between abbot and monk. It suggests that the subject of obedience, in taking the abbot's function, makes himself master to himself. In short, Æthelwold's charge of theft accuses Ælfstan not simply of being disobedient, but of something more consequential – undoing himself by exercising improper agent action.

Against the backdrop of the renewal of Benedictine monasticism, this episode in the life of one of its great reformers asks attention to that virtue – obedience – through which Benedictine monastic life was identified and structured. But it also asks attention – perhaps despite itself – to the expression of agency that elicited so dramatic a reaction from Æthelwold. In what follows, I argue that attention to narratives of monastic obedience in both the polish of their surfaces and the fractures those surfaces

---

no documentation. Just such a sentiment is found in Basil's *Sermo asceticus et exhortatio de renuntiantione saeculi*, cap. 4 (PG 31.634 = *CPG* 2889): 'Si igitur Dei auxilio repereris (prorsus autem si quaeras, reperies) bonorum operum doctorem, observa apud teipsum, ut nihil praeter ejus sententiam peragas. Quidquid enim sine ipso efficitur, furtum est et sacrilegium, quod mortem infert, non utilitatem, tametsi tibi videtur esse bonum. Etenim si bonum est, cur fit clanculum, non in aperto? Interroga animum tuum, te ad praedandum industrie provocantem: siquidem dum bonis non obtemperas, te ad sinistras actiones instruit.' However, the Latin translation offered in the PG is the work of a much later translator. Closer to Wulfstan's time, in an eighth-century commentary on the *RSB*, Hildemar of Civate connects monastic disobedience and theft: '*Non facere furtum.* Numquid ille solummodo facit furtum, qui alienam rem absconse tollit? Verum etiam ille furtum facit, qui rem sibi ab abbate delegatam, i.e. deputatam vel datam aliis sine licentia tribuit, nec non etiam ille furtum facit, qui se subtrahit de servitio Dei, quantum ad minora peccata attinet; aut etiam ille furtum facit, qui aliis malum exemplum praebet aut hortatur agere, quantum similiter ad minora peccata attinet, v[erbi] gr[atia] si hora tacendi loqueris, aut hora legendi aut aliquid agendi te subtrahis, furtum agis. Quod si aliis istud exemplum praebes, furtum facis, vel si hortaris illos, istud agere, pejus furtum facis.' Rupert Mittermüller, ed., *Expositio Regulae ab Hildemaro Tradita*, vol. 3 of *Vita et Regula SS. P. Benedicti* (Regensburg, 1880), 142–3 [Thou shalt not steal. Does he alone commit theft, who secretly takes another's property? But certainly, with respect to lesser sins, he also commits theft who transfers to others without permission something assigned (that is, allotted or given) to him by the abbot, and he also commits theft who withdraws himself from God's service; or he even commits theft, who offers a bad example to others or urges them to act badly, similarly with respect to lesser sins. For example, if you speak during the time of silence or the time of reading or you withdraw yourself from doing anything, you commit theft. But if you offer that bad example to others you commit theft, or if you urge others to do that, you commit a worse theft.] On Hildemar's commentary (hereafter cited as Hildemar, *Expositio*) see below, pp. 37–42. Wulfstan's narrative is unique in identifying theft as taking the abbot's function.

conceal shows us the intimate interconnection between monastic identity and a construction of agency markedly different from our own. The interconnection between monastic identity and the expression of agency that drives it lies in the discipline of obedience. Such obedience is particular and textually constructed – by citation and variation on the sayings of the desert fathers, in the development of coenobitic monastic Rules by Pachomius and Basil of Caesaria, through the transmission (and attendant development) of coenobitic monasticism by Cassian, and in its subsequent articulations in the Rule of the Master and the *RSB*. My goal here is not a genealogy of obedience in Western monasticism – the source work for such a pursuit has been ably produced by Albert de Vogüé and others.[11] Rather, in what follows I attend to the discourse of monastic obedience, particularly the paradox underlying the monastic configuration of obedience – as sacrifice and as freedom – as well as in its intimate connection to choice. If obedience was understood as the sacrifice of personal freedom (a sacrifice understood to lead to spiritual freedom), obedience was also understood as the product of choice. While sacrificial obedience reduced a monk's or nun's freedom of action, so that every action of every day was to be undertaken at the command of another, that reduction, even if to a vanishingly small degree, still required the exercise of choice to obey. It is here that we find a point of most interesting complexity. The relation of subject to abbot (or abbess) is a relation of complete obedience, modelled on the perfect obedience of Christ the Son to God the Father. It is the central virtue (along with humility) of monasticism designed as a corrective to the central failing of humankind through Adam and Eve in the

11 For an overview of early Western monastic rules, see Adalbert de Vogüé, ed., *Les règles monastiques anciennes 400–700*, Typologie des sources du Moyen Âge occidental 46 (Turnhout: Brepols, 1985). For Benedict's use of the Rule of the Master, see Adalbert de Vogüé and Jean Neufville, eds., *La règle de Saint Benoît*, 6 vols., Sources chrétiennes 181–6 (Paris: Éditions du Cerf, 1971–7), IV: 181–6. For a review of obedience in scripture, in early religious communities, and in late antique and early medieval writers see Adalbert de Vogüé, 'Obéissance et autorité dans le monachisme ancien jusqu'á Saint Benoît,' in *'Imaginer la théologie catholique,' permanence et transformations de la foi en attendant Jésus-Christ: Mélanges offerts à Ghislain Lafont*, ed. Jeremy Driscoll (Rome: Centro Studi S. Anselmo, 2000), 565–600. On obedience and the development of a religious vow see Catherine Capelle, *Le voeu d'obéissance des origines au XIIe siècle: Étude juridique*. Bibliothèque d'histoire du droit et droit romain 2 (Paris: R. Pichon et R. Durand-Auzias, 1959). For an overview of obedience in the Christian East see Tomáš Špidlík, S.J., *The Spirituality of the Christian East: A Systematic Handbook*, trans. Anthony P. Gythiel (Kalamazoo, MI: Cistercian Publications, 1986).

primal disobedience that produced its fallen, sinful nature. As the primary duty of humankind is obedience to the will of God, the monk's (or nun's) primary duty is obedience to the abbot (or abbess) through whom they show obedience to God. But while God sees the hearts of all and discerns dispositions and intentions, men and women must interpret God's will (and their superiors' will) before exercising their own wills in choice. It is in the space of that interpretation that agency may appear.

The reformed Benedictine monastic community, structured as 'schola' as well as 'familia' by the Rule governing it, remade the identity of all who lived within its walls. As a 'familia' distinct from blood kin, such a community refigured its members as spiritual fathers and brothers or mothers and sisters, and it set them apart as both servants and soldiers of Christ. As 'schola' it aspired to a particular textual identity, played out ritually and somatically in relation to a written Rule and scripted liturgical performance. If obedience to the will of God is a general marker of Christian identity, the members of a Benedictine community pursued an ideal and a special case of such obedience. The *RSB*, cap. 5.6 embraced Christ's words commissioning the seventy-two disciples in Luke 10:16: 'Qui vos audit, me audit' ['He that heareth you, heareth me'], using it to model the relation of disciple to master on the Gospel's relation of disciple to God.[12] Wholehearted obedience to a monastic superior was precisely obedience given to God (*RSB* 5.15). Among those following the Rule, agent action as such was understood, narrowly, as an iteration of his or her original commitment to obey, as we will see below. However narrow the dimensions of agent action exercised in doing the will of another, the agency it presupposed comes into existence in a space of uncertainty where an agent desiring to obey interprets the command of his or her superior. And the negotiation of that command (be it in the form of God's will or that of an abbot or abbess) requires subjects of obedience to draw on their knowledge of monastic structures – the Rule as memorized and read aloud, the observed behaviours of brothers or sisters, texts read or heard, examples remembered, scriptures internalized – for their performance. It is in this uncertain space of interpretation and through these means that agency may make its appearance. But for Æthelwold as for us, the difficulty is in knowing whether we have seen it. The sections that follow address the terms in which we can approach these problems.

12 Rudolf Hanslik, ed., *Benedicti Regula*, 2nd rev. ed., CSEL 75 (Vienna: Hoelder-Pichler-Tempsky, 1977), 38. Unless otherwise indicated, I cite the Vulgate text of the Bible and provide the Douay-Rheims translation.

Agency

Agency is as slippery a concept as it is ubiquitous, and the difficulty in defining it is compounded by the multiple discourses within which the word is used. In its broadest formulation, agency is the capacity for responsible individual action. But the structure within which such responsibility might be possible, the identification of who is an agent or whether a collective might have agency, the discrete behaviours that might exhibit agency, or the very possibility of agency *tout court* are all matters of contemporary debate and all yield different definitions of the term.[13] Given the definitional latitude of the term and the difficulty of determining whether for any given actor agency can be discerned in a particular action, 'agency' is often levelled to a common denominator: an agent is a human actor exhibiting some degree of autonomy. Or agency is inferred to be at work in individual actions from a liberatory political commitment. Such approaches have much merit in giving visibility to non-traditional actors but either beg the question of agency as such or appear, at least, to identify the agent actions studied with our own.

In analytic philosophy, an agent is a particular kind of actor capable of free, deliberated, intentional action. Agent action is such an action within this discourse. The problem of agent action in analytic philosophy centres around determinism and the possibility of free action: given a deterministic universe, is agency as defined above possible? That is, are what appear to be choices for individuals actually free?[14] The two main approaches to this question – compatibilism and incompatibilism – are

13 For example, when Mary Swan, 'Identity and Ideology in Ælfric's Prefaces,' in *A Companion to Ælfric*, ed. Hugh Magennis and Mary Swan (Leiden: Brill, 2009), 249–69 at 253 and 255, refers to Ælfric 'foreground[ing] his agency,' the word must refer to his ability or power. Clare A. Lees and Gillian R. Overing, *Double Agents: Women and Clerical Culture in Anglo-Saxon England* (Philadelphia: University of Pennsylvania Press, 2001), in 'trac[ing] the activities of the female agent' attributed even if 'we occasionally hallucinate' (2), would seem to resolve agency into simple action. Andrew Rabin, 'Female Advocacy and Royal Protection in Tenth-Century England: The Legal Career of Queen Ælfthryth,' *Speculum* 84.2 (2009): 261–88, usefully investigates the queen's limited legal agency by examining her '"room for manoeuvre"' (at 263). In this he follows Janet Nelson in seeing 'female agency' as less a measure of power than as 'room for manoeuvre in shaping the future for herself.' See Janet Nelson, 'The Wary Widow' in *Property and Power in the Early Middle Ages*, ed. Wendy Davies and Paul Fouracre (Cambridge: Cambridge University Press, 1995), 82–113 at 83 and 94.

14 For an overview of the current major philosophical arguments on free will, see Robert Kane, *A Contemporary Introduction to Free Will* (Oxford: Oxford University Press, 2005).

mutually exclusive and divide on the truth or falsity of determinism and whether and under what circumstances agency could be compatible with determinism.[15] Incompatibilism itself divides on the issue of determinism: those accepting determinism and arguing against the existence of free will, and those who reject determinism in order to argue for free will. The latter are called libertarians. The critical ideas in such philosophical analyses of agency are the operations of human will, choice, reason, deliberation, and intention. Within this language of argument, contemporary philosophy's strategies of analysing agency have been usefully applied to various posings of the question of determinism (in the form of divine predestination and omniscience) and free will in the Middle Ages, notwithstanding the predominantly theological approach to the problem by early medieval thinkers. Thus Eleonore Stump has argued strongly that Augustine was a 'modified' libertarian in at least some of his positions on free will, although others have judged him a compatibilist.[16] And Katherin Rogers has claimed Anselm for full libertarianism.[17] Because its terms of art fit comfortably with the language of early medieval engagement with questions of

---

15 For a clear, schematic overview of the positions on the issue of free will, see Galen Strawson, 'Free Will,' in *Routledge Encyclopedia of Philosophy*, ed. E. Craig (London: Routledge, 1998), http://www.rep.routledge.com/article/V014 (accessed 9 November 2009). For a defence of compatibilism, see Daniel C. Dennett, *Elbow Room: The Varieties of Free Will Worth Wanting* (Oxford: Clarendon Press, 1984). For a libertarian argument see Robert Kane, *The Significance of Free Will* (New York: Oxford University Press, 1999). For a range of approaches see Gary Watson, ed., *Free Will*, 2nd ed. (Oxford: Oxford University Press, 2003). On Frankfurt-style examples see David Widerker and Michael McKenna, eds., *Moral Responsibility and Alternative Possibilities: Essays on the Importance of Alternative Possibilities* (Burlington, VT: Ashgate, 2003).

16 Eleonore Stump, 'Augustine on Free Will,' in *The Cambridge Companion to Augustine*, ed. Eleonore Stump and Norman Kretzmann (Cambridge: Cambridge University Press, 2001), 124–47 at 125. Stump modifies the usual position that there are simply compatibilism and libertarianism by arguing that there is a middle position, which she calls 'modified libertarianism,' that judges an agent to be morally responsible for an act even if he could not have done otherwise. Given this middle position, she argues Augustine's view of free will was a 'modified' libertarianism. For the argument that Augustine was a compatibilist see Gerard O'Daly, 'Predestination and Freedom in Augustine's Ethics,' in Godfrey Vesey, ed., *The Philosophy in Christianity*, Royal Institute of Philosophy Lecture Series 25 (Cambridge: Cambridge University Press, 1989), 85–97 at 92–3, 96. For an attempt to navigate between compatibilism and libertarianism see James Wetzel, 'The Recovery of Free Agency in the Theology of St Augustine,' *Harvard Theological Review* 80 (1987): 101–25 at 111.

17 Katherin Rogers, *Anselm on Freedom* (Oxford: Oxford University Press, 2008), esp. 99–101. At 4–5 (and throughout) she considers Augustine a compatibilist.

will, choice, and intention, I will on occasion borrow the language of analytic philosophy to clarify some ways in which 'will' and 'intention' might have been imagined to operate in particular monastic settings or to disambiguate strands of argument in a particular narrative. However, because analytic philosophy is preoccupied with trans-historical questions – and free will is fundamentally a subject of metaphysics – my engagement with agency in this book looks elsewhere for its strategies of analysis.[18] Because this book is concerned with narratives about religious life in a specific cultural setting – the reformed Benedictine communities of later Anglo-Saxon England – it does not pursue the linked metaphysical questions 'Does free will exist?' and 'If so, under what circumstances?' In fact, although the word 'will' appears rather freely in the book (and necessarily, as a key, if vexed, term in all the religious narratives of the book), I do not examine 'free will' as such but rather narratives in which historical notions of and claims for 'free will' play a central role. The critical concept I use to perform that analysis is 'agency' as it is understood in cultural critique. As I will discuss below, to consider 'agency' in this arena is to consider the imbrications of individuals in their historical, cultural circumstances.

From the perspective of cultural critique, in contradistinction to that of analytic philosophy, the question of agency centres on the relation of individual to structure, that is, to those forces (e.g., language, culture, ideology) that shape individuals and circumscribe not simply action but the very possibility of thought. As Sherry Ortner has phrased it: 'Agency is not some natural or originary will; it takes shape as specific desires and intentions within a matrix of subjectivity – of (culturally constituted) feelings, thoughts, and meanings.'[19] Interest in agency from the perspective of cultural studies developed in reaction to the extremes of structuralism, which construed subjects as nodal points within numerous planes of discourse through which they were 'spoken' by their language and culture.[20] In explicitly political terms, such 'speaking' was a function of the pervasive reach of ideology. The *locus classicus* for the hidden and all-encompassing operation of ideology is Althusser's formulation of 'freedom' within

18 Kane, *A Contemporary Introduction to Free Will*, 123.

19 Sherry B. Ortner, 'Subjectivity and Cultural Critique,' *Anthropological Theory* 5.1 (2005): 31–52 at 34.

20 On the 'overplaying' of structure in structuralism and post-structuralism, see Anthony Appiah, 'Tolerable Falsehoods: Agency and the Interests of Theory,' in *Consequences of Theory*, ed. Jonathan Arac and Barbara Johnson, Selected Papers from the English Institute, 1987–88, n.s., 14 (Baltimore: Johns Hopkins University Press, 1991), 63–90 at 70.

subjectivity (significantly articulated within his analysis of the 'Christian Religious Ideology': 'the individual *is interpellated as a (free) subject in order that he shall submit freely to the commandments of the Subject* [viz. God], *i.e. in order that he shall (freely) accept his subjection*, i.e. in order that he shall make the gestures and actions of his subjection "all by himself"' (italics in original).[21]

The pressing question of agency in *Stealing Obedience* is not its possibility, which in current debate (outside of philosophical determinism) is generally conceded.[22] Rather, the question I pursue is double-edged: first, in historical terms, how do the texts commemorating the religious men, women, and children who are the subjects of this book represent what was, for their culture, agent action? And second, in terms of cultural critique, how can we discern in these representations the operation of what *we* might adjudge agency? In the framing of these questions, I will use two terms, 'agent action' and 'agency,' to disambiguate the two interests. 'Agent action,' a label I adapt from analytic philosophy, is the term I will use when exploring and referring to the nexus of (free) will and obedience in the Christian master narrative of choice and responsibility inherited by the early Middle Ages. I do so because of the centrality of 'will' and 'intention' to medieval analyses of responsible human action. I will reserve 'agency' as the term of art when asking a different kind of question emerging not from philosophy but from cultural critique: can we discern in these narratives of religious life an action which appears to show agency by our own, contemporary definition? Asking such a question demands attention severally to narrative (in its textualization of culture), identity (as a structure that forms the individual and acts as an interface between

21 Louis Althusser, 'Ideology and Ideological State Apparatuses' in his *Lenin and Philosophy and Other Essays*, trans. Ben Brewster, with an introduction by Frederic Jameson (New York: Monthly Review Press, 2001), 85–126 at 123. In a memorable formulation, Anthony Giddens, *Central Problems in Social Theory* (Berkeley: University of California Press, 1979), 52, calls the Althusserian subject a 'structural dope.'

22 See Paul Smith, *Discerning the Subject* (Minneapolis: University of Minnesota Press, 1988), xxxv, who locates the possibility of agency in terms of contradiction and resistance: 'by virtue of the contradictions and disturbances in and among subject-positions, the possibility (indeed, the actuality) of resistance to ideological pressure is allowed for (even though that resistance too must be produced in an ideological context).' Judith Butler, *The Psychic Life of Power: Theories in Subjection* (Stanford: Stanford University Press, 1997), argues the possibility of agency because the forces of ideology are not monolithic: 'agency is the assumption of a purpose *unintended* by power' (15; italics in original).

culture and self), and the individual man or woman (as represented in specific genres of texts).

In pursuing the question of agency in the context of identity, I have found helpful the approach of Dorothy Holland and colleagues in their study of identity and human agency in attending to 'processes whereby human collectives and individuals often move themselves – led by hope, desperation, or even playfulness, but certainly by no rational plan – from one set of socially and culturally formed subjectivities to another.'[23] For Holland and colleagues, human behaviour is always mediated by identity, and the construction of identities is a process of formation and re-formation over a lifetime.[24] What they call the 'space of authoring' (in homage to Bakhtin) is a practice of identity formation where 'authorship' is an orchestration of social discourses, at times virtually rote and at other times improvised. 'Human agency comes through this art of improvisation … The histories that give shape to spaces of authoring, besides being both personal and public, are thus also compulsory and liberatory, in degrees that vary greatly.'[25] Agency is not opposed to cultural structure, but is enabled by it. To exercise agency requires actors to have knowledge of the cultural forms within which they are enmeshed and some ability to affect them.[26] But the temporal distance between our moment and the last century of Anglo-Saxon England and the nature of the materials available to us mean that even when we are dealing with historical actors (as Dunstan, or Gunhild, or Eve of Wilton), we are left only with representations of their actions in narratives that pursue their own interests. Thus, the challenge for the present study is precisely to discern the improvisation that produces and indexes human agency (in our terms): charting the discursive structures that emplot actions, the texts that articulate structure for particular identities, and the narrative moments of contradiction and surprise that point us to the orchestration of agency. Thus 'agent action' as a descriptor in this book points to the metaphysics of free will

23 Dorothy Holland, William Lachicotte Jr, Debra Skinner, and Carole Cain, *Identity and Agency in Cultural Worlds* (Cambridge, MA: Harvard University Press, 1998), 6–7.

24 Ibid., 270.

25 Ibid., 272.

26 See William H. Sewell, Jr, *Logics of History: Social Theory and Social Transformation* (Chicago: University of Chicago Press, 2005), 143: 'To be an agent means to be capable of exerting some degree of control over the social relations in which one is enmeshed, which in turn implies the ability to transform those social relations in some degree … [A]gents are empowered to act with and against others by structures.'

structuring early medieval beliefs, and 'agency' points, by contrast, to the pragmatics underlying questions about individual improvisation within cultural structures in our own moment.

To ask the question of agency in the historical circumstances I am framing, however, is not to inquire into human liberation, to celebrate freedom, or individuality, or any of the ideas bequeathed to us by Enlightenment notions of humanity. In this study of agency in Anglo-Saxon England I have wanted to avoid too easily finding contemporary ideas of agency (as empowerment, individuality, free choice, resistance) in the texts available to us for analysis.[27] And so I have focused on what might otherwise appear to be a counter-intuitive set of writings in Latin and Old English to ground this investigation: writings from the last century of Anglo-Saxon England associated with the Benedictine Reform and its aftermath. But to read these texts is to read accounts of an explicit form of self-fashioning: inward looking, yet institutionally framed; self-conscious yet denying the self; using the will to deny the will. These are texts that locate freedom in obedience, plot choice as a function of knowledge (rather than potency), and remake identity in terms of texts rather than blood. The monastic identity studied in this book is a function of coenobitic community, whose set of practices (somatic practices of food, sleep, postures, and time; ritual practices of prayer, fasts, penitence, and celebration; textual practices of commemoration, identification, study, 'publication,' and replication of the community) were designed to 'make' the monk or nun in a specific, textualized identity, and in so doing free him or her from the present world to ensure a place in the world to come. They are texts that focus on living in community, making scripture (in the ways interpreted by the larger Benedictine community) the roadmap of life. The central tenet of that life models the critical relation in a Benedictine community as a relation between abbot and monk which self-consciously replicates the one between man and God. That relation makes obedience the central virtue of Benedictine life as obedience is the central, Pauline, virtue of Christian life. But that obedience, understood as an unending set of behavioural choices, presupposes that each choice is unconstrained by external necessity. As we will see, obedience thus works doubly: in the language of the texts we will examine, it deliberately aims to crush the will (or put in a more positive

27 See Talal Asad, *Formations of the Secular: Christianity, Islam, Modernity* (Stanford, CA: Stanford University Press, 2003), 71, who argues against the notion that the 'agent as "active subject" has both the desire to oppose power and the responsibility to become more powerful so that disempowerment – suffering – can be overcome.'

light structures sacrifice of the will) in following the will of another (the abbot or abbess) and in so doing to free individuals from the more dangerous parts of their own possibilities; and it also insists on locating that freedom precisely in the sacrifice that was obedience. What follows is an inquiry about a world long gone and about languages of inquiry – Latin and Old English – whose analytical terms, words like 'freedom,' 'will,' and 'choice,' sound comfortably familiar but on examination stake out a territory that is strange and at times contradictory.

Insofar as the coenobitic relation of monk and abbot models the larger Christian relation between the individual and God, studying what texts from the Reform movement and after have to say about monastic life and the work of obedience tells us a great deal about the larger culture and its expectations. To pose the question of agency in these texts is to study the circumstances under which monks and nuns were understood to be responsible, for their language of freedom and choice is, ultimately, a language about circumstances under which people are held morally responsible. Framing the question in this way shows how an important strand of this book is a story of agent action imposed as a cultural demand, that is, as a capacity installed in people in order to exact responsibility. The circumstances in which we find these demands – oblated children whose 'choice' of religious life was made by others, women whose families had conveyed them to the church, men commanded to take holy orders by a king – show us 'choice' driven by the demands of social identity and the expectations of obedience.

The Language of Will and Choice

An axial figure in this study is Ælfric of Eynsham, whose extensive writings in the two languages of culture in Anglo-Saxon England draw on a range of patristic writings, either directly or indirectly. For Ælfric, as an inheritor of Augustinian thought, the world is a space of moral actions in which the will and its choices, understood to be free, are evaluated for what they reveal about a person's interior disposition. Although Ælfric draws on a superstructure of free will and its juxtaposition with grace (within the larger questions of God's omniscience and predestination) to explain both the operation of choice and the moral responsibility of one who chooses, Ælfric is considerably more interested in the pragmatics of choice than in the metaphysics of free will. I suggest that this interest is primarily pragmatic, because it is driven by the greater accessibility of the outcomes of choice to external judgment.

The discourse of human freedom associated with Augustine, a freedom underpinning moral responsibility, focused on the will as the faculty by which human beings made choices.[28] This interest in the will provided a rich legacy to medieval theology, but by the twelfth century interest shifted from free will (*libera uoluntas*) as such to the question of free choice (*liberum arbitrium*).[29] *Liberum arbitrium* or *libertas arbitrii* thus forms the centrepiece of Anselm's arguments for responsible human action in a set of treatises in which he explores the essential freedom of human choice.[30] Although Ælfric draws on a wide range of Augustinian texts (often indirectly), there is a substantial set of his writings that distinguishes sharply – linguistically and conceptually – between 'will' and 'choice.' Ælfric's arguments on choice (*cyre*) though lacking the philosophical rigour that would later inform Anselm's treatises, nonetheless mark a distance between Ælfric and the Augustinian theology he inherited. As we will see, Ælfric's insistence on human freedom of choice focuses our attention on the pragmatics of judging moral behaviour from a pastoral concern that attends to choice as the instrument of action. Assessing the operation of will in the Augustinian terminology Ælfric inherited is considerably less straightforward. 'Choice,' that part of the Augustinian formula *liberum uoluntatis arbitrium* specifically labelled 'free' (or as John Rist would term it 'morally responsible'), can be pointed to and labelled 'good' or 'bad.' 'Choice' with its implication of options and alternatives (although there may be none) becomes the mechanism by which moral responsibility is assigned. The will as disposition may be good or bad, but choice, the endpoint of any process of the will, is the action in the world. It is through the theological assertion that choice exists and that choice is free that men and women are deemed agents in Anglo-Saxon England. As we will see in subsequent chapters, more often than not, that *liberum arbitrium*, the *agen cyre* attributed to (and demanded of) men and women, points less to agency than to its phantoms.

Augustine's concept of freedom of the will (what Gerard O'Daly has memorably called 'a glorious and influential failure') profoundly affected

28 I consider this topic in detail at pp. 17–26, below.

29 Giles Constable, 'Liberty and Free Choice in Monastic Thought and Life, Especially in the Eleventh and Twelfth Centuries,' in his *Monks, Hermits and Crusaders in Medieval Europe* (London: Variorum Reprints, 1988), chap. IV, pp. 99–118 at 103.

30 Sandra Visser and Thomas Williams, 'Anselm's Account of Freedom,' in *The Cambridge Companion to Anselm*, ed. Brian Davies and Brian Leftow (Cambridge: Cambridge University Press, 2004), 179–203.

the development of the Christian theology of individual responsibility.[31] The influence of his great volume of writings is shown by their dissemination throughout the Middle Ages, although the texts themselves need not have been known for their ideas to have been at work. Aaron Kleist, in his study of grace and free will in Anglo-Saxon England, points out that Augustine's major writings on free will were themselves unknown to Bede, Alfred, and Ælfric, though Augustine's theology of free will was pervasive.[32] Because Augustine's views developed over his lifetime from the early arguments in *De libero arbitrio* (388X95), through the polemics in response to Pelagius and Pelagians, to the late *De correptione et gratia* (426), his position on key terms changed, and his language itself presents considerable difficulty for those who would interpret his terms of art.[33] The expression 'liberum uoluntatis arbitrium' fully translated as 'free choice of the will' is often, at least in English, reduced to 'free will,' and this shorthand can give rise to further interpretative difficulties, since the words 'liber' and 'uoluntas' do not translate unproblematically. In his classic study of Augustine's views of predestination and free will, John Rist pointed out that 'uoluntas' does not refer to 'a part of the psyche.' Rather, Augustine understood 'uoluntas' to be 'the human *psyche* in its role as a moral agent. As in Seneca, the word *uoluntas* is in Augustine almost to be translated as "moral self" or "moral personality"' (emphasis in original).[34] Such an understanding, collapsing the will with the person, underlies the Augustinian characterization of the will (as person) as either good or bad. To make matters more complex, Augustine himself used 'uoluntas' in several different senses. It could mean, in different circumstances, the faculty

---

31 O'Daly, 'Predestination and Freedom in Augustine's Ethics,' 97.

32 Aaron Kleist, *Striving with Grace: Views of Free Will in Anglo-Saxon England* (Toronto: University of Toronto Press, 2008), 31. Kleist's larger study traces the various approaches to free will as inflected by Bede and Gregory and realized in the range of Latin and vernacular writings in Anglo-Saxon England. Michael Lapidge, *The Anglo-Saxon Library* (Oxford: Oxford University Press, 2006), 282–91, shows that surviving manuscripts of Augustine's major works on predestination and free will (*De gratia et libero arbitrio, De correptione et gratia, De praedestinatione sanctorum*, and *De dono perseuerantiae*) are post-Conquest, provenanced to St Augustine's, Canterbury and Salisbury. There are two surviving manuscripts of the early *De libero arbitrio* (Oxford, Trinity College 4 [s. x/xi] and Salisbury, Cathedral Library 106 [s. xi^{ex}]).

33 I follow the chronology in John M. Rist, *Augustine: Ancient Thought Baptized* (Cambridge: Cambridge University Press, 1994), xvii–xviii.

34 John M. Rist, 'Augustine on Free Will and Predestination,' *Journal of Theological Studies*, n.s., 20.2 (1969): 420–47 at 421.

of will, an act of that faculty (i.e., choice), an intention, or a person's predominant disposition.[35]

In his treatment of freedom of will and choice, Anselm, himself a careful scholar of Augustine, takes care to distinguish the various ways in which 'uoluntas' is used: 'Voluntas utique dici videtur aequivoce tripliciter. Aliud est enim instrumentum volendi, aliud affectio instrumenti, aliud usus eiusdem instrumenti'[36] [Doubtless, 'uoluntas' seems to be used equivocally in three ways. For one way is as the instrument of willing, another is as the affection of that instrument, and another is the use of that same instrument]. Such distinctions enable Anselm to maintain, in *De libertate arbitrii*, that even when someone through sinning is a 'slave to sin,' freedom of choice is still conserved (cap. 12).[37]

Ælfric distinguishes between *agen cyre* and *agen willa* throughout his career. We see this distinction richly illustrated in *CH* I and II (990X95),[38] and it appears as well in *Lives of Saints, Interrogationes Sigeuulfi, Hexameron* (decade of 992X1002); Belfour Homily IX (1002); Assmann Homily III (1005–6 [the period of *Vita S. Æthelwoldi*]); and *De creatore et creatura* (1006), among others.[39] The freedom of that 'cyre' is of foremost concern to him, and he defends against arguments of any sort of determinism, either fate

35 See the careful distinctions in Scott MacDonald, 'Primal Sin,' in Gareth B. Matthews, ed., *The Augustinian Tradition* (Berkeley: University of California Press, 1999), 110–39 at 117.

36 F.S. Schmitt, ed., *De concordia praescientiae et praedestinationis et gratiae Dei cum libero arbitrio*, St Anselm, Opera Omnia, Electronic Edition, 5 vols. (Charlottesville, VA: InteLex Corp., 2002), II: 279. In the earlier *De libertate arbitrii*, cap. 7, with less clarity, Anselm distinguishes between two senses of 'uoluntas': as instrument of willing and activity of willing. See Schmitt, *De libertate arbitrii*, Anselm, Opera Omnia, I: 219: 'ita voluntas, i[n]strumentum scilicet volendi, semper est in anima, etiam cum non vult aliquid, velut cum dormit; voluntatem vero quam dico usum sive opus eiusdem instrumenti, non habemus nisi quando volumus aliquid.' Thomas Williams, trans., *Anselm: Three Philosophical Dialogues* (Indianapolis: Hackett, 2002), 44, translates: 'Similarly, the will that is the instrument for willing is always in the soul, even when it is not willing anything – for example, when one is asleep – but we have the will that I am calling the exercise or activity of that instrument only when we are willing something.'

37 For a discussion of the distinction between *liberum arbitrium* and *libertas* in Augustine's thought see Étienne Gilson, *The Christian Philosophy of Saint Augustine*, trans. L.E.M. Lynch (New York: Random House, 1960), 323–4. Gilson notes that Anselm 'clarified' Augustine's terminology.

38 On this dating, at variance with that of Clemoes, see Godden, *CH* III, xxxv.

39 The Chronology is from Peter Clemoes, 'The Chronology of Ælfric's Works,' in *The Anglo-Saxons: Studies in Some Aspects of Their History and Culture*, ed. Peter Clemoes (London: Bowes and Bowes, 1959), 212–47 at 244–5.

or predestination. The explanation for God's endowing of humankind with *agen cyre*, is his profound justice ('deope rihtwisnys') and the requirement that individuals be morally responsible for their actions. Such responsibility would be impossible if God either forced created beings by necessity into his service ('þeowte') or if he forced them ('bescufe') into evil.[40] In his rendition of Alcuin's *Interrogationes Sigeuulfi*, Ælfric explains this concept in catechetical format, stressing the importance of individual responsibility: 'Hwi wæs se man betæht to his agenum cyre? To þan þæt he wære him sylfum ealdor swa to life, swa to deaðe. forþon gif he wære neadunga gode geunderþeod, þonne næfde he nan wuldor for godum weorcum, ne nan wite for yfelum, ac wære þonne swilce nyten'[41] [Why was man given responsibility for his own choice? So that he would be his own master for life as for death, because if he were subjected to God of necessity, then he would have no glory for good works nor punishment for evil works, but would be like a beast]. In this translation, Ælfric increases the precision of Alcuin's question by focusing on the function of choice as the instrument of moral accountability. His answer explains that Adam was created his own master so that he could be responsible for his own (eternal) life or death. Were he subjected to God of necessity, he would not be responsible for his actions and, capable of neither reward nor punishment, would be no better than an animal.

Ælfric considers 'cyre' in the *Interrogationes* a second time, and this instance highlights the important distinction of 'cyre' and 'willa': 'Hwi wolde se æþela scyppend æfre þone mannan to his agenum cyre lætan? Forþon þe se scyppend nolde þæt se man þeow wære, se þe to his anlicnysse

---

40 *CH* I.7, line 147. See further lines 143–6: 'His deope rihtwisnys nolde hi neadian to naþrum; ac forgeaf him agenne cyre; for þan ðe þæt is rihtwisnyss þæt gehwylcum sy his agen [in mss. T and K 'cyre' is supplied here] geþafod.' Here and in subsequent citations of *CH* I and II, I silently expand abbreviations and replace the punctus elevatus with a semicolon.

41 George E. MacLean, 'Ælfric's Version of *Alcuini interrogationes Sigeuulfi in Genesin*,' *Anglia* 7 (1884): 1–59 at pp. 4–6, lines 36–41. (I have silently expanded abbreviations and modernized the punctuation.) It translates Alcuin's question V: 'Cur homo suae potestatis auctor est creatus? R. Ut sibi ipse auctor esset ad vitam, sive ad mortem. Si vero necessitate esset subjectus, tunc nec boni operis haberet gloriam, nec mali poenam: sed esset quasi unus ex pecoribus' [Q. Why was man created to be his own master? A. So that he would be his own master for life or death. For if he were obedient by compulsion, then he would have no merit for a good deed or penalty for a bad one; but he would be just like one of the animals]. Lewis and Short, s.v. 'potestas', I.B.2 'esse in sua potestate,' 'to be one's own master.'

gesceapen wæs, ac wære þurh godne willan hergenlic, oððe of yfelum willan nyðergendlic'[42] [Why did the holy Creator desire to leave man always to his own free choice? Because the Creator did not wish that man, who was created in his likeness, would be a slave, but would be praiseworthy through a good will, or worthy of condemnation through an evil will]. In this distinction, 'cyre' is the act of choice (where Ælfric uses *agen cyre* to translate 'liberum arbitrium'), and 'willa' is the disposition developed through individual choices.[43] This understanding of 'willa' as disposition is even clearer in a Rogationtide homily, where Ælfric uses 'godne willan' to gloss 'godne gast,' itself referring to a disposition assisted to goodness by grace.[44] Elsewhere, 'cyre' and 'willa' both are in the domain of the soul, which acquires either a good or bad will, according to the choices it makes.[45] Ælfric's pejorative use of *willa* in the homily 'De auguriis' requires some discussion in the context of will and choice in agent action. The unprincipled, those deserving of punishment, are those who 'wadað on heora agenum willan' (line 239), a failing that is further specified by the following line: 'and on heora lustum heora lif aspendað.' That is, living according to their own will is tantamount to squandering their lives in their own pleasure. *Willa*, here, as in the earlier examples, is more specific than the modern English word 'will' and refers less to the act of choice than to a disposition of behaviour. When modified with 'agen' (own, with the sense of 'self') it shows *willa* as a dangerous and wayward disposition, directing the individual to himself and his desires and away from God. As we will see below in the discussion of a set of Ælfric's homilies, it is the act, *cyre*

42 MacLean, 'Ælfric's Version of *Alcuini interrogationes,*' p. 24, lines 230–5.

43 Ælfric repeats 'willa' for the parallel, but Alcuin has 'voluntario bono' for good will, and 'appetitu malo' for the bad will.

44 *CH* I.18, lines 150–2: 'Ac se gooda heofenlica fæder; forgifð us geleafan. 7 hiht. 7 þa soðan lufe; 7 deð þæt we habbað godne gast. þæt is godne willan' [But the good, heavenly father gives us belief and hope and true love, and makes us to have a good spirit, that is a good will]. For a discussion of this homily in terms of prevenient grace, see Kleist, *Striving with Grace*, 172–6.

45 W.W. Skeat, ed., *Ælfric's Lives of Saints*, vol. 1, EETS o.s. 76, 82 (Oxford, 1881–5; reprinted as one volume, Oxford: Oxford University Press, 1966), I.1 (p. 20, lines 171–2): 'Seo sawul is gesceadwis gast. æfre cucu and mæg underfon ge godne wyllan. and yfelne. æfter agenum cyre' [the soul is a rational, immortal spirit and can acquire either a good or evil will according to its own choice]. The effect of a good or bad disposition on the choices made is clarified by the phrase 'and let hi [scil., the evil servants of Matt. 21:33–46] habban cyre agenes willan' in John C. Pope, ed., *Homilies of Ælfric: A Supplementary Collection*, 2 vols., EETS 259, 260 (London: Oxford University Press, 1967), I.3 (p. 253, line 111).

[choice], rather than the faculty or disposition, *willa* [will], that occupies Ælfric's interest in the operation of agent action.[46] In this, Ælfric maps *willa* on *uoluntas*, and *cyre* on *arbitrium*. As 'agen' increases the potency of 'cyre' so does it increase the negative reference of 'willa.'

Like angels, human beings were created with *agen cyre*, which Ælfric stresses repeatedly is not compelled by God.[47] Ælfric offers several possible explanations for the freedom of choice given to mankind: the service that men and women might render to God is only pleasing if it is free.[48] On this understanding, the virginity of the Blessed Virgin was more pleasing to God because she consecrated herself 'be hyre agenum cyre' [by her own choice].[49] And Ælfric borrows from the Old English translation of Boethius's *De consolatione Philosophiae* the explanation that because it is only fitting that a great king be served by free men, God cannot be served by compulsion.[50] But of all the reasons for *agen cyre*, Ælfric returns again and again to choice as that capacity by which man is responsible for his every behaviour, behaviour that is judged by the degree to which man is obedient to God. This emphasis on answerable human choice, compelled neither by fate nor by God, is fully explored in the early homily 'Epiphania Domini' (*CH* I.7). Ælfric defends against the claim that God compels men to evil through fate by explaining the force of *agen cyre*.[51] His refutation

46 Kleist, *Striving with Grace*, provides a table of Ælfric's references to will, merit, and grace (206–9). His tally of references to 'will' collapses *agen willa* and *agen cyre* into a single category.

47 *CH* I.1 (p. 180, lines 53–5): '7 let hi habban agenne cyre. 7 hi næfre ne gebigde ne ne nydde mid nanum þingum to ðam yfelan ræde' [and he let them have their own choice, and never forced nor compelled them in any way to that evil counsel].

48 See *CH* II.33 (p. 284, lines 146–7): 'Nele se ælmihtiga god habban genydne þeowdom' [Almighty God does not wish to have forced service].

49 Bruno Assmann, ed., *Angelsächsische Homilien und Heiligenleben*, Bibliothek der angelsächsischen Prosa 3 (Kassel, 1889; repr. with intro. by Peter Clemoes [Darmstadt: Wissenschaftliche Buchgesellschaft, 1964]), pp. 24–48 at 32, line 203.

50 Skeat, *Lives of Saints* I.17, p. 382, lines 260–5. See Malcolm R. Godden, 'Ælfric and the Alfredian Precedents,' in *A Companion to Ælfric*, ed. Hugh Magennis and Mary Swan (Leiden: Brill, 2009), 139–63 at 151–7; see also Malcolm Godden and Susan Irvine, eds., *The Old English Boethius*, 2 vols. (Oxford: Oxford University Press, 2009), II: 489–90 for a comment on how Ælfric used the Old English Consolation, cap. 41. The 'De auguriis' is discussed by Kleist, *Striving with Grace*, pp. 210–11 and pp. 356–7, nn. 157–61.

51 *CH* I.7, p. 236, lines 137–8). For the sources and background to this homily see Godden, *CH* III, pp. 53–60. Godden doubts that Ælfric was directly familiar with the Carolingian treatises on predestination (p. 58). For a general overview of Ælfric's angelology see Michael Fox, 'Ælfric on the Creation and Fall of the Angels,' *ASE* 31 (2002): 175–200.

of the operation of fate entails an account of the creation of angels and men as the two types of rational beings who, by virtue of their reason, are also agents. In creating angels, God 'forgeaf him agenne cyre þæt hi moston þurhwunian on ecere gesælðe þurh gehyrsumnysse; 7 mihton eac þa gesælða forleosan na for gewyrde. ac for ungehyrsumnysse'[52] [gave them their own choice that they might live continually in eternal happiness through obedience and they might also lose that happiness not because of fate but for disobedience]. Ælfric founds his discussion of agent action not on the question of freedom as such or of will, as we might expect, but on the question of choice framed in terms of obedience and compulsion.[53] The cause of the fall of angels is their disobedience (that is, improper choice), which was not compelled by God, and the point of his excursus on the angelic behaviour is the defence of human freedom to choose.[54] For human beings, as for angels, choice is free ('nolde hi neadian to naþrum,' l. 144 [[God] did not wish to compel them to anything]), and that choice is completely proper to the creature ('*agenne* cyre' [emphasis added]). Here, *agen cyre* as the instrument of moral responsibility is intimately connected to obedience or disobedience: 'þa forgeaf he adame 7 euan agenne cyre. swa hi þurh gehyrsumnysse a on ecnysse buton deaðe on gesælðe wunodon mid eallum heora ofspringe. swa hi þurh ungehyrsumnysse deadlice wurdon'[55] [Then he gave Adam and Eve free choice, whether through obedience they would live forever in happiness with their offspring without death or through disobedience would become mortal]. Human mortality and guilt were the result of choice ('þurh agenum cyre' l. 155), itself understood in terms of obedience or disobedience to God.

Those who abandon God through their own choice and the devil's incitement, God will abandon to eternal damnation.[56] As the homily continues, Ælfric affirms that God knows the number of the elect angels and elect men as well as the fallen angels and wicked men, but does not predestine ('gestihte,' l. 167) anyone to damnation, because he himself is life. Yet

52 *CH* I.7, p. 236, lines 141–3.

53 His arguments are the same as in *CH* I.1, except that his example of compulsion is 'gewyrde' – that is, a force by which God might *neadian* [compel] angels or men.

54 Godden, *CH* III, p. 58, notes some general similarities to Augustine, *De correptione et gratia*, 'but little that suggests a direct debt.'

55 *CH* I.7, pp. 236–7, lines 150–3.

56 *CH* I.7, p. 237, lines 160–1: 'Witodlice þa ðe nu þurh agenne cyre. 7 deofles tihtinge god forlætað; god forlæt hi eac to þam ecum forwyrde' [truly, those who now abandon God through their own choice and the devil's prompting, God will abandon also to eternal damnation].

'He predestined ['forestihte,' l. 167] the chosen to eternal life because he knew in advance they were such through his grace and their own obedience; he did not wish to predestine the wicked to his kingdom, because he knew in advance they were such through their own sin and perversity.'[57] In this passage the language of predestination structures the argument yet offers no explanation of how it could be that God could predestine and man could be free. For Ælfric in this passage the simultaneous possibility of a specific form of predestination and *agen cyre* is a matter not for reason but belief.[58]

In 'De auguriis,' however, Ælfric uses an entirely different form of argument. Here, Ælfric creates a frame that addresses the Christian's relation to divine law, freedom, and human responsibility, and adds this to his adaptation of a homily of Caesarius of Arles on auguries and witchcraft.[59] In refuting the logic of divination, Ælfric observes that some men believe that what happens in their lives must happen because it was destined for them ('þæt him sceole gelimpan / swa swa him gesceapan wæs. and geset æt fruman').[60] His vigorous counterargument proceeds, however, by a telling inversion, in which the moral consequences of determinism, in this case the claim that our behaviour is determined by fate, are laid out in order to be refuted:

> Nu secge we to soðan. gif hit swa beon sceall
> [þæt hit is unnyt bebod] ðe god bebead ðurh dauid. Declina a malo et
> fac bonum

57 Ibid., lines 167–71: 'He forestihte þa gecorenan to þam ecan life; for þan þe he wiste hi swilce towearde þurh his gife. 7 agenre gehyrsumnysse; He nolde forestihtan þa arleasan to his rice. for þan ðe he wiste hi swilce towearde þurh heora agenre forgægednysse 7 þwyrnysse.'

58 Kleist, *Striving with Grace*, 182, argues that 'Ælfric understands human choice in Gregorian rather than Augustinian terms' in *CH* 1.7, which he interprets as choice in refusing grace.

59 M.R. Godden, 'The Sources of Ælfric's *Lives of Saints* 17 (On Auguries) (C.B.1.3.18),' Fontes Anglo-Saxonici: World Wide Web Register, http://fontes.english.ox.ac.uk/ (accessed July 2009), accepts the three Pauline epistles, Caesarius's Sermo 54, and the passages from the Old English *Boethius* as clear borrowings. On this homily and its augmented version, see Mary Clayton, 'Ælfric's *De auguriis* and Cambridge, Corpus Christi College 178,' in *Latin Learning and English Lore*, ed. Katherine O'Brien O'Keeffe and Andy Orchard, 2 vols. (Toronto: University of Toronto Press, 2005), II: 376–94.

60 Skeat, *Ælfric's Lives of Saints*, I.17, pp. 378–80, lines 222–3. Kleist, *Striving with Grace*, 210–11, discusses *LS* I.17, lines 222–71 from the perspective of prevenient grace.

Buh fram yfle. and do god. And eft se apostol cwæð.
swa man swyðor swincð for gode. swa he selran mede hæfð.
Gif ælces mannes life æfre sceola swa gan.
þæt he ne mæge forbugan bysmorlice dæda.
þonne bið unrihtlic þæt ða unrihtwisan onfon
ænigne witnunge for heora wohnysse.
Eac ða arfæstan beoð wolice gearwurðode.
gif þæt soð beon mæg þæt him swa gesceapen wæs.
and on unnyt we swincað on urum þeowdome.
oððe on ælmyssum. oþþe on oðrum dædum.
gif we his na maran edlean æt urum drihtne nabbað.
þonne receleasan menn. þe butan gerade lybbað.
and on eallum þingum wadað on heora agenum willan.
and on heora lustum heora lif aspendað.[61]

[Now we say truly, that what God commanded through David, 'turn from evil and do good,' is a useless command, as is what the apostle said 'the more a man labours for good, the better reward he will have,' if it must be the case that each man's life must always proceed so that he cannot turn away from shameful deeds. Then it is unjust that the unrighteous receive any punishment for their wickedness, and also the good are wrongly rewarded if it can be true that it [viz. their virtuous deed] was determined for them, and we labour uselessly in our service or in almsgiving, or in other deeds, if we cannot have a greater reward from our lord than negligent men who live without reflection, and go in all things according to their own wills and squander their lives on their own pleasures.]

Ælfric's intuition, that if people could not avoid evil punishment would be unjust, is the crux of the question of moral agency.[62] His argument depends on a claim that God's command that man must avoid evil and do

---

61 Skeat, *Ælfric's Lives of Saints*, I.17, p. 380, lines 225–40.

62 Stump, 'Augustine on Free Will,' pp. 133–4 and n. 37, points out that Augustine argues that scriptural exhortations to good actions would be pointless without human free will in *De gratia et libero arbitrio* II.2. An example closer to Ælfric's logic is *De gratia et libero arbitrio* II.4 (PL 44.883): 'Quid illud, quod tam multis locis omnia mandata sua custodiri et fieri jubet Deus? quomodo jubet, si non est liberum arbitrium?' [And what of this, that in so many places God orders all his commands to be kept and carried out. In what way does he order, if there is no free will?] By comparison to Augustine, who wishes to preserve both free will and knowledge of the law, Ælfric in *LS* I.17 is pursuing the notion of human responsibility in terms of good works and reward.

good is both clear and possible to obey.[63] In this understanding, the divine command in Psalm 36:27 necessarily means that man *can* avoid evil and do good. But the moral consequence of such behaviour is only possible if human behaviour is not determined, that is, if men are neither destined to do evil or to do good. The second part of Ælfric's argument, based on 1 Cor. 3:8 (that all will be rewarded according to merits) reveals something more about the human context of Ælfric's thought experiment. Agent action (though these would not be Ælfric's words) is a necessary condition for reward and punishment to be just. Ælfric argues even further that anything considered meritorious behaviour (the giving of alms or the practice of other good deeds) would be pointless without the assurance that appropriate consequences followed individual deeds. Otherwise the *receleasan* (those who live an unprincipled life) and the *arfæstan* (those who are virtuous) would be just as likely to receive reward as punishment.

The other part of the frame, the introduction to the homily, lines 1–66, shows Ælfric citing three Epistles of Paul on divine law (*æ*).[64] Though his citations of Gal. 5:8 and 1 Tim. 1:9 both call on Paul's distinction between the law and the spirit as well as the exemption of the Christian from the Mosaic Law, Ælfric is especially interested in that aspect of the law that punishes, explaining that the law brings no evil to the righteous, but 'heo gewitnað þa unrihtwisan be heora gewyrhtum' (lines 20–1) [it punishes the unrighteous according to their deserts]. The idea of just deserts for the sinner is the converse of his later citation of 1 Cor. 3:8 where Paul teaches that every man is rewarded according to his merits.[65] Just as the homily's introductory lines call on the law, freedom, and responsibility through the Epistles, Ælfric combines these three ideas when he observes, vis-à-vis 1 Tim. 1:9, that 'se rihtwisa soðlice ne þearf him ondrædan þa stiðan steora þe godes æ. tæcð. gif he him sylfum styrð fram eallum stuntnyssum' (21–3) [the righteous man truly need not fear the strict regulation of God's law, if he restrains himself from all foolishness (with word play on *steora* and *styrð*)]. This assumes, of course, as Ælfric will assert in the conclusion to the homily, that the deeds of men are their own, because they are free to

63 Ælfric is adapting a passage from the Old English translation of Boethius's *De consolatione Philosophiae*. See Godden, 'Ælfric and the Alfredian Precedents,' 152–3. In his argument from Ps. 36:27 he anticipates a subsidiary argument for free choice in Anselm's *De concordia*, 3.1.

64 Galatians, 1 Timothy, and 1 Corinthians.

65 'Qui autem plantat, et qui rigat, unum sunt. Unusquisque autem propriam mercedem accipiet secundum suum laborem.'

choose good behaviour or bad. Were this not the case, reward and punishment would be arbitrary or random.

Although it is not initially clear from the homily's opening articulation of man's relation to the law – that merit earns reward and sin earns punishment – Ælfric offers an explanatory framework for the understanding of agent action in Anglo-Saxon England that is formally at some distance from Augustine's late formulations. Ælfric's argument, carefully based in scripture, refutes determinism (in the form of fate) by arguing that the actions which incur punishment or reward must be free. His distinction between *cyre* and *willa* is innocent of the philosophical rigour of Anselm's later definitions, but he shares Anselm's interest in choice as the judgable act of the will. His reference to *agen willa* implicitly sets the self-will (as a destructive disposition) of 'receleasan men' against Christian obedience.

Obedience

In both Latin and Old English writings, the early medieval notion of agent action (understood as responsible action enabled by a particular kind of freedom) is measured by the yardstick of obedience, and this notion has a rich history beginning with St Paul.[66] As Albrecht Dihle puts it succinctly: 'To St. Paul, every factual fulfilment of the Law is primarily an act of obedience, appropriate in every creature towards the Creator. It can be performed, as St. Paul observes, with and without the explicit knowledge of the divine commandment, and it is only the act itself that really matters.'[67] This idea finds its most compelling formulations in Augustine; as Evodius is made to say in Augustine's early treatise *De libero arbitrio*, 'Voluntas illius [scil. Dei] mihi est necessitas.'[68] True freedom lies in obedience; otherwise one is enslaved to sin (Rom. 6:16–23; John 8:34).[69] Prosper

66 On the language of obedience in the writings of St Paul see Cynthia Briggs Kittredge, *Community and Authority: The Rhetoric of Obedience in the Pauline Tradition*, Harvard Theological Studies (Harrisburg, PA: Trinity Press International, 1998), esp. chapters 1 and 2.

67 Albrecht Dihle, *The Theory of Will in Classical Antiquity* (Berkeley and Los Angeles: University of California Press, 1982), 80, writing on Romans 2.

68 [His will is my necessity.] W.M. Green, ed., *Sancti Aurelii Augustini, De Libero Arbitrio*, CCSL 29 (Turnhout: Brepols, 1970), 211–321 at 279 (III.iii.26).

69 See also, Augustine's *Enchiridion*: 'Liberaliter enim seruit qui sui domini uoluntatem libenter facit, ac per hoc ad peccandum liber est qui peccati seruus est. Vnde ad iuste faciendum liber non erit nisi a peccato liberatus esse iustitiae coeperit seruus. Ipsa est uera libertas propter recte facti laetitiam, simul et pia seruitus propter praecepti obedientiam.' E. Evans, ed., *Enchiridion ad Laurentium de Fide et Spe et Caritate*, Aurelii

of Aquitaine, who softened many of Augustine's more rigid formulations in popularizing the works of the bishop, explains how we do God's will and our own at the same time: 'Suam uoluntatem homines faciunt non Dei, quando id agunt quod Deo displicet. Quando autem ita faciunt quod uolunt, ut diuinae seruiant uoluntati, quamuis uolentes agant quod agunt, illius tamen uoluntas est, a quo et praeparatur et iubetur quod uolunt'[70] [Men do their own will, not God's, when they do what displeases God. However, when they do what they will in such a way that they serve the divine will, even though they will what they do, they do His will, by whom what they will is both foreseen and appointed]. In such an understanding of and demand for responsible action, freedom of action was measured retrospectively by the degree to which one's every choice was in alignment with the will of God.

The intrinsic if vexed connection of Christian obedience and the rebellious will was theorized and modified over time in many works of Augustine, who located the origin of evil in a misuse of will that resulted in catastrophic disobedience.[71] Satan became a devil through his disobedience – 'Sed ceteri angeli in [s]ua obedientia perstiterunt; ille inobediendo et superbiendo lapsus est angelus, et factus est diabolus'[72] [But the other angels persisted in their obedience; he, through pride and disobedience, fell as an angel and was made a devil] – where the pride that accompanied that disobedience was understood as the reflex of self-will. The parents of all humankind, Adam and Eve, had but a single command to obey: not to eat of the tree of the knowledge of good and evil (Gen. 2:16–17). This command, given to Adam and Eve while they were still in paradise showed,

---

Augustini Opera, part 13.2, CCSL 46 (Turnhout: Brepols, 1969), pp. 21–114 at 65–6 (IX.30.45–50) [For he serves freely, who willingly does his lord's will, and for this reason, he who is the servant of sin, is free to sin. Whence he will not be free to act rightly unless, freed from sin, he begins to be the servant of justice. It is true freedom because of the pleasure in doing right and at the same time devout subjection because of obedience to a command].

70 M. Gastaldo, ed., *Sancti Prosperi Aquitani Liber Sententiarum*, CCSL 68A (Turnhout: Brepols, 1972), 213–365 at 344 (CCCXL): Prosper here is working from *Tractates on the Gospel of John*. See Radbod Willems, ed., *Sancti Aurelii Augustini in Iohannis Evangelium Tractatus CXXIV*, CCSL 36 (Turnhout: Brepols, 1954), XIX.19.11–15 (p. 202).

71 For a survey of the direct and indirect knowledge in Anglo-Saxon England of the works of Augustine on will and grace see Kleist, *Striving with Grace*, esp. 37–8.

72 See Augustine, *In Iohannis Evangelium Tractatus CXXIV*, ed. R. Willems, XLII.10.34–6. Godden, *CH* III, p. 9, observes that this passage, available in Haymo, Homily 32, PL 118, 216D, lies behind Ælfric's explanation of creation and fall in *CH* I.1.

Augustine thought, the advantage of obedience to rational beings and the concomitant disadvantage of self-will.[73] God's prohibition to Adam and Eve was understood in positive terms by Bede, in his comment on Gen. 2:17, as a command to follow God's will, not human will.[74] Transgressing that command led not simply to the loss of immortality, but to a fatal damaging of human will, ignorance of right, and a persistent desire for what is sinful.[75] Through the sin of mankind's first parents – Original Sin – the penalty of primal disobedience ('inobedientiae poena') was inherited by all mankind.[76] For Augustine, this original sin was the consequence of an act of will, freely undertaken by Adam and Eve.[77] Calling on the nexus of agency and identity, Ælfric tellingly contextualizes the prohibition in the Garden by making obedience central to the fashioning of human identity. Asking why God would forbid mankind 'such a little thing' ('swa lytles þinges'), Ælfric concludes that the purpose of the divine command was to teach Adam his own identity: 'hu mihte adam tocnawan hwæt he wære. buton he wære gehyrsum on sumum þincge his hlaforde; swilce

73 'Sed oboedientia commendata est in praecepto, quae uirtus in creatura rationali mater quodam modo est omnium custosque uirtutum; quando quidem ita facta est, ut ei subditam esse sit utile; perniciosum autem suam, non eius a quo creata est facere uoluntatem.' Bernard Dombart and Alfonsus Kalb, eds., *Sancti Aurelii Augustini De Ciuitate Dei Libri XXII*, 2 vols., CCSL 47–8 (Turnhout: Brepols, 1955), II: 434 (XIV.12.12–16) [But in his command, [God] established obedience, the virtue that in a rational created being is the mother and guardian of all the virtues: particularly since it was created so that it would be useful to the created being subject to it; on the contrary, it would be destructive for that being to do his own will and not the will of him by whom he was created].

74 Bede, *Libri Quatuor in Principium Genesis*, in *Bedae Venerabilis Opera*, part 2.1, *Opera Exegetica*, ed. Charles W. Jones, CCSL 118A (Turnhout: Brepols, 1967), p. 52, lines 1637–8. Bede is citing Augustine, *De Genesi ad litteram*, 8.13: 'quid aliud quam dei uoluntas humanae uoluntati praeponeretur?' (*Sancti Aureli Augustini De Genesi ad Litteram Libri Duodecim*, ed. Joseph Zycha, CSEL 28.1 [Vienna, 1894], p. 252, lines 10–11).

75 Evans, *Aurelii Augustini Enchiridion*, cap. 24, p. 63. For Gregory the Great, primal sin was an attempt to imitate God in seeking satisfaction from oneself ('sufficere ad se'): see Carole Straw, *Gregory the Great: Perfection in Imperfection* (Berkeley: University of California Press, 1988), 112–13.

76 Evans, *Aurelii Augustini Enchiridion*, cap. 26, p. 63, line 32.

77 For a good general overview of Original Sin, the function of will in it, and the consequence damage to the will, see Étienne Gilson, *The Christian Philosophy of Saint Augustine*, trans. L.E.M. Lynch (New York: Random House, 1960), 150–1. See also J.N.D. Kelly, *Early Christian Doctrines*, 5th rev. ed. (London: Continuum, 2000), 362–6.

god cwæde to him; Nast ðu þæt ic eom þin hlaford 7 þæt ðu eart min þeowa buton ðu do þæt ic ðe hate. 7 forgang þæt ic ðe forbeode'[78] [How might Adam know what he was, unless he was obedient in something to his lord? It is as if God had said to him, 'You will not know that I am your lord and that you are my servant unless you do what I command you and refrain from what I forbid you']. In Ælfric's view the prohibition and the command to obedience are integral to Adam's identity as a created being, and such identity is articulated as a relation between a subject and a lord.[79] This emphasis on obedience as a vertical relation and as a marker of identity reacts to the Christian master narrative of unruly wills and persistent disobedience of the fallen children of Adam and Eve (that is, the catastrophic consequences of the Fall) and marks conditions that the monastic life was designed to address.

The pre-eminent figure of obedience in the Old Testament is Abraham, whose willingness to sacrifice his only son, Isaac, earned him God's blessing and the reward of innumerable progeny (Gen. 22:1–18).[80] Abraham's obedience models the ideal response of mankind to the Old Testament God, where to hear God's word is to obey.[81] As such, Abraham's unquestioning obedience is a function of faith not knowledge, entailing a sacrifice of self-will in favour of God's will. In other terms, Abraham's response to God's command that he sacrifice his son is the fruit not of deliberation

78 *CH* I.1, p. 181, lines 74, 75–8. Compare Ælfric's emphasis on the conferral of identity with Augustine's stress on knowing that man had a lord: 'Non esset ergo, unde se homo dominum habere cogitaret atque sentiret, nisi ei aliquid iuberetur' [Thus there would be nothing whereby man might know and understand that he had a lord, unless he was ordered to do something]. See Augustine, *De Genesi ad litteram*, 8.6, ed. Zycha, p. 240, lines 4–5.

79 On this homily and Ælfric's contrast of *cyre* [choice] and *willa* [will] see above, pp. 19–22.

80 On Abraham as a model for monastic obedience see de Vogüé, 'Obéissance et autorité,' 566. Writing on the examples of the patriarchs, Ælfric commends Abraham's faith and obedience: 'Abraham for his micclan geleafan to gode. and for his gehyrsumnysse underfeng swilce bletsunge æt gode. þæt eall mancynn ða þe gelyfað on god is gebletsod on his cynne. and his sunu Isaac æfter him leofode mid bletsunge. and god hine lufode' [For his great faith in God and for his obedience, Abraham received such a blessing from God, that all mankind who believe in God are blessed in his kindred, and his son Isaac lived after him with God's blessing, and God loved him]. Skeat, *Lives of Saints*, I.16, p. 338, lines 25–9, my translation. See also Ælfric's comment in MacLean, 'Ælfric's Version of *Alcuini Interrogationes*,' p. 52, lines 495–500.

81 Karl Suso Frank, 'Gehorsam,' in *Reallexikon für Antike und Cristentum* (Stuttgart: Anton Hiersemann, 1976), at 399.

but of reflexive obedience.[82] In Christian appropriations of the Hebrew Bible, the relation of Abraham to Isaac would come to figure the relation of God the Father to his only Son, whom he sacrificed for the redemption of humankind (Rom. 8:32).[83] But in the New Testament, it is Christ himself who, in his complete accession to the will of the Father, models perfect obedience for the Christian: 'Quia descendi de caelo, non ut faciam voluntatem meam, sed voluntatem eius, qui misit me' (John 6:38) [Because I came down from heaven, not to do my own will, but the will of him that sent me]. And through Christ's kenosis, by his incarnation and then death on the cross, Paul proclaims him 'obedient unto death' (Phil. 2:8).[84] Although obedience is commanded of all Christians, the penitential life of monks and nuns makes that virtue the centre of their religious life and a critical marker of their identity.[85]

Obedience in the Rule of St Benedict

Although monastic behaviour in general was learned by imitating other, senior monks,[86] as the monastic virtue of self-perfection, obedience was especially a virtue of textual *imitatio*. *RSB* 5.13 is explicit in specifying that monastic obedience imitates Christ's obedience to the Father

82 Dihle, *Theory of Will*, 15: 'Since it is only the will of God which can be ascertained in the relation between God and man, man cannot possibly give his response to God through an act of thinking or perceiving but only by his being obedient or disobedient, that is to say by his will. Any attempt to understand intellectually the motives behind an order given by Yahveh is doomed to fail and even to lead to fatal disobedience. Knowledge can only be expected as a result of obedience, as was shown in the case of Abraham.'

83 See, for example, Isidore, *Quaestiones in Vetus Testamentum*, cap. 18, PL 83.249–50.

84 'Humiliavit semetipsum factus obediens usque ad mortem, mortem autem crucis.'

85 Luke 10:16 is generally understood to command general Christian obedience to the word of God through God's messengers. In his commentary on this verse, Bede stresses that spurning the teachers of the Gospel is spurning God. See Bede, *In Lucae Evangelium Expositio*, ed. D[avid] Hurst, *Bedae Venerabilis Opera*, Part 2.3, CCSL 120 (Turnhout: Brepols, 1960), p. 218, lines 2044–7. Wulfstan, in his brief homily 'Lectio secundum Lucam' (Dorothy Bethurum, ed., *The Homilies of Wulfstan* [Oxford: Clarendon Press, 1957], Homily 17, pp. 242–5 at 244, lines 50–2), raises the stakes by claiming: 'se ðe nele Godes bodan hyran mid rihte ne godcundre lare gyman swa he sceolde, he sceal hyran feondan, gif he nele freondan' [whoever does not wish to obey God's prophets, will obey his enemies, if he doesn't wish to obey his friends].

86 For a sociological analysis of the learning of virtue, see Talal Asad, *Genealogies of Religion: Discipline and Reasons of Power in Christianity and Islam* (Baltimore and London: Johns Hopkins University Press, 1993), 63.

(John 6:38).[87] The perfection of such obedience structures a vision of the monastic actor who is simultaneously heroic (in the magnitude of his sacrifice) and passive (in the sacrifice of his will) since his goal is to disregard every prompting of desire and focus his will on the single action of obedience. That is virtuous action taken in both the fear of punishment and the love for God.[88] Obedience unto death means, precisely, that the individual, for whom this obedience is *the* defining virtue, is in the process of emptying himself of everything, especially of self-will.[89] To imitate Christ is thus always to do the will of the Father, never to follow the vagaries of one's own desires. This practice is a recognized form of emptying to counter the most difficult and most dangerous kind of *proprium, propria uoluntas*. And as Talal Asad has observed, its goal was to 'reorganiz[e] the basis on which choices were to be made.'[90]

The Prologue of the *RSB*, calling the hearer to a life of penitential obedience, addresses those who, by loving Christ, wish to pursue eternal life: 'Obsculta, o fili, praecepta magistri et inclina aurem cordis tui et admonitionem pii patris libenter excipe et efficaciter comple, / ut ad eum per oboedientiae laborem redeas, a quo per inoboedientiae desidiam recesseras. / Ad te ergo nunc mihi sermo dirigitur, quisquis abrenuntians propriis uoluntatibus domino Christo uero regi militaturus oboedientiae fortissima atque praeclara arma sumis'[91] [Listen my son to the precepts of your master and incline the ears of your heart, and willingly receive the admonition of your affectionate father and carry it out effectively, that you may return to him through the labour of your obedience, from whom

87 Hanslik, *Benedicti Regula*, 5.13, pp. 39–40: 'Sine dubio hii tales illam domini imitantur sententiam, qua dicit: *Non ueni facere uoluntatem meam, sed eius, qui misit me*' [Without doubt, such as these imitate that statement of the Lord which says, 'I came down from heaven, not to do my own will, but the will of him that sent me'].

88 For obedience and the fear of God see *RSB* 5.9; for fear of eternal punishment see *RSB* 5.3. On obedience for love of Christ see *RSB* 5.2. For Augustine, obedience, necessary as it is, also arises from love for God. See John M. Rist, *Augustine: Ancient Thought Baptized* (Cambridge: Cambridge University Press, 1994), 181.

89 *RSB* 7.10–33 (on humility) treats the importance of abandoning self-will. For early commentaries on the application of 'obedience unto death' see below, pp. 41–2. In a memorable comment apropos St Augustine's desire to abandon self-will, Karmen MacKendrick observes '[the will] wills its own overtaking not as the desire to evade responsibility but as the desire to perfect itself by becoming (one with) God's will, in an impossible perfection of subordination.' *Fragmentation and Memory: Meditations on Christian Doctrine* (New York: Fordham University Press, 2008), 50.

90 Asad, *Genealogies of Religion*, 135.

91 Hanslik, *Benedicti Regula*, prol. 1–3, pp. 1–2.

you departed through the idleness of disobedience. So to you, now is my message directed, whoever leaves behind his own will and takes up the splendid and most strong arms of obedience to serve the true king, the lord Christ]. These lines combine a number of potent ideas about obedience and will that find themselves repeated in varying combinations throughout the *RSB*. The 'son' addressed here is admonished to hear the precepts of a teacher figured also as a father.[92] Not only must this 'son' hear these teachings, but he must carry them out effectively, thus placing the opening admonition within the biblical identification of hearing with obedience. His (or for the women who would come to live under the Rule, her) obedience had a double purpose. As Cassian pointed out in his observations on the obedience required by the desert fathers, the discipline of such conduct had a practical use in testing and strengthening those who sought admission to monastic communities.[93] But Adalbert de Vogüé has pointed out that Benedict draws on two other models for his call to obedience: a social model of monastic community which constructs the relation of subject to abbot as the relation of son to father, and Christian to pastor; and an ascetic model found in the Rule of the Master, which frames obedience as the

92 Æthelwold's Old English translation of the opening words of the Prologue, 'Gehyr ðu min bearn geboda' uses the gender-neutral 'bearn' (child). See Arnold Schröer, ed., *Die angelsächsischen Prosabearbeitungen der Benedictinerregel*, Bibliothek der angelsächsischen Prosa 2, 2nd ed., with supplement by Helmut Gneuss (Kassel, 1885–1888; Darmstadt: Wissenschaftliche Buchgesellschaft, 1964), p. 1, line 1. Manuscripts of the translation show its having been adapted for use by nuns, although priority of the version for monks or for nuns is an open question. See Mechthild Gretsch, 'The Benedictine Rule in Old English: A Document of Bishop Æthelwold's Reform Politics,' in *Words, Texts and Manuscripts: Studies in Anglo-Saxon Culture Presented to Helmut Gneuss on the Occasion of His Sixty-Fifth Birthday*, ed. Michael Korhammer, with the assistance of Karl Reichl and Hans Sauer (Cambridge: D.S. Brewer, 1992), 131–58 at 143. See also her 'Æthelwold's Translation of the *Regula Sancti Benedicti* and Its Latin Exemplar,' *ASE* 3 (1974): 125–51, at 138–9. For an argument that Æthelwold's translation was at least originally intended for novices, and 'may have been particularly needed in female communities,' see Rohini Jayatilaka, 'The *Regula Sancti Benedicti* in Late Anglo-Saxon England: The Manuscripts and Their Readers' (D.Phil. thesis, University of Oxford, 1996), 354.

93 Michael Petschenig, ed., *Iohannis Cassiani, De Institutis Coenobiorum et De Octo Principalium Vitiorum Remediis Libri XII*, CSEL 17.1 (Vienna, 1888), IV.8, pp. 52–3. See de Vogüé, 'Obéissance et autorité,' 582–3. For a sociological analysis of the function of obedience in the early medieval monastery see Annette Kehnel, 'Das Gehorsamsparadox: Vorüberlegungen zu einer Kulturhistorischen Interpretation der evangelischen Räte,' in *Oboedientia: Zu Formen und Grenzen von Macht und Unterordnung im mittelalterlichen Religiosentum*, ed. Sébastien Barret and Gert Melville, Vita regularis 27 (Münster: Lit Verlag, 2005), 69–82.

annihilation of self-will in submission to the will of God.[94] This higher goal of obedience required a different form of spiritual balancing: within an understanding of the consequence of Adam's sin of disobedience as alienation from God and an attendant corruption of the human will, the continuing, radical obedience of monastic men and women who answer the call of the *RSB* was aimed to address the wrong of Adam's primal sin and this goal was understood as a salvific act.[95] That such obedience was characterized as *labor* ('per oboedientiae laborem') pointed less to the virtue itself than to the continuing effort involved in lifelong obedience to another.[96] And this labour was precisely the work of overcoming self-will.[97] Thus obedience, now refigured in the *RSB* as the arms by which the prospective monk will fight for his true king, Christ, was the instrument by which that monk might accomplish the renunciation of self-will.[98] The multiple references to obedience in these verses show us monastic obedience as a vertical social relation (of son to father, disciple to teacher) and an ascetic practice of renouncing self-will, both linked to the understanding of primal sin as a disobedience which placed human will before the will of God.

Obedience, given pride of place in the Prologue, is the first of the monastic disciplines to be treated in full in an individual chapter (*RSB* 5). Its practice is the pre-eminent concern of the abbot, whose responsibility for the salvation of his flock is measured by their obedience (*RSB* 2.6), and it emerges as a disciplinary practice not simply linking the monk to the abbot vertically (*RSB* 2, 5, and 68) but also linking the monk with his spiritual brothers in the humility of mutual obedience (*RSB* 71).[99]

---

94 Adalbert de Vogüé, *The Rule of Saint Benedict: A Doctrinal and Spiritual Commentary*, trans. John Baptist Hasbrouck (Paris, 1977; Kalamazoo, MI: Cistercian Publications, 1983) [first published as *La Règle de saint Benoît, VII, commentaire doctrinal et spirituel*], 104.

95 de Vogüé, *The Rule of Saint Benedict*, 106.

96 For an argument that 'obedience' means 'labor' in the *RSB* see Basilius Steidle, '"Per oboedientiae laborem ... per inoboedientiae desidiam" (I): Zu Prolog 2 der Regel St. Benedikts,' *Erbe und Auftrag* 53 (1977): 428–35 at 430.

97 Basilius Steidle, '"Per oboedientiae laborem ... per inoboedientiae desidiam" (II): Zu Prolog 2 der Regel St. Benedikts,' *Erbe und Auftrag* 54 (1978): 200–16 at 211.

98 Eug[ène] Manning, 'La signification de "militare-militia-miles" dans la Règle de saint Benoît,' *Revue Bénédictine* 72 (1962): 135–8 at 137, argues that '*militare*, dans la Règle de saint Benoît, ne se comprend que dans le sens où "service" est une "manière de vivre," une "obéissance."'

99 Stephen M. Hildebrand, '*Oboedientia* and *Oboedire* in the Rule of St. Benedict: A Study of Their Theological and Monastic Meanings,' *American Benedictine Review* 52.4 (2001): 421–36, provides a useful survey of the work of 'obedience' outside *RSB* cap. 5, and 68.

The most striking of this chapter's statements on obedience (*RSB* 5.12) illustrates its fundamental character as a denial of the will, its construction as a social relation, and its requirement that the monk (or nun) *desire* the obedience demanded of them. Those following the Rule choose the narrow way 'ut non suo arbitrio uiuentes uel desideriis suis et uoluptatibus oboedientes, sed ambulantes alieno iudicio et imperio in coenobiis degentes abbatem sibi praeesse desiderant' (*RSB* 5.12) [so that not living by their own choice or desires and obeying their own wills, but walking in the judgment and command of another and living in monasteries they desire to have an abbot rule over them]. 'Ambulantes alieno iudicio et imperio' looks forward and backward in the verse: it is the striking image of leaving behind one's own will (expressed as individual choice, desire, and pleasure, which all exact their own obedience) in order to live communally under the command of an abbot. Such an abandonment of self-will, constructed as a self-conscious imitation of Christ, is also obedience given to God, since the abbot takes the place of Christ in the monastery (*RSB* 2.2) and obedience given to a superior is given to God (*RSB* 5.15), by the pattern of Luke 10:16, 'Qui vos audit, me audit' [he that heareth you, heareth me]. This double valence of obedience (where obedience to every command of the abbot is obedience given to God) shows how the relation between monk and abbot models the ideal relation of Christian to God.

In directions on the exercise of obedience, the Rule is concerned to extend obedience beyond the externals of simple behavioural compliance to a transformation of the individual's will itself. In a Benedictine community, true obedience (which is to say obedience that is effective toward salvation) must be immediate, cheerful, and complete. It is obedience without delay (*RSB* 5.1), carried out as soon as a task is commanded, as if given from heaven itself (*RSB* 5.4). It is cheerful, that is to say carried out without private reserve or public grumbling, because God loves a cheerful giver (*RSB* 5.14, 16). This second idea, along with the specification that such obedience will only be acceptable if it is accomplished in the proper spirit, neither slow, half-hearted, hesitating, nor grudging, has as its goal the eradication of the subject's own desires. And the completeness of obedience is also a function of its execution *sine mora*. The swiftness of its accomplishment and the degree of its success in overcoming self-will is measured by the subject's abandonment of any activity he was engaged in. *RSB* 5.8, specifying that those who truly obey leave unfinished whatever they were doing, meant to recall the much-repeated story of the obedient scribe Marcus, who when given a task, left unfinished the letter 'o' he was copying, in order to obey the command of his superior.[100] In striving to effect a cheerful, immediate, and complete execution of each act of obedience, the ideal monk cannot permit himself to take an attitude toward any order, cannot choose when to execute the order, and cannot decide how much of what he is ordered he will do.

Obedience to the abbot is thus the monk's vehicle for the imitation of Christ. As the *RSB* will later explain, such obedience is given to God through obedience to the abbot, who is believed to act in Christ's place in the monastery ('Christi enim agere uices in monasterio creditur'),[101] and who is responsible for the salvation of those in his charge.[102] In the daily exercise of emptying himself of self-will, the monk strove to make himself more and more Christ-like in being obedient even unto death. (Hence the heroic examples in narratives of the desert fathers where monks under obedience walk into a furnace or fire, or face a wild beast.) This is a specifically textual obedience, in that it is a behaviour developed from an interpretation of scripture and then exemplified in narratives of its heroic execution. In such an understanding, a successful act of obedience is one that collapses the will of the subject into the will of the abbot and permits no interval between command and execution. 'Et ueluti uno momento praedicta magistri iussio et perfecta discipuli opera in uelocitate timoris dei ambae res communiter citius explicantur'[103] [and as if at one moment – the master's command uttered and the works of the disciple completed – both are achieved together swiftly, in the speed of the fear of God]. Such temporal oneness of command and act imagines a unity of will and intention for both abbot and subject. It is to this imagined unity that Anselm refers when he urges the nuns of Shaftesbury to be obedient:

> Vos, sorores dilectae et filiae meae, hortor et moneo, quatenus matri vestrae subiectae et oboedientes sitis, non tantum ad oculum humanum, sed etiam ad oculum dei, cui nihil est secretum. Tunc autem est vera oboedientia, quando voluntas subiecti oboedit voluntati praelati, ut, ubicumque sit subiectus, hoc velit quod intelligit velle praelatum, quod non sit contra voluntatem dei.[104]

---

100 *Verba seniorum*, PL 73.949. The story is repeated in Cassian, *De institutis*, IV.12.

101 Hanslik, *Benedicti Regula*, 2.2, p. 21.

102 Hanslik, *Benedicti Regula*, 2.7, p. 22.

103 Hanslik, *Benedicti Regula*, 5.9, p. 39.

104 Schmitt, Letter 403, St Anselm, Opera Omnia, V: 347. Obedience was a continuing concern in monastic life. For an argument on the centrality of obedience in the discourse of Lotharingian reformers at the beginning of the eleventh century see Steven

> [My beloved sisters and daughters, I urge and admonish you, that you be subject and obedient to your mother [viz. the abbess] not just before human eyes, but also before the eyes of God, from whom nothing is hidden. For it is true obedience when the will of the subject obeys the will of the superior so that wherever the subject may be, she wills what she knows her superior wills, provided that is it not against the will of God.]

This Benedictine vision of obedience seeks to make repeated, immediate, and ungrudging acquiescence to a superior's command the instrument by which the monk may return to God from disobedience (inherited as Original Sin from Adam's first disobedience) by renouncing self-will ['abrenuntians propriis uoluntatibus'] in a life of obedience.[105] This invitation to the life of the *RSB* by summoning prospective monks or nuns, paradoxically, to use their wills to deny their wills[106] sets the stage for an agonistic performance of humble obedience.

'Ambulantes alieno iudicio et imperio'

Although obedience is a virtue practised by an individual, obedience both produces a relation and is the continuing product of that relation. In his study of the pastoral relation in Christianity, Michel Foucault observed that the principle characteristic of Christian obedience is a subordination that entailed complete submission of the individual not to the law but to a person in a relationship that was never finalized.[107] The *RSB* strengthened the power of the abbot over previous rules, and it is precisely the dimensions of this pastoral relation that the early commentaries on the Rule endeavoured to elucidate.[108] The first of these commentaries, the *Expositio in Regulam S. Benedicti* by Smaragdus of St Mihiel, was composed not long after the Synod of Aachen (816–17) and Benedict of Aniane's compilation of the *Concordia regularum*.[109] While Smaragdus's commentary was

---

Vanderputten, '*Oboedientia*. Réformes et discipline monastique au début du XIe siècle,' *Cahiers de civilisation médiévale* 53 (2010): 255–66, esp. 263 and 265.

105 Hanslik, *Benedicti Regula*, Prologue, 3, pp. 1–2.

106 Kehnel, 'Das Gehorsamsparadox,' 78.

107 Michel Foucault, *Security, Territory, Population: Lectures at the Collège de France, 1977-78*, ed. Michel Senellart, trans. Graham Burchell (London: Palgrave, 2007), 175–7.

108 On the increased power of the abbot see Marilyn Dunn, *The Emergence of Monasticism: From the Desert Fathers to the Early Middle Ages* (Oxford: Blackwell, 2000), 127.

109 Smaragdus of St Mihiel, *Smaragdi Abbatis Expositio in Regulam S. Benedicti*, ed. Alfred Spannagel and Pius Engelbert, CCM 8 (Siegburg: F. Schmitt, 1974).

known in Anglo-Saxon England,[110] it is fairly derivative, given to quoting extensively from scripture, and overly fond of philological exposition.[111] The commentary by Hildemar of Civate, by contrast, though apparently unknown in Anglo-Saxon England, is particularly insightful about the relation between abbot and subject and thus asks our attention.[112]

The commentary of Hildemar of Civate offers important insight into obedience, identity, and the vexed question of agent action from three perspectives: it treats obedience as a relation between abbot and subject, explores the responsibilities of the abbot vis-à-vis his subject, and, in posing the possibility of latitude in the interpretation of an order, raises the problem of reading both order and execution within the relation of obedience. The relation between abbot and subject formed through obedience begins with the understanding that the abbot holds the place of Christ in the monastery (*RSB* 2.2). To explain how this understanding builds the relation between abbot and monk, in his commentary on *RSB* 2.2 Hildemar offers as model the relation of Christ to his disciples given in John 15:10.

See Terrence G. Kardong, O.S.B., 'The Earliest Commentator on RB: Smaragdus on Benedict's Prologue,' *American Benedictine Review* 55.2 (June 2004): 171–93, at 172, who follows Spannagel and Engelbert, CCM 8, pp. xxix–xxx, in believing that the work was composed shortly after 817. The *Concordia regularum* is printed in PL 103. There is a translation of the commentary into English: *Smaragdus of Saint-Mihiel, Commentary on the Rule of Saint Benedict*, trans. David Barry (Kalamazoo, MI: Cistercian Publications, 2007).

110 Surviving manuscripts of Smaragdus's commentary include Cambridge, Cambridge University Library Ee. 2. 4 (with Oxford, Bodleian Library, Lat. th. c. 3, fols. 1, 1*, and 2), s. x med. (Gneuss, *Handlist*, no. 3); and Paris, Bibliothèque Nationale, lat. 4210, s. x/xi (Gneuss, *Handlist*, no. 883). On Æthelwold's use of this commentary see Gretsch, 'The Benedictine Rule in Old English,' 132 and n. 6.

111 For a positive assessment of Smaragdus's intellectual engagements in the commentary see Matthew D. Ponesse, 'Editorial Practice in Smaragdus of St Mihiel's Commentary on the Rule of St Benedict,' *Early Medieval Europe* 18.1 (2010): 61–91 at 78.

112 Hildemar's *Expositio*, composed slightly later than Smaragdus's commentary, survives in three redactions and has a complicated text history. One redaction was attributed to 'Paulus Diaconus' (edited as *Pauli Warnefridi Diaconi Casinensis in Sanctam Regulam Commentarium* [Monte Cassino, 1880]), and another, unedited, attributed to one Basilius. For a survey of the manuscripts of the commentary in its three redactions see Wolfgang Hafner, *Der Basiliuskommentar zur Regula S. Benedicti*, Beiträge zur Geschichte des alten Mönchtums und des Benediktinerordens 23 (Münster Westfalen: Aschendorffsche Verlagsbuchhandlung, 1959), 7–51. Mechthild Gretsch, 'Æthelwold's Translation of the *Regula Sancti Benedicti* and Its Latin Exemplar,' *ASE* 3 (1974): 125–51 at 146, regards the possibility of Æthelwold's use of Hildemar's commentary 'not very likely.'

This verse founds the relation between Christ and his disciples in love and obedience: 'Si praecepta mea servaveritis, manebitis in dilectione mea, sicut et ego Patris mei praecepta servavi, et maneo in eius dilectione' ['If you keep my commandments, you shall abide in my love; as I also have kept my Father's commandments, and do abide in his love']. To develop this idea Hildemar evokes John 16:27 to connect love of the Father with love of Christ: as Christ chose his apostles, loved them and taught them, the abbot, acting in the place of Christ, chooses his monks to iterate this relation:

> Et iterum ad hoc elegit [scil. Christus], ut illos doceret … Et iterum ideo apostoli elegerunt Dominum, ut diligerent illum, et obedirent ei … [M]onachi ad hoc debent eligere abbatem suum, ut ament illum et obediant ei, sicut discipuli Christum; nam si aliter elegerint, i.e. non ut abbatem suum ament et obediant, non vicem discipulorum tenent, sed aliorum.[113]
>
> [And again, Christ chose for this reason, that he might teach them … and again therefore the apostles chose the Lord, that they might love him and obey him. Monks ought to choose their abbot for this reason, that they might love him and obey him, as did the disciples Christ; for if they chose in another fashion, i.e. so as not to love and obey their abbot, they would not hold the place of disciples, but of others.]

The responsibility of the abbot for the members of his flock is total. Their salvation depends on his care and direction, and his salvation depends on shepherding them to heaven. *RSB* 2.6 reminds the abbot that his teaching (*doctrina*) and their obedience (*oboedientia*) will be weighed on the Day of Judgment. Hildemar writes that this warning should never be far from the abbot's thoughts, so that he will always be solicitous about his teaching and his monks be solicitous about their obedience. As Hildemar develops this theme he observes that the unsuccessful abbot will be liable for a double punishment at the Last Judgment, as penalty for the sin of his own negligence and for his sin in failing to get his monks to correct their errors.[114] Even though the Rule specifies that a diligent abbot will be held harmless if his flock remains stubbornly restless and disobedient, the measure of that diligence could only have been the conduct of the individual

113 Hildemar, *Expositio*, 87.

114 Ibid., 92. In *RSB* 2.8–9, however, the abbot will be held harmless if he can give a satisfactory account of his own care and his flock's disregard of his shepherding.

monks. Interpreting the monks' behaviour (a question of reading both external actions and private intentions) was of vital importance to the abbot.

Commenting on *RSB* 2.25 Hildemar divides obedience into categories of behaviour to suggest how the abbot may discern its performance. The first category comprises those who obey the abbot or other superiors for fear or desire for praise – they may be discerned by their refusal to obey others. If their obedience were sound, Hildemar observes, they would obey others according to the directive of *RSB* 71: selective obedience is the sign for the abbot of their lack of virtue. The second category comprises those who will obey a few brothers to garner praise or for other reasons, but decline to obey the abbot or other superiors. The abbot can tell their obedience is not sound, because if it were, their obedience would stem from the love for God, and they would obey others. Hildemar recommends reproving such monks harshly. The third category comprises monks who obey abbot, superiors, and all brothers for love of God. These should be encouraged to advance to a still better life.[115] Set against the ideal of conduct laid out in the *RSB*, Hildemar's examples of observed behaviours an abbot might have to discern in his monks raises the difficult problem of reading intentions as well as behaviours. Because obedience rendered superficially or from the wrong motives is worthless, it is critical for the abbot (whose pastoral oversight will be weighed at the Last Judgment) to see past appearance, so that he can admonish and correct when necessary:

> Sunt enim multi, qui videntur coram hominibus sine mora, i.e. sine tarditate agere obedientiam, tamen coram Deo cum mora agunt, i.e. aut pro vana gloria, aut pro timore, aut certe pro alia aliqua ratione obediunt. Iterum sunt alii, qui cum mora coram hominibus videntur obedire, tamen coram Deo sine mora obediunt, quia pro impossibilitate hoc faciunt. Isti tales probandi sunt. Probandus est ille, qui sine mora obedit coram hominibus isto modo: ut securus sit abbas de illo, coram Deo debet illum admonere, ne hoc, quod facit, non pro vana gloria aut pro timore faciat. Et ut securior sit, debet illum probare in aliis operibus. Si illum cognoverit studiosum esse in lectione, in mortificatione, in jejunio, et reliq., tunc potest causa Dei etiam sine mora obediens esse. Quodsi illum non cognoverit esse studiosum in aliis rebus, poterit etiam suspicari, non ejus intentionem sanam esse in hoc loco. Illum vero, qui videtur cum mora agere obedientiam, potest isto modo abbas probare,

115 Hildemar, *Expositio*, 110–11.

i.e. debet cognoscere, qualis sit illa obedientia, quae illi injungitur a decano aut praeposito vel ab aliquo priore. Si cognoverit, illam obedientiam esse rectam et bonam, tunc debet illum interrogare, quare cum mora obedit. Ille vero si dixerit: causa impossibilitatis hoc ago, iterum debet illum probare in aliis rebus, i.e. si invenerit illum studiosum et mortificatum in aliis operibus, tunc poterit illum cognoscere causa impossibilitatis hoc agere; si autem cognoverit, illum non studiosum esse, tunc poterit in illo suspicari, hoc desidiae causa agere, et postea, prout cognoverit abbas illum delinquere, potest illum regulari disciplina constringere.[116]

[For there are many who obey without delay in the eyes of men, but before God, they delay, that is, they act either for vainglory or for fear, or doubtless obey for some other reason. And again there are others who seem to obey with delay before men, but before God obey without delay, seeing as they do this because of the task's impossibility. Such ones ought to be tested. The one who obeys without delay before men should be tested in this manner: that the abbot might be untroubled concerning him, he ought to admonish him before God, that he not do what he does for vainglory or for fear. And that he might be more assured, he ought to test him in other actions. If he knows that he is zealous in reading, in mortification, in fasting, and so forth, then he can be obedient for the sake of God also without delay. But if [the abbot] has not known that he is zealous in other things, he could suspect that his intention is not pure in this instance. However, the abbot can test the one who seems to obey with delay in this way: i.e. he ought to know what sort of obedience it is, that was enjoined on him by the deacon, the provost, or by another superior. If he knows that obedience is right and good, then he ought to ask him, why he obeys with delay. But if he says, I do it because of its impossibility, again he [the abbot] ought to test him in other things, i.e. if he discovered that he was zealous and mortified himself [i.e. *mortificatus*, from Rom. 8:13] in other actions, then he could know that he did this because of its impossibility; if, however, he knew that he was not zealous, then he could suspect of him that he did this because of slothfulness, and afterwards, to the extent that the abbot knows that he has transgressed, he can restrain him with regular discipline.][117]

Evaluating behaviour for its surface effects and its motivating forces is a continuing problem for the abbot. The distinctions Hildemar makes here are meant to help the abbot discern whether apparent compliance is

116 Ibid., 185–6.
117 For a further consideration of the types of insufficient obedience see ibid., 195.

true obedience or simply the show of obedience. He must monitor those brothers who are negligent or contemptuous in their duty of obedience, but discern which monks are humble, and punish the sins of the delinquent.[118] To do otherwise would be to call down the terrible punishment of Eli, who did not reprove his sons out of mistaken fatherly affection (1Kings 2:29–34; 4:17–18).[119]

However delicate and fraught the abbot's responsibility for interpreting his subjects' behaviour, such difficult reading must also be inherent in the monk's interpretation of his abbot's command. Hildemar's commentary explores this problem in commenting on the meaning of 'obedient unto death' for the monk, found in *RSB* 7.34: 'Tertius humilitatis gradus est, ut quis pro dei amore omni oboedientia se subdat maiori imitans dominum, de quo dicit apostolus: *factus oboediens usque ad mortem*' [The third degree of humility is that someone subject himself to a superior in all obedience, imitating the Lord, of whom the apostle [scil. Paul, Phil. 2.8] says: He 'bec[ame] obedient unto death'].[120] For this, Hildemar's commentary investigates a situation where the abbot sends a monk into extreme danger, and he suggests, pragmatically, that if the monk finds danger where the abbot had not expected it, he should return to the monastery, not from disobedience but because the abbot might not have known what the monk would encounter.[121] He goes on to explore the possibility that the monk sent on a task might realize that he was about to fall among thieves, and at that point should return to the monastery to inform the abbot:

> quia cum obedit monachus, magis debet ad intentionem respicere abbatis, quam ad verba sola; nam sunt multi abbates sive sapientes sive simplices, cum mittunt monachum suum causa profectus monasterii longe, dicunt illi, quae aut qualiter agere debeat; deinde cum pervenit monachus ad illum locum, non invenit aut tempus nec locum, ut ita agat, sicut ei imperatum est, et ideo non debet ad verba, quae audivit, respicere, sed ad intentionem abbatis sui, hoc est, ut faciat, quod abbatem suum cognoverit velle, quamvis non possit eo modo perficere, sicuti audivit, eo quod melior est illa obedientia, quae ad intentionem respicit, quam illa, quae ad verba sine intentione.[122]

118 Ibid., 111–12.

119 Ibid., 112–14. See also Smaragdus, *Expositio*, CCM 8, p. 73, lines 3–10.

120 Hanslik, *Benedicti Regula*, p. 50.

121 Hildemar, *Expositio*, 226: '[D]ebet abbati suo manifestare ipsum periculum, non inobediendi causa, sed solummodo, quia ille abbas forte non vult, ut eat in illud periculum.'

122 Ibid., 227. (I have silently omitted two redundant 'et's.)

> [For when a monk obeys, he ought to consider the intention of the abbot more than the words alone. For there are many abbots, either shrewd or artless who, when they send their monk far away for the monastery's profit, tell him what or how he ought to perform; afterwards, when the monk arrives at that place, he does not find either the time or the place that he might do just as he was ordered, and for this reason he ought not to pay attention to the words he heard but to his abbot's intention, that is, so that he might accomplish what he understands the abbot wishes, although he cannot do it just as he heard it, because obedience mindful of intention is better than obedience mindful of words without intention.]

Such advice offers a humane, if sharp, counterpoint to the heroics of obedience explored in commentary on *RSB* 5, heroics memorialized in the oft-repeated stories of the desert fathers and recommended in Smaragdus's own commentary on *RSB* 7.34: 'Si enim deum ut decet diligimus, non solum in omni oboedientia subdi maiori, sed si necesse fuerit parati debemus esse etiam pro illo mori, sicut et ille pro nobis mortuus est'[123] [But if we love God, as is right, we are not only subject to our superior in all obedience, but, if it were necessary, we ought to be prepared also to die for Him, just as He died for us]. By contrast, Hildemar's commentary recognizes that abbots may not always understand the full circumstances of their commands and suggests that the spirit of the command rather than the letter should guide the monk who desires to obey his abbot in such a circumstance. His understanding recognizes that despite the ideal of *RSB* 5.9, the relation of monk to abbot within obedience is a space of interpretation.

These early observations on the meaning of the *RSB* and the circumstances of monks' behaviour return us to the problem of obedience and will. The obedience presupposed in the *RSB* necessitates the monk's self-will operating in the fulfilment of a command. He must, in other words, insert himself into the command to interpret what his abbot actually wants. In fact, within the relation of obedience the problem of interpretation is always present: the subject must always interpret his abbot's command, even while desiring to complete his obedience without delay. And the abbot, as we shall see, must interpret his subject's actions even to understand the terms of his own order.

123 Smaragdus, *Expositio*, p. 178, lines 14–18.

On the Stories of Obedience in the *Verba seniorum*

As coenobitic forms of monasticism took inspiration from heroic asceticism in the desert, the virtue of obedience to a spiritual father developed as an essential element of monastic life. While the naturalization of religious identity for new and continuing members of a monastic *familia* depended on the imitation of other brothers in the house, the ideals of behaviour circulated textually in the many stories of the heroic obedience of the pioneers of monasticism. One important source of information on the wisdom and practice of the desert fathers was a collection of texts commonly known as the *Verba seniorum*.[124] Many of the stories collected in cap. 14 (*De obedientia*) of the *Verba seniorum* were widely known, incorporated by Cassian in his *De institutis* and by Sulpicius Severus in the *Dialogi*, and echoed in the *RSB*.[125] Some versions of the *Verba seniorum* were copied in Anglo-Saxon England, though the five surviving manuscripts transmit extracts.[126] And it was known and used by Ælfric on some eight occasions.[127] The collection of sayings on obedience show us different aspects of the relation of spiritual master to subject, illustrate various modes of command, but always show the heroism of exacting obedience and celebrate it as among the most precious in the monk's spiritual arsenal.

124 PL 73, 855–1022 (*BHL* 6527) reprints the seventeenth-century edition of Heribert Rosweyde.

125 See below, pp. 44–6.

126 Gneuss, *Handlist*: London, British Library Additional 15350, fols. 1 and 121 (no. 281); British Library, Cotton Otho C. i, vol. ii (no. 359); Cotton Vespasian D. vi, fols. 2–77 (no. 389); Worcester, Cathedral Library F. 48 (no. 761); Brussels, Bibliothèque Royale 9850–2 (no. 808.2). For knowledge of the *Vitas patrum* in Anglo-Saxon England, see Peter Jackson, 'The *Vitas Patrum* in Eleventh-Century Worcester,' in *England in the Eleventh Century: Proceedings of the 1990 Harlaxton Symposium*, ed. Carola Hicks, Harlaxton Medieval Studies 2 (Stamford: Paul Watkins, 1992), 119–34, esp. 123. On the problem of 'secondhand' use of the *Vitas patrum* see also Peter Jackson, 'Vitae Patrum,' in *Sources of Anglo-Saxon Culture: A Trial Version*, ed. Frederick M. Biggs, Thomas D. Hill, and Paul E. Szarmach, with the assistance of Karen Hammond, Medieval and Renaissance Texts and Studies 74 (Binghamton: State University of New York at Binghamton, 1992), 162–5.

127 Peter Jackson, 'Ælfric and the "Uita Patrum" in Catholic Homily I.36,' in *Essays on Anglo-Saxon and Related Themes in Memory of Lynne Grundy*, ed. Jane Roberts and Janet Nelson, King's College London Medieval Studies 17 (London: King's College London, Centre for Late Antique & Medieval Studies, 2000), 259–72 at 263 and n. 11.

The key to the relation of spiritual master to subject is the severity of the trial exacted out of love and regard. We see this in the story of Abba Ares and the brother who asks what he must do to be saved (XIV.2). Abba Ares first tells him to eat bread and salt each evening for a year. After the year is completed, he tells him to eat bread and salt but fast every other day. When Abba Ares is asked why he imposed so harsh a burden on the younger man, Ares replies: 'hic vero quia propter Deum venit audire verbum, operarius autem est magnus, et quidquid ei dixero, cum omni sollicitudine facit, propterea et ego loquor ei verbum Dei' [but he comes to hear a word for the love of God, and indeed he is a great labourer, and whatever I will say to him, he does with every care. For this reason I speak the word of God to him]. Recasting the terms of the question, Abba Ares explains the harshness of his tests as a sign of his love for the monk he is trying and a sign of his spiritual regard for him. In other words, so difficult a test is an index of the relation between master and disciple.

Other stories show the importance of obedience in coenobitic communities. St Syncletica is remembered to have valued obedience over continence for those living in community: 'quoniam continentia arrogantiam habet, obedientia autem humilitatem congruam pollicetur' [for continence produces arrogance, but obedience promises appropriate humility (XIV.9)].[128] Such obedience, linked to humility, surfaces again in the context of living in community, when Syncletica observes that living in a congregation requires a self-denial that abandons both possessions and self-will: 'in congregatione manentes, [oportet] non quae nostra sunt quaerere, neque servire propriae voluntati' [when living in community, it is necessary that we not seek after our own goods nor gratify self-will (XIV.10)]. The pre-eminence of obedience in comparison to the other, characteristic ascetic virtues of monastic life is illustrated by a brief narrative told of Abba Pambo, who is visited by four brothers dressed in skin tunics, each of whom showed a different virtue:

> Unus namque ex eis jejunabat multum, alter vero nihil possidebat, tertius autem habebat charitatem plurimam; de quarto vero dixerunt quia viginti duos annos haberet in obedientia permanens seniorum. Respondit autem ei abbas Pambo: Dico vobis quia istius virtus major est quam caeterorum: quoniam unusquisque vestrum virtutem quam possidet, voluntate propria eam

128 Yet another of the sayings places obedience before continence. See XIV.17, where a man is raised from the dead by the prayers of an obedient monk.

retinuit; hic autem suam voluntatem abscindens, alienae voluntatis se servum fecit. Tales enim viri confessores sunt, si usque ad finem ita permanserint.[129]

[For one of them fasted a great deal, another owned nothing; and yet a third had great charity; about the fourth, though, they said that he had spent twenty-two years living in obedience to the elders. Then Abba Pambo replied: 'I say to you that the virtue of this man is greater than that of the others since each one of you keeps the virtue that he has by keeping self-will. But he has stripped away his self-will and made himself subject to another's will. Indeed, such men, if they remain in that state until death, will be confessors.]

Abba Pambo's formulation is startling from the outset, since it appears to contravene 1 Cor. 13:13 by asserting that obedience is a greater virtue than charity. But the explanation for the advantage of obedience over poverty, fasting, and charity in this context is the radically transformative nature of obedience. In Pambo's valuation, obedience means giving away all that one has and all that one is. The other three men in the story, though remarkable in their practice of individual virtue, *chose* to practise those virtues, and in so doing kept as their own ('propria') the will to be virtuous. The fourth man, however, stripping himself ('abscindens') of will in the continued practice of obedience, negated his self-will by subjecting himself (and the word is *seruus*, servant) to the will and command of another. By emptying himself he filled himself with virtue.[130] Elsewhere in the *Verba seniorum*, some abbots observe that God wants nothing as much as obedience from those who have recently converted to monastic life (XIV.15).[131] The moral effect of such obedience (and the radical effect of the denial of the will required by such obedience) is suggested by another saying, 'Quia si habet quis in aliquo fidem, et tradit se ei ad subjectionem, non debet attendere in mandatis Dei, sed Patri suo spirituali omnem voluntatem suam

129 PL 73, 949, cap. XIV.7.

130 *Verba seniorum* XIV.19 explains that the obedient will have greater glory in heaven than any others, because unlike others who are virtuous by their own wills ('secundum propriam voluntatem') or by their own choice ('arbitrio suo'), 'Hic autem ordo, qui se ad obediendum dedit, omnes voluntates suas abjiciens, pendet ad Deum et ad jussionem Patris spiritualis, propterea et majorem gloriam aliis habet' [But this cohort, that gives itself to obedience, casting away all self-will, and depends on God and the commands of a spiritual father, will have, for this reason, greater glory than those others].

131 *Verba seniorum* XIV.13 observes that God requires Christians to obey the scriptures, since they contain the pattern of behaviour, and to conform to the pronouncements of the fathers and bishops.

committere; quia illi per omnia obediens, non incurret peccatum apud Deum'[132] [If someone has faith in another and subjects himself to him, he should not strive after the commands of God, but entrust all his will to his spiritual father, because by obeying him in all things, he will not sin before God]. This observation about the demands of obedience shows obedience as a relation where the spiritual father stands in the place of God, and diligence in obeying his commands translates into suitable obedience to God. It suggests that the wholly obedient subject is absolved of responsibility for himself to the degree that he rids himself of his self-will. For even something as praiseworthy as striving to obey the commandments lessens the object of obedience, that is, the eradication of self-will.

The value accorded to obedience, its place at the forefront of ascetic virtues, and its function in the relation between spiritual father and subject illustrated in these stories make comprehensible the heroic dimensions of perfect obedience extolled in this chapter of the *Verba seniorum*. A number of these illustrative stories were adopted by later writers.

Stealing Obedience

With these observations on agency, identity, and obedience, we can return to the problems posed by Wulfstan's narrative of Æthelwold's prudence and Ælfstan's great obedience. Rather than one, there are three, incommensurable, narratives at work in Æthelwold's test of Ælfstan and of his obedience. The first is a narrative of pastoral rule. The disconcerting detail that Æthelwold makes his demand of Ælfstan 'hilari uultu' (with a cheerful countenance) at first blush seems to portray the abbot as a sadist whose contemplation of his subject's present discomfort and future pain brought obvious pleasure. But the following events of Wulfstan's account, where Ælfstan's unhesitating obedience does him no harm, clarifies the *uita*'s positioning of Æthelwold within traditional monastic narratives of abbatial command. From just such a store of narratives, richly illustrated – for example, in the *Vitas patrum,* as well as in Cassian's *De institutis*[133] – Smaragdus of St Mihiel drew in the *Diadema* to illustrate the heroism of monastic obedience in the face of commands that appear either

132 *Verba seniorum*, XIV.12. Such severity is not matched in later commentaries on the *RSB*.

133 Michael Petschenig, ed., *Iohannis Cassiani Opera: De Institutis Coenobiorum et de Octo Principalium Vitiorum Remediis Libri XII*, CSEL 17 (Vienna, 1888), IV.24 (Abbot John and the dry stick); 27 (Abbot Patermutus and the child tossed into the river).

pointless or impossible.[134] In one such story, an abbot commands a would-be monk to water a dead stick in the desert until it blooms; in another an abbot orders a father to toss his infant son into a furnace.[135] Of particular interest to the framing of Æthelwold's test of Ælfstan, however, is one such narrative that Sulpicius Severus offers in his *Dialogues*.[136] Here he tells of a postulant who wishes to illustrate the extent of his proffered obedience. Increasingly anxious at the prospect of being denied entry into the monastery, the postulant assures the master that he would walk through fire if the master so ordered him. By chance, the narrative explains, nearby was an oven glowing with heat, ready for cooking some loaves of bread. As the flames lick outside its open door, the master orders the would-be monk to walk into the burning oven. The postulant's immediate obedience is rewarded just as was the faith of the boys in the fiery furnace (Dan. 3:50). Unharmed, the young man is welcomed into the monastery.

As Wulfstan's narrative calls upon these earlier stories of heroic monastic obedience to affirm Æthelwold's status as *pater monachorum* and *errantium corrector* [father of monks and corrector of those who have strayed], Æthelwold is shown to give an order that both illustrates obedience and tests it. In the context of pastoral narrative, his comment, 'you have stolen this obedience from me,' made 'hilari uultu,' means to show not pleasure in anticipation of pain, but serenity in the knowledge that perfect obedience – an obedience that would confirm Ælfstan's identity as a monk – would keep the monk unharmed. Æthelwold's cheerful countenance is thus meant to show his good will (that he is not angry with the monk), his confidence in his command, and his assurance in the dimensions of the pastoral relationship, abbot to monk, superior to subject.[137] And yet his radical test of obedience has more complex work to do,

134 See, for example, Smaragdus, *Diadema monachorum*, PL 102, 610, who retells the tests of watering a dead stick and tossing a beloved son into an oven. Compare Cassian, *De institutis coenobiorum*, IV.27 (cited above, n. 133).

135 See *Vitas patrum*, PL 73, 948; 952. See also Jacques Fontaine, ed., with Nicole Dupré, *Gallus, Dialogues sur les 'Vertus' de Saint Martin*, Sources chrétiennes 510 (Paris: Éditions du Cerf, 2006), I.19, pp. 177–80 (on the dry stick).

136 Fontaine, *Gallus, Dialogues*, cap. 18, pp. 172–7.

137 But see Hildemar, *Expositio*, 594, commenting on *RSB* 64.16 ('Non sit turbulentus et anxius'): 'Turbulentus enim dicitur ille, qui in vultu suo hilaritatem non ostendit' [For he is said to be agitated, who does not show cheerfulness in his face]. Compare the version of 'Paulus Diaconus' (*Pauli Warnefridi Diaconi . . . Commentarium*, p. 482), who adds 'et semper incedit iratus et vultu orribili' [and always appears angry and with a fearsome countenance]. Smaragdus, *Expositio*, p. 317, lines 5–6, gives simply

for the further strands of the narrative show us, by contrast, a different Æthelwold, disturbed by his subject's apparent insubordination and anxious to settle the issue.

The second strand of the narrative comprises Wulfstan's presentation of Ælfstan. While Wulfstan makes it clear that Ælfstan will go on to a distinguished religious career, as abbot of the Old Minster, Winchester, and later, bishop of Ramsbury,[138] it is also clear that the younger man's energetic response to his command troubles Æthelwold. Wulfstan phrases the abbot's command simply: 'praeuidere cibaria artificum monasterii,' that is, to provide food for the monastery's workmen.[139] If we look for a moment at this command (and we are only given Wulfstan's paraphrase to work with), we can see Ælfstan's dilemma. What, exactly, might the abbot mean by 'praeuidere'? To oversee, to see to, to provide? If Ælfstan asks himself, 'What does he want?' he will calibrate his own obedience (immediate and cheerful) with his own history in the house (to which we have no access) but also with the textual examples of monastic obedience against which Wulfstan and his readers would judge the monk's compliance. And further, he will wonder how Æthelwold will judge his performance. Will his obedience fall short (if he merely 'oversees' when more was expected) or will it exceed the scope of the original command (if he 'provides' when overseeing had been expected). Ælfstan improvises, bringing to Æthelwold's command the heroic obedience of narratives from the *Vitas patrum*. Beyond overseeing the preparation of food, the monk cooked, served, lit the fire, fetched water, cleaned the pans so that they sparkled, and swept the floor – in short, he performed all the tasks associated with providing food from the kitchen. But such energetic work, however cheerfully and immediately performed, not only gained Ælfstan no merit, it opened him to Æthelwold's charge of theft. By doing more than the abbot's literal order to oversee the food, Ælfstan appears to keep for himself his own will in exceeding what was commanded of him. That excess, appearing to be the product of self-will (however praiseworthy the object of the exercise), would remove him from the structured relation of superior and subject, in that by willing other than he was ordered, he would, in fact, be acting as abbot to himself. In that refiguring of the

---

'Turbulentus dicitur commotionis ira turbatus, mestus, molestus vel atrox.' For a discussion of these commentaries, see above, pp. 36–42.

138 See Lapidge and Winterbottom, eds., *Life of St Æthelwold*, p. 28, n. 1.

139 Ibid., cap. 14, p. 26. Ælfric's language is identical: cap. 10, p. 74. See Lewis and Short, s.v. *praevideo*, sense II.B, late Latin 'to provide.'

relation between abbot and subject (where the abbot wills and the subject obeys), through the improper use of his will, Ælfstan would not only steal obedience but would steal his abbot's function. Such a reading of Ælfstan's act and Æthelwold's charge inserts the two men in a contest driven by the master–slave dialectic. In suspecting Ælfstan's response to his command, Æthelwold interprets the monk's behaviour as a challenge to his authority and a threat to his identity as abbot. His order that Ælfstan plunge his hand into the cauldron demands both recognition of his own identity as abbot and simultaneous confirmation of Ælfstan's identity as monk, which is to say his subject position. Even further, however, Æthelwold's strange claim to *own* the obedience due him reacts to what can only be perceived as improper agent action arising in Ælfstan's attempt to carry out the abbot's command. In refusing the latitude of the monk's interpretation of his command, Æthelwold, as abbot, acts also as the God who tried Abraham's faith by testing his unquestioning obedience (Gen. 22:1–14).

As the *RSB* 5.7 specifies, the obedience owed to a superior meant an abandoning of one's own will,[140] and Ælfstan's industry, by contrast, appears to contravene that requirement.[141] If he has indeed anticipated Æthelwold's command, Ælfstan has made it impossible for himself to obey Æthelwold and has diminished Æthelwold's ability to direct him. In so doing, he will have taken from Æthelwold the obedience due him as abbot, disrupted the relationship of subordinate to superior, and undone his own identity as monk and brother of the community, for his identity is precisely dependent on repeated acts of obedience. Such expected behaviour is made clear by the Rule's criticism of the detested Sarabaites, who live in groups of two or three, but have no abbot or rule to direct them:[142] 'for them, the pleasure of their own desires is law.' The threatened inversion of the monastic relation in Ælfstan's act is hinted at in the expression on Æthelwold's face

140 'uoluntatem propriam deseren[s].' Hanslik, *Benedicti Regula*, 5.7, p. 38.

141 'mox aliquid imperatum a maiore fuerit, ac si diuinitus imperetur, moram pati nesciant in faciendo.' Hanslik, *Benedicti Regula*, 5.4, p. 38. Further, the third degree of humility is obedience to a superior. Ibid., 7.34, p. 50.

142 Ibid., 1.8, p. 20: 'Qui bini aut terni aut certe singuli sine pastore, non dominicis, sed suis inclusi obilibus pro lege eis est desideriorum uoluptas, cum, quidquid putauerint uel elegerint, hoc dicunt sanctum et, quod noluerint, hoc putant non licere.' For a reading of the *RSB*'s portrayal of the Sarabaite's nature as both 'soft and feminine' as well as 'uncultivated and bestial' see Lynda L. Coon, *Dark Age Bodies: Gender and Monastic Practice in the Early Medieval West* (Philadelphia: University of Pennsylvania Press, 2011), 78.

('hilari uultu'), which is that expression expected of the compliant monk in the *RSB* ('hilarem datorem').[143]

The third strand of the narrative – in which Æthelwold commands Ælfstan to reach into the boiling pot and retrieve a morsel of food – is structured as a judicial ordeal.[144] Of the several possible forms of ordeal, this trial by stewpot evokes the ordeal by boiling water.[145] This particular ordeal took place in a church, where the water was heated to a boil. No one might enter the church after the water was set to boil, except the priest overseeing the ordeal and the subject of the trial. This form of the ordeal required a stone to be suspended in the boiling water: for a 'single' accusation, the proband had to plunge his hand in up to the wrist; for a 'threefold' accusation, up to the elbow.[146] In Wulfstan's account, Æthelwold as priest and Ælfstan as proband stand before the cauldron as the two parties in this ritual. The instrument of Ælfstan's ordeal is the kitchen's boiling cauldron ('feruens caldarium'), and his order, to draw the morsel from the *bottom* of the stewpot, suggests the severity of a 'threefold' accusation, where Ælfstan would have had to reach into the boiling liquid up to his elbow. In Robert Bartlett's elegant formulation, ordeal was resorted to when 'certain knowledge was impossible but uncertainty was intolerable,'[147] and its

143 The Rule echoes 2 Cor. 9:7: 'Hilarem enim datorem diligit Deus,' and Sir. 35:11: 'In omni dato hilarem fac vultum tuum.'

144 Patrick Wormald, 'Æthelwold and His Continental Counterparts: Contact, Comparison, Contrast,' in Yorke, ed., *Bishop Æthelwold: His Career and Influence*, 13–42 at 13–14, lists the incident of the stewpot as a type of ordeal without further comment. Robert Bartlett, *Trial by Fire and Water: The Medieval Judicial Ordeal* (Oxford: Clarendon Press, 1986), 9, discusses trial by cauldron as the early Frankish form of proof. See Bruno Krusch, ed., *Gregorii Episcopi Turonensis Libri Octo Miraculorum*, MGH, SRM 1.2 (Hannover, 1885; repr. Hannover: Hahn, 1969), I.80, pp. 92–3. See also Paul R. Hyams, 'Trial by Ordeal: The Key to Proof in the Early Common Law,' in *On the Laws and Customs of England: Essays in Honor of Samuel E. Thorne*, ed. Morris S. Arnold, et al. (Chapel Hill: University of North Carolina Press, 1981), pp. 90–126 at 93, n. 13.

145 See DOE, *A-G*, s.v. *ceac*, sense 'c.' Where the word for 'vessel for water or another liquid' stands for the ordeal itself. See Patrick Wormald, *The Making of English Law: King Alfred to the Twelfth Century*, vol. 1 (Oxford: Blackwell, 1999), 172 and n. 40.

146 F. Liebermann, ed., *Die Gesetze der Angelsachsen*, 3 vols. (Halle: Max Niemeyer, 1903–16), I: 386–7, 'Dom be haten isene and wætre.' For a translation into English see F.L. Attenborough, ed. and trans., *The Laws of the Earliest English Kings* (Cambridge: Cambridge University Press, 1922; facs. repr. Felinfach: Llanerch Publishers, 2000), Appendix II, 'Dom be hatan isene and wætre,' 170–3. See also II Æthelstan 23.1 (Liebermann, *Gesetze*, I: 162 and Wormald, *The Making of English Law*, 374).

147 Bartlett, *Trial by Fire and Water*, 33.

use in the episode shows us an abbot unable to interpret the conundrum of Ælfstan's actions, that is, the unreadable intention behind his subject's performance of obedience. In short, Æthelwold's problem as abbot is a problem of knowledge whose resolution can only be achieved by appealing for divine intervention. Ælfstan, whose guilt or innocence of *furtum* is being assessed, is kept harmless from the boiling water in two dimensions: by virtue of an act of obedience perfect and swift that affirms his identity as Æthelwold's subject, and by the judgment of God, who read the innocent intention of Ælfstan's prior act. His present, perfect obedience makes plausible his earlier obedience; his unscalded hand and arm confirm it.[148]

We see in this story, repeated almost verbatim in Ælfric of Eynsham's version,[149] the crucial importance of obedience as surrender of the will in monastic life. Such ideal surrender of the will is repeatedly illustrated in the *uita* by several instances of Æthelwold's own submission to the king's orders (for example, in being tonsured and in accepting monastic life away from Glastonbury), the implication being that his obedience put him in harmony with God's plan.[150] If we find these instances of behaviour strangely passive, their point was to demonstrate that the saint's life was not determined by his own will, but by direction from above.

Æthelwold's test of Ælfstan is multiple: at its simplest it is a test of his subject's obedience. If, on the model of *RSB* 5.9 and the trials of obedience of the desert fathers, Ælfstan complies immediately, he will demonstrate his own obedience and in so doing show his identity as a monk and subject of Æthelwold. But the scripting of the test as an ordeal shows a great deal more. The mapping of ordeal on trial of obedience shows Æthelwold's command to be an invocation of God's judgment to clarify the unreadable intention of the abbot's subject, that is, to determine whether Ælfstan's previous behaviour was true obedience or theft. Because he is pastor to his flock, Æthelwold's own salvation depends

148 The immediate plunging of his hand into the stewpot was done, as the *RSB* specifies, 'ueluti uno momento' (*RSB* 5.9) with Æthelwold's order. In Wulfstan of Winchester's *Narratio metrica de S. Swithuno*, St Swithun shows mercy to an apparently guilty slave (=Wulfstan of Winchester II.viii, Lantfred, *Translatio et miracula S. Swithuni*, cap. 25), who was condemned to the ordeal of hot iron, perhaps for theft. When the slave's hand is unbandaged, the reeve sees a whole hand and declares him innocent, but the slave's owner, who had prayed to St Swithun, sees a putrified hand and thus the slave's guilt. See Lapidge, *The Cult of St Swithun*, 508–15. See also Katherine O'Brien O'Keeffe, 'Body and Law in Late Anglo-Saxon England,' *ASE* 27 (1998): 209–32 at 223–4.

149 See Lapidge and Winterbottom, *Life of St Æthelwold*, Appendix A, cap. 10, p. 74.

150 See ibid., cap. 7 ('iubente rege,' p. 10) and cap. 11 ('secundum regis uoluntatem,' p. 20).

on his conducting all in his charge to heaven by carefully supervising their obedience,[151] and Ælfstan's possible disobedience puts his abbot at risk. A successful negotiation of the ordeal will also have confirmed to Æthelwold the true relation of abbot and subject in the good will (which is to say dead will) of the younger monk.[152] But the test was meant to establish something further – Ælfstan's true identity as a monk in the *familia* of Abingdon. We see this in the words that preface Æthelwold's testing command: 'si talis miles Christi es qualem te ostendis' [if you are the soldier of Christ that you show yourself to be] makes obedience *the* critical test of monastic identity. But as obedience is never finished, such identity is always subject to fracture, uncertainty, and anxiety within the dynamic relation of superior and subject.

Ælfstan's story, showing the obedience of a professed monk, is driven by an understanding of the nature and function of obedience as a practice that consistently denied the will in order to structure and ensure the monk's identity. And the degree to which a monk's life of obedience was, in fact, praiseworthy, was measured by his cheerful and immediate accession to his superior's will. In such a circumstance, will, as we might understand its operation, did not operate in the choice of individual activities (praying, writing, fetching water, and so forth) but was contracted into a willing to obey, in the language of analytic philosophy, a second-order volition in which the monk desires to be obedient.[153] The monk's ideal agent action

151 *RSB* 2.5–7. See Hildemar, *Expositio*, 91–3; see also Smaragdus, *Expositio*, p. 63, lines 15–21.

152 As Michel Foucault observes of the pastoral relation, 'Being humble is basically, and above all, knowing that any will of one's own is a bad will. So if there is an end to obedience, it is a state of obedience defined by the definitive and complete renunciation of one's own will. The aim of obedience is the mortification of one's will; it is to act so that one's will, as one's own will, is dead, that is to say, so that there is no other will but not to have any will' (*Security, Territory, Population*, 177–8).

153 In his classic argument for a new approach to compatibilism (that is, the philosophical position that free will, and thus, moral responsibility, do not require the ability to do otherwise), Harry Frankfurt distinguishes between first-order and second-order desires: a first-order desire might be 'I want to exercise daily.' A second-order desire forms a desire about a desire: 'I desire to want to exercise daily.' In the case where a person wants that second-order desire to be his/her will, Frankfurt terms it 'second-order volition.' In this understanding, moral responsibility lies in forming what he would call 'reflective self-evaluation.' See Harry Frankfurt, 'Freedom of the Will and the Concept of a Person,' *Journal of Philosophy* 68.1 (1971): 5–20, esp. 7–10. The essay has been widely reprinted. My interest here lies not in the merits of compatibilism, nor necessarily in the reality of the phenomenon of free will, but rather in the usefulness of the distinction of second-order volition in arguments about agency.

(his 'free' will) in this understanding of moral responsibility, lies solely at this level, not at the first-order level of individual, daily behaviours. But in this account of abbot and monk we see another face of obedience that the narrative will not acknowledge: that monastic obedience is a dynamic relation where agency, however narrow the space for improvisation, emerges as an effect of the mutual interpretation of an abbot's command and a subject's act. It is a space of possibility where abbot and subject act in the negotiations of interpretation. The *RSB*, in prescribing that the abbot's command and the resulting obedient act take place *ueluti uno momento* [as if at one moment], would foreclose that possibility, in imagining not only a temporal oneness of command and act, but a unity of will and intention for abbot and subject. Yet, as it celebrates Æthelwold's zealous pursuit of just such an obedience and offers for our admiration an exemplary relation within obedience, Wulfstan's *uita* (as well as the *uita* of Ælfric) shows just as clearly the fissures of the central, imagined unity of monastic obedience. Instead of a unity of action between superior and subject, as the *RSB* imagines and prescribes, we see a dynamic relation where subject and superior are joined in complementary acts of citation, performance, and interpretation. Instead of unity of will, we see a contest of reading, where intention and will are continually at play in the relation between superior and subject. In short, we see in the imagined unity of obedience a space of uncertainty opened for the possibility of agency.

In pursuing questions of agency raised by the dimensions of Anglo-Saxon monastic identities (shaped variously by familial relations, gender, practices of space, ritual, and performance), *Stealing Obedience* engages a set of interlocking questions: how was agent action understood and figured in Anglo-Saxon England? And what contradictions do these notions of agent action instigate? If we define human agency as an improvisation within conflicting structures, how can we discern agency in the actors represented in our texts? What conflicting structures offer the most persistent loci for their anxieties about agency? Connected to these issues is a question that approaches identity from both its social and its intimate aspects: what are the frames in which religious identity is 'known' by the self and by which the self is 'known' by the society of which it is a part? Given the relatively rigid boundaries by which the identities of monk and nun were structured, how is desire within such identities figured and regulated? The individual chapters of *Stealing Obedience* address themselves variously to these questions and arrange these questions in different configurations. In so doing, they extend the considerations of obedience in the pastoral relation of superior and subject explored in this introduction to the larger question of obedience to the will of God, on which the monastic relation was modelled. The reading of the abbot's or the abbess's will in the act of obedience was precisely analogous to the reading of the will of God ('Qui vos audit, me audit'). The following chapters attend to the narratives of the taking up of religious identity framed as a discourse of simultaneous willing (by God and by the saint); explore the contradictions of the practice of oblation that ascribes agency to a child conveyed as an object; read the building of textual identity in the monastic classroom through the order to 'be what you are'; investigate the legal situation of nuns (ritually analogous to that of oblated children); and argue that the attendant demands on them required investing them with what I term 'phantom' agency. And they investigate the ambiguous relationship between Eve, once a nun of Wilton, and Goscelin, her spiritual adviser, and the play of identity and agency at work in her move to reclusion in Angers.

The smooth surface of Wulfstan's narrative of great obedience does not quite contain the disquiet at work within his account. The startling charge of stealing obedience that Æthelwold levels points us to other disruptions: to the uncertainties in performance, to the fragility of identity, and to the ambiguity of reading. While all of these confront Æthelwold in his direction of the monk Ælfstan, the narrative shows us, in the saint's recourse to ordeal, that the disjunction producing the greatest anxiety for him was the ambiguity of reading. What, precisely, did Ælfstan's energetic performance mean? Did it signify a humble undertaking of the abbot's command, or a cunning undercutting of his authority? Was it a sign of dead will or self-will? Did it show Ælfstan on the path to salvation or damnation? Did it affirm or deny the identities of the two men? Æthelwold's conundrum, driven by the improvisory terms of Ælfstan's performance, enacts a problem that the narrative reveals despite itself: that agency as such resists our interpretation. The miracle of Ælfstan's preservation from the boiling cauldron marks in the narrative divine approbation for the monk's behaviour. But what was approved: sedulous conformity or successful improvisation? In different ways, the chapters that follow show that Æthelwold's problem of reading is also our own.

1 Dunstan in the Theatre of Choice

It cannot be said that St Dunstan's time at the court of King Athelstan was uniformly comfortable. Shining in accomplishment and knowing the favour of the king (as B., the first of his hagiographers explains it), Dunstan aroused the envy of enemies at court who contrived to drive him from the king's favour. Having succeeded in expelling him from court, they then added insult to injury by dumping him in a filthy swamp, further dishonouring him by pressing him into the mire – what B. terms 'in foetenti uolutabro' [in a stinking wallowing hole].[1] After this distressing misadventure, Dunstan went to stay with his kinsman, Bishop Ælfheah, who, thinking that the young man's unhappy experience at court would dispose him favourably to withdrawing from the world, urged him to become a monk. In the four versions of Dunstan's *uita* with which this chapter is concerned – those by B., Osbern, Eadmer, and William of Malmesbury – the saint, quite remarkably, is shown to resist conversion to the monastic way of life.[2] And in each account, somewhat later after

1 Michael Winterbottom and Michael Lapidge, eds., *The Early Lives of St Dunstan*, OMT (Oxford: Clarendon Press, 2011) forthcoming, cap. 6.6, p. 22. I am grateful to them for making available to me in advance their text of B.'s *uita* of St Dunstan.

2 The four versions are printed in *Memorials of Saint Dunstan*, ed. William Stubbs, RS 63 (London: Longman, 1874). Osbern's *Vita Sancti Dunstani* is edited by Stubbs, *Memorials of Saint Dunstan*, pp. 69–128. For Eadmer's account see now Andrew J. Turner and Bernard J. Muir, eds., *Eadmer of Canterbury: Lives and Miracles of Saints Oda, Dunstan, and Oswald*, OMT (Oxford: Clarendon Press, 2006). For William's account see M. Winterbottom and R.M. Thomson, eds., *William of Malmesbury, Saints' Lives: Lives of SS. Wulfstan, Dunstan, Patrick, Benignus and Indract*, OMT (Oxford: Clarendon Press, 2002). The lections in Adelard's *Epistola ad Elfegum* (Stubbs, *Memorials of Saint Dunstan*, pp. 53–68) do not contain this incident.

a bout of illness, Dunstan agrees to become a monk. While each inflects this process with a different emphasis, it is Osbern's account of monastic conversion that exposes most starkly the ideological template for conversion to monastic life, cast in the language of will and choice. The peculiarities of his account – its loving attention to the hesitations of conversion, its departure from convention, its use of direct address, and its shocking critique of monastic obedience – draw on and react to the larger narrative of monastic identity and obedience that characterized Benedictine life. In examining the obedience understood to be proper to monastic identity and the agent action it presupposed and demanded, this chapter focuses on Osbern's narrative of Dunstan's monastic conversion, the models on which he draws for portraying a saintly life, the changes he makes in the source material from which he worked, and the shocked reaction of the two writers who shortly followed. In trying to reconcile the predestinarian elements at work in hagiographical narratives of saintly accession to the divine will with newer articulations of agent action, Osbern inserts Dunstan in a theatre of choice, where he stages the play of will and obedience.

Osbern's striking presentation of Dunstan's conversion to monastic life takes its force from a remarkable exchange dramatized between the future saint and the bishop who desires his conversion. In this account, Dunstan, leaving behind the envy and hatred at court, visits his kinsman Ælfheah, bishop of Winchester (934–51), who urges him to become a monk by this argument: since Dunstan's conduct demonstrated that he had in him the beginnings of angelic life ('angelicae conversationis initia haberet'), he should show steadfastness in the conduct of his life ('perseverantiam in habitu demonstraret') by taking the habit.[3] It is possible that Ælfheah himself was a monk.[4] But in striking contrast to the exemplary behaviour of other saints (and his contemporary Æthelwold comes immediately to

3 Stubbs, *Memorials of Saint Dunstan*, cap. 12, p. 82. Osbern got the detail about kinship from B., who describes Ælfheah as 'propinquus ipsius' (Winterbottom and Lapidge, *Early Lives of St Dunstan*, cap. 7.2, p. 26). But see Nicholas Brooks, 'The Career of St Dunstan,' in *St Dunstan: His Life, Times and Cult*, ed. Nigel Ramsay, Margaret Sparks, and Tim Tatton-Brown (Woodbridge: Boydell Press, 1992), pp. 1–23 at 7, who suggests that B. was either exaggerating the significance of a distant relationship or misinterpreting adoptive kinship in the bishop's *familia*.

4 William of Malmesbury regards him as such. See his *Vita S. Dunstani*, in Winterbottom and Thompson, *William of Malmesbury, Saints' Lives*, I.7.1 (p. 184). For information on Bishop Ælfheah see Michael Lapidge and Michael Winterbottom, eds., *Wulfstan of Winchester, The Life of St Æthelwold*, OMT (Oxford: Clarendon Press, 1991), cap. 8, p. 12, n. 1.

mind) and perhaps in contrast to the bishop's own example, Dunstan does not obey:

> respondit ille excellentioris gratiae esse qui in saeculo consenuit et tamen quae monacho digna sunt fecit, eo qui se monasterio dedit, nec quicquam aliud praeterquam quod sibi statutum est post haec facere potuit. 'Alterum,' inquit, 'necessitatis est, alterum libertatis.'[5]
>
> [He responded that that man who grew old in the world and nevertheless did what was proper for a monk would be of superior quality, because the one who gave himself to a monastery was not able after that to do anything other than what was commanded him. The one, he said, is a matter of necessity, the other of freedom.]

In this response to Bishop Ælfheah's persistent urgings that Dunstan become a monk, Osbern makes Dunstan's refusal the result of a principled, ethical argument on the better way to lead one's life, an argument that radically undercuts the central rationale of Benedictine monasticism. 'Libertas' in this argument is that freedom to choose good or evil with which man is endowed. In possession of such freedom, Dunstan is made to argue, at each moment of his life, any act of monastic discipline he undertook would be the product of moral choice arising from individual intention and could thus be regarded as agent action. In short, Dunstan's reply to the bishop argues, shockingly, in context, that any act of monastic discipline independently initiated and freely willed by the individual was of greater intrinsic merit than the same act performed under the rule of obedience. Under the condition of freedom that he describes, there would be no need for an abbot to read his intention, judge his achievement, or mediate between him and God. The multiplicity of free acts that Dunstan is made to imagine in this anecdote would, by virtue of their superior individual merit, produce a life of greater worth than the bound life of a monk, who had irrevocably committed himself to a monastery. In claiming that the latter acts by necessity and the former from free choice, Dunstan appears to deny agent action to a monk bound by the vow of monastic obedience. The description of a monk as one 'qui se monasterio dedit' is not innocent: the monk's conveyance to the monastery makes him a gift to God like an oblate, and as gift each acts at the command of another. After such a commitment, Dunstan is made to argue in Osbern's account, the

5 Stubbs, *Memorials of Saint Dunstan*, cap. 12, p. 82.

monk's act can be no more praiseworthy than merely carrying out what he is ordered to do, because he lacks the full capacity for agent action of those not bound by his vow of obedience, immediate and complete.

Following this claim, Osbern has Ælfheah frame an answer to Dunstan's objection. But in so doing, the bishop builds his case by redefining Dunstan's key terms – *necessitas* and *libertas* – to argue a different, fundamental, necessity and a new goal for freedom. Ælfheah's focus is the fires of concupiscence leading to the fires of Hell, and a salvation that requires removing the 'tinder' ('fomenta' [for *fomes*]) igniting such fires:

> Ad haec episcopus, 'Omnibus,' ait, 'in commune summa necessitas est, ut qui ignem gehennae voluerit effugere, ignem concupiscentiae studeat extinguere. Ignis vero concupiscentiae non multum extinguitur, si fomenta illius humanis sensibus non subtrahuntur. Sicut enim ligna ad ignem, sic ea quae sensibus subjacent, ad concupiscentiam. Sed nulla erit fomentorum subtractio, si saecularium negotiorum non fuerit renunciatio. Ex quibus omnibus id elicitur; ut si ignem gehennae volueris effugere, saeculo studeas renunciare. Ad haec quod praecipue in mundo appetitur, libertas est hominis. Hac enim omissa, caetera possideri nequeunt. Quod si possidentur, illa non desinit haberi. Quapropter quamdiu illam retinueris, illud Deo non dedisti, quod maxime dilexisti: ut ergo des quod maxime diligis, illa desinat haberi.'[6]
>
> [To these things the bishop replies: for all people in general it is of the highest necessity that whoever wishes to escape the fire of Gehenna should strive to extinguish the fire of concupiscence. In fact, the fire of concupiscence is rarely extinguished if its tinder is not removed from the human senses, for things of the senses are to concupiscence as wood to the fire. But there will be no removal of the tinder, if there is no renunciation of the things of this world. From all this it is ascertained: if you wish to avoid the fire of Gehenna, you should strive to renounce the world. In this connection, what is especially sought after in the world is human freedom. Absent this, the rest cannot be possessed. For if they are possessed, then that [=freedom] does not cease to be had. Wherefore, for as long as you retain that [=freedom], what you have not given to God is what you have loved most of all: therefore, that you may give what you love most of all, let freedom cease to be possessed.]

In the rhetoric of his answer Ælfheah changes the grounds of the argument, even while denying Dunstan's premises that there is spiritual value

6 Ibid.

in the actions of a man in the world and that obedience is unhelpful and unnecessary. Here 'libertas' and 'necessitas' no longer signify as they did when they functioned as the logical poles of Dunstan's description of two contrasting existential conditions. In Ælfheah's rebuttal, 'necessitas,' altered from its first sense as 'necessity' or 'compulsion' to a secondary sense, 'need,' is subordinated to a moral argument about avoiding the consequences of concupiscence.[7] Attacking the second logical pole of Dunstan's description, Ælfheah calls on the argument of sacrificial obedience (though without using the specific language of sacrifice) to assert that obedience is central to salvation. In doing so, he recuperates Dunstan's hapless straw monk, who gave himself to the monastery ('se monasterio dedit') and was unable to do anything thereafter, by redefining the monk's sacrificial gift as what a man loves most in the world, his freedom. As an oblate is the sacrifice of his parents, freedom is the sacrifice of the monk. Absent that ultimate gift, Ælfheah claims, there can be no renunciation of the world. Freedom, it would appear, has vanished.

As Osbern develops the account, there is further (though unreported) argument between the two men, and Dunstan hesitates, perhaps unsurprisingly, considering that Ælfheah's reply hardly met his formal objections. Agitated by his indecision, he contracts a terrible fever, leaving him and all who saw him in doubt of his life. Upon his recovery (and not, it should be noted, in the throes of his illness), he leaves behind the prospect of pleasure and a wife on the argument that such things leave the living unsatisfied and the dead without hope. He thereafter devotes himself to virginity in the monastic life.

Osbern's dramatization of Dunstan's reason for refusing conversion is shocking in itself, but even more so when read against the language of predestination he uses in the earlier part of the *uita* and the contemporary hagiographical conventions he employs in recounting a saint's pursuit of the religious life. As we will see, the resulting picture of Dunstan contrasts markedly as well with those in the *uitae* of Æthelwold and Oswald, the other two great reformers of English Benedictine monasticism. Fully to appreciate the implications of Osbern's narrative strategy, we must first take a closer look at the conventions for presenting the trajectory of a saint's life. In these conventions – prodigies of nature, precocious spiritual

7 Lewis and Short, s.v. *necessitas*, sense I; sense II.C. Although Ælfheah does not make the explicit connection, the context understands concupiscence as an immediate consequence of the Fall, the result of mankind's primal disobedience.

development, perinatal dreams – hagiographical narratives abound not only to underline the sanctity of their subjects, but more importantly to embed them in a master narrative of God's will and exemplary human response. Obedience to the will of God is only possible if that will is made readable, and conventional signs perform that function in the narrative, both for the saint and for the reader. By contrast with the plenitude of signs to be read, the small interest that early medieval hagiography shows in saints' acts of choice in monastic conversion asks attention to their portrayal of agency in such obedience.

Obedience and Agency in the Lives of Saints

One came to the religious life in the early Middle Ages by one of two routes, as a child or as an adult.[8] The operation of choice and the engagement of will in each instance were radically different, although the validity of both ways to religious life was vigorously defended. A child might be ritually dedicated to God and given to a monastic foundation by his or her parents through oblation, an act of piety by which a child was committed to a life in religion.[9] References to such forms of piety can be found widely in contemporary histories, hagiographies, and ecclesiastical legislation. According to the 'Kentish Royal Legend,' when Domne Eafe and her husband, King Merwald, dissolved their marriage to live chaste lives, they gave their children, three daughters and a son, to God. '7 hi þa æfter ðan for godes lufan 7 for þisse worlde him todældon, 7 hiora bearn 7 hiora woruldæhta gode forgeafan'[10] [and after that (viz. the begetting of their

8 For the distinction between 'conversus' and 'nutritus' see Du Cange, *Glossarium* s.v. *conversio*. See also Mayke de Jong, 'Growing Up in a Carolingian Monastery: Magister Hildemar and His Oblates,' *Journal of Medieval History* 9 (1983): 99–128 at 99.

9 Mayke de Jong, *In Samuel's Image: Child Oblation in the Early Medieval West* (Leiden: E.J. Brill, 1996), gives the standard account of oblation in the early Middle Ages. See also Maria Lahaye-Geusen, *Das Opfer der Kinder: Ein Beitrag zur Liturgie- und Sozialgeschichte des Mönchtums im Hohen Mittelalter*, Münsteraner theologische Abhandlungen 13 (Altenberge: Oros Verlag, 1991) for a review of early oblation practices. An earlier treatment is Patricia A. Quinn, *Better Than the Sons of Kings: Boys and Monks in the Early Middle Ages* (New York: Peter Lang, 1989). I consider the implication of oblation for agency and identity in chapter 2 and its legal ramifications in chapter 3.

10 [Thomas] Oswald Cockayne, ed., *Leechdoms, Wortcunning, and Starcraft of Early England*, vol. 3, RS 35 (London, 1866), 422–32 at 422–4. I have modified spacing and punctuation in the citation. On Domne Eafe see D.W. Rollason, *The Mildreth Legend: A Study in Early Medieval Hagiography in England* (Leicester: Leicester University Press, 1982).

children, Sts Mildburg, Mildrith, Mildgith, and Merefin) they separated and gave their children and all their worldly possessions to God]. The account's combination of children and worldly possessions as the objects of the parents' pious gift suggests, at least to us, the potential difficulties posed by giving a gift that has self-will. The Northumbrian King Oswiu (d. 670) promised to oblate his infant daughter Ælfflæd if he was victorious in battle against the heathen Mercian king, Penda. After his victory, in fulfilment of his vow, he gave the child to Hild, then abbess of Hartlepool. Later Ælfflæd would become abbess of Whitby, Hild's subsequent foundation.[11] According to Goscelin, her hagiographer, St Edith, first child of King Edgar, was given by her father to the convent of Wilton as sacrificial 'first fruits.'[12] Bede himself tells us that his kinsmen gave him at the age of seven to Benedict Biscop, abbot of the twin foundation Monkwearmouth and Jarrow, to be educated. Thereafter, he remained for the rest of his life 'inter obseruantiam disciplinae regularis' [within the observance of the discipline of the rule].[13] Alcuin reports that his teacher, Archbishop Ælberht (767–80) was given to a monastery in childhood.[14] Alcuin, reportedly of noble birth, was educated from an early age by the religious community of York Minster.[15] Asser, the biographer of King Alfred, indicates that he was brought up, educated, and tonsured in the monastery of St David's in western Wales.[16] Writing of the translation of St Swithun (971), Wulfstan of Winchester reveals that he himself had been an oblate in the Old Minster

11 Bertram Colgrave and R.A.B. Mynors, eds., *Bede's Ecclesiastical History of the English People*, OMT (Oxford: Clarendon Press, 1969), III.24, pp. 290–2. In an earlier chapter (III.8, p. 238), Bede indicates that in the seventh century, families sent girls to Brie, Chelles, and Andelys-sur-Seine for education and oblation ('sed et filias suas eisdem erudiendas ac sponso caelesti copulandas mittebant'). The royal daughters Sæthryth and Æthelburh were among this number.

12 See chapter 3 below.

13 Colgrave and Mynors, *Bede's Ecclesiastical History of the English People*, V.24, p. 566. Alcuin described Bede's entry into Jarrow: 'utpote septennem quem fecit cura parentum / arta monasterii Girvensis claustra subire' ['With loving concern his parents had made him enter at the age / of seven the cloistered precincts of the monastery of Jarrow,' trans. Godman]. See *Versus de patribus regibus et sanctis Euboricensis ecclesiae*, ed. Peter Godman, *Alcuin, The Bishops, Kings and Saints of York*, OMT (Oxford: Clarendon Press, 1982), lines 1293–4, pp. 102–3.

14 *Versus de patribus regibus et sanctis Euboricensis ecclesiae*, ed. Godman, lines 1415–18, p. 110.

15 *Acta SS*, Mai iv, cols. 335–6 (*BHL* 242).

16 William Henry Stevenson, ed., *Asser's Life of King Alfred*, with an introductory article by Dorothy Whitelock (Oxford: Clarendon Press, 1959), cap. 79, p. 64.

at the time.[17] And Osbern, hagiographer of Sts Ælfheah and Dunstan, had been an oblate in the community of Christ Church, Canterbury, as his vivid accounts of miracles at the shrine of St Dunstan attest.[18]

An oblated child would be given to a religious foundation at around the age of seven for education and naturalization in the monastic life. The act of oblation was understood to be irrevocable, and not only did the parent (usually the father) by his gift commit the child to a continuing life under the Rule, he also promised never to try to revoke that gift. A standard formula for this promise is found in London, British Library, Cotton Tiberius C. i, 93r–93v: 'Et ut hæc nostra traditio inconuulsa permaneat, promitto cum iure iurando coram eadem Sancta MARIA quia nunquam per me, nunquam per suspectam personam, nec quolibet modo per rerum mearum facultates aliquando egrediendi ei de monasterio tribuam occasionem' [And that our gift may remain intact, I promise by oath before this same Saint Mary that never through me nor any respected person, nor in any way through the power of my possessions will I provide opportunity for him to leave the monastery].[19] The specificity of this triple promise hints at how tempting it could have been for parents to change their minds. Although Anglo-Saxon England did not have a case of such dramatic dimensions as that of Gottschalk, Ælfric's cautionary tale of the runaway *munuccild* and Goscelin's confection of infant choice in his *uita* of St Edith suggest that for the children as well as parents return to the world must have posed a temptation.[20]

By contrast, for the adult *conuersus*, like Guthlac or Cuthbert, both of whom turned to religious life after military service, or for the founders of

17 Lapidge and Winterbottom, *Wulfstan of Winchester, Life of St Æthelwold*, xiv.

18 Osbern, *Miracula S. Dunstani*, cap. 11–12, ed. Stubbs, *Memorials of Saint Dunstan*, pp. 136–9, writes of 'nos pueri' and describes a miracle whereby Dunstan spares the boys a whipping. In cap. 12 he refers to himself and another boy in the monastery as 'puerul[i]' [little boys], and that a widow calls them 'pueri Dei.' On what little is known of Osbern's early life see Jay Rubenstein, 'The Life and Writings of Osbern of Canterbury,' in *Canterbury and the Norman Conquest: Churches, Saints and Scholars 1066–1109*, ed. Richard Eales and Richard Sharpe (London: Hambledon Press, 1995), 27–40.

19 For the full text of the ritual and a translation see my 'Goscelin and the Consecration of Eve,' *ASE* 35 (2006): 251–70 at 259. This would appear to be a standard formulation for oblations: see De Jong, *In Samuel's Image*, 176–85. Such stipulations are repeated in Lanfranc's *Decreta* (ca 1077): *The Monastic Constitutions of Lanfranc*, ed. and trans. Dom David Knowles, rev. ed. Christopher N.L. Brooke (Oxford: Clarendon Press, 2002), cap. 105, pp. 162–4.

20 See below, chapters 2 and 3. On the famous case of Gottschalk, see De Jong, *In Samuel's Image*, 77–91.

the Benedictine Reform – Dunstan, Æthelwold, Oswald – two of whom served at court before entering monastic life, embracing the *RSB* meant a *conuersio morum*.[21] Such a change in the habits of one's life, change understood to be ongoing in the following of the Rule, appears to us to constitute a radically different experience than that of the child committed to a monastery. But as we will see, the Anglo-Saxon accounts of adult entry into monastic life assume meaning by being recounted in a narrative not of 'conversion' as such but of fulfilment.[22] The former finds drama inherent in the disposition of the will in the act of choice; the latter focuses on patterned acts of obedience. In a narrative of fulfilment, where the saint is shown to be living fully the purposes of divine providence, agent action was understood as praiseworthy acceptance of the divine plan.[23] And so, the accounts of adult entry into monastic life more or less contemporary with the Reform – those of Dunstan, pre-eminently, but also of Æthelwold and Oswald – show narratives not of desire and choice, but of obedience.

In the *uitae* of the saints of Anglo-Saxon England, narrative interest in the painful process of conversion – whether psychological or social – barely registers.[24] Because a saint was understood as the chosen of God (as, for example, Æthelwold, while still in his mother's womb is

21 'Conversio morum' was part of the commitment of profession. See Smaragdus of St Mihiel, *Smaragdi Abbatis Expositio in Regulam S. Benedicti*, ed. Alfred Spannagel and Pius Engelbert, CCM 8 (Siegburg: F. Schmitt, 1974), cap. 5.4, p. 150, lines 25–9. For a survey of continental formulas of Benedictine profession containing 'conuersio morum,' see Catherine Capelle, *Le voeu d'obéissance des origines au XIIe siècle* (Paris: R. Pichon et R. Durand-Auzias, 1959), 103–10.

22 For a different approach and terminology see Clare Stancliffe, 'Cuthbert and the Polarity between Pastor and Solitary,' in *St Cuthbert: His Cult and His Community to A.D. 1200*, ed. Gerald Bonner, David Rollason, and Clare Stancliffe (Woodbridge: Boydell Press, 1989), 21–44 at 25, who contrasts static and developmental models of narrative. See below, pp. 67–72.

23 See James Wetzel, 'The Recovery of Free Agency in the Theology of St Augustine,' *Harvard Theological Review* 80 (1987): 101–25 at 121: 'In so far as another agent (God) is continually and necessarily involved in their moral successes, members of the elect are never strongly commendable for what they manage to accomplish. They are weakly commendable, however, simply for being the agents of their own actions and for being the sorts of people God has led them to become.'

24 Karl F. Morrison, *Understanding Conversion* (Charlottesville: University of Virginia Press, 1992), xii, observes of the eleventh and twelfth centuries: 'It is striking how little attention was then given to conversion as a single event, a dramatic peripety, shattering and reforming at the same time.' Morrison examines conversion as a continuing process.

described as 'Deo electum'),[25] narratives of a saint's life required copious illustration not simply of holy qualities and remarkable miracles but, more important, of the degree to which the events of the saint's life conformed to divine providence.[26] In crafting *uitae* of saints who entered religious life as an adult, early writers found it necessary to fit the life into a pattern of readable signs, recognizable temptations, and Christ-like miracles. Such normalization affirmed God's choice of the saint and confirmed both the saint's triumphant completion of his or her life and its worthiness for imitation. Thus perinatal prodigies and signs often furnished at the beginning of saints' *uitae* both set such saints apart from the ordinary and simultaneously insert them in a reassuring narrative of interpretable distinction. There are miracles of fire or light: when Wilfrid's mother was giving birth, people outside saw her house in flames reaching the heavens though not consumed by them.[27] Before Dunstan's birth, on the feast of the Purification, all the candles in the church went out except his mother's, miraculously rekindled.[28] Goscelin records that at St Edith's birth a light appeared in her parents' bedchamber.[29] There are prodigies of nature: when Guthlac's mother was in labour, a hand, shining in golden red, appeared in the sky and reaching down marked the door of the house where Guthlac

25 Lapidge and Winterbottom, *Wulfstan of Winchester, Life of St Æthelwold*, cap. 4, p. 8.

26 On the function of miracles and visions in hagiography, see David Rollason, 'The Concept of Sanctity in the Early Lives of St Dunstan,' in *St Dunstan: His Life, Times and Cult*, ed. Nigel Ramsay, Margaret Sparks, and Tim Tatton-Brown (Woodbridge: Boydell Press, 1992), 261–72 at 263. Saints' lives routinely iterated biblical miracles and, on occasion, the lives of other saints.

27 Bertram Colgrave, ed., *The Life of Bishop Wilfrid by Eddius Stephanus* (1927; repr. Cambridge: Cambridge University Press, 1985), cap. 1, p. 4. The attribution of the *Vita S. Wilfridi* (*BHL* 8889) to 'Eddius Stephanus' is now rejected, and the author of the work is now known as 'Stephen of Ripon.' Stephen, who specifically compares the miracle to that of Moses and the burning bush, goes on to interpret the sign: 'Et hoc per beatum pontificem nostrum omnibus paene Brittanniae ecclesiis palam effulsit, sicut praesagia futurorum prodiderunt et rei eventus postmodum probavit' ['… and through our blessed bishop it [scil. Wilfrid's light] has shone openly upon almost all the churches of Britain, even as the omens foretold: and events afterwards gave proof of them,' pp. 4–5. On the narrative significance of the miracle see Bertram Colgrave, 'The Earliest Saints' Lives Written in England,' *PBA* 44 (1958): 35–60, at 56.

28 Stubbs, *Memorials of Saint Dunstan*, p. 54 (Adelard); p. 72 (Osbern); Turner and Muir, *Eadmer of Canterbury: Lives*, cap. 1, pp. 50–2; Winterbottom and Thomson, *William of Malmesbury, Saints' Lives*, cap. 1.2, p. 172.

29 André Wilmart, ed., 'La légende de Ste Édith en prose et vers par le moine Goscelin,' *AB* 56 (1938): 5–101, 265–307, cap. 3, p. 42.

would be born.[30] Christina of Markyate's pregnant mother was visited for a week by a tame dove.[31] There are also prenatal dreams: St Willibrord's pregnant mother dreamt of a waxing moon, which, as she watched, fell into her mouth and suffused her with light.[32] Similarly, Æthelwold's pregnant mother had prophetic dreams of a banner touching the heavens and of a golden eagle emerging from her mouth and flying away.[33] Æthelwold's hagiographer, Wulfstan, interprets the banner as a sign that the boy would be God's standard bearer and interprets the eagle as a complex sign of the saint's greatness.[34] Before her conception, St Wulfhild's parents, who had given up conjugal relations for a life of married chastity, were warned in separate angelic visions that it was necessary for them to resume married life to beget a virgin bride of Christ. Their child, after weaning, was given to Wilton for her education and subsequent religious life.[35] Such wonders mark God's favour to the saint but more importantly underscore the belief that God's will, if inscrutable in purpose, is readable in its demand.

For similar reasons, hagiographers often portray their saints with preternatural spiritual gifts while children, and these gifts require interpretation and correct action by their parents. Willibald, one of St Boniface's hagiographers, reports that the saint at around four or five years of age applied himself to God's service and yearned to take on monastic life.[36] St Cuthbert practised ascetic discipline while just a child.[37] Christina, though

30 Bertram Colgrave, ed. and trans., *Felix's Life of Saint Guthlac* (Cambridge: Cambridge University Press, 1956), cap. 5–7, pp. 74, 76. Colgrave, ibid., p. 177, connects this portent with the iconography of the Hand of God.

31 C.H. Talbot, ed. and trans., *The Life of Christina of Markyate, A Twelfth-Century Recluse*, rev. ed., Medieval Academy Reprints for Teaching 39 (Toronto: University of Toronto Press, 1997), cap. 1, p. 34.

32 W. Levison, ed., *Vita Willibrordi Archiepiscopi Traiectensis Auctore Alcuino*, MGH, SRM 7 (Hannover: Hahn, 1920), 81–141 at 117. On this dream see below, 73–4.

33 Lapidge and Winterbottom, *Wulfstan of Winchester, Life of St Æthelwold*, cap. 2, p. 4 (Ælfric's version, cap. 2, p. 71).

34 Ibid., cap. 3, p. 6 (Ælfric's version, cap. 2, p. 71).

35 Marvin L. Colker, 'Texts of Jocelyn of Canterbury Which Relate to the History of Barking Abbey,' *Studia Monastica* 7 (1965): 383–460 at 420.

36 Wilhelm Levison, ed., 'Vita Bonifatii Auctore Willibaldo,' in *Vitae Sancti Bonifatii Archiepiscopi Moguntini*, MGH, SRG 57 (Hannover: Hahn, 1905), cap. 1, p. 4, lines 29–31, to p. 5, lines 1–4.

37 See below, p. 69. See also Alcuin, *Versus de patribus regibus et sanctis Euboricensis ecclesiae*, ed. Godman, *Alcuin, The Bishops, Kings and Saints of York*, line 648, p. 54: 'qui fuit a puero signis insignis apertis' ['From boyhood he was set apart by manifest signs'; Godman's translation].

not even of the age of reason, flagellated herself for perceived transgressions.[38] In the moment of his birth, Rumwold cried out three times 'I am a Christian' and preached for three days before his predestined death.[39] The royal saint Edith chose the veil of virginity when only two years old.[40] William of Malmesbury reports that Wulfstan II, bishop of Worcester (1062–95), when barely out of infancy ('uix dum primum pueritiae limen egressus'), fasted, prayed, and offered his hands for correction if he did any wrong ('si quid perperam faceret').[41]

In those narratives of saints given to the church as children, the saints' parents are shown either to recognize divine intervention in the life of their child themselves or to have the signs interpreted for them. When the three-year-old Willibald was in danger of death, his parents offered him to God to save his life. For this promise God healed the boy, and in fulfilment of their vow, when Willibald was five years old, 'venerandoque abba illius monasterii qui vocatur Egwald offerebant, ast illum sui condicionis iure iuniorem seu oboediendo discipulum suo subdiderunt imperio' [they brought him to the venerable abbot of the monastery, who was called Egwald, and they set him as a novice on account of his age or a disciple, to obey his authority].[42] St Leoba was oblated by her parents after her mother's old nurse prophesied that she would conceive a daughter. The mother then gave Leoba to the convent of Wimbourne under Abbess Tetta.[43] By contrast, it took an act of God (through which Boniface's father contracted a fatal illness) to move Boniface's family to permit him to enter religious life.[44] Dunstan's parents arranged to have him tonsured when they recognized his 'excellence.'[45] What for us is the drama of conversion to religious life – the operation of agency in the crafting of an identity, movingly recorded in the anguish of Augustine, the journeys of Francis of

38 Talbot, *The Life of Christina of Markyate,* cap. 2, p. 36.

39 Rosalind C. Love, ed. and trans., *Three Eleventh-Century Anglo-Latin Saints' Lives,* OMT (Oxford: Clarendon Press, 1996), cap. 3, p. 98.

40 Wilmart, 'La légende de Ste Édith,' cap. 5, pp. 43–5.

41 Winterbottom and Thomson, *William of Malmesbury, Saints' Lives,* I.1, 2–3, pp. 14–16.

42 See, for example, O. Holder-Egger, ed., *Vitae Willibaldi et Wynnebaldi auctore Sanctimoniali Heidenheimensi,* MGH, Scriptores 15.1 (Hannover, 1887), pp. 80–117 (cap. 2, p. 89, lines 9–11).

43 G. Waitz, ed., *Vita Leobae Abbatissae Biscofesheimensis, auctore Rudolfo Fuldensi,* MGH, Scriptores 15.1 (Hannover, 1887), pp. 118–31, at cap. 6, p. 124. On the infant Edith's 'choice' of religious life see below, 161.

44 Willibald indicates that the saint's father only relented when he recognized his illness as a sign (Levison, 'Vita Bonifatii Auctore Willibaldo,' cap. 1, p. 6, line 20, to p. 7, line 2).

45 See below, p. 79.

Assisi, or the spiritual quest of the wounded Ignatius Loyola – occupied the early medieval English hagiographer very little.[46]

The small interest the circumstances of saintly conversion held for early Anglo-Saxon hagiographers is pointedly illustrated by the two Latin prose lives of St Cuthbert (b. ca 635, d. 687), the earlier written by an anonymous monk of Lindisfarne and the later by Bede.[47] After apparently seeing some military service, Cuthbert entered the monastery of Melrose in 651.[48] Yet the Anonymous is sublimely indifferent to Cuthbert's process of conversion to monastic life, for he understands the unfolding of Cuthbert's life as the realization of divine providence, where he locates the drama of his narrative.[49] By contrast with his later, perfunctory mention of Cuthbert's entry into religious life, the Anonymous lavishes detail on the account of a three-year-old child admonishing the eight-year-old Cuthbert for playing frivolous sports and games, since he reads it as an index of the saint's election. The infant reproves the future saint: 'O sancte episcope et presbiter Cuðberhte, hec tibi et tuo gradui contraria nature propter agilitatem non conueniunt' ['O holy Bishop and priest Cuthbert, these unnatural

46 Karl F. Morrison, *Conversion and Text: The Cases of Augustine of Hippo, Herman-Judah, and Constantine Tsatsos* (Charlottesville: University Press of Virginia, 1992), 10–11, argues that Augustine was not interested in giving a historical account of his conversion, but rather in writing a polemic defending his legitimacy as bishop. See also Karl F. Morrison, *Understanding Conversion* (Charlottesville: University of Virginia Press, 1992), 14: 'the moment in which one entered a monastery was not the full *conversio*, but only its beginning, the *initium conversionis* according to the *Rule* of St Benedict.' While this observation is, of course, correct, *conversio morum* was understood in a fundamental way as a change in identity that could not be undone.

47 Bertram Colgrave, ed. and trans., *Two Lives of Saint Cuthbert* (Cambridge: Cambridge University Press, 1940). Bede wrote a metrical Life of Cuthbert early in his career. See Werner Jaager, ed., *Bedas metrische Vita Sancti Cuthberti*, Palaestra 198 (Leipzig: Mayer and Müller, 1935). Michael Lapidge, 'Bede's Metrical *Vita S. Cuthberti*,' in *St Cuthbert, His Cult and His Community*, 77–93 at 78, dates its composition to 'within a year (or two at most) of 705.' The verse life is significantly lacking in concrete detail, aiming at a text suited for meditation. See Lapidge, ibid. p. 93.

48 The Anonymous mentions military service (I.7): 'quomodo in castris contra hostem cum exercitu sedens' (p. 72) in the context of divine aid when the saint found himself with meagre food, but this information is not mentioned in Bede's Life.

49 See Catherine Cubitt, 'Memory and Narrative in the Cult of Early Anglo-Saxon Saints,' in *The Uses of the Past in the Early Middle Ages*, ed. Yitzhak Hen and Matthew Innes (Cambridge: Cambridge University Press, 2000), 29–66 at 39–40, on the Anonymous's disinterest in conversion. Clare Stancliffe, 'Cuthbert and the Polarity between Pastor and Solitary,' in *St Cuthbert, His Cult and His Community*, 25, argues that the Anonymous's Irish-influenced understanding of Cuthbert as predestined from childhood is responsible for the *uita*'s lack of sequential development.

tricks done to show off your agility are not befitting to you or your high office'].[50] Placing this event in the context of Jacob's, Samuel's, and David's early calling by God, the Anonymous interprets the weeping child's behaviour as a sign of divine providence and confirmation that Cuthbert 'per prouidentiam Dei electus ostenditur'[51] [was shown to be elect by the providence of God]. His further citation of Romans 8:30 ('And whom he predestinated, them he also called') is most likely meant to connect providence and calling, rather than to pronounce on Cuthbert's predestination as such.[52] When Cuthbert stops his games to console the child, the narrative explains that the saint did not understand what had been said to him, but he complied nonetheless. This action, potent in its illustration of reflexive obedience in the face of a sign and a call, is only praiseworthy as agent action within the Anonymous's narrative frame, structured as it is by the Augustinian concept of aligning the will with the divine.[53] But the conversion itself to monastic life is merely presented as *having* occurred: 'Bene ergo disponens duriori se uite lege in monasterio constringere, a populari uita reuertens, religiosa tamen atque immaculata ad meliora proficiens, sanctum laborem tolleranter ferebat, quia uoluntariae seruitutis longum in Dei opere studium consuetudinemque in naturam uerterat' ['So having arranged to bind himself by the more rigid rule of life in a monastery, leaving his secular life, pious and undefiled though it was, he advanced to better things and patiently bore the holy labour for, by long-standing zeal for voluntary bond-service in the work of God and by custom, it had become part of his nature'].[54] The language of his conversion cites the *Vita Antonii* directly: 'Disponens igitur duriori se vitae lege constringere, cum omnes infatigabilem adolescentis mirarentur instantiam, sanctum toleranter ferebat laborem, quia voluntariae servitutis longum in Dei opere studium, consuetudinem in naturam verterat'[55] [Therefore deciding to bind himself to a stricter law of life, when all were wondering at

50 Colgrave, *Two Lives*, I.iii, pp. 64–5 (trans. Colgrave). On prophecy by a child see Pierre Courcelle, 'L'enfant et les "sorts bibliques,"' *Vigiliae Christianae* 7 (1953): 194–220 at 201–10. See also his *Les confessions de saint Augustin dans la tradition littéraire* (Paris: Études Augustiniennes, 1963), 143–54, for a consideration of child prophecy.

51 Colgrave, *Two Lives*, I.iii, p. 66.

52 Stancliffe, 'Cuthbert and the Polarity,' 25, sees the predestination of Irish hagiography at work in this Life.

53 See Albrecht Dihle, *The Theory of Will in Classical Antiquity* (Berkeley and Los Angeles: University of California Press, 1982), 123–32 at 129.

54 Colgrave, *Two Lives*, II.i, pp. 74–5.

55 PL 73.130. Noted by Colgrave, *Two Lives*, 74.

the indefatigable perseverance of the youth, he carried on his holy labour patiently, because the long exertion of voluntary servitude in the work of God had turned habit into nature]. Yet the citation is hardly apposite in its details: at this point the Evagrian translation shows Antony increasing his mortifications following his first successful combat with the devil. But the borrowed language asserts connection and thus meaning by claiming for Cuthbert the agent action of obedience in *uoluntaria servitudo*.

Bede's account of the prophetic infant, substantially indebted to the Anonymous, although rhetorically more subtle, is equally committed to presenting Cuthbert's life as the unfolding of the divine will.[56] Here the saint's preternatural commitment to ascetic practices in his early youth is attributed to heavenly grace ('superna … gratia'), and Cuthbert's response to the wailing child, though initially uncomprehending, is shown to have been guided by the Holy Spirit ('illo nimirum spiritu interius eius praecordia docente' ['that Spirit assuredly instructed his heart from within']).[57] Bede's narrative of Cuthbert's progress towards monastic life connects sign

---

56 Though Stancliffe, 'Cuthbert and the Polarity,' 27, claims that the 'predestinarianism' in the Anonymous account is gone in Bede's prose life, Bede's verse life of Cuthbert (Jaager, *Bedas metrische Vita Sancti Cuthberti*, cap. 1, pp. 61–3) devotes 75 lines to this incident. On the stylistic differences between the two accounts see Walter Berschin, *Biographie und Epochenstil im lateinischen Mittelalter*, vol. 2, Merowingische Biographie. Italien, Spanien und die Inseln im frühen Mittelalter (Stuttgart: A. Hiersemann, 1988), pp. 278–81.

57 Colgrave, *Two Lives*, cap. 1, p. 154; pp. 158–9. Ælfric, while making complex use of the earlier Latin *uitae*, shows little interest in either Cuthbert's encounter with the weeping child or his conversion: 'Se eadiga cuþberhtus æfter ðisum ealle woruldðing eallunge forlet. and mid halgum ðeawum hine sylfne to munuclife geðeodde. and he hrædlice siððan he munuc wæs wearð geset cumena ðen.' See Godden, ed., *CH* II.10, lines 59–62 (pp. 82–3). On Ælfric's uses of the earlier lives see Godden, *CH* III, pp. 412–29, and E. Gordon Whatley, 'Acta Sanctorum,' in *Sources of Anglo-Saxon Literary Culture I: Abbo of Fleury, Abbo of Saint-Germain-des-Prés, and Acta Sanctorum*, ed. Frederick M. Biggs, Thomas D. Hill, Paul E. Szarmach, and E. Gordon Whatley (Kalamazoo: Medieval Institute Publications, Western Michigan University, 2001), 22–486 at 159. See also B.A. Blokhuis, 'Bede and Ælfric: The Sources of the Homily on St Cuthbert,' in *Beda Venerabilis: Historian, Monk, and Northumbrian*, ed. L.A.J.R. Houwen and A.A. MacDonald (Groningen: Egbert Forsten, 1996), 107–38 at 115, 117, 129, 131; and Alex I. Jones, 'Ælfric's Life of Saint Cuthbert,' *Parergon* 10.1 (1992): 35–43. Peter Jackson argues that for Ælfric, Cuthbert was 'another paradigmatic hermit' in 'Ælfric and the "Uita Patrum" in Catholic Homily I.36,' in *Essays on Anglo-Saxon and Related Themes in Memory of Lynne Grundy*, ed. Jane Roberts and Janet Nelson, King's College London Medieval Studies 17 (London: King's College London, Centre for Late Antique and Medieval Studies, 2000), 259–72 at 269.

and saintly action more explicitly than does the Anonymous; indeed Bede's narrative is more explicitly theological than that of the Anonymous.[58] Bede confirms the connection among sign, call, and response in the aftermath of the miraculous healing of Cuthbert's infected knee, making the saint's response the narrative connection between chapters.[59]

A substantial distinction between Bede's narrative approach and that of the Anonymous lies in their different handlings of Cuthbert's formal embrace of monastic life. The Anonymous offers no antecedent or specific motivation for it and defines no triggering event. While the Anonymous simply narrates Cuthbert's vision of Bishop Aidan's soul ascending to heaven (I.v), Bede explicitly makes this vision part of Cuthbert's conversion.[60] Cuthbert, in the company of other shepherds, had a vision of Aidan's soul and is moved 'ad subeundum gratiam spiritualis exercitii' [to submit to the grace of spiritual practice].[61] The following morning, having given over his sheep, he 'monasterium petere decreuit' [determined to seek out a monastery].[62] Bede continues in this vein, linking Cuthbert's embrace of monastic life with the vision of Aidan's soul 'coelesti uisione ad appetenda perpetuae gaudia beatitudinis incitatus' [inspired by the heavenly vision to seek the joys of perpetual happiness].[63] With both the wailing child and the vision of Aidan's soul, Bede makes it clear that Cuthbert's entry into religious life is a playing out of divine will whereby the saint acts in response to signs from God. If the saint does not always understand the full significance of the sign (because obedience is required for Christian action, not full knowledge), the sign is made fully readable to the audience of the *uita* by its appeal to their familiarity with the schema or by its naturalization to key events of the Old Testament (the call to David or Samuel, for example), or the New (healings of the blind, the deaf,

58 Walter Goffart, 'Bede's *uera lex historiae* Explained,' *ASE* 34 (2005): 111–16 at 113–14. Lapidge, 'Bede's Metrical *Vita S. Cuthberti*,' 88–90, discusses Bede's approach in terms of the exegetical influence of Arator.

59 To open the following chapter Bede shows Cuthbert 'ab hoc autem tempore deuotus Domino' [from this time devoted to the Lord]. See Colgrave, *Two Lives*, cap. 3, p. 160.

60 Stancliffe, 'Cuthbert and the Polarity,' p. 29, n. 57, notes that only Bede makes this vision a determinant of Cuthbert's religious commitment.

61 Colgrave, *Two Lives*, cap. 4, p. 166.

62 Ibid. Similarly, Ælfric (who follows Bede) devotes a single sentence to Cuthbert's entry into the monastery: 'Se eadiga cuþberhtus æfter ðisum ealle woruldðing eallunge forlet. and mid halgum ðeawum hine sylfne to munuclife geðeodde' (Godden, *CH* II, pp. 82–3).

63 Colgrave, *Two Lives*, cap. 6, p. 172.

or the crippled). That Cuthbert came formally to the monastic life after some time in the world is of lesser significance to the narrative than that he could be shown to have embraced monastic discipline from his early years: 'superna illum gratia ad uiam ueritatis paulatim a primis iam puericiae incitauerat annis'[64] [already divine grace had spurred him little by little to the way of truth from the first years of his childhood]. The miraculous loaf that Cuthbert finds in Bede's account showed the operation of a heavenly spirit that 'manifestis edoceret indiciis quia quaerentibus regnum Dei et iustitiam eius, ea quae ad uictum corporis pertinent, beneficio diuinae prouisionis adiciuntur'[65] [teaches by clear signs that for those seeking the kingdom of God and his justice, the things that pertain to the nourishment of the body would be provided through the blessing of divine providence].

In their lives of Cuthbert both Bede and the Anonymous drew from Evagrius's translation of Athanasius's life of Antony. In this influential *uita*, the saint as a child is shown to have precocious sanctity burning with desire for God ('Dei desiderio flagrans').[66] Yet its account of the moment of the saint's conversion is framed with a careful hesitation about the relationship between precipitating event and the choice of monastic life. While the young Antony had been thinking about how the apostles had left everything behind to follow Christ, he enters a church, where he hears the words of the Gospel, 'Si vis perfectus esse, vade, vende quae habes, et da pauperibus, et habebis thesaurum in caelo' [If thou wilt be perfect, go sell what thou hast, and give to the poor, and thou shalt have treasure in heaven (Matt. 19:21)]. That day he sold all he had. But the account asks closer attention to its conditionals: 'Quo audito, *quasi* divinitus hujusmodi ante memoriam concepisset, et *veluti* propter se haec esset Scriptura recitata, ad se Dominicum traxit imperium; statimque regressus, possessiones quas habebat vendidit' [emphasis added][67] [Hearing that, *as if* he thought that his memory earlier had been divinely inspired, and *as if* that scripture had been recited on account of him, he took to himself the Lord's command and immediately upon his return sold all his possessions]. While floating the possibility of divine intervention in the saint's decision, the narrative's 'quasi' and 'veluti' inflect a careful neutrality about whether Antony's thoughts prior to going into the church were actually the result of divine inspiration, and the narrative is equally non-committal on the coincidence of the Gospel reading and

64 Cf. Lam. 3:27, 28; Colgrave, *Two Lives*, cap. 1, p. 154.
65 Ibid., cap. 5, p. 168.
66 PL 73.127a.
67 PL 73.127c.

the saint's prior thoughts. But such hesitation is not to be found in the lives of Cuthbert, whose narratives are driven by God's readable action in the life of the saint and the saint's conformity to God's will.

We see this commitment at work in the *uitae* in a wide variety of Anglo-Saxon saints. Bede lavished considerable attention on Æthelthryth's preservation of her virginity and ascetic practice after her retirement to the convent, but the actual narrative of her conversion to monastic life is brief, merely recording the final accession of King Ecgfrith to the queen's twelve-year requests: 'Quae multum diu regem postulans, ut saeculi curas relinquere atque in monasterio tantum uero regi Christo seruire permitteretur, ubi uix aliquando impetrauit, intrauit monasterium Aebbae abbatissae, quae erat amita regis Ecgfridi'[68] [Having asked the king for a very long time that she might be allowed to leave behind the cares of the world and in a monastery serve the only true king, Christ, when she finally and with difficulty succeeded, she entered the monastery of Abbess Æbbe, King Ecgfrith's aunt]. The poem Bede had earlier written on the saint suggests that her virginity had long before been dedicated to Christ: 'Quid petis, alma, uirum, sponso iam dedita summo? / sponsus adest Christus; quid petis, alma, uirum?'[69] [Holy lady, already given to the best bridegroom, why do you seek a husband? Christ is with you, why, holy lady, do you seek a husband?]. And in his later version of Æthelthryth's life, Ælfric adds nothing to Bede's account of her conversion beyond indicating that she had asked the king to serve Christ 'on mynsterlicre drohtnunge swa hire mod hire tospeon'[70] [in the monastic life as her mind urged her].

Judged by the spare standards of either early *uita* of Cuthbert, or Bede's account of St Æthelthryth, the conversion of Guthlac to the monastic life approaches the dramatic, but it too is designed to illustrate entry into monastic life as an act in conformity with the divine plan. In Felix's *uita*, a sign accompanying the child's birth foretells Guthlac's special status in God's plan. Thereafter, unsurprisingly, the boy shows exemplary conduct and evinces a string of virtues. Nonetheless, Guthlac exerts himself for nine years in military actions.[71] When, having conquered his enemies, Guthlac finds himself in his accustomed contemplation of the sorry lot of

68 Colgrave and Mynors, *Bede's Ecclesiastical History*, IV.19, p. 392.

69 Ibid., IV.20, p. 398.

70 Walter W. Skeat, ed., *Ælfric's Lives of Saints*, EETS o.s. 76, 82, 94, 114 (Oxford, 1881–1900; repr. as 2 vols., London: Oxford University Press, 1966), I.20, p. 434, line 33.

71 Colgrave, *Felix's Life of Saint Guthlac*, cap. 12–14, p. 78: He never troubled his parents, did not shout or chatter, but was wise, cheerful, gentle, and frank. For his military exploits see cap. 16–18.

man, 'extimplo velut perculsus pectore, spiritalis flamma omnia praecordia supra memorati viri incendere coepit'[72] [suddenly, as though he had been struck in his heart, a spiritual flame began to burn the whole body of the aforementioned man]. Felix ascribes Guthlac's conversion to the sudden prompting of God ('subito instigante divino numine'),[73] and driven by divine grace, he leaves behind parents, homeland, and comrades ('in illo divinae gratiae inflammatio flagrabat').[74] Similarly, when he chooses to become a hermit, his desire for the eremitic life is driven by divine inspiration ('tum inluminato cordis gremio avida cupidine heremum quaerere fervebat'),[75] but only undertaken with the permission of his superiors.[76]

The underlying expectations of all these early narratives are neatly explicated by Alcuin's life of Willibrord, which illustrates the way grace, providence, and signs interact to chart the events of the saint's life, signpost for the saint a proper course of action, and illustrate for others that the events of the saint's life were directed by God. As we have seen, Willibrord's mother while pregnant had a prophetic dream. Looking into the heavens she saw the crescent moon grow to a full moon, which suddenly fell into her mouth. When she swallowed it, in the dream, her breast shone with light. A priest thereafter interpreted the dream to signify that the son she conceived that night would draw many to him by the brightness of his life.[77] Understanding the dream as a sign of Willibrord's divine election, his parents gave the child to the community of Ripon: 'statim ablactatum infantulum, tradidit eum pater Hrypensis ecclesiae fratribus relegiosis studiis et sacris litteris erudiendum, ut fragilior aetas validioribus invalesceret disciplinis, ubi nihil videret nisi honesta, nihil audiret nisi sancta'[78] [As soon as he was weaned, his father gave him to the brothers of the church of Ripon to be trained in religious studies and sacred letters, that the weakness of his age might grow strong with more vigorous teachings, where he

---

72 Ibid., cap. 18, p. 80.

73 Ibid., cap. 18, p. 82.

74 Ibid., cap. 19, p. 82.

75 Ibid., cap. 24, p. 86.

76 On Felix's use of his sources to craft a recognizable *uita*, see Cubitt, 'Memory and Narrative,' pp. 51–3. On this point Cubitt cites Alan T. Thacker, 'The Social and Continental Background to Early Anglo-Saxon Hagiography' (unpublished DPhil thesis, University of Oxford, 1976), which I have not been able to consult.

77 Levison, *Vita Willibrordi*, cap. 2, p. 117.

78 Ibid., cap. 3, p. 117, line 26 to p. 118, line 3. C.H. Talbot, ed. and trans., *The Anglo-Saxon Missionaries in Germany* (London: Sheed and Ward, 1954), p. 5, n. 1, suggests that 'ablactatum infantulum' means that he was given when he 'had reached the age of reason,' as he translates it.

would see nothing but moral and hear nothing but holy things]. At Ripon, divine grace enabled Willibrord to advance in mind and character and surpass all the other youth of the monastery. Alcuin records that at twenty the saint desired a more rigorous life 'artioris vitae ardore succensus,'[79] and thereafter he decided to evangelize the Frisians. Significantly, Alcuin frames the saint's desire in terms of his mother's dream and its relationship to divine providence: 'Sed ut somnii, Deo dispensante, inpleretur veritas, quod mater olim de eo se vidisse testatur, suae conscius voluntatis, licet adhuc divinae dispensationis ignarus, illas in partes navigare cogitavit'[80] [So that the truth of the dream which his mother testified that she had once had concerning him might be fulfilled in accordance with God's providence, aware of his own purpose, although ignorant of divine providence, he decided that he would travel into those parts]. That is, Willibrord decides to set out on a mission and does so both in fulfilment of and in order to fulfil his mother's dream. His action confirms his mother's dream as prophetic, though his parents had already recognized its significance and oblated Willibrord on the strength of it. Their action at his birth and Willibrord's action in his young manhood are separate events. Alcuin is careful to align Willibrord's will with divine providence but in so doing underlines the difference in knowledge between the saint and God. As Alcuin portrays Willibrord aware of his own will ('suae conscius voluntatis'), he shows him to be ignorant of God's direction: in this way the saint is shown to act in obedience rather than knowledge.

We are fortunate in having other, contemporary *uitae* against which to evaluate Osbern's handling of Dunstan's choice. Early *uitae* of the three great tenth-century reformers of monastic life in England – Dunstan, Æthelwold, and Oswald – were written within a decade of each other and within living memory of each man's death. Wulfstan is thought to have composed the *uita* for the translation of St Æthelwold (d. 984) in 996 or soon thereafter.[81] Byrhtferth wrote a life of Oswald within a decade of Oswald's death in 992.[82] And Michael Lapidge has dated B.'s composition of the *uita* of Dunstan (d. 988) to early in the decade 995–1005.[83] These late tenth-century

79 Levison, *Vita Willibrordi*, cap. 4, p. 118, lines 15–16.

80 Ibid., cap. 5, p. 119, lines 16–18.

81 Lapidge and Winterbottom, *Wulfstan of Winchester, Life of St Æthelwold*, p. xvi.

82 Michael Lapidge, 'Byrhtferth and Oswald,' in *St Oswald of Worcester: His Life and Influence*, ed. Nicholas Brooks and Catherine Cubitt (London: Leicester University Press, 1996), 64–83 at 65.

83 See Michael Lapidge, 'B. and the *Vita S. Dunstani*,' in his *ALL* II, pp. 279–91 and 487 at 279 and n. 2.

lives fit comfortably within the hagiographical traditions of the earlier lives of Anglo-Saxon saints in their deployment of miracles and signs, indifference to the process of monastic conversion, and use of the narrative of fulfilment.

In addition to her prenatal dreams of a magnificent banner and a golden eagle,[84] Æthelwold's mother was vouchsafed knowledge of the entry of her son's soul into his body within her womb. Wulfstan interprets this event (which he claims Æthelwold himself used to recount) as a sign that 'eum Deo electum extitisse etiam antequam nasceretur' [that he was 'elect of God' even before he was born].[85] His nurse, prevented from attending church by violent weather, is miraculously transported to Mass, with the infant Æthelwold still in her arms. Wulfstan reads this prodigy as a sign that just as Habbakuk was transported to feed Daniel, so Æthelwold would feed thousands within the church.[86] And although there is no mention in the *uita* of a moment of decision in which Æthelwold chose monastic life, for Wulfstan the index of the saint's fulfilment of God's will, in what would become his monastic life, was his precocious learning of scripture. Wulfstan records that 'studebat … diuinis semper obsequiis omnia membra sua mancipare et ad Dei implendam uoluntatem totam mentis suae intentionem dirigere'[87] [he endeavoured always to commit his entire body to divine service and to direct the intention of his mind to fulfilling entirely the will of God]. However, the will of God, shown in the various signs that Wulfstan records, is carried out, in part, by the king, who orders ('iubente rege') Æthelwold to be tonsured, to take minor orders, and then to be ordained a priest.[88] Thereafter the saint studies with Bishop Ælfheah, again 'praecipiente rege' [at the king's direction], and somewhat later goes to Glastonbury to study with Dunstan. And finally, in an anticlimactic clause, 'tandem monastici ordinis habitum ab ipso [scil. Dunstano] suscepit'[89] [at length he received the habit of the monastic order from him (Dunstan)]. Wulfstan's disinterest in the personal details of Æthelwold's conversion to monastic life serves a higher purpose in plotting his saint's spiritual progress within a narrative of the fulfilment of God's will.

Byrhtferth's lengthy *uita* of Oswald abounds in information on the saint's uncle Oda, Oswald's study at Fleury, and his energetic work in the Reform

84 See above, p. 65.
85 Lapidge and Winterbottom, *Wulfstan of Winchester, Life of St Æthelwold*, cap. 4, p. 8.
86 Ibid., cap. 5, p. 8.
87 Ibid., cap 6, p. 10.
88 Ibid., cap 7, p. 10.
89 Ibid., cap 9, p. 14.

movement, but shows scant interest in Oswald's life before his departure for Fleury beyond the saint's studies under his uncle, Archbishop Oda (whose life takes up section 1 of the *uita*), and Oda's gift enabling Oswald to get a minster in Winchester.[90] And even for these events, there is no real detail, for the work is so overwhelmed by Byrhtferth's bombastic Latin style that the *uita* is all surface and manner.[91] While the standard prodigies and miracles that attend the youth of Anglo-Saxon saints are nowhere to be found, Byrhtferth is nonetheless careful to emplot Oswald's early life in a narrative of fulfilling God's will. Oswald shares with Æthelwold and Dunstan a fervent love for learning, which Byrhtferth attributes to the gift of the Holy Spirit, explaining: 'Sitiebant ipsius penetralia cordis largiter haurire semper doctrinam sacre eruditionis, quam conditor clementius contulit in pectore beati tyronis – quem "presciuit et predestinauit" ante sue natiuitatis tempora preesse ecclesie filiis'[92] [The recesses of his heart thirsted always to drink abundantly the teaching of holy learning which the Creator kindly fixed in the breast of the blessed youth, whom 'he foreknew and predestined' before the time of his birth to rule over the sons of the church]. After Archbishop Oda gives his nephew the means to acquire a minster in Winchester (at this point occupied by secular canons), Oswald lives luxuriously until he ponders how best to please Christ, and his conclusions are attributed to an outpouring of divine grace.[93] At this point, Byrhtferth records a meeting between Oswald and the archbishop where Oswald reveals that he wishes to go across the sea to take up monastic life. And this, too, is the gift of the Holy Spirit.[94] Oswald's desire, as it was placed in his mind by God, is necessarily in complete accord with God's will. Byrhtferth explains Odo's lack of surprise at Oswald's decision: 'Non magnopere tamen de ipsius mirabatur uoluntate, quia "omnis subita mutatio rerum" non fit sine persuasione creatoris piissimi omnium creaturarum'[95] [Yet he was not particularly surprised at his wish, because

---

90 Michael Lapidge, ed. and trans., *Byrhtferth of Ramsey, The Lives of St Oswald and St Edgwine* (Oxford: Clarendon Press, 2009), ii.1, pp. 32–4.

91 Lapidge, 'Byrhtferth and Oswald,' 68, remarks that the *uita* 'frequently becomes a patchwork of quotations from the Bible, Bede, Boethius, Aldhelm and others.'

92 Lapidge, *Byrhtferth of Ramsey, Lives,* ii.1, pp. 32–4. Byrhtferth cites Rom. 8:29.

93 Ibid., ii.2, p. 36: '[C]ontulit suo electo famulo congruam consilii gratiam, per quod naufragium posset aufugere et ad suum confugere portum' [He bestowed on his chosen servant grace suited to the plan, through which he was able to flee shipwreck and take refuge in his (scil. Christ's) port].

94 Ibid., ii.3, p. 36: 'in eius corde … sancti spiritus donum.'

95 Ibid.

no sudden change of things comes about without the persuasion of the most holy Creator of all creatures]. Byrhtferth's account of Oswald's journey to Fleury, the gifts he brought, his warm reception there, and his embrace of Fleury custom is offered with a stylistic excess that must have been intended to match Oswald's own strenuous religious exercises. As a result, however, the saint's monastic profession finds mention only as an anticlimactic insertion in a riot of spiritual weeds which anticipate a quotation of Aldhelm's riddle 'De urtica': 'Pretiosus famulus saluatoris Iesu Christi, postquam uepres et spinas et zizania et omnia frutecta dumosi ruris sui cordis a se expulit et alternum sancti baptismatis uelamen suscepit (quod "monasticum" pii uiri "habitum" dicunt), cepit cordetenus, ut prephati sumus, lolium et urticas exstirpare'[96] [The splendid servant of the saviour, Jesus Christ, after he removed from himself the brambles, thorns, cockle, and all the thickets of the thorny fields of his heart, and received a second robe of holy baptism, which pious men call the monastic habit, began to uproot from his heart, as we said before, tares and nettles].

The narrative pattern to which these *uitae* conform presents prodigies and signs as indicators of God's will and as assurances (in their repetitions and predictability) that if God's will is inscrutable, it is at least readable in its demands for human action. These *uitae* thus generally portray the assumption of religious life (insofar as it is handled at all) as untroubled, obedient accession to divine providence. In this light, Osbern's departure from the script in his staging of Dunstan's choice of religious life is both shocking and puzzling. By portraying Dunstan struggling over the direction of his life and deriding monastic life as having no value, Osbern brings troubling drama to the *conuersio morum* precisely by focusing attention on the moment of choice.

Osbern's Theatre of Choice

The earliest surviving account of the life of St Dunstan, addressed to Archbishop Ælfric by an author known only by the initial 'B' proved influential.[97] It was known to Adelard, and later used by Osbern, Eadmer, and William of Malmesbury in their *uitae* of the saint.[98] Michael Lapidge

96 Ibid., iii.1, p. 52. For Enigma 46 ('De urtica') see Rudolf Ehwald, *Aldhelmi Opera*, MGH, AA 15 (Berlin: Weidmann, 1919), 117.
97 Lapidge, 'B. and the *Vita S. Dunstani*,' p. 279 and n. 2.
98 Osbern makes cryptic references to deficiencies in the works of the two unnamed authors (B. and Adelard) he used in writing his account. See Stubbs, *Memorials of*

has argued that B. must have been a member of Dunstan's retinue, since many instances in the *uita* appear to be eyewitness accounts or first-hand observations.[99] He further argues that B. was an Englishman who took minor orders at Glastonbury but was a secular cleric rather than a monk. Most likely having accompanied Dunstan to the Continent, B. then went to Liège, where he remained.[100] Whatever B. may have known at first-hand about Dunstan's later career, his narrative is sketchy at best on the details of the saint's early life. He records that Dunstan was born in the reign of Athelstan to pious parents, Heorstan and Cynethryth, who lived in the vicinity of Glastonbury, although modern historians suppose the saint's birth to be some fifteen years earlier, ca 909 or 910.[101] B. makes little mention of Dunstan's earliest life, and it is noteworthy that B. alone of Dunstan's hagiographers does not record the miracle of his mother's candle on the feast of the Purification. He does record, however, that Heorstan brought him on a visit to Glastonbury, where the child had a miraculous vision. B. provides no particular reason why father and son should be at Glastonbury ('Contigit ergo huiuscemodi causis predictum uirum Heorstanum comitante secum beato puero Dunstano etiam transisse Glæstoniam')[102] [It happened, therefore, for reasons of this sort (i.e., that crowds of faithful worshipped at Glastonbury) that the aforementioned man Heorstan with the blessed boy Dunstan also travelled to Glastonbury]. While they spent the night there, the child Dunstan had a vision of an old man in shining white garments, who showed him the future monastic buildings there and the order in which they would be built under Dunstan's direction. Although B. does not interpret this miraculous vision further, its detail and position in the *uita* indicate that it was understood to be a prophetic vision, similar in type to the dream of Willibrord's mother.[103]

Saint Dunstan, 70; Turner and Muir, *Eadmer of Canterbury, Lives and Miracles*, list Eadmer's sources for his life of Dunstan (including B. and Adelard, as well as Osbern), lxx; Winterbottom and Thomson, *William of Malmesbury, Saints' Lives*, xvii, state that William had access to the lives by B., Adelard, Osbern, and Eadmer.

99 See Lapidge, 'B. and the *Vita S. Dunstani*,' 280 and 291.

100 Ibid., 286–7 and 291.

101 Brooks, 'The Career of St Dunstan,' 4.

102 Winterbottom and Lapidge, *Early Lives of St Dunstan*, cap. 3.4, p. 12.

103 B. does not mention the prenatal miracle of the candles in the church when the saint's pregnant mother was celebrating the feast of the Purification. It is found in Adelard's set of lections, commissioned by Archbishop Ælfheah, 1006–11 (see Stubbs, *Memorials of St Dunstan*, pp. xxxi and 54), and in the subsequent *uitae* by Osbern (Stubbs, *Memorials of St Dunstan*, 72), Eadmer (Turner and Muir, *Eadmer of Canterbury,*

Thereafter Dunstan's parents set him to study sacred letters. He surpasses his peers in every way, and when in his vigorous studies he is stricken by a raging fever and while delirious climbs to the roof of the church, he is found safe and asleep in the locked church, having been brought down from the roof by a miracle. This further miracle, as B. recounts it, predicted the distinction of Dunstan's future religious career and was a crucial part of that 'excellence' on whose basis Dunstan's parents committed the boy to minor orders: 'Videntes itaque parentes praenominati tantam sui excellentiam filii, dignam sibi clericatus officii inposuere tonsuram, inque famoso Glæstoniensis aecclesiae sociauerunt coenobio; quatinus ibidem die noctuque Deo Deique genitrici deseruiret Mariae tempore continuo. Iamque disciplinis deificis innexus florentes suae pubertatis annos euicta iuuentute calcauit'[104] [And so, seeing such excellence in their son, the aforementioned parents imposed on him the tonsure of the holy office of ordination and joined him to the famous monastery of the church of Glastonbury; that there he would day and night without interruption serve God and Mary the mother of God. And now with his youth behind him, he completed the flowering years of his young manhood bound to sacred studies].

From its juxtaposition of events, B.'s narrative firmly connects Dunstan's parents' commitments on Dunstan's behalf with their interpretation of events in Dunstan's life – the vision of monastic building and Dunstan's learning and miraculous rescue – as signs. Dunstan's entry into minor orders (a first step in a religious career) is thus arranged by his parents after they acknowledge such signs. In fact, the only actions taken in the narrative at this point are by the parents: they impose tonsure ('inposuere') and commit ('sociauerunt') the child to Glastonbury. From the following account of Dunstan's flourishing in virtue, readers would understand that Dunstan's acceptance of tonsure in minor orders was a praiseworthy act of obedience, itself a sign that he was of good will. But Dunstan's conversion to monastic life is presented by B. in considerably more detail than we have seen in earlier saints' lives, and certainly in the contemporary *uitae* of Æthelwold and Oswald. In B's account, Dunstan distinguishes himself at court, while nonetheless continuing his ascetic practices. Upon his expulsion from court (a reversal contrived by jealousy courtiers), he visits his

Lives and Miracles, 50–2), and William of Malmesbury (Winterbottom and Thomson, *William of Malmesbury: Saints' Lives*, 172).

104 Winterbottom and Lapidge, *Early Lives of St Dunstan*, cap. 5.1, pp. 16–18.

kinsman ('propinquus'), Bishop Ælfheah, and the narrative of his conversion begins. B. structures his account of Dunstan's conversion in terms of 'struggles with temptation' ('temptamentorum luctamina') in which the devil determines to subvert Dunstan by infecting him with sexual desire for women ('mulierum illi iniecit amorem').[105] The devil hopes by this means to get Dunstan to decline Ælfheah's many requests and spiritual admonitions that he become a monk. And so Dunstan's resistance to conversion is presented rather luridly as a preference to marry so that he could be cherished daily by his wife's caresses, rather than to assume the cowl of a monk.[106] It should be noted that the course upon which Dunstan's parents set him was the life of the secular clergy, who were free to marry.[107] But B., himself a secular cleric, explains the devil's stratagem in leading Dunstan to prefer the pleasures of the flesh was that such pleasure would lead him to embrace all the rest of the delights of this world.

B.'s presentation of Dunstan's conversion to the monastic life illustrates the contemporary understanding of the operation of individual will within an individual's orientation to the divine will. The elements in the narrative structure Dunstan's 'choice' as a morally fraught exercise where preference (as we might view it) runs athwart obedience to God's will. Thus Dunstan's inclination to marry is presented not as an option (however free he was to marry in minor orders) but as an occasion of sin. The verb that B. uses, 'maluit,' expresses preference to be sure, but that preference is shown to be counter to God's plans for the saint, as Dunstan's ensuing illness makes clear. When Bishop Ælfheah learns of Dunstan's decision to decline monastic life, he prays that God will send a sign of his disapproval ('correctionum suarum indicia')[108] that Dunstan might heed the bishop's advice he had earlier disregarded.[109] God obliges, and Dunstan is afflicted with such desperate pain and swelling over his whole body that he believes that he is suffering from elephantiasis (a virulent form of leprosy) and despairs of his life. B.'s choice of word for the onset of Dunstan's experience, 'correptus,'

105 Ibid., cap. 7.1, p. 26.

106 Ibid., cap. 7.2, p. 26: 'maluit sponsare iuuenculam cuius cotidie blanditiis foueretur.'

107 Brooks, 'The Career of St Dunstan,' 13, notes that even under Dunstan's abbacy secular clerks remained at Glastonbury.

108 Winterbottom and Lapidge, *Early Lives of St Dunstan*, cap. 7.2, p. 26, print 'indicia' based on MS C (the St Gallen manuscript), which they demonstrate preserves B.'s original text of the *uita*. Stubbs's reading, 'judicia' (*Memorials of Saint Dunstan*, cap. 7, p. 13), is that of the later redactions.

109 B. uses 'abnuens' to describe Dunstan in his refusal, perhaps also with the sense the participle had of declining military service. See Lewis and Short, s.v. 'abnuo,' sense B.

captures the word's double sense of 'attacked' and 'reproached,' and the saint's subsequent behaviour is framed in terms of obedience.[110] In great distress and despairing of his life, Dunstan now sends for the bishop and begs to obey his beneficial advice: 'Tunc ergo festinanter, magno angore correptus misit, et ad se prescriptum pontificem iam antea se spretum humili prece uocauit et oboedire se uelle eius salutaribus monitis nuntiauit'[111] [Consequently, then, attacked by great torment, he quickly sent for the aforementioned bishop he had earlier disregarded, summoning him with humble entreaty, and declared that he wished to obey his salvation-giving counsels]. Dunstan's will now is to obey, and his obedience underscores that the bishop's 'salvation-giving counsels' are not suggestions but the articulation of God's will. In his mercy, B. explains, God 'brought him back' ('retraxit') from the love for women, and Dunstan was saved by God's chastisement ('correctione') and the bishop's warning ('documento').[112]

In B.'s narrative the bishop stands in the place of an abbot, and to obey him is to obey God in precisely the way the *RSB* understands obedience ('qui vos audit, me audit'). Dunstan is set between two forces: temptation and salvation, the devil and the bishop. He interprets his illness correctly as the monitory sign that it is, and the virtue of his subsequent decision to become a monk lies in obeying (and B. uses the word *oboedire*) the bishop's advice, thus aligning his will with God's plan. These actions, taken, significantly, when he thought he was about to die, show how the larger narrative structures Dunstan's 'choice' as an exercise in interpreting the obedience required of him.[113] As we saw in B.'s earlier account of Dunstan's tonsuring, the saint's ritual admission to minor orders as a secular cleric was his parents' doing. Similarly here, the exercise of volition in Dunstan's conversion contracts into a *willing* to obey ('oboedire se uelle ... nuntiauit').[114] To put it analytically, in B.'s narrative, Dunstan's choice is the choice of obedience. That such obedience might seem to have been coerced by a mortal illness sent by God troubled B. not at all, for his presentation of Dunstan's conversion to monastic life understands the operation of agent action as an individual's assent to the divine will.

110 Lewis and Short, s.v. 'corripio,' senses IB3 and IIA.
111 Winterbottom and Lapidge, *The Early Lives of St Dunstan*, cap. 7.3, p. 26.
112 Ibid., cap. 8.1, p. 26.
113 Dunstan's earlier inclination to marry is presented as contrary to God's will. Although the verb that B. uses, *maluit*, expresses preference, ensuing events make clear that this preference is not in line with God's plans for the saint (ibid., cap. 7.2, p. 26).
114 Winterbottom and Lapidge, *The Early Lives of St Dunstan*, cap. 7.2, p. 26.

This is the account that Osbern inherited from B., and as he did elsewhere in his life of Dunstan, he proceeded to add to and modify it.[115] Chapters 3 through 11 in Osbern's version emphasize that Dunstan was predestined by God for spiritual greatness. The miracle experienced by his pregnant mother and the boy's vision when accompanying his father to Glastonbury, recognizable to Osbern's readers from the prodigies that mark earlier saints' lives, were also read by Dunstan's parents. Through them his parents recognize God's will for the boy, and offer him as a 'Levi' consecrated to God (Num. 3:11–13). Osbern makes a further assertion of the operation of God's will in the boy by using *praevidere* and *praevenire* to emphasize the trajectory of Dunstan's life as a function of God's eternal will:

> Magnum quippe Deus illum futurum praevidebat, quem ibi dulcedinis Suae benedictionibus praevenerat, ubi omnes filii Adam nativae maledictionis sententiam excipiunt, si non per assumptam a Filio Dei humani habitus formam ad pristinam reformentur beatitudinem. Magnum inquam Deus illum futurum praevidebat, cui tantum muneris donatum est, ut ante mundo signis innotesceret quam hunc in hujus mundi lucem mater fudisset.[116]
>
> [Certainly God foresaw that he would be great, whom he then aided with the blessings of His love, since all the sons of Adam draw on themselves the judgment of their inborn punishment if they are not restored to original blessedness through the human form taken by the Son of God. I say that God foresaw that he would be great, to whom he gave such a gift, that he would become known by signs in the world before his mother brought him forth into the light of this world.]

Osbern's choice of language is by now familiar, calling on God's omniscience ('praevidebat'), his prevenient grace ('praevenerat'), and the penalty of Adam's primal sin that required redemption by Christ's incarnation and death. And his second use of *praevidere* underscores the expectation that the trajectory of such a life should be readable – by the saint, by his parents, by his contemporaries, and by the readers of the *uita* – through the signs that attend it. When Osbern writes in cap. 5 that Dunstan's

115 See David Townsend, 'Anglo-Latin Hagiography and the Norman Transition,' *Exemplaria* 3.2 (1991): 385–433 at 396–403.

116 Stubbs, *Memorials of Saint Dunstan*, cap. 3, p. 72. Later, cap. 11, p. 81, Osbern will use *praedestinare* in describing God's will for the saint.

parents offered him 'as a Levi,' it does not mean that he was oblated at Glastonbury (which was not at this point a reformed house), but explains that his parents simply intended him for a life in the church. It is meant to account for his education at Glastonbury and, of course, his parents' wish that he take minor orders. Dunstan's obedience is then shown in conforming his will to theirs ('quorum ille voluntate humiliter parens').[117] Similarly, when he goes to visit his paternal uncle, Archbishop Athelm, he does so 'permissu parentum suorum' [with the permission of his parents].[118] All of this makes his unwillingness to become a monk, when urged by Bishop Ælfheah, the more unusual and dramatic.

The choice dramatized in cap. 12 is all the more unlikely precisely because it is cast not simply as a choice of embracing monastic actions, but of embracing obedience itself. By vivid contrast with B.'s account, Osbern's treatment of Dunstan's choice makes no mention of God's predestination or omniscience. This absence is notable, since God's predestination is prominently featured in the preceding chapter, where the devil, attempting to defeat Dunstan, defeats himself, 'ignorans malam voluntatem suam Deo famulari, ad perficiendam Dei bonam voluntatem in homine, quem ad conregnandum et congaudendum ipse praedestinaverat' [unaware that his evil will served God by accomplishing the good will of God in the man whom he had predestined for reigning and rejoicing with him].[119] By this language we are meant to understand that Dunstan's expulsion from court was the doing of divine providence. Yet, if the devil himself finds his will co-opted by God, in what way is Dunstan to be understood as free in his choice of monastic life? In what way does Osbern portray Dunstan as morally responsible for his decision? In short, in what way can Dunstan's choice be seen as agent action?

In counterpoint to the language of divine predestination that Osbern uses so carefully in earlier chapters of the *uita*, Dunstan's choice (marriage or the monastery) in cap. 12 is nonetheless portrayed as free. In Osbern's theatre of choice, Dunstan is free to choose what God wills. This is the only way in which we can understand Osbern's careful emplotting of Dunstan's free choice within a divine providence that has predestined Dunstan for eternal glory. The theatricality of Dunstan's choice is found not only in its direct address (the speeches by Dunstan and the bishop) but

117 Ibid., cap. 8, p. 77.
118 Ibid., cap. 9, p. 79.
119 Ibid., cap. 11, p. 81.

also in its staging of Dunstan's illness. In this chapter, Osbern puts aside the language of predestination and divine intervention to show a Dunstan deliberating on his future:

> Cum ergo hiis et hujuscemodi verbis per singulos dies episcopus insisteret; et Dunstanus aut veris aut verisimillimis rationibus insistentem differret, quadam die vehementer hoc cogitationis ambiguo pulsatus est, ut quid in vita quam maxime appetendum fuisset, virtus an voluptas, uxor an virginitas, magnopere deliberaret. Quem sub tali ambiguo positum gravissima febris invasit, atque ad desperationem vitae perduxit.[120]

> [And therefore while the bishop urged him every day with these or similar words, and Dunstan put off his urging with true arguments or arguments very like the truth, on a certain day he was stricken by the uncertainty of his thought, that he should consider carefully what should most be sought in life – virtue or pleasure, a wife or virginity. While put in such uncertainty, a very severe fever attacked him and led him to despair of his life.]

Gone is B.'s leprous illness sent by God at the bishop's request. Instead, Dunstan is stricken by a fever while in the middle of his deliberations. And in contrast with B.'s account, where Dunstan makes his choice in the throes of illness, in Osbern's account, though Dunstan's illness is certainly severe, the saint makes his decision to accept monastic life *after* he recovers ('tum ex insperato recalescens'), not while on the point of death. In Osbern's version of Dunstan's choice, there is no direct 'reading' of the illness as a sign, simply a presentation of the decision that followed it. Its decoupling of chastening sign from decision taken portrays a freedom nowhere to be seen in the earlier *uita*. Through its careful departures from B.'s account (where Dunstan, chastened for his disinclination to become a monk makes amends while still in the throes of a mortal illness), Osbern's narrative works to reconcile choice to predestination, agent action to God's will. Yet the freedom that Osbern accords to Dunstan is not, at least in Osbern's terms, merely a theatrical gesture. Rather, Osbern dramatizes what his master Anselm will work out in philosophical dialogues, an argument for an essential human freedom of choice. To understand the orthodoxy within Osbern's radical departure from the presentation of a saint's good will, we must look at Anselm, Osbern's teacher and patron

120 Ibid., cap. 12, p. 82.

at Bec, for two complementary arguments: the first of moral exhortation, the second of logic.

The Discourse of Freedom and Necessity

As we have seen, in his dialogue with the bishop, Dunstan uses the opposing conditions of freedom and necessity (*libertas* and *necessitas*) to argue against the worth of monastic obedience. The sacrifices of monastic life exacted under the condition of necessity (here, the result of an irrevocable promise of obedience), he is made to argue, lack the quality of freedom required for worthy acts. (The argument is that the man who acts freely is of a better quality ['excellentioris gratiae'] than the man who acts from necessity.) The meaning of 'libertas' is left formally undefined in Dunstan's critique of monastic life, but its context locates that 'libertas' legally in the condition of a free man whose acts are his own. In his counterargument, as we have seen, Bishop Ælfheah changes the terms by equivocating on the senses of 'libertas' and 'necessitas.' In exhorting Dunstan that to avoid the fires of concupiscence it is necessary for a man to leave the world and sacrifice what he holds most dear, his freedom, the bishop makes not a philosophical but a moral argument on the need for salvation. Just such an argument is made in an early letter from Anselm to Henry, a young monk of Christ Church, Canterbury, who wished to leave the monastery to rescue his sister, who had been forced unjustly into servitude.[121] Written before 1074, the letter gives a sense of the values Anselm attached to monastic life and the spurning of the world: that there is nothing in the world that is worth giving up monastic life and jeopardizing eternal salvation.[122] Reminding Henry that monks should have no concern with the world, Anselm claims that nearly everyone in the world serves, and what difference does the label make under which one serves? Anselm's argument about servitude and freedom depends on 1 Cor. 7:21–2 for its force: 'Servus vocatus es? non sit tibi curae: sed et si potes fieri liber, magis utere. Qui enim in Domino vocatus est servus, libertus est Domini: similiter qui liber vocatus est, servus est Christi' [Wast

121 F.S. Schmitt, ed., *S. Anselmi Cantuariensis Archiepiscopi Opera Omnia*, 6 vols. (Edinburgh: Thomas Nelson and Sons, 1946–61), Letter 17 (III: 122–4 at 123), 'indebitae servituti.' Henry left Canterbury and later returned to be made prior by Lanfranc. See R.W. Southern, *Saint Anselm: A Portrait in a Landscape* (Cambridge: Cambridge University Press, 1990), 168.

122 On the dating of the letter see Walter Fröhlich, trans., *The Letters of Saint Anselm of Canterbury*, 3 vols. (Kalamazoo, MI: Cistercian Publications, 1990–94), I: 107.

thou called, being a bondman? care not for it; but if thou mayest be made free, use it rather. For he that is called in the Lord, being a bondman, is the freeman of the Lord. Likewise he that is called, being free, is the bondman of Christ]. In this difficult text, Paul articulates the paradox of being freed by serving the Lord. Since, Anselm argues, all serve in this world, the name under which one serves is of no significance except for pride. Freedom, in a legal or a political sense, has no value for salvation.

While it is doubtful that such an argument would have been of much comfort to Henry's sister (and Henry did leave Canterbury to go to her aid), its attitude towards freedom in the world underlies the counter that the bishop offers to Dunstan's argument about the value of free actions outside monastic service. The sacrifice of freedom is necessary for salvation. Henry's intention to help his sister is characterized by Anselm as that prime monastic sin, *propria uoluntas,* whose antidote is obedience to the wishes of the abbot of Bec (who joined Anselm in his sentiments) and of his friends.[123] A second letter that Anselm writes, this time to one William, argues the case for the value of leaving the world and embracing monastic life.[124] William, on the point of entering the monastery of Bec, had received a call for help from his brother, who asked him to join him in fighting for Jerusalem. Once again, Anselm makes the argument for monastic life a matter of salvation, warning William that his decision may cost him his soul. Love of the world, even of his brother, is nothing compared with love for Christ. 'Ne pudeat te rumpere vincula propositae vanitatis, quia non dedecus, sed honor est transire in libertatem veritatis'[125] [Do not be ashamed to break the chains of your intended vanity, because it is not a shame but an honour to enter into the liberty of truth]. Worldly concern and love for a brother are here accounted vanities, whose claims, in binding William, make him unfree. To break such bonds, although it might seem dishonourable in the world, will permit him true liberty, which is the service of truth. To be the poor man of Christ will earn him the heavenly kingdom; to be a soldier of Christ will ensure that the king will be with him in every danger.

Such are the moral arguments for leaving the apparent freedoms of the world for monastic service. But Osbern's *libertas* has a further burden, untouched by Bishop Ælfheah's fervent arguments. This antinomy between *libertas* and *necessitas* plays out in a logical field where the possibility of freedom is set against the apparent necessity posed by God's

---

123 Schmitt, *Anselmi Opera Omnia*, III: 124.

124 Ibid., III: 252–5 (Letter 117). Fröhlich, *The Letters of Saint Anselm*, I: 281, dates the letter to spring 1086.

125 Schmitt, *Anselmi Opera Omnia*, III: 254.

predestination and foreknowledge. It is likely that Osbern was familiar with the argument of Anselm's letter to Henry: Osbern was an inmate of Christ Church at the time, and such letters were designed to be read aloud.[126] Since Osbern spent time at Bec, from about 1076 to 1080, where he studied with Anselm,[127] it is likely as well that he knew something of the concerns about will and choice that Anselm explored in a set of texts, *De libertate arbitrii, De veritate*, and *De casu diaboli*, composed between 1080 and 1085.[128] *De libertate arbitrii* begins, precisely, with a student posing the question of the apparent incompatibility of human freedom with divine omniscience and predestination:

> Quoniam liberum arbitrium videtur repugnare gratiæ et prædestinationi et præscientiæ dei: ipsa libertas arbitrii quid sit nosse desidero, et utrum semper illam habeamus. Si enim libertas arbitrii est, 'posse peccare et non peccare,' sicut a quibusdam solet dici, et hoc semper habemus: quomodo aliquando gratia indigemus? Si autem hoc non semper habemus: cur nobis imputatur peccatum, quando sine libero arbitrio peccamus?[129]

> [Since free choice seems to be incompatible with the grace, predestination, and foreknowledge of God, I want to know what this freedom of choice is, and whether we always have it. For if freedom of choice is 'the ability to sin and not to sin,' as some are accustomed to say, and we always have that ability, then how is it that we ever need grace? On the other hand, if we do not always have it, why is sin imputed to us when we sin without free choice?][130]

The teacher in the dialogue immediately disputes the student's definition of 'libertas arbitrii,' for a power shared with God and the good angels cannot be a power to sin. The teacher then leads the student into defining the concept in terms of its purpose:

> M. Ad quid tibi videntur illam habuisse libertatem arbitrii: an ad assequendum quod vellent, an ad volendum quod deberent et quod illis velle expediret?

---

126 Fröhlich, *The Letters of Saint Anselm*, I: 25.

127 Rubenstein, 'Life and Writings of Osbern,' 34–5.

128 These texts are edited in Schmitt, *Anselmi Opera Omnia*, I: 170–276. On the dating of these dialogues see Southern, *Saint Anselm, A Portrait in a Landscape*, 172. On the early publication of these texts see Richard Sharpe, 'Anselm as Author: Publishing in the Late Eleventh Century,' *JML* 19 (2009): 1–87.

129 Schmitt, *Anselmi Opera Omnia*, I: 207.

130 Thomas Williams, trans., *Anselm: Three Philosophical Dialogues* (Indianapolis, IN: Hackett, 2002), 32.

D. Ad volendum quod deberent et quod expediret velle.

M. Ergo ad rectitudinem voluntatis habuerunt libertatem arbitrii. Quamdiu namque voluerunt quod debuerunt, rectitudinem habuerunt voluntatis.[131]

[T. For what purpose do you think they had this freedom of choice: in order to attain what they willed, or in order to will what they ought to and what was expedient for them to will?

S. In order to will what they ought to and what was expedient to will.

T. So they had freedom of choice for the sake of rectitude of will – since as long as they willed what they ought to, they had rectitude of will.][132]

While Anselm never directly answers in *De libertate arbitrii* the student's opening question about the incompatibility of free choice and predestination, his definition is designed to resolve the apparent conflict.[133] He does so by locating the operation of that *libertas* solely in the moral realm, defining it as a power to preserve rectitude of will for its own sake and confining its operation to a particular end: 'ad volendum quod deberent' [willing what they ought to will]. In this understanding of freedom of choice, Anselm takes what we have seen is a compatibilist position on the possibility of freedom, asserting that the 'right' choice – i.e., what God wills – is always made freely.[134] In such an understanding, Dunstan's choice of monastic life may be both free and in accord with God's eternal will.

---

131 Schmitt, *Anselmi Opera Omnia*, I: 211.

132 Williams, *Three Philosophical Dialogues*, 35.

133 His great attempt at reconciling grace, predestination, and free choice is made in the late *De concordia praescientiae et praedestinationis et gratiae dei cum libero arbitrio*, which Southern, *Saint Anselm, A Portrait*, xxix, dates to 1107–8. See Schmitt, *Anselmi Opera Omnia*, II.245–88.

134 Sandra Visser and Thomas Williams, 'Anselm's Account of Freedom,' in *The Cambridge Companion to Anselm*, ed. Brian Davies and Brian Leftow (Cambridge: Cambridge University Press, 2004), 179–203 at 197, observe that Anselm's definition (inflected by the other two dialogues of the trio), though denying the principle of alternate possibilities (see Frankfurt examples, above, p. 10, n. 15), satisfies some intuitions of both incompatibilists and compatibilists: 'What is central to Anselm's definition is that the action be self-initiated and consciously chosen, not that it be one of at least two possibilities. This aspect of Anselm's theory partially satisfies the intuition that as long as a person knows what he is doing and why he is doing it, his action is free, regardless of whether the agent had some other option available to him … What is relevant to freedom is not the source of the motivations, but whether, when there is a decision to be made among competing goals, it is the agent himself who is doing the deciding.' By contrast, Katherin Rogers, *Anselm on Freedom* (Oxford: Oxford University Press, 2008), chap. 8, argues that Anselm reconciles libertarian freedom with God's foreknowledge.

With this information in hand, we may see that Osbern's innovations in his version of the saint's commitment to monastic life lie not in rejecting predestination (which he clearly does not do), but in exploring freedom and obedience in the context of Dunstan's choice. He does this in two ways: through the dialogue between Dunstan and Ælfheah and through the staging of Dunstan's decision. It will be recalled that B. had Dunstan choose monastic life when he was in doubt of his own, having been stricken by a terrible illness by God's will. By vivid contrast, in Osbern's account the etiology of the illness that befalls Dunstan in cap. 12 is the same that befalls him in cap. 7 when he was a boy at Glastonbury. God is not portrayed as the agent of Dunstan's fever in cap. 12, nor is the fever shown to be the instrument of Dunstan's choice. Osbern's Dunstan decides to become a monk *after* he begins to recover from his illness, not while the illness threatens to kill him. In short, Osbern stages for Dunstan a compatibilist freedom of choice: the saint is seen to choose what God has willed for him, but to choose freely. It is for this reason that Osbern eliminates the language of predestination from the chapter and removes as well B.'s explanation that the fever attacked Dunstan by God's intervention.

Later Accounts

The two early-twelfth-century versions of Dunstan's *uita* by Eadmer of Canterbury and William of Malmesbury are elegantly crafted versions that reshape B.'s narrative line and carefully avoid Osbern's. Neither later version reports a conversation between Dunstan and the bishop. Eadmer's account is particularly undramatic. In his rewriting, while Ælfheah is said to have urged Dunstan vigorously to become a monk, there is no direct exchange between the two men, and Ælfheah is given but a few lines of direct discourse. Ælfheah is reported to have cited Mark 10:21 (and also Matt. 19:21), Christ's words of admonition to the young man who would be perfect, that he should leave all and follow him. The bishop is then made to say 'Ita, fili, si uis ut ea quae in te iam magni boni spem praestant perfectionis culmen attingant, necesse habes omnia quae in saeculo possides relinquere, et Christi uestigia nudus sequi'[135] [So, my son, if you wish that those things that already show the hope of great good in you will attain the pinnacle of perfection, it necessary for you to give up all you possess in the world and follow naked in the footsteps of Christ]. In reply to this

135 Turner and Muir, *Eadmer of Canterbury: Lives and Miracles*, cap. 10, p. 64.

urging, Eadmer's Dunstan does not refuse monastic life, but much influenced by the bishop, nonetheless vacillates about a previously contracted marriage. There is nothing here that hints at Dunstan's spirited objection in Osbern's *uita*. Eadmer carefully purges Dunstan's speech in the earlier account and records him only as making objections to conversion 'which seemed reasonable to him' ['quae sibi rationis uidebantur'].[136] Still wavering about the contracted marriage, Dunstan is afflicted by a fever, and the order of events in this version of Dunstan's conversion contrasts importantly with those in Osbern's account:

> In qua dubietate constitutum, nutu Dei ualida febris inuasit, et in tantum corpus eius attenuauit, ut nichil minus quam de ducenda uxore cogitaret. Cum autem, iam aliquantum sopito languore, et uerba pontificis et duriciam sui cordis in se reuersus ad mentem reduceret, suspirans grauiter erubuit, quod potentior in eo fuit tercianae febris igniculus ad extinguendam carnis suae concupiscentiam, quam ille ignis quem, ut in cordibus fidelium uehementer arderet, Dominus uenit mittere in terram. Versa igitur uice, ardorem ignis diuini in se succendens carnalibus illecebris funditus renunciauit, seque perpetuo uirginem perseueraturum diuinitatis confisus auxilio uouit.[137]
>
> [In such uncertainty of mind, a serious fever assailed him by God's will and weakened his body to such a degree that he thought of nothing less than taking a wife. But when, now that his illness had diminished somewhat, he recovered himself and recalled to mind both the words of the bishop and the hardness of his own heart, sighing deeply he blushed that the spark of a tertian fever was more powerful in extinguishing in him the concupiscence of his flesh than that fire, which the Lord came to send into this world to burn earnestly in the hearts of the faithful. Quite the contrary, he kindled in himself the flame of divine fire and entirely renounced fleshly enticements and vowed that he would preserve his virginity forever, trusting in God's help.]

As in B.'s account, Eadmer makes Dunstan's illness a function of God's will ('nutu Dei') although there is no indication that the bishop prayed for this outcome. The illness is serious, but not apparently life-threatening – there is no suggestion of swelling or leprosy, nor are there people attending who despair of Dunstan's life. Rather, the fever is an opportunity for a rhetorical figure (the heat of fever versus the effects of the ardour of divine love). That the fever was the result of God's will suggests that the illness was

136 Ibid.
137 Ibid.

monitory, and Dunstan interprets its effects as burning out of his body the fire of concupiscence. While his embarrassment lies in the earlier weakness in him of the divine flame that Christ came to kindle on earth,[138] Dunstan calls the bishop to him to do penance for his having not obeyed immediately (Eadmer's word is 'obtemperauerit').[139] That is, Dunstan holds himself liable for an infraction of obedience even before his conversion to monastic life. But his obedience is double: that the bishop's counsel to take the habit was also the will of God was confirmed for Dunstan by his fever. Obedience to the bishop was obedience to God.

William of Malmesbury[140] follows B.'s narrative line by presenting a Dunstan much influenced by the possibilities of unspecified pleasure (although no mention is made of marriage). William keeps a censorious corrector's eye on Osbern's version and gives Dunstan no direct speech, though he reports that the young man put the bishop off with witty remarks ('facetis responsis').[141] As disapproving as William is of Osbern's version, he is also concerned to report facts gleaned from earlier accounts, and he edges around the scandal of Dunstan's reply in the earlier *uita*, reporting that 'sometimes also he mocked that the life of monks did not please God any more than that of laymen.'[142] This, of course, grossly understates his source. Osbern's Dunstan argued that the life of an equally observant layperson was *more* pleasing than that of a monk because it was not obligated by obedience. Unlike Osbern, William follows B. in having Ælfheah pray for a bodily sign to warn Dunstan. And so, after a terrible inflammation covers his whole body, Dunstan calls for the bishop and becomes a monk.

Common to both accounts (and Adelard does not treat the incident) are the following: insistent urging of the bishop, temptation to pleasure, a refusal or a deferral of some magnitude, illness as a divine sign, and conversion during the illness. Both William and Eadmer knew Osbern's account and were clearly scandalized by it. In reaction, they return to the scripting of B., where Dunstan's illness comes as a chastisement from God's hand and where obedient action is the result of reading the sign of God's will.

138 See Luke 12:49, 'Ignem veni mittere in terram' [I am come to cast fire on the earth].

139 Turner and Muir, *Eadmer of Canterbury: Lives and Miracles*, cap. 10, p. 64: 'quod sibi uiam perfectionis suadenti non statim obtemperauerit, quod habitum religionis monasticae ad uerbum eius non susceperit.'

140 Ignoring Eadmer's account (see Winterbottom and Thomson, *William of Malmesbury, Saints' Lives*, xxii).

141 Winterbottom and Thomson, *William of Malmesbury, Saints' Lives*, cap. 7, p. 184.

142 Ibid., 'nonnumquam etiam monachorum uitam non magis placere Deo quam laicorum cauillatus.'

Clearly influenced by B., William has the bishop pray for God to inflict an illness on Dunstan as a readable sign. William is careful to mark out the connections between the bishop's prayer and Dunstan's illness. The bishop's earnest prayer, described as a 'scintilla caritatis' [spark of love] kindles a 'flammam egrotationis' [flame of illness] so severe that it covered Dunstan's body with swelling blisters.[143] The course of action that William now describes shows us both a conservative preference for B.'s account of divine intervention and a negative reaction to Osbern's account: 'Hoc periculo territus nuntiis missis rogauit eius aduentum. Maturauit iter episcopus, et ueniens audit quod diu optauerat, Dunstanum anxie expetere quod ante rogatus supersederat facere. Datur ergo effectus desiderio: alteratur Dunstanus et fit monachus'[144] [Terrified by the danger, he sent messages begging the bishop to come. The bishop rushed to him and reaching him heard what he had long desired, that Dunstan sought anxiously to do what he earlier, when asked, had declined to do. Thus his desire was accomplished: Dunstan was changed and made a monk.]

William's account (as does B.'s) portrays Dunstan's monastic conversion as action taken directly following a manifestation of God's will. To make the motivation for Dunstan's action readable, William narrates purposive action by the bishop in his praying specifically for direct action by God in sending an illness ('flagello ammoneretur corporeo'), and a clear understanding of that illness as a chastising sign.[145] The divine warning made clear to his readers by William's prose is painfully clear to Dunstan on his body, since he agrees to become a monk while still in the grips of his terrible illness. God's will and the bishop's desire are one, and Dunstan's decision to accept monastic life is shown as obedient alignment with God's will. In contrast, Osbern shows us Dunstan choosing monastic conversion without an immediate divine sign and without God's causing his illness; he shows us a choice made freely by rational argument, not as a result of the bishop's prayer for divine intervention. But this behaviour of Dunstan contrasts even with that in earlier chapters of Osbern's *uita*, where Dunstan is shown conforming his will to that of his parents, who, in turn, are fulfilling God's will for Dunstan.[146] Such careful portrayal of divine will, and of the saint humbly deferring to the will of others, makes

143 Ibid. Winterbottom and Thomson translate Dunstan's affliction as 'dropsy or the King's Evil' (185).

144 Ibid., cap. 7, p. 184.

145 Ibid.

146 On Osbern's language of predestination see above, pp. 82–3.

his subsequent unwillingness to become a monk, when urged by Bishop Ælfheah, and his scandalous argument the more unusual and dramatic.

Osbern constructs a story of resistance (however conventionally it is resolved) centred on Dunstan's desire to retain his *self-will*, and the question that Osbern has Dunstan frame undercuts the entire monastic enterprise. Acknowledging that obedience is the fundamental identifying characteristic of a monk, Dunstan's question challenges the value of that obedience and the necessity of that identity. Rather than ensuring value to each act of the obedient monk, obedience, in this argument, by transforming each act of a monk into the valueless activity of a drone, makes monastic life of less value than the life of one for whom each religious act is a praiseworthy act of the will. In our terms, Dunstan's objection thus aims at the linkage of monastic identity and agency. While Dunstan's speech challenged the value of obedience, Ælfheah's argued its utility. But the larger, unspoken issue in the episode is the way in which individual acts work within God's providential will. Here is where Osbern shows a particular anxiety in trying to portray that Dunstan's decision to become a monk is free at the same time as it is directed by God. This anxiety explains why there is no place in his narrative for the chastising sign in B. sent at the prayerful entreaty of Ælfheah. If the heroism of Dunstan's conversion in Osbern's narrative is magnified by the gravity of his objections, nonetheless the scandal of his objection to an obedience without agency hovers over the text.

Obedience is both the stuff of monastic identity and the test of this cardinal virtue's successful incorporation in the monastic subject. Obedience is never perfected, never finally achieved, for its end is only continued obedience. Its aim, as Foucault observed in his study of the pastoral relation, 'is to act ... so that there is no other will but not to have any will.'[147] Obedience is thus the performative through which monastic identity is installed, tested, and ensured, an identity in which self-will is left behind and agent action is conceived to lie in the cheerful, immediate, and complete accession to the will of another. While Osbern's Dunstan shows us self-will as a temptation more seductive than sex, his narrative wrestles to portray Dunstan's obedient submission to the will of God as an act that can, nonetheless, be seen as completely free.

147 Michel Foucault, *Security, Territory, Population: Lectures at the Collège de France, 1977–78*, ed. Michel Senellart, trans. Graham Burchell (London: Palgrave, 2007), 178.

2 'Esto quod es': Ælfric's *Colloquy* and the Imperatives of Monastic Identity

The Latin command 'Esto quod es' [Be what you are] begins an admonition to the fictional pupils in Ælfric's *Colloquy.* 'Be what you are,' the Consiliarius tells the boys, 'because it is a wrong and a shame for a man to want not to be what he is.' What the pupils within the *Colloquy* are meant to be (oblates in a post-Reform Benedictine monastery) and the text in which this admonition is found (an early classroom exercise to train those oblates in the Latin language) make the shape of its advice particularly rich in its implications for identity and agency in the late tenth century and for the desire that mediates between them. Oblates, by definition, were children given to a monastery by their parents as gifts to God. The act of giving, understood as irrevocable, was also understood to change the child's religious, legal, and social status forever.[1] Although such children might be dedicated at birth, they would not be brought to live in the monastery until around the age of seven. And at that point, these children would have to learn to regard themselves as no longer part of their blood family, but as members of the new, spiritual *familia* of the monastery. The process of assuming and naturalizing this new identity happened across a spectrum of activities.[2] In somatic terms the children acquired new repertoires of gestures and postures, habits of eating, practices of silence, and disciplines of

1 On oblation see the excellent study of Mayke de Jong, *In Samuel's Image: Child Oblation in the Early Medieval West* (Leiden: E.J. Brill, 1996); see also her earlier study on *pueri nutriti* in the commentary of Hildemar, 'Growing Up in a Carolingian Monastery: Magister Hildemar and His Oblates,' *Journal of Medieval History* 9 (1983): 99–128; for a discussion of the canonical issues connected to oblation, see chapter 3.

2 From the perspective of developmental psychology, late childhood (ages six to twelve) is a critical period in identity formation. See Roy F. Baumeister, *Identity: Cultural Change*

living corporately in the rhythms of the monastic day and year.[3] In intellectual terms they were tasked with memorizing key texts, learning their meaning and the tropes through which to interpret them, and learning the language – Latin – fundamental to all these skills. The naturalizing of these activities would mark the child as a member of the monastic community as surely as (and more profoundly than) their wearing of the monastic tunic and cowl. The pupils of the *Colloquy*, and by extension the children voicing their parts in this classroom exercise, portray for us this fundamental activity – the learning of Latin – in a way that illustrates perception of its acquisition as a crucial marker of identity.

My interest in the *Colloquy* is in *its* interest in these boys, the children of the monastic community. In what follows I wish to trace the *Colloquy*'s role in the formation of monastic identity for the youngest members of a monastic *familia*, that is, the family in religion to which these boys had been irrevocably given. While the linguistic exercises of the *Colloquy* show it to be an elementary text for language acquisition, I argue that it had other work to do. 'Esto quod es' [Be what you are] is the phrase that shows that work to us; it speaks to the need for forming identity while claiming that identity is always already formed; it shows us the nexus between language learning and naturalization into monastic life; most remarkably, it speaks to anxieties over the will of oblates, whose religious commitments were made by others. 'Be what you are,' in commanding the children to embrace what they were made, exposes the fissures in the construction of agent action for a child – indeed, for an adult – conveyed as an object but expected to will what was willed by others. 'Esto quod es' shows us a moment when a particular form of agency is installed in and demanded of a child given to religious life. The form of that agency and its installation are the interests of this chapter.

The unspoken of the Consiliarius's[4] command 'esto quod es' is a narrative of identity and agency that connects, often in unexpected ways, notions of

---

and the Struggle for Self (Oxford: Oxford University Press, 1986), 173–97, esp. 182–6 and 196–7.

3 On the training of the body see Isabelle Cochelin, 'Besides the Book: Using the Body to Mould the Mind – Cluny in the Tenth and Eleventh Centuries,' in *Medieval Monastic Education*, ed. George Ferzoco and Carolyn Muessig (London: Leicester University Press, 2000), 21–34.

4 The Latin word means 'counsellor' or 'adviser' (see Lewis and Short, sense I). Patrizia Lendinara, 'The *Colloquy* of Ælfric and the *Colloquy* of Ælfric Bata,' in her *Anglo-Saxon Glosses and Glossaries* (Aldershot: Ashgate, 1999), 207–87 [trans. 'Il Colloquio di Ælfric e il colloquio de Ælfric Bata,' in '*Feor ond neah*,' *Scritti di Filologia Germanica in*

will and choice, desire and obligation, structure and individual, obedience and freedom. The statement of which it is a part: 'Siue sis sacerdos, siue monachus, seu laicus, seu miles, exerce temet ipsum in hoc, et esto quod es; quia magnum dampnum et uerecundia est homini nolle esse quod est et quod esse debet'[5] [Whether you are a priest, or a monk, or a layman, or a warrior, train yourself in that, and be what you are, because it is a wrong and a shame for a man to want not to be what he is] proffers an immediate social context for the command in the conceptually overlapping social categories of monk, priest, layman, and warrior that it offers as illustrations. These occupations – imagined to be unchangeable identities that nonetheless are threatened by the desire to be other – are offered as models to children whose identity had been formally changed in the gesture of the gift that was their oblation and whose identity was, in fact, being formed in the speaking of the *Colloquy* itself. If 'esto quod es' frames itself as an exhortation to perseverance, it does so by imagining the period of education as a time of fulfilment in which the child trained himself in 'that,' that is, the naturalizing of practices and skills required for being a monk.[6] The monastic classroom taught at once both the fundamentals of text and language and the life in which they were lived.[7]

---

memoria di Augusto Scaffidi Abbate, ed. Patrizia Lendinara and Lucio Melazzo, Annali della Facoltà di Lettere e Filosofia dell'Università di Palermo, Studi e ricerche 3 (Palermo, STASS, 1983), 173–249], at 232, notes that the OE gloss to 'consiliarius' ('geþeahtend') indicates not an official post but someone in the role of peacemaker in a dispute.

5 G.N. Garmonsway, ed., *Ælfric's Colloquy*, rev. ed. (Exeter: University of Exeter Press, 1978), pp. 41–2, lines 240–3. On the Old English glosses for these occupations see Patrizia Lendinara, 'The *Colloquy* of Ælfric and the *Colloquy* of Ælfric Bata,' 232–3. On the notion of three orders of society in Anglo-Saxon England see Timothy E. Powell, 'The "Three Orders" of Society in Anglo-Saxon England,' *ASE* 23 (1994): 103–32, esp. 110–15. John Ruffing sees 'esto quod es' as 'curiously circular reasoning' that 'deliberately exclud[es] the problematic interrelations of roles' in 'The Labor Structure of Ælfric's *Colloquy*,' in *The Work of Work: Servitude, Slavery, and Labor in Medieval England*, ed. Allen J. Frantzen and Douglas Moffat (Glasgow: Cruithne Press, 1994), 55–70 at 68.

6 On monastic perseverance see Adalbert de Vogüé, 'Persévérer au monastère jusqu'à la mort. La stabilité chez saint Benoît et autour de lui,' *Collectanea Cisterciensia* 43 (1981): 337–65. On the monastery as *dominici scola* see See Rudolf Hanslik, ed., *Benedicti Regula*, 2nd rev. ed., CSEL 75 (Vienna: Hoelder-Pichler-Tempsky, 1977), prol. 45–8 (p. 9); see also Adalbert de Vogüé, ed. and trans., *La Règle du Maître*, 3 vols., SC 105–7 (Paris: Les Éditions du Cerf, 1964–5), I, p. 326 (Ths 45–6) and pp. 115–16.

7 The Rule made special allowance for children in the monastery, and this latitude, in recognition of their youth and their inexperience, is recognized by the child's reply in the *Colloquy* that he may eat meat 'quia puer sum sub uirga degens' [because I am a child

Examining the narrative of will, choice, and obedience in the formation of monastic identity that underlies the Consiliarius's command to his pupils will take us first to the imagined classroom of the *Colloquy* and to the ways in which the teaching of Latin it bespeaks functioned in the building and maintaining of monastic life.[8] The monastic identity to which Ælfric appeals through the Consiliarius in the *Colloquy* is, I propose, a specifically textual identity for which learning in Latin is both its idealized, essential component and its measure and index. In the most general sense, such an identity is textual in that its corporate performance is driven and judged by a written Rule (a portion of which was recited daily), centred on the voicing of sacred texts in the round of monastic liturgies, and on the reading and hearing of scripture and religious writings.[9] The

---

living under the rod] (Garmonsway, *Ælfric's Colloquy*, p. 46, lines 285–6). In effect, 'living under the rod' defines 'child,' since beating was the punishment deemed appropriate for children in the *RSB*; see pp. 121–3 below.

8 The Old English verb for such action is *drohtnian*. See DOE, s.v. *drohtnian*, sense 5, 'to live according to a rule, a teaching, a will or purpose.' The noun form is *drohtnung*.

9 For the monastic communities of the Benedictine Reform, the *RSB* was the written text governing the minutia of their lives. In addition, the *Regularis concordia*, as the written agreement designed to regulate all reformed houses in England, sought to regularize monasteries and convents through enhanced liturgical performance beyond what was specified in the *RSB*. See Dom Thomas Symons, ed. and trans., *Regularis Concordia* (London: Thomas Nelson and Sons, 1953), cap. 6, p. 4. On the impact of reciting portions of the *RSB* daily see Dom David Knowles, *The Monastic Order in England*, 2nd ed. (Cambridge, 1963; repr. Cambridge: Cambridge University Press, 1966), 14. For a magisterial analysis of Ælfric's understanding of monasticism and the 'surprisingly elastic terms' of his theorizing of the *ordo monasticus* see Christopher A. Jones, 'Ælfric and the Limits of "Benedictine Reform,"' in *A Companion to Ælfric*, ed. Hugh Magennis and Mary Swan, Brill's Companions to the Christian Tradition 18 (Leiden: Brill, 2009), 67–108 at 69. On the monastery as a 'textual community' see Catherine Cubitt, 'Memory and Narrative in the Cult of Early Anglo-Saxon Saints,' in *The Uses of the Past in the Early Middle Ages*, ed. Yitzhak Hen and Matthew Innes (Cambridge: Cambridge University Press, 2000), 29–66 at 33. On the collective memory arising from communally memorized liturgical texts see Janet Coleman, *Ancient and Medieval Memories: Studies in the Reconstruction of the Past* (Cambridge: Cambridge University Press, 1992), 133. However, Coleman's emphasis on forgetting within the monastery is, perhaps, excessive. On the mediation of monastic education through the moral example of the teacher see Catherine Cubitt, 'Monastic Memory and Identity in Early Anglo-Saxon England,' in *Social Identity in Early Medieval Britain*, ed. William O. Frazer and Andrew Tyrrell (London: Leicester University Press, 2000), 253–76 at 262–5. See also Brian Stock, *The Implications of Literacy: Written Language and Models of Interpretation in the Eleventh and Twelfth Centuries* (Princeton: Princeton University Press, 1983), 90–1, on the transformative dynamics of 'textual communities.'

strong distinction between monks and secular clergy, made in the wake of the Benedictine Reform, is that the former were literate, conducted their struggle against the clerics in a variety of ideological texts, and defined themselves and their program through texts in Latin and the vernacular.[10] In the case of Ælfric, the *textual* dimension of monastic identity is clear from the commitments of the writings in his educational projects, his pervasive and enduring concern for a sufficient understanding of Latin in the clergy, and, supremely, his often-stated anxiety over correct interpretation.[11] These concerns show that the monastic identity Ælfric imagines in the shadow of the Benedictine Reform was defined, however briefly, by an orientation toward fundamental Christian texts and an ability to read and interpret them that differentiated the members of that community from all outside it. That Ælfric may have perceived his own Latinity never to have reached the heroic stature of his master's, Æthelwold, lends poignancy to his pedagogical commitment and explains, perhaps, the urgency with which he states it.[12] The building of such textual identity required the oblates of the community to obey their masters, persevere in their studies, and exercise their wills in becoming what they were.

The consequence of doing otherwise – that is, acting on the desire to be something other – Ælfric dramatizes in a vignette in his homily on St Benedict of Nursia. In translating Gregory's account of a miracle attributed to the eponymous father of Benedictine monasticism, Ælfric reframes the

10 On the effect of 'reform polemic' see John Blair, *The Church in Anglo-Saxon Society* (Oxford: Oxford University Press, 2005), 353–4. For a sympathetic account of the reform see Knowles, *The Monastic Order in England*, 31–56. On the use of language in Reform culture as a means of creating difference see Catherine Cubitt, 'The Tenth-Century Benedictine Reform in England,' *Early Medieval Europe* 6 (1997): 77–94 at 89. On the importance of Latin to reformed Benedictine identity, see Rebecca Stephenson, 'Scapegoating the Secular Clergy: The Hermeneutic Style as a Form of Monastic Self-Definition,' *ASE* 38 (2010): 101–35, esp. 128.

11 On Ælfric's concern for interpretation and orthodoxy see Jonathan Wilcox, ed., *Ælfric's Prefaces*, Durham Medieval Texts 9 (Durham: Durham Medieval Texts, 1994), 65–71, and Robert Stanton, *The Culture of Translation in Anglo-Saxon England* (Cambridge: D.S. Brewer, 2002), 131–71.

12 On Ælfric's 'unease' with and 'sincere diffidence' about his ability in Latin see Christopher A. Jones, '*Meatim sed et rustica*: Ælfric of Eynsham as a Medieval Latin Author,' *JML* 8 (1998): 1–57 at 54–5 and 57. But see Rebecca Stephenson, 'Ælfric of Eynsham and Hermeneutic Latin: *Meatim sed et rustica* Reconsidered,' *JML* 16 (2006): 111–41, who argues convincingly that Ælfric's syntax is capable of subtlety and complexity and that his refusal of hermeneutic vocabulary should be ascribed not to poor education but to a desire for clear prose.

pope's narrative in the context of the tenth-century Benedictine Reform. His changes refashion the story of a runaway oblate, a *munuccild*, as a cautionary tale of dangerous desire, lost identity, and the importance of obedience for the oblates of a monastic house.[13]

As Gregory the Great presents the story of the runaway oblate in *Dialogi* II.24, the point of the narrative is to show Benedict's spiritual merits and the favour in which he is held by God.[14] Ælfric's translation and adaptation give the story a more dramatic profile than its source, focusing on a single act and its results. His alterations highlight the runaway's wilful behaviour and the consequences of his disobedience:

> Sum munuccild drohtnode on his mynstre. and hæfde micele lufe to his fæder and to his meder. swiðor for ðære sibbe þonne for godes dæle. wearð þa oflangod ungemetlice. and arn buton bletsunge of mynstre to his magum. and swa hraðe swa he him to com ydæges swa gewat he of ðisum andwerdum life; Þa he bebyriged wæs. ða ne mihte seo byrgen hine gehealdan. ac wearð his lic on merigen afunden bufon þære byrgenne; His magas hine eft bebirigdon. and he wearð eft up aworpen. and swa gelomlice; Þa magas ða comon and mid micclum wope þæs halgan weres fet gesohton. his gife biddende; Se halga benedictus him sealde godes husel mid his agenre handa. and cwæð; Lecgað þis halige husel uppon his breoste. and bebyriað hine swa; Ða þis gedon wæs. ða heold seo eorðe þone lichaman. and syððan ne awearp.[15]

> [An oblate was leading the monastic life in his [= Benedict's] monastery and he had great love for his father and his mother, more for the bond of kinship than for God's inheritance. He was immoderately afflicted by longing and he ran without blessing from the monastery to his kinsmen. And as soon as he got to them, on the same day he departed this present life. When he was buried, then the grave could not hold him, but his body was discovered in the morning above the grave. His kinsmen buried him again, and again

13 On the importance of obedience in monastic life see Smaragdus, *Diadema monachorum*, cap. 13, PL 102, 609–10.

14 Adalbert de Vogüé, ed., Paul Antin trans., *Grégoire le Grand, Dialogues*, vol. 2, SC 260 (Paris: Les Éditions du Cerf, 1979), 210, 212.

15 Malcolm Godden, ed. *Ælfric's Catholic Homilies: The Second Series, Text*, EETS s.s. 5 (Oxford: Oxford University Press, 1979), pp. 102–3, lines 362–75 (= *CH* II). Godden, *Ælfric's Catholic Homilies: Introduction, Commentary and Gloss*, EETS s.s. 18 (Oxford: Oxford University Press 2000), p. 442 (= *CH* III), comments: 'Ælfric expands Gregory's brief reference to the boy "loving his parents more than he ought," apparently to explain in what ways this might be sinful and make his fate more justifiable (lines 362–4).'

> afterwards he was tossed out, and so on continuously. Then his kinsmen came with great weeping and sought the feet of the holy man, begging his favour. Saint Benedict gave them the Eucharist with his own hand and said 'Lay this holy Eucharist upon his breast and bury him that way.' When this was done, the earth then held the body and didn't toss it out thereafter.]

The narrative's juxtaposition of the boy's untimely death and his wilful departure from the monastery presses the inference, *post hoc ergo propter hoc*, that he died *because* he ran away.[16] The child's wilful action has a further, uncanny consequence: no matter how many times his family buried him, the grave wouldn't keep him and his body was tossed out. As the narrative structures it, the condign punishment for the child's leaving God's place *sua sponte* was that in death the earth kept returning him to his family. Having left his proper place, abandoning the *familia* of the monastery for the family of his own blood, he could not, in death, have a place until St Benedict intervened with a miracle. The account in the *Dialogi* emphasizes the offence to Benedict of the child's leaving without his blessing, and Gregory draws the conclusion for Deacon Peter and his readers that the incident shows Benedict's extraordinary saintly merits: 'Perpendis, Petre, apud Iesum Christum Dominum cuius meriti iste uir fuerit, ut eius corpus etiam terra proiecerit, qui Benedicti gratiam non haberet'[17] [Think, Peter, what merit this man had with the Lord, Jesus Christ, that even the earth would reject the body of someone who did not have Benedict's favour].

While Ælfric is clearly interested in Benedict's miracle-working record in this homily, by contrast with that of Gregory, his structuring of the narrative places primary emphasis on monastic institutional issues – the boy's transgression, his ante- and post-mortem punishment – and the saint's miraculous power plays out in a conflict between agency and identity. In using the technical word 'drohtnode,' with its sense of living under a rule, Ælfric makes clear that the boy was a member of the monastic community and was practising monastic life.[18] 'Drohtnian,' with its extensive use in Ælfric's corpus, speaks of the boy in terms of a lived monastic identity, for 'drohtnian' means, precisely, living the life, with the implication that the child, by wearing the habit, rising, retiring, eating, and worshipping by the bell, though technically a monk by his oblation, was becoming

16 On punishment and Gregory's hierarchical reasoning see Charles M. Radding, *A World Made by Men: Cognition and Society, 400–1200* (Chapel Hill: University of North Carolina Press, 1985), 67–9.

17 De Vogüé, *Grégoire le Grand, Dialogues*, II.xxiv.16–19 (p. 212).

18 On *drohtnian* see note 8 above.

a monk in actuality by his practice. The tension between agency and identity emerges starkly in the opposition Ælfric establishes in his translation between 'drohtnode,' with its sense of the stability of the repeated daily actions of monastic life, and the OE verb 'arn' [ran]. That contrast throws into stark relief the child's spontaneous departure. He ran. In the contrast between 'drohtnode' [lived the life] and 'arn' [ran] Ælfric sets up the oppositions that define the horizons of the boy's world and the range of his desires: family and monastery, or more precisely the family of his blood and his spiritual family, flesh and spirit, proper and improper love, desire, will, and obedience.

Ælfric's dramatic revisions to Gregory's narrative are even clearer when seen in the context of Wærferth's Old English translation of the *Dialogi*.[19] Wærferth's close translation preserves the habitual nature of the boy's visits home featured clearly in Gregory's Latin: 'atque eorum habitaculum tendens' becomes '7 geneahhe higode 7 ferde to heora huse.'[20] Wærferth's translation carefully preserves the significant detail of Gregory's Latin account, that the boy appears to have gone home often by Benedict's indulgence. But because *this* departure was without a blessing, that is, without Benedict's permission, its fatal result (and the subsequent miracle) show Gregory's narrative revolves around the child's offence to his abbot, St Benedict.[21] By contrast, the omitted blessing takes on an additional institutional meaning for monastic performance in Ælfric's version, in the wake of the Benedictine Reform in England, given the insistence of the *Regularis concordia* that any action of a monk, temporal or spiritual,

19 Hans Hecht, ed., *Bischofs Waerferth von Worcester Übersetzung der Dialoge Gregors des Grossen*, Bibliothek der angelsächsischen Prosa 5 (Leipzig: Georg H. Wigland, 1900–7).

20 Ibid., p. 154, lines 12–13a. De Vogüé, *Grégoire le Grand, Dialogues*, II.xxiv.3 (p. 210). Wærferth's translation underwent a comprehensive revision in the tenth century at an unknown centre. For a meticulous study of the two versions see David Yerkes, *The Two Versions of Waerferth's Translation of Gregory's Dialogues: An Old English Thesaurus* (Toronto: University of Toronto Press, 1979). Mechthild Gretsch, *Ælfric and the Cult of Saints in Late Anglo-Saxon England*, Cambridge Studies in Anglo-Saxon England 34 (Cambridge: Cambridge University Press, 2005), 140–1, shows that Ælfric knew the translation, but that we cannot know which version. The revision has 'for yrnende,' making the continuing nature of the action explicit. On the durative character of the periphrastic + *faran* see Bruce Mitchell, *Old English Syntax*, 2 vols. (Oxford: Clarendon Press, 1985), I, § 691. This usage is especially significant since the reviser regularly reduces the numbers of periphrastics but in this instance has introduced one. See Mitchell, *Old English Syntax*, I, § 686.

21 Compare the behaviour of the obedient child, Maurus, who asks Benedict's blessing before running to save the boy Placidus, swept away by the current: De Vogüé, *Grégoire le Grand, Dialogues*, II.vii; Godden, *CH* II, homily 11, p. 95, line 99.

should begin with a blessing.[22] Ælfric's revision to the simple preterite *arn* (a word choice distinct from Wærferth's 'eode' [went, walked]) highlights the punctual nature of the boy's act, the one-off, impulsive quality of a single, defining event. In so doing, he contrasts the child's running with his habitus, the *drohtnung*, of his life. As Ælfric elaborates Gregory's spare account[23] in bringing the story into English, he affectively particularizes 'parentes' as mother and father, expands 'ultra quam debebat diligens' to 'had more [love] for his kindred than for God's inheritance' and intensifies the neutral 'exisset' to 'ran.' In these added particulars, Ælfric dramatizes the child's sin as an act of choice.[24] His judgment that a misplaced love drove the child to choose the bond of kinship (*sib*) over 'Godes dæle' [God's portion (=inheritance)] lays out the institutional terms in which the boy violates his identity.[25] The boy's perverse choice, then, was to return to the family of his blood, rejecting the (spiritual) inheritance that would be his expectation were he to continue his life with the *familia* of Benedict's monastery. The moral valence of such a choice is made clear by Ælfric's identification of what we would call 'free will' with choice. The word 'cyre' [choice], a cognate of *ceosan* [to choose], is his preferred translation for Augustine's 'liberum arbitrium,' and in that context, a word he often coupled with *gehyrsumnes* [obedience].[26]

---

22 Symons, *Regularis Concordia*, cap. 14 (p. 11): 'omnia ... spiritualia siue corporalia ... cum benedictione incohentur.'

23 De Vogüé, *Grégoire le Grand, Dialogues*, II.xxiv.1–4 (p. 210): 'dum quidam eius [scil. S. Benedicti] puerulus monachus, parentes suos ultra quam debebat diligens atque ad eorum habitaculum tendens, sine benedictione de monasterio exisset.' See also the following story in Godden, *CH* II.11, on the monk who does not wish to remain in the monastery (from *Grégoire le Grand, Dialogues*, II.xxv.1–19 (p. 212).

24 On Ælfric's understanding of human responsibility for actions taken, and his ascription of choice to action see above, Introduction, pp. 19–22.

25 For *dæl* in the sense of *portio* as religious inheritance see DOE, s.v. *dæl*, sense B1. Æthelwold's Old English translation of the Rule of St Benedict stresses eligibility to inherit the heavenly kingdom as the goal of monastic life. See Arnold Schröer, ed., *Die angelsächsischen Prosabearbeitungen der Benedictinerregel*, 2nd ed. with supplement by Helmut Gneuss, Bibliothek der angelsächsischen Prosa 2 (Kassel, 1885; Darmstadt: Wissenschaftliche Buchgesellschaft, 1964), p. 4, lines 21–5. His conclusion, 'mid gefylled-nesse goddere þenunge we weorðaþ heofena rices yrfeweardes' [with the fulfilment of divine service we will become heirs of the kingdom of heaven] specifies inheritance beyond what appears in the *textus purus* (cf. Hanslik, ed. *Benedicti Regula*, prol. 39 (p. 8).

26 The DOE indicates that with approximately sixty occurrences, *cyre* is 'disproportionately freq[uent]' in Ælfric's works (DOE, s.v. *cyre*). On the work of choice in Ælfric's thought see the Introduction, pp. 15–26.

If we return for a moment to the child's departure, we might imagine him frozen in mid-run, suspended between *monasterium* and *habitaculum*, between his spiritual father and brothers on the one side and his mother and father on the other, neither sent by St Benedict nor taken by his family. In the space between his former and current home he is attached to nothing; the habit he wears functions only negatively: it marks him as no longer of his blood family. By his wilful departure the habit can no longer mark belonging under the sign of *stabilitas* within the monastery, and instead is rendered merely a badge of his incoherence. Suspended in the space between the two structures shaping who he might be – the family of his birth and the *familia* of his spiritual life – the child's improvisation in leaving may suggest to us a moment of agency played out in the empty space between the two places of his life, for as he runs he acts outside the script of both his blood family and the *familia* of Benedict's monastery.[27] But his running, for Ælfric, only constitutes a sinful choice, undoing the identity imposed on him by his punctual oblation and by the naturalizing, obedient actions of the habitus he is meant to acquire. Driving the boy is desire: he 'ran' because he was 'oflangod ungemetlice' [immoderately afflicted by longing],[28] and Ælfric diagnoses that longing as a symptom of his misplaced love, more for his mother and father than for God's inheritance. The child, unmindful of the consequence of the desire to be other than he is, ends up with no place at all. No longer belonging to his family, the child cannot be properly buried by them. Because he lacks a proper place, even the earth won't have him.

Ælfric's revision of Gregory's miracle story shows us the consequence of imperfectly realized monastic identity – the child disobediently returns to the family of his blood rather than stay with the *familia* of the

27 Dorothy Holland, William Lachicotte Jr, Debra Skinner, and Carole Cain, *Identity and Agency in Cultural Worlds* (Cambridge, MA: Harvard University Press, 1998), 272: 'authorship is not a choice – but the form of the answer is not predetermined … [A]uthorship is a matter of orchestration: of arranging the identifiable social discourses/practices that are one's resources (which Bakhtin glossed as "voices") in order to craft a response in time and space defined by others' standpoints in activity, that is, in a social field conceived as the ground of responsiveness. Human agency comes through this art of improvisation … This vision of human activity makes a mockery of any notion of individual authorship, if that means a kind of independent or autonomous creativity. But it fills personal authorship with social efficacy, for identities take us back and forth from intimate to public spaces.'

28 In this usage, 'oflangod' ascribes to the child the same class of longing as the speaker has in the *Wife's Lament* 29b.

monastery – and in so doing he illustrates action arising from problematic desire, a desire, from the monastic perspective, to be other than what he is by both God's will and his parents' gift. If in our own moment we may identify agency in the child's improvisation and are tempted to admire the freedom from institutional constraints that shows the act as truly his, Ælfric's narrative assesses the act as a transgression arising from disordered love, a misprision of identity that leads to placing the self before the community, an indulgence of desire that leads to destruction, and a catastrophic failure of obedience within a structure that supports identity and promises the reward of eternal life. Such disobedience, read within the monastic context of Ælfric's thought as the product of a bad will, showed not freedom but slavery to sin, the persistence of the 'old' man (Eph. 4:22; Col. 3:9), and the hopeless chaining of the will to destructive patterns of behaviour.[29] True freedom lay in obedience to God and in the freely given, obedient bending of the will to one's monastic superiors.[30] Such an understanding of the dialectic of freedom and obedience was fundamental to the training of a young oblate, whether found in the realm of the practical, as the *RSB* was read in chapter, or in the many iterations of Augustine's thought, found in curriculum authors such as Prosper of Aquitaine.

Let us return to the *Colloquy* and our opening problem: 'Siue sis sacerdos, siue monachus, seu laicus, seu miles, exerce temet ipsum in hoc, et esto quod es; quia magnum dampnum et uerecundia est homini nolle esse quod est et quod esse debet.'[31] For this, as for the rest of the *Colloquy*, an Old English gloss provides a careful translation, whether done by Ælfric's pupil, Ælfric Bata, or by some other hand: 'Swa hwæðer þu sy, swa mæsseprest, swa munuc, swa ceorl, swa kempa, bega oþþe behwyrf þe sylfne on þisum, 7 beo þæt þu eart; forþam micel hynð 7 sceamu hyt is menn nellan wesan þæt þæt he ys 7 þæt þe he wesan sceal.'[32] I should like to look closer at the command 'Esto quod es' ('Beo þæt þu eart') [Be what you are] to examine the work it does in the *Colloquy*. I suggest that the command operates from a nodal point of intersecting expectations connecting identity and agency. Launched within the fiction of the grammar classroom, 'esto quod es,' offering practice in the Latin imperative mood, has richer work to do. In teaching the patterns of language, it teaches a

29 On Ælfric's understanding of choice in the context of good and bad will see the Introduction, pp. 18–21.

30 Hanslik, *Benedicti Regula*, prol. 2; cap. 5; cap. 71.

31 Garmonsway, *Ælfric's Colloquy*, pp. 41–2, lines 240–3.

32 Ibid.

pattern of life. The *Colloquy*'s existential imperative 'Be what you are' is simultaneously a demand to assume monastic identity and a defence against the operation of a desire the *Colloquy* itself installs as the child first memorizes and then voices the words and life of another. This imperative takes on additional point and force by sharing the grammatical and syntactic pattern of a second, underlying imperative. 'Esto quod factus es' [Be what you were made] is at once a political and religious imperative taken from Isidore's *Synonyma*, a widely popular moral vocabulary builder and fundamental classroom text.[33] The Consiliarius's imperative takes not only its grammatical pattern from Isidore, but also, and more importantly, its applicability to the monastic context of the oblates' lives. These imperatives are linked conceptually by an understanding of the operation of identity that is also explicitly articulated in the *Colloquy*. The Consiliarius's advice leading up to our imperative is addressed to all who have a *cræft* (here, an occupation within the widest social understanding of the term), whether peasant, warrior, or religious.[34] He tells the pupils 'let each one go about his *cræft* eagerly, because whoever abandons his *cræft*, will be abandoned by his *cræft*' ['7 þis geþeaht ic sylle eallum wyrhtum, þæt anra gehwylc cræft his geornlice begange, forþam se þe cræft his forlæt, he byþ forlæten fram þam cræfte'].[35] The consequence of not practising one's *cræft* is being abandoned by it, being left incoherent and without substance. In the Consiliarius's message, the threat of abandonment by one's *cræft* is a fundamental threat to identity itself within the understanding that 'You are what you do.' These interlocking apprehensions of identity – how it is built, recognized, threatened, and maintained – understand monastic identity as something at once punctually conferred (in the act of oblation) and acquired (in the performance of monastic habitus and the labour of the

33 Isidore of Seville, *Synonyma*, PL 83.827–68 at 845b. See Claudia Di Sciacca, *Finding the Right Words: Isidore's 'Synonyma' in Anglo-Saxon England* (Toronto: University of Toronto Press, 2008). Gneuss, *Handlist*, 169, lists seven manuscripts of the *Synonyma* and one fragment surviving from Anglo-Saxon England. On the *Synonyma* as one of 'a small core of staple patristic texts,' see Lapidge, *The Anglo-Saxon Library* (Oxford: Oxford University Press, 2006), 127. 'Esto quod factus es' is found in its context in the *Synonyma*, book II in London, BL, Harley 110, fol. 37v, line 28. As will be discussed below, this manuscript also contains Prosper of Aquitaine's *Epigrammata*, a fundamental classroom text. The larger context of this portion of the *Synonyma* is translated into Old English in Vercelli Homily 22. D.G. Scragg, ed., *The Vercelli Homilies and Related Texts*, EETS o.s. 300 (Oxford: Oxford University Press, 1992), 368–78 at 374–5.

34 On the use of 'cræft' within religious life see *CH* II.34, p. 291, lines 125–6.

35 Garmonsway, *Ælfric's Colloquy*, p. 41, lines 237–40.

monastic schoolroom). Between the ritual conferral of identity and the continuous labour of naturalizing its content is the space imagined for the action of the obedient agent.

By its nature as a text to be memorized and then performed in interaction with others, the *Colloquy* is at once a schoolroom exercise in language learning and a means for building and installing identity in the oblates who perform it after committing it to memory. That such identity is critically and fundamentally acquired through language learning and its corollary practices of interpretation tells us much about the monastic community that Ælfric knew, shaped, and sought to perpetuate. 'Be what you are' (with its corollaries) commands obedience of its hearers and, simultaneously, an understanding of their identity at the very moment of installing it. The following section examines the way in which the identity of the English monastic community to which Ælfric refers was explicitly textual, the role of the classroom in forming that identity, and the ways agency was imagined to operate both with it and against it.

Colloquy, Classroom, Schooling

Ælfric's *Colloquy,* a Latin classroom text, survives in three versions: London, BL, Cotton Tiberius A. iii (C); Oxford, St John's College 154 (J); and Antwerp, Plantin-Moretus Museum M.16.2 (47) + London, BL, Add. 32246 (R_1+R_2).[36] The text in C is furnished with a full Old English gloss

36 Gneuss, *Handlist*, nos. 363, 686, 775; Ker, *Catalogue*, nos. 186, 362. Garmonsway, *Ælfric's Colloquy,* edits the text in the form most familiar to modern readers, using C (Tiberius A. iii) as his base text though reversing the order of text. His edition makes the Old English gloss the main text and uses the Latin text as its gloss. C is the only text with a continuous gloss. J is edited by W.H. Stevenson, *Early Scholastic Colloquies* (Oxford: Clarendon Press, 1929), 75–101, with interlinear glosses in Old English supplied from C. R_1+R_2 was edited for the first time by Joyce Hill, ed., 'Ælfric's *Colloquy*: The Antwerp/London Version,' in *Latin Learning and English Lore: Studies in Anglo-Saxon Literature for Michael Lapidge*, ed. Katherine O'Brien O'Keeffe and Andy Orchard (Toronto: University of Toronto Press, 2005), II: 331–48. For an analysis of the relationships among the versions see David W. Porter, 'Ælfric's *Colloquy* and Ælfric Bata,' *Neophilologus* 80 (1996): 639–60. Porter argues that the order of production was C, R, and J, that there were other versions, given the differences among the existing witnesses, and that Ælfric Bata made editorial changes to all three versions of the *Colloquy* including supplying the interlinear gloss to C (at 641, 651, 656). By contrast, Lendinara, 'The *Colloquy* of Ælfric and the *Colloquy* of Ælfric Bata,' 236, argues that Ælfric himself glossed his *Colloquy* and that Ælfric Bata used Ælfric's *Glossary* in expanding the *Colloquy* (239). Joyce Hill, 'Winchester Pedagogy and the *Colloquy* of Ælfric,' *Leeds Studies in English*, n.s., 29 (1998): 137–52, at 145–6, argues, in part based on the

(most familiar to modern readers as the 'main' text of the *Colloquy*), though Ælfric wrote the text in Latin, as a way of teaching the elements of spoken Latin to oblates. The text in J, with only sporadic glosses in Old English, shows augmentation for vocabulary by Ælfric Bata, a one-time pupil of Ælfric. The *Colloquy* formed part of Ælfric's pedagogical writings, probably following the *Grammar* and the *Glossary*, and all three projects date from between 992 and 1002, when Ælfric was at Cerne Abbas.[37] In them we see Ælfric's concern for the training of boys in the monastic *familia*, both to initiate the young into Latin textual culture and to reproduce the textual community of the Benedictine reformed monastery of late Anglo-Saxon England. The Latin preface to the *Grammar*, addressed to the little boys ('pueruli') for whom the work was conceived, takes, nonetheless, a defensive posture towards this pedagogical enterprise, no doubt because the intended audience of the Latin preface were men literate in Latin:

> noui namque multos me reprehensuros, quod talibus studiis meum ingenium occupare uoluissem, scilicet grammaticam artem ad anglicam linguam uertendo. sed ego deputo hanc lectionem inscientibus puerulis, non senibus, aptandam fore.[38]
>
> [I know that many will criticize me because I have wished to employ my talent with such works, that is, by translating the art of grammar into the

---

Latinity of the exordium, that the gloss is not by Ælfric. On Ælfric's use of 'Winchester' vocabulary as an element of his education at the Old Minster see Walter Hofstetter, 'Winchester and the Standardization of Old English Vocabulary,' *ASE* 17 (1988): 139–61 at 157 and 161. For a survey of Ælfric's educational project see Thomas N. Hall, 'Ælfric as Pedagogue,' in *A Companion to Ælfric*, ed. Hugh Magennis and Mary Swan, Brill's Companions to the Christian Tradition 18 (Leiden: Brill, 2009), 193–216.

37 On the dating see P.A.M. Clemoes, 'The Chronology of Ælfric's Works,' in *The Anglo-Saxons: Studies in Some Aspects of Their History and Culture Presented to Bruce Dickins*, ed. Peter Clemoes (London: Bowes and Bowes, 1959), 212–47 at 244. For the *Grammar* and *Glossary* see Julius Zupitza, ed., *Aelfrics Grammatik und Glossar: Text und Varianten*, 4th ed. with an introduction by Helmut Gneuss (Hildesheim: Weidmann, 2003). On the Glossary, Grammar, and Colloquy as a pedagogic 'set' see Joyce Hill, 'Learning Latin in Anglo-Saxon England: Traditions, Texts and Techniques,' in *Learning and Literacy in Medieval England and Abroad*, ed. Sarah Rees Jones, Utrecht Studies in Medieval Literacy 3 (Turnhout: Brepols, 2003), 7–29 at 28, and also her 'Ælfric's Grammatical Triad' in *Form and Content of Instruction in Anglo-Saxon England in the Light of Contemporary Manuscript Evidence*, ed. Patrizia Lendinara, Loredana Lazzari, and Maria Amalia D'Aronco (Turnhout: Brepols, 2007), 285–307.

38 Zupitza, *Aelfrics Grammatik und Glossar*, p. 1, lines 8–12. I have silently normalized 'j' to 'i' and surpressed diacritical marks throughout.

English language. But I consider such a text to be suitable for ignorant little boys, not seniors.]

Acknowledging that his revision and translation of *Excerptiones de Prisciano* was not an advanced work, Ælfric promotes the enterprise instead as a work of pedagogy, carefully positioned in the line of Æthelwold's own teaching practice.[39] By this we must understand not adherence to Æthelwold's preference for hermeneutic vocabulary, but rather Ælfric's acknowledgment of his own place in a particular textual community, the 'Winchester School' that produced the late Old English standard literary dialect.[40] The ethical commitment of a pedagogy that measures learning (and teaching) by lived behaviour, implicit in the description of Æthelwold as one 'qui multos ad bonum imbuit,' is more deliberately laid out in the Old English preface to the *Grammar*.[41] Here Latin grammar is described as 'seo cæg, ðe ðæra boca andgit unlicð'[42] [the key that unlocks the meaning of books], and Ælfric's personal commitment to conveying that *cæg* is framed in the language of the parable of the talents (Matt. 25:14–30), where the servant who did not increase what was entrusted to him by his master was judged 'lyðre' [wicked] and cast out. The fundamental principle that Ælfric advances in this preface is that it is incumbent on anyone

39 Ibid., lines 16–17: 'sicut didicimus in scola Aðelwoldi, uenerabilis praesulis, qui multos ad bonum imbuit' [as we learned in the school of Æthelwold, the venerable bishop, who inspired many to good].

40 On Æthelwold and hermeneutic style see Michael Lapidge, 'The Hermeneutic Style in Tenth-Century Anglo-Latin Literature,' in *ALL* II: 105–49 and 474–9 at 126; on the pedagogical relationship between Æthelwold and Ælfric see Michael Lapidge, 'Æthelwold as Scholar and Teacher,' in *ALL* II, 183–211 and 482 at 201–4; on Æthelwold and Standard Old English see Helmut Gneuss, 'The Origin of Standard Old English and Æthelwold's School at Winchester,' *ASE* 1 (1972): 63–83; and Walter Hofstetter, *Winchester und der spätaltenglische Sprachgebrauch, Untersuchungen zur geographischen und zeitlichen Verbreitung altenglischer Synonyme,* Texte und Untersuchungen zur Englischen Philologie 14 (Munich: Wilhelm Fink, 1987).

41 Both prefaces circulated with the *Grammar*. See Wilcox, *Ælfric's Prefaces*, 77–8. For a list of the manuscripts see Gneuss's introduction to Zupitza, *Aelfrics Grammatik und Glossar,* iv–xii. Melinda J. Menzer usefully points out the connection of grammar to Christian learning in 'Ælfric's *Grammar*: Solving the Problem of the English-Language Text,' *Neophilologus* 83.4 (1999): 637–52 at 641.

42 Zupitza, *Aelfrics Grammatik und Glossar*, p. 2, lines 16–17. Melinda J. Menzer's argument that Ælfric intended the *Grammar* to teach English and interpretation of vernacular texts is difficult to sustain. See her 'Ælfric's *Grammar*' above and her 'Ælfric's English *Grammar*,' *JEGP* 103.1 (2004): 106–24.

who has a good 'cræft' [here, skill or ability] to multiply it by teaching it to others.[43]

From this principle, Ælfric advances a spiritual economy of the monastic community: 'iungum mannum gedafenað, þæt hi leornion sumne wisdom and ðam ealdum gedafenað, þæt hi tæcon sum gerad heora iunglingum, forðan ðe ðurh lare byð se geleafa gehealden'[44] [It is fitting for young men that they learn some knowledge, and it is fitting for the old, that they teach some wisdom to their juniors, because belief is preserved through teaching]. In this model, the 'wisdom' achieved by the older members of the community must be passed to the young by teaching, and the young are obliged to receive it and preserve it by learning.[45] The content of the community's wisdom is belief.[46] The man who loves such wisdom is 'gesælig' ['happy' in the sense of 'blessed'], but the consequence for either young or

43 Ernst Robert Curtius, *European Literature and the Latin Middle Ages*, trans. Willard R. Trask (Princeton: Princeton University Press, 1953), 87, notes that this is a 'favorite topos' of the Latin Middle Ages. See also *Distichs of Cato*, IV.23, below, n. 44.

44 Zupitza, *Aelfrics Grammatik und Glossar*, p. 2, line 24–p. 3, line 2. The advice to learn from the learned and teach the unlearned may be found in the *Disticha Catonis* IV.23: 'Disce sed a doctis, indoctos ipse doceto: / propaganda etenim est rerum doctrina bonarum.' Marcus Boas, ed., *Disticha Catonis*, rev. H.J. Botschuyver (Amsterdam: North-Holland, 1952), p. 219. Boas notes (p. 220) that Alcuin changes the second line to 'Semper *amanda* quidem est rerum doctrina bonarum' (emphasis added). An Old English translation was made in 'Dicts' 58. On the *Disticha Catonis* see below, pp. 125–7. On the 'Dicts' see below, pp. 127–8.

45 In his homily on St Benedict (*CH* II.11, p. 92, lines 3–6), Ælfric changes the emphasis of Gregory's text in *Dialogi* II and fits Benedict more clearly into the contemporary ideology of monastic formation; on which see Mechthild Gretsch, *Ælfric and the Cult of Saints*, 146). The *Dialogi* makes it very clear that Benedict refuses the education that his parents set him to ('despectis … studiis' [de Vogüé, *Grégoire le Grand, Dialogues*, II, p. 126, lines 11–12]) and the text makes the summary judgment, 'recessit igitur scienter nescius et sapienter indoctus' (14–15) [And so he returned, wisely ignorant and prudently unlearned].

Ælfric's alterations here are carefully in line with the textual identity that underlies both his education projects (*Grammar, Glossary, Colloquy*) and his various writings on monastic saints. For an argument on the Reformers' self-understanding as teachers see Wilhelm G. Busse, '"Sua gað ða lareowas beforan ðæm folce, & ðæt folc æfter": The Self-Understanding of the Reformers as Teachers in Late Tenth-Century England,' in *Schriftlichkeit im frühen Mittelalter*, ed. Ursula Schaefer, ScriptOralia 53 (Tübingen: Gunter Narr Verlag, 1993), 58–106.

46 For a discussion of the application of grammar to study of the Bible in the Carolingian Renaissance see Vivien Law, 'The Study of Grammar,' in *Carolingian Culture: Emulation and Innovation*, ed. Rosamond McKitterick (Cambridge: Cambridge University Press, 1994), 88–110 at 99–103.

old of neglecting his duty to knowledge is moral decay, for the individual and the community:

> se ðe naðor nele ne leornian ne tæcan, gif he mæg, þonne acolað his andgyt fram ðære halgan lare, and he gewit swa lytlum and lytlum fram gode. hwanon sceolon cuman wise lareowas on godes folce, buton hi on iugoðe leornion? and hu mæg se geleafa beon forðgenge, gif seo lar and ða lareowas ateoriað?[47]

> [[as to] the one who wishes neither to learn nor teach, if he is able, then his understanding will grow cool from that holy learning, and little by little he will depart from God. Where will good teachers come from among God's people, unless they learn in their youth? And how can belief advance, if teaching and teachers lose heart?]

The Old English preface to the *Grammar* thus explains what Ælfric leaves unspoken in the Latin preface: that the ethical imperative of preparing the boys of the community to learn by teaching them the language of learning and the grammar of interpretation is of the highest value.[48] Such teaching is a moral activity within Ælfric's interpretation of Matt. 25:14–30, and by assimilating the boys of the monastery to its corporate life and belief, he takes his place as *lareow* in the line of Æthelwold and Dunstan.[49]

Of Ælfric's three teaching texts, the *Colloquy* is the most elementary, designed to initiate young boys in the beginnings of spoken Latin.[50] And as we have seen, such instruction and such learning were understood as fundamental to the continued life of the monastic community. Without it, the community of brothers in religion would cease to exist. Thus the learning of Latin was the foundation on which the textual life of the community

---

47 Zupitza, *Aelfrics Grammatik und Glossar*, p. 3, lines 3–9.

48 On the sophisticated application of 'grammar' to theological dispute in the ninth century see G.R. Evans, 'The Grammar of Predestination in the Ninth Century,' *Journal of Theological Studies*, n.s., 33 (1982): 134–45. Lynne Grundy argues that for Ælfric grammar is a 'theological issue': 'Ælfric's Grammatical Theology and Theological Grammar,' in *Essays on Anglo-Saxon and Related Themes in Memory of Lynne Grundy*, ed. Jane Roberts and Janet Nelson, King's College London Medieval Studies 17 (London: King's College London, Centre for Late Antique & Medieval Studies, 2000), 1–14 at 5.

49 On Ælfric as a 'master teacher' see David W. Porter, *Excerptiones de Prisciano: The Sources for Ælfric's Latin-Old English Grammar*, Anglo-Saxon Texts 4 (Cambridge: D.S. Brewer, 2002), 31.

50 David W. Porter, 'The Latin Syllabus in Anglo-Saxon Monastic Schools,' *Neophilologus* 78.3 (1994): 463–82 at 464.

depended, and as such, I argue, the learning of Latin in the first instance, and thereafter the learning and interpretation of other fundamental texts, constituted the indispensable building blocks of the textual identity of the members of the monastic community. Ælfric's *Colloquy* as a teaching tool is part of a long tradition of using a dialogue for Latin language learning.[51] By memorizing lines of dialogue on various topics, children learned lexicon and syntax.[52] Yet Ælfric's development of the form is quite distinct from what preceded it. As Patrizia Lendinara points out in her analysis of the *Colloquy*, '[its] important innovation ... lies in his giving prominence to the minor characters of the other dialogues, such as the shepherd and the cook, and allowing them to speak.'[53] In the imagined classroom of the *Colloquy*, children learn to speak Latin by memorizing, internalizing, and then voicing the lines of a range of characters. But in this process of transmitting and acquiring the *cæg* to the community's knowledge, something else is also produced. By its nature as a text to be memorized and then performed in interaction with others, the *Colloquy* is at once a schoolroom exercise in language learning and a means for building and installing identity in the oblates who perform it after committing it to memory. That such identity is critically and fundamentally acquired through language learning and its corollary practices of interpretation tells us much about the monastic community that Ælfric knew, shaped, and sought to perpetuate.

The idealized classroom of the *Colloquy*, complete with master, pupils, and a 'consiliarius' (*geþeahtend* in the Old English gloss), is imagined as a space of both acculturation and obedience. It opens with the pupils

51 On colloquies in pre-Conquest Britain see Scott Gwara, ed., *Latin Colloquies from Pre-Conquest Britain*, Toronto Medieval Latin Texts 22 (Toronto: Pontifical Institute of Mediaeval Studies, 1996), 10–14; see also Scott Gwara, 'The *Hermeneumata pseudodositheana*, Latin Oral Fluency, and the Social Function of the Cambro-Latin Dialogues Called *De raris fabulis*,' in *Latin Grammar and Rhetoric: From Classical Theory to Medieval Practice*, ed. Carol Dana Lanham (London: Continuum, 2002), 109–38, esp. 110–17. See also Pierre Riché, 'La vie quotidienne dans les écoles monastiques d'après les colloques scolaires,' in *Sous la règle de saint Benoît: structures monastiques et sociétés en France du Moyen Âge à l'époque moderne* [no editor given] (Geneva: Librairie Droz, 1982), 417–26 at 418.

52 Gwara, *Latin Colloquies*, points out that earlier Anglo-Saxon colloquies mostly confined themselves to grammatical topics, whereas the *Colloquia retractata* and Ælfric Bata's *Colloquia* are indebted to the *Hermeneumata pseudositheana* by focusing on the events of an ordinary day (14).

53 Lendinara, '*Colloquy* of Ælfric,' 222.

begging their master (*lareow*) to teach them to speak Latin and confessing their willingness to be beaten to ensure a good result. The interactions the *Colloquy* represents point us further to a structure of inculcation in which the dialogue performed, memorized, and thus internalized is an instrument of installing in the boys Latin, the language of power and of monastic identity, and, thereafter, the forms of interpretation – tropes of words and thought – leading to techniques of reading, and through a critical use of memory, the internalization of proper discourses and bodies of knowledge. Such forms of interpretation were tied primarily to interpretation of scripture and, in contradistinction to the practice of antiquity, were the province of grammarians.[54] Formally, they were the province of advanced study; practically, the pupils of the *Colloquy*, as we will see, learned apt scriptural citation as the entrée into community. The learning of Latin enables the boys to understand the liturgy they voice, to interpret the scripture they hear and read, to desire the right life (i.e., to be of good will), and to perpetuate the textual community to which they had been given. But the opening scene of instruction in which the boys are made to speak their desire to have their learning beaten into them, to have failure marked on their bodies that learning might be marked on their minds, opens up as well, perhaps perversely, a space of play in the *Colloquy* as the boys are made to voice characters far removed from their social ambit. While earlier colloquies confined themselves to matters grammatical or to the daily round of the monastic routine, each of the characters in the *Colloquy* opens an alternative world of identity: the enslaved ploughman with his hoarse young helper, the king's hunter who speaks the economics of exchange, the cowardly fisherman, the merchant anxious for profit, the salter eager for recognition – all of these require the boys who voice their dialogue to perform *their* words, assume *their* positions, and take on, for a time, another, imagined, life. The threat of this activity, whose express goal is to produce the boys as fully fledged members of the monastic community, is that it provides them the means – fantasy – to undo the very work that they are labouring to produce.[55]

The command itself, 'esto quod es,' addressed to the oblates in the implied classroom of the colloquy, imagines, of course, the opposite – the

54 See Gabriele Knappe, 'Classical Rhetoric in Anglo-Saxon England,' *ASE* 27 (1998): 5–29 at 17.

55 I cannot agree with Earl R. Anderson, 'Social Idealism in Ælfric's *Colloquy*,' *ASE* 3 (1974): 153–62 at 160, who regards the occupations as primarily monastic.

possibility of being something else. In the very moment of awakening that dangerous desire in its actors, the *Colloquy* explicitly defends against it. The relationship between fantasy and desire (and it is the desire itself that Ælfric warns against) is a constitutive one as fantasy structures and enables desire. Being a ploughman, being a hunter means, precisely, *not being* an oblate. The danger of fantasy as such does not lie in *being* a ploughman. Rather, the moment of voicing another's life (that is, acting the fantasy) structures the very desire that would undo the oblate's life. As he voices their words, the oblate's performing the hunter, say (or the salter or the blacksmith), opens for him a space of being other than what he is. Ælfric identifies the problem when the Consiliarius warns the boys that it is a shame and a sin to *want* to be other than what you are, to desire to be other. And the desire which fantasy structures in performing hunter or fowler or merchant is the desire to constitute one's self outside the monastic community. The desire to be other brings with it the illusion (from Ælfric's perspective) that such self-authoring is possible. The paradox, of course, is that the children of the dialogue (and the *pueri* who were set to memorize and perform it) are engaging exactly in self-authoring by their acquisition of the rudiments of the hieratic language of power, the *cæg* to the textual identity they are to assume. But as such self-authoring is imagined by the *Colloquy* to take place within the structures of their parents' commitment on their behalf, within the Benedictine community of the Rule, the dangers of desire and self-will are defended against by the primary virtue and habit of the Rule, obedience: 'be what you were made' speaks to the actions of the obedient agent.

The phrase 'be what you are' ('esto quod es'; 'beo þæt þu eart') returns us to the positivity of language learning in the *Colloquy* and its goal of making good monks. As an exercise, the *Colloquy* is one in a set of steps to educate and thus produce fully integrated members of the monastic community. 'Be what you are' shows the *Colloquy*'s relation to the institutional production of monastic identity and its dedication to the careful formation of boys as members of the monastic *familia*, as brothers not by blood but through shared textual identity.

Ælfric and the Foundations of Textual Identity

Though by Ælfric's time Latin learning had progressed remarkably since the dark days of Alfred's grim complaint in the Preface to the OE translation of the *Regula pastoralis*, Michael Lapidge has observed that even at the height of learning in the later tenth century, there was, at any given time, only a small number of centres of learning.[56] The pre-eminent centre of learning in late tenth-century England was Æthelwold's school at Winchester, of which Ælfric was an alumnus.[57] In his *uita* of his former master, Ælfric goes on to describe Æthelwold as a powerful teacher: 'dulce namque erat ei adolescentes et iuuenes semper docere, et libros Anglice eis soluere, et iocundis alloquiis ad meliora hortari; unde factum est ut perplures ex eius discipulis fierent abbates et episcopi in gente Anglorum'[58] [For it was sweet to him to teach the youth and young men and to translate books for them into English, and to urge them to better things with pleasant encouragements; whence it came about that very many of his students became abbots and bishops among the Anglo-Saxons]. In framing this portrait of Æthelwold, Ælfric presents as well an ideal of teaching.[59] Æthelwold shows his excellence in forming his young monks by translating texts that are beyond them (or likely using translation as a technique of exposition) and, equally important, using his teaching as a means of inspiring his students to 'meliora.' Just what those 'meliora' are – the learning of doctrine, embracing a more ascetic life – and how productive Æthelwold's teaching was are suggested by Ælfric's following claim that among the abbot bishop's former students are now English abbots and bishops. True learning (driven by true teaching) advances the students' moral life and produces leaders indispensable to the church and the kingdom. The model

56 Henry Sweet, ed., *King Alfred's West-Saxon Version of Gregory's Pastoral Care,* EETS o.s. 45, 50 (London, 1871–2; repr. with corrections by N.R. Ker, London: Oxford University Press, 1958), I, p. 3, line 13, to p. 5, line 18. Michael Lapidge, 'Schools, Learning and Literature in Tenth-Century England,' in his *ALL* II, 1–48 and 469 at 3. For a survey of education in Anglo-Saxon England see D.A. Bullough, 'The Educational Tradition in England from Alfred to Ælfric: Teaching *utriusque linguae*,' in his *Carolingian Renewal: Sources and Heritage* (Manchester: Manchester University Press, 1991), 297–334 (updated from its original version in *La Scuola nell'occidente latino dell'alto medioevo*, in *Settimane di studio del Centro italiano di studi sull'alto medioevo 19* [Spoleto, 1972], II: 453–94).

57 'Wintoniensis alumnus'; see 'Ælfric's *Vita S. Æthelwoldi*,' cap. 1, in Michael Lapidge and Michael Winterbottom, eds., *Wulfstan of Winchester: The Life of St Æthelwold* (Oxford: Clarendon Press, 1991), Appendix A, p. 71.

58 Lapidge and Winterbottom, 'Ælfric's *Vita S. Æthelwoldi*,' cap. 20 (p. 77). Compare Wulfstan's *uita* of St Æthelwold, in Lapidge and Winterbottom, *Wulfstan of Winchester, the Life of St Æthelwold*, cap. 31 (p. 48), where Wulfstan continues between 'soluere' and 'et iocundis' – 'et regulas grammaticae artis ac metricae rationis tradere' [and teach the rules of grammar and metrics].

59 In the Latin Preface to his *Grammar*, Ælfric indicates that his method follows what he learned in 'scola Aðelwoldi' (Zupitza, *Aelfrics Grammatik und Glossar*, p. 1, lines 16–17).

of teaching that Ælfric advances here connects learning with a religious life of service and rule, whose practical effect is the moral life in action, both within the monastic community and in the larger English church.[60]

His memory of Æthelwold's teaching contrasts starkly with the modest achievements of an early master that Ælfric recalls in his Preface to Genesis. There, concerned about two linked problems – the relationship between poor Latinity and an improper grasp of the techniques of scriptural interpretation – Ælfric remembers a priest 'se þe min magister wæs on þam timan, hæfde þa boc Genesis, 7 he cuðe be dæle Lyden understandan … ac he nyste, ne ic þa git, hu micel todal ys betweohx þære ealdan æ 7 þære niwan'[61] [who was, at that time, my teacher; he had the book of Genesis, and he could understand a little Latin … but he did not know, nor did I yet, how great a difference there is between the Old Law and the New]. In this passage, and in the Preface to Genesis as a whole, Ælfric is haunted by the difficulties of correct scriptural interpretation, the grave consequences to the faithful of not distinguishing between literal and spiritual meanings, and the necessity of interpreters with adequate learning in Latin to mediate between the text and the faithful who required instruction in its elements. He is especially troubled by clergy whose ignorant interpretations may mislead the people who depend on them for knowledge: 'ungelæredan preostas, gif hi hwæt litles understandað of þam Lydenbocum, þonne þingð him sona þæt hi magon mære lareowas beon'[62] [unlearned priests, if they understand a little bit of Latin books, then it seems to them immediately that they may be famous teachers]. Ælfric's concern in the Preface to Genesis is not simply that it is unwise to increase the access of so difficult a book by translating it into English, but also that those to whom

60 On grammar and the road to salvation in the monastery see Coleman, *Ancient and Medieval Memories*, 144–5.

61 S.J. Crawford, ed., *The Old English Version of the Heptateuch, Ælfric's Treatise on the Old and New Testament and His Preface to Genesis*, EETS o.s. 160 (London: Oxford University Press, 1922), p. 76, lines 12–17. There is some question about the interpretation of 'be dæle,' which I have rendered 'a little.' On this point see Richard Marsden, *The Cambridge Old English Reader* (Cambridge: Cambridge University Press, 2004), 124, n. 13. By contrast, Mark Griffith, 'How Much Latin Did Ælfric's *Magister* Know?' *Notes and Queries*, n.s., 46.2 (1999): 176–81 at 180, argues that 'be dæle' does not have its literal meaning here (as 'in part, to some extent') and should be translated as an understatement. Jones, 'Ælfric and the Limits of "Benedictine Reform,"' 104–5, explores the intriguing possibility that this early master was outside the ambit of the Benedictine Reform and thus that Ælfric only came to the monastic life at some later point.

62 Crawford, *Preface to Genesis*, p. 77, lines 23–5.

the interpretation of such a text is entrusted are often ill-trained for such a responsibility.[63] As we have seen, in the *Grammar* Ælfric makes learning the task of young men and teaching the task of the old. Through this relation, he claims, belief is retained. But without it, as knowledge is lost, right conduct is lost with it. Such an understanding makes moral conduct the product of right teaching and right learning, as it echoes Alfred's bitter complaint in his Preface to the translation of the *Regula pastoralis*:

> [I]s nu for ði godes þeowum and mynstermannum georne to warnigenne, þæt seo halige lar on urum dagum ne acolige oððe ateorige, swaswa it wæs gedon on Angelcynne nu for anum feawum gearum, swa þæt nan englisc preost ne cuðe dihtan oððe asmeagean anne pistol on leden, oðþæt Dunstan arcebisceop and Aðelwold bisceop eft þa lare on munuclifum arærdon.[64]
>
> [Therefore are God's monks and servants to be warned zealously that holy learning in our day not cool and vanish, just as had happened in England for a number of years, when no English priest knew how to compose or understand a letter in Latin, until Archbishop Dunstan and Bishop Æthelwold revived learning in monastic life.]

The twin concern for the responsibility of teaching and appreciation of his position in the direct line of education from Dunstan to Æthelwold likely made Ælfric's educational program a self-conscious one, for the personal and the institutional components of teaching lie in the *making* of the monastic pupil.[65]

The *Colloquy* would not have been Ælfric's students' first step in learning Latin.[66] Boys entrusted to monasteries began their education in Latin

63 Ælfric presents an ideal. For an assessment of the situation in the countryside, with priests 'devolved' from the monasteries and their humbler village counterparts, see Blair, *The Church in Anglo-Saxon Society*, 491–3.

64 Zupitza, *Aelfrics Grammatik und Glossar*, p. 3, lines 9–16.

65 On this point, Nicholas Brooks, 'The Anglo-Saxon Cathedral Community, 597–1070,' in *A History of Canterbury Cathedral*, ed. Patrick Collinson, Nigel Ramsay, and Margaret Sparks (Oxford: Oxford University Press, 1995), 1–37 at 28, observes of the contents of the library of Christ Church, Canterbury, between ca 990 and 1066 (some sixty-two manuscript books): 'It was a library intended to produce devout and humble Benedictine monks, who would know the psalms and much of the New Testament by heart and who would appreciate the skills of Latin hexameters and hymns. It does not seem to have encouraged intellectual curiosity or, indeed, new writing.'

66 Vivien Law, *Grammar and Grammarians in the Early Middle Ages* (London: Longman, 1997), 203, indicates that children ready to learn Latin as a language would learn the

with the recitation of the Psalms as part of the performance of the Divine Office.[67] In the daily round of liturgical performance, the children would begin to learn verses and psalms by heart, and it is clear that memorial performance was expected.[68] Though he entered the monastery as a young man, according to his hagiographer, Felix, Guthlac's first two years at Repton were dedicated first to learning his letters, then to learning the Psalms, and then to learning the texts of liturgical performance. What he learned he brought with him to Crowland.[69] From his Irish education, the young Wilfrid (later bishop of York, 669–78) had learned the *Gallicanum* version of the Psalter by heart, as well as other books, and when he was in Canterbury in the 650s he had to learn the Psalter anew 'memoraliter,' this time in the *Romanum* version.[70] The point of Stephen of Ripon's anecdote was not the memorization of the Psalms – that was virtually a given – but that Wilfrid had learned the version *more Romanorum* as well. Such feats of memorial learning are, to be sure, common features in *uitae* of English saints; their frequent appearance strongly suggests that such ability and performance were both recognized as desirable and accepted as accurate by contemporary readers and listeners. Byrhtferth's *uita* of St Oswald records that the saint, before returning from Fleury to England, learns by heart the Office as it was practised there: 'Coepit

forms of the language from the *Grammar*, and then they would work on vocabulary from the *Glossary* and *Colloquy*.

67 Mechthild Gretsch, *The Intellectual Foundations of the English Benedictine Reform* (Cambridge: Cambridge University Press, 1999), 16–17; Pierre Riché, 'L'étude du vocabulaire latin dans les écoles Anglo-Saxonnes au début du Xe siècle,' in *La lexicographie du latin médiéval et ses rapports avec les recherches actuelles sur la civilisation du moyen-âge* (Paris: Centre National de la Recherche Scientifique, 1981), 115–24 at 115. George Hardin Brown, 'The Dynamics of Literacy in Anglo-Saxon England,' in *Textual and Material Culture in Anglo-Saxon England*, ed. Donald Scragg (Cambridge: D.S. Brewer, 2003), 183–212 at 194–5. See also Pierre Riché, *Éducation et culture dans l'Occident barbare VIe–VIIIe siècle*, 4th ed. (Paris: Éditions du Seuil, 1995), 374–5 (on learning the Psalter by memory).

68 Lendinara, 'The *Colloquy* of Ælfric,' 219–20: the children learned the alphabet, simple prayers and chants, then the Psalter: '[U]p to this stage in their instruction it was still possible for them to remain ignorant of Latin and to learn all the texts by heart' (220).

69 Bertram Colgrave, ed. and trans., *Felix's Life of Saint Guthlac* (Cambridge: Cambridge University Press, 1956), cap. 22–3, pp. 84–6.

70 Gretsch, *Intellectual Foundations*, 24. Bertram Colgrave, ed., *The Life of Bishop Wilfrid by Eddius Stephanus* (1927; Cambridge: Cambridge University Press, 1985), cap. 2, p. 6; cap. 3, p. 8.

more sancte monastice legis memoriter agnoscere et ecclesiastica digniter officia retinere, desiderans (Domino clementi annuente) in patria docere suis que extra proprium solum didicit ab extraneis'[71] [He undertook to learn by memory the custom of holy monastic law [at Fleury], and to remember worthily the church offices, desiring, with the Lord kindly helping, to teach his own (followers) in his native country, what he learned abroad from foreigners]. Similarly, his associate Germanus remains longer in Fleury to learn the Fleury customs *memoriter*.[72] This is not to say, however, that memorial learning of the Psalter indicated oral fluency in Latin.[73]

Memorial learning in the medieval classroom was a given, though fine-grained detail on particular techniques of teaching have been lost to us. Pierre Riché has pieced together details from England and the Continent, presenting a picture of boys admitted to the monastery for study around the age of seven.[74] In the monastic classroom, pupils would sit on stools around the master's chair for lessons primarily oral and memorial; only rarely did a pupil copy out the master's lecture and grammar lessons. Copying, when it was done, would be done on wax tablets, since the expense of parchment reserved that medium for experienced writers.[75] Whatever lesson the student had been set the master would examine on the following day, and in the case of imperfect learning, the teacher would demand to know why he had not been given back what the pupil had

71 Michael Lapidge, ed. and trans., *Byrhtferth of Ramsey, The Lives of St Oswald and St Edgwine* (Oxford: Clarendon Press, 2009), iii.2, p. 54.

72 Ibid., iii.7, p. 66. On Germanus and his later career see Michael Lapidge, 'Abbot Germanus, Winchcombe, Ramsey and the Cambridge Psalter,' in *ALL* II, 387–417 and 490 at 405–14.

73 Law, *Grammar and Grammarians*, 189–90, observes that even St Boniface's spoken Latin was 'at best shaky,' and the oral fluency of contemporary (i.e., eighth-century) literate clergy is uncertain. Roger Wright, 'Foreigners' Latin and Romance: Boniface and Pope Gregory II,' in his *A Sociophilological Study of Late Latin*, Utrecht Studies in Medieval Literacy 10 (Turnhout: Brepols, 2002), 95–109, at 102, ascribes the difficulty to Boniface's speaking a Latin derived from 'traditional written forms' while Gregory spoke a 'natural language.'

74 The standard account of early medieval education is by Pierre Riché, *Éducation et culture*. For the teaching of reading in tenth-century St Gall, see Anna A. Grotans, *Reading in Medieval St Gall* (Cambridge: Cambridge University Press, 2006).

75 See Michelle P. Brown, 'The Role of the Wax Tablet in Medieval Literacy: A Reconsideration in Light of a Recent Find from York,' *British Library Journal* 20 (1994): 1–16. See Riché, *Éducation et culture*, 371–2, and Michael Lapidge, 'The Study of Latin Texts in Late Anglo-Saxon England,' *ALL* I, 455–98 and 516 at 458.

received (*acceptum*) the day before.[76] Such memory work is the subject of advice a master in Ælfric Bata's colloquies gives his pupils: 'Rogo uos, pueri, et iubeo, ut duriter et instanter legatis quicquid heri didicistis a magistris uestris, et id bene firmate, ut possitis cras quantotius reddere et coria uestra sic reseruare sana'[77] ['I beseech and command you, boys, read with concentration and vigor what you learned from your teachers yesterday. Memorize it well so tomorrow you can recite it as fast as possible and that way keep your hides in one piece'].[78] The goal here clearly is to commit the set text to memory, to 'firmare,' that is, shore up the *acceptum* of the day before. The further connection of 'legere' and 'firmare' elsewhere in this colloquy underlines this central fact of medieval education – that reading and memorization were taught as a single activity.[79] This practice is clear from pedagogical techniques continued from antiquity: set texts were taught to children twice, first to learn the text by memory at the level of syllable, and then separately to learn its significance.[80] Ælfric Bata has one of his pupils explain the utility of such memorization: 'ut quando senes eritis, tunc memoriter in cunctis libris latinis legere possitis et aliquid intellegere in illis' ['so that when you're old you'll be able to read from memory in all Latin books and understand something in them'].[81] It is unlikely that the boy is suggesting in this statement that his fellow will have learned all Latin books by the time he is a *senex*. Rather, the combination 'memoriter ... legere' suggests that the books themselves were understood as prompts to what was already learned and retained in memory.[82]

76 See Pierre Riché, *Écoles et enseignement dans le Haut Moyen Âge* (Paris: Picard, 1989; repr. with additional bibliography of *Les écoles et l'enseignement dans l'Occident chrétien*, Paris, 1979), 218–36, esp. 218–23.

77 Scott Gwara, ed. *Latin Colloquies*, Colloquy 3, p. 40, lines 1–4.

78 Scott Gwara ed. and David W. Porter, trans., *Anglo-Saxon Conversations: The Colloquies of Ælfric Bata* (Woodbridge: The Boydell Press, 1997), 83.

79 Gwara, *Latin Colloquies*, Colloquy 3, p. 40, lines 11–12. On the integration of reading and memorizing see Mary J. Carruthers, *The Book of Memory: A Study of Memory in Medieval Culture*, 2nd ed. (Cambridge: Cambridge University Press, 2008), 129.

80 Mary Carruthers, 'Reading with Attitude: Remembering the Book,' in *The Book and the Body*, ed. Dolores W. Frese and Katherine O'Brien O'Keeffe (Notre Dame, IN: University of Notre Dame Press, 1997), 1–33 at 14–15. Porter, 'The Latin Syllabus in Anglo-Saxon Monastic Schools,' 479, infers from Ælfric Bata's Colloquies that the children had practice sessions with cooperative study, perhaps supervised by an 'apprentice teacher.'

81 Gwara, *Latin Colloquies*, Colloquy 4, lines 4–6; Gwara and Porter, *Anglo-Saxon Conversations*, 87.

82 On the book as a support for memory see Carruthers, *The Book of Memory*, 199.

Learning *memoriter* meant that what was learnt was expected to stay with the learner for a lifetime.[83] Memory, the faculty that made such learning possible, was often conceptualized as a splendid container, both guardian of knowledge and its treasure house.[84] Committed to memory were not simply the words of a book but a comprehension of its text, for to learn a text *memoriter* was not to learn a text by rote, but to be formed by the text in terms of understanding and will. Both remembering and committing to memory were functions of the will. So closely connected are these three functions of the soul – *gemynd, andgyt, wylla* (*memoria, intelligentia, uoluntas*) – understood to be that Ælfric (following Alcuin, himself drawing on Augustine) uses their interconnection to explain the mystery of the Trinity, three persons in one undivided God:

> And þas ðreo þing habbað annysse him betwynan. Ic undergyte . þæt ic wylle undergytan and gemunan . and ic wylle þæt ic undergyte and gemune . þær þær þæt gemynd bið . þær bið þæt andgyt and se wylla.[85]
>
> [And these three things have a unity among themselves. I understand what I will to understand and remember, and I will what I understand and remember. Where memory is, there are understanding and will.]

Elsewhere, he explains their interaction in terms of linked functions: that memory ('gemynd') enables the mind to think ('geþencð') what it has seen, heard, or learned; understanding ('andgit') permits comprehension of what it has seen or heard; and will produces thoughts, words, and deeds, whether good or bad.[86] Without memory, there would be nothing for understanding to comprehend; without will there would be nothing to remember or understand. Ælfric's apprehension of the critical connection of will to the operation of both memory and understanding underpins the

---

83 In *Wulfstan's Canons of Edgar*, ed. Roger Fowler, EETS o.s. 266 (London: Oxford University Press, 1972), cap. 32, pp. 8, 9, a priest was instructed to say Mass with the book before him 'þi læs þe him misse' [lest he forget].

84 On late antique and early medieval metaphors for memory as a repository see Gillian R. Evans, 'Two Aspects of *Memoria* in Eleventh and Twelfth Century Writings,' *Classica et Mediaevalia* (Copenhagen) 32 (1971–80): 263–78 at 270–1.

85 *LS*, I.1, p. 18, lines 119–22. Ælfric's use of this analogy in *Lives of Saints* repeats his earlier usage in the homily 'Feria IIII De Fide Catholica,' *CH* I.20, p. 342, lines 195–212, both of which translate Ælfric's earlier translation and adaptation of Alcuin's *De ratione animae* (here, PL 101.641–2). See also *CH* III, 164–5.

86 'Feria IIII De Fide Catholica,' *CH* I.20, p. 342, lines 195–212.

moral function of learning. Will, itself either good or bad, is responsible for the moral content of an individual's thoughts and actions, and so the exercise of memory in the storing of formative texts both supplies thought to understanding and assists in the formation of a right will. The location of these three functions in the soul (a modification that Ælfric makes to Alcuin's treatment)[87] makes clear, as well, the fundamental moral orientation of learning both for the individual and for the community.

Beyond the training of an individual memory, memorial learning of a set of commonly received texts supported and perpetuated a conservative community of intellectual exchange, where citation of scripture or the writings of the fathers affirmed membership in the community and ensured its continuance. So fundamental was this modality that Carruthers suggests that 'instead of the word "self" or even "individual," we might better speak of a "subject-who-remembers," and in remembering also feels and thinks and judges.'[88]

To accomplish this end, the permanent impression of particular texts on a child's mind, the rod was not far from the monastic classroom, as Ælfric Bata's *Colloquies* richly illustrate. While the extravagances of these *Colloquies* in vocabulary and behaviour urge caution in reading his dialogues as social record (for example, what customary would allow a boy to accompany a senior monk to the toilet!),[89] nonetheless, the sheer number of references to beating the boys suggests, at least, that such discipline was a daily expectation. One boy complains to his fellow that the other boy's

87 See Malcolm R. Godden, 'Anglo-Saxons on the Mind,' in *Learning and Literature in Anglo-Saxon England: Studies Presented to Peter Clemoes on the Occasion of His Sixty-Fifth Birthday*, ed. Michael Lapidge and Helmut Gneuss (Cambridge: Cambridge University Press, 1985), 271–98 at 278. (On the abridgement of *De ratione animae* see his p. 298.)

88 Carruthers, *Book of Memory*, 226. Carruthers also cites Gregory the Great to illustrate the notion of permanent transformation in what is read: 'We ought to transform what we read within our very selves, so that when our mind is stirred by what it hears, our life may concur by practicing what has been heard' (205) (citing, at p. 424, n. 32, *Moralia in Job*, 1.33 [PL 75.542C]).

89 Gwara, *Latin Colloquies*, Colloquy 9, pp. 49–50. While Gwara and Porter, *Anglo-Saxon Conversations*, note the excesses in Ælfric Bata's colloquies and their distance from the ideals of Benedictine monasticism, they consider him 'a valuable historical witness' (15). However, whatever information for social history Ælfric Bata's colloquies may provide must be carefully teased from what can only be regarded as burlesques of contemporary practice. See now Christopher A. Jones, 'The Irregular Life in Ælfric Bata's *Colloquies*,' *Leeds Studies in English*, n.s., 37 (2006): 241–60, for the contemporary monastic context of Ælfric Bata's *Colloquies*.

stupidity earned his classmates a corporate beating, 'pene omni die.'[90] In Colloquy 24, the boys nervously await the appearance of their master with a whip in one hand and rods in the other; in Colloquy 6, a boy manages to wheedle his way out of a whipping; but Colloquy 28 stages a sadistic scene of two boys whipping a third at the detailed direction of the master.[91] Beatings were a fact of life for the recalcitrant schoolboy Augustine. Despite his memorable account of his childhood distaste for the classroom, in adulthood, at least, Augustine seems to have thought some of his beatings were deserved.[92] Not so for Guibert of Nogent, who protests that his ignorant first tutor regularly beat the boy savagely for his own inability to understand his pupil's *acceptum*: 'dum ipse me cogeret discere, quae docere nequiverat'[93] [while he forced me to learn what he didn't know how to teach]. The docile children of Ælfric's idealized classroom in the *Colloquy* accept the necessity of being beaten, claiming to prefer to be whipped for the sake of learning ('flagellari pro doctrina quam nescire') rather than not to learn. Although they speak of the master beating them only if *they* force him ('nisi cogaris a nobis'), nonetheless, the wider understanding of whipping, caning, and other forms of corporal punishment indicates that learning, and particularly memorial learning, was a bodily process believed to require pain for its accomplishment.[94] Successful learning equipped the boy

---

90 Gwara, *Latin Colloquies*, Colloquy 3, p. 41, line 28.

91 Gwara and Porter, *Anglo-Saxon Conversations*, 132, 92, 166–70.

92 Lucas Verheijen, ed., *Sancti Augustini Confessionum Libri XIII*, CCSL 27 (Turnhout: Brepols, 1981), I.ix.6–7, p. 8: 'Et tamen, si segnis in discendo essem, uapulabam' [still, if I was dilatory in learning, I was flogged].

93 Guibert de Nogent, *Autobiographie*, ed. and trans. Edmond-René Labande (Paris: Belles Lettres, 1981), 32. For a translation see Paul J. Archambault, *A Monk's Confession: The Memoirs of Guibert of Nogent* (University Park: The Pennsylvania State University Press, 1996).

94 Garmonsway, *Colloquy*, p. 18, line 8, to p. 19, line 10. Towards the end of the *Colloquy* the Consiliarius inquires whether the boys had been beaten that day and gets a rather sassy reply (p. 45, lines 279–83). Law, *Grammar and Grammarians*, 209, in another context cites Ælfric's illustration of the accusative plural of 'puer': 'hos pueros flagello; ðas cild ic swinge … I beat these children,' as an example of the monastic context of instruction. In his *Grammar* (Zupitza, *Aelfrics Grammatik und Glossar*, 125), Ælfric illustrates the imperative voice similarly: '*flagella istum puerum* beswing ðis cild; *flagelletur* sy he beswungen' [beat this child; let him be beaten]. In the *Miracula S. Dunstani*, Osbern records how the oblates of Christ Church were spared a scheduled whipping on the day following a miracle at Dunstan's shrine (William Stubbs, ed., *Memorials of St Dunstan*, RS 63 (London, 1874), cap. 11, pp. 137–8; in cap. 15 (pp. 140–2) the boys escape a whipping through the intervention of Dunstan. *RSB*, cap. 30, explains the appropriateness of beatings for boys and adolescents; cap. 45.3 specifies beating for a child who makes an

with texts, a shared body of traditional interpretation, a set of master tropes for processing new information and communicating it to others, and an ethics of living. In short, it incorporated him into the monastic community.

The moral content of such education is apparent when the Consiliarius asks the children of the *Colloquy* what they want from their studies. One replies for all that they wish to be wise ['Uolumus esse sapientes'].[95] To challenge them on their practical understanding of the noun from which the adjective 'sapiens' derives, and combining both lexical and moral instruction, he queries what knowledge they seek (as 'sapientia' includes intelligence, wisdom, as well as discrete bodies of knowledge). Not surprisingly, the form of this challenge focuses on the goal of the *Colloquy*, the acquisition of Latin itself.[96] The Consiliarius suggests that the pupils' desire is the morally corrupt goal of acquiring a rhetorical skill to make the worse thing seem the better: 'Uultis esse uersipelles aut milleformes in mendaciis, astuti in loquelis, astuti, uersuti, bene loquentes et male cogitantes, dulcibus uerbis dediti, dolum intus alentes, sicut sepulchrum depicto mausoleo, intus plenum fetore?'[97] [Do you want to be sly or shifty in lies, subtle in conversations, crafty, deceitful, speaking fairly and thinking wickedly, given to sweet words, filled with guile within, as a painted sepulchre, inside full of stench?]. With his tendentious version of 'sapientes' (and its trailing echo of Matt. 23:27) the Consiliarius probes to see that the boys are *bonae uoluntatis* [of good will], for a good moral disposition will ensure their good (=moral) behaviour.[98] There is no such thing as morally neutral learning: it must be used for good or for bad. Learning, as

error reading in the oratory. See Hanslik, *Benedicti Regula*, pp. 94 and 123. On the role of pain in memory work see Carruthers, 'Reading with Attitude.'

95 Garmonsway, *Colloquy*, p. 43, line 253. The Old English translation of *De consolatione Philosophiae* explicitly connects *cræft* and *wisdom* in a lengthy exposition. See Malcolm Godden and Susan Irvine, eds., *The Old English Boethius: An Edition of the Old English Versions of Boethius's 'De Consolatione Philosophiae,'* 2 vols. (Oxford: Oxford University Press, 2009), B, cap. 17 (I: 277–8, lines 20–5) and C, prose 9 (I: 422, lines 21–4). For the commentary tradition on this connection see II: 318–19.

96 Helmut Gneuss, 'The Study of Language in Anglo-Saxon England,' in *Textual and Material Culture in Anglo-Saxon England: Thomas Northcote Toller and the Toller Memorial Lectures*, ed. Donald Scragg (Cambridge: D.S. Brewer, 2003), 75–105 at 86, points out that Ælfric was clearly aware of the tensions between the language of scripture and the strictures of the classical grammarians but 'was able to unite reverence for the work of God with the patent necessity of Latin instruction.'

97 Garmonsway, *Colloquy*, p. 43, lines 254–8.

98 See John M. Rist, 'Augustine on Free Will and Predestination,' *Journal of Theological Studies*, n.s., 20 (1969): 420–47 at 421–2.

we have seen, implies praxis, and the learning of the monastic classroom was simultaneously an education in the moral life and formation in the life of the community. The child makes a morally correct reply: 'Nolumus sic esse sapientes, quia non est sapiens, qui simulatione semet ipsum decipit ... Uolumus esse simplices sine hipochrisi, et sapientes ut declinemus a malo et faciamus bona'[99] [We don't want to be wise that way, because the one who deceives himself by delusion is not wise ... We wish to be sincere without hypocrisy and wise so that we may avoid evil and do good]. But beyond the simple moral, his answer's echo of Matt. 23:29, with its connection of 'hypocritae' with 'sepulchra,' identifies him through the scriptural coding of his reply. It shows that he has not merely memorized the Gospel verse and its sequelae; his pertinent citation works doubly – its iteration both marks him as a member of the community and reinforces his membership in it.

After the child pleads that the Consiliarius return to simpler issues, more suited to the children's age and knowledge, the *Colloquy* makes a turn from the voicing of characters to a more traditional discussion of the order of the monastic day – the round of prayer, liturgical ritual, and learning that shape the lives of the boys. But the preceding catechesis on 'sapientes' tells us much about the centrality of language learning to the shaping of the oblates, and the larger issues of the relation of language learning to the moral formation of the children as oblates and later monks of a reformed Benedictine community.[100] Learning to speak is empty without a morally formed praxis of everyday life. The praxis of that life, lived bodily in the regular cycles of eating, sleeping, working, and praying, made and maintained the community and understood and defined itself through texts.

Learning to Live

The two elements driving the narrative of identity and agency that the *Colloquy* addresses – 'be what you are' and 'you are what you do' – are lessons carefully taught and reinforced in the elementary classroom texts that oblates were expected to learn. After the basics of conversational Latin, monastic pupils' study of Latin grammar continued with the

---

99 Garmonsway, *Colloquy*, p. 43, lines 259–63.

100 Hill, 'Winchester Pedagogy and the *Colloquy* of Ælfric,' 143, observes that Ælfric pays as much attention in the *Colloquy* to the boys' training in the regular life as he does to matters of grammar and lexis.

Disticha Catonis and Prosper's *Epigrammata.*[101] Quite apart from proverbial wisdom so admired in the early Middle Ages, these texts provided their learners, along with training in vocabulary and syntax, rhetorically structured concepts fundamental to developing the textual identity of the oblates tasked with learning them. Assimilating these texts in a foundational process of memorization equipped the boys with life scripts, ready packets of wisdom, and conventional tropes of interpretation. The memorization, parsing, and explication of such texts comprised the *cæg* to the understanding of books that Ælfric considered the product of grammatical study. In this way, the *cæg* that the boys received in the learning of Latin grammar combined in memory both content and technique: it furnished them with common understandings and equipped them with the shibboleths of conventual life (as, for example, the pupil's scripturally coded reply in *Colloquy,* line 262). In short the learning of the monastic classroom was designed to initiate boys into the community's vision of the world and incorporate them in that vision.

'Esto quod es' and its corollaries call the oblated children in the monastic classroom to the willed labour of becoming in life what they had been made by their gift. That the labour of the classroom is the labour of

101 Lapidge, 'The Study of Latin Texts,' in *ALL* I, 459, lists five works 'which formed part of what may be called the Anglo-Saxon curriculum.' In addition to the two basic works, the *Disticha Catonis* and the *Epigrammata*, he lists Juvencus's *Euangelia*, Caelius Sedulius's *Carmen paschale*, and Arator's *De actibus Apostolorum*, noting that further work remains to be done on the Anglo-Saxon curriculum. For an overview of the Anglo-Saxon schools and the limitations of our knowledge see now Patrizia Lendinara, 'Instructional Manuscripts in England: The Tenth- and Eleventh-Century Codices and the Early Norman Ones,' in *Form and Content of Instruction in Anglo-Saxon England*, 59–113 at 71–83, and also her 'The World of Anglo-Saxon Learning,' in *The Cambridge Companion to Old English Literature*, ed. Malcolm Godden and Michael Lapidge (Cambridge: Cambridge University Press, 1991), 264–81 at 271–2. On pedagogical practice in language instruction see Porter, 'The Latin Syllabus in Anglo-Saxon Monastic Schools.' Gneuss, *Handlist*, lists five surviving manuscripts of the *Disticha Catonis*: Cambridge, University Library Gg. 5. 35 (s. xi med.) (no. 12); Cambridge, Trinity College O. 2. 31 (s. x/xi) (no. 190); London, BL, Cotton Vespasian D. vi, fols. 2–77 (s. x med. [or x^2]) (no. 389); Oxford, Bodleian Library, Rawlinson G. 57 (s. xi ex. or xi/xii) (no. 664); there is an Old English translation in Cambridge, Trinity College R. 9. 17 (xi/xii) (no. 182). Four manuscripts of Prosper's *Epigrammata* and fragments of a fifth survive from Anglo-Saxon England: Gneuss, *Handlist*, lists Cambridge, University Library Gg. 5. 35 (s. xi med.) (no. 12); Cambridge, Corpus Christi College 448 (s. x^1 or x med.) (no. 114); Cambridge, Trinity College, O. 2. 31 (1135) (s. x/xi) (no. 190); London, BL, Harley 110 (s. x ex.) (no. 415); and the fragmentary London, BL, Cotton Tiberius A. vii, fols. 165–66 (s. xi^1) (no. 365).

becoming emerges clearly from the repeated commonplaces in their beginners' texts. In line with the *Colloquy*'s connection of work (as *cræft*) and identity, both the *Disticha Catonis* and Prosper's *Epigrammata* understand the linked activities of learning and interpretation as an indispensable part of an ethics of identity. If the first asserts that practising what you learn is a good in itself, the second insists that it is indispensable to salvation. As rote memory of texts has no merit without action on the principles learned in their elementary texts, the learning of texts is also the development of habitus.

As an elementary text, the *Disticha Catonis,* with its simple units of proverbial wisdom, fits tidily into the understanding of learning and doing in the *Colloquy.*[102] While a number of distichs treat the importance of education and the necessity of doing what one learns, Distichs IV.21 makes the same point as the Consiliarius in warning the boys to practise what they learn:[103]

> Exerce studium, quamvis perceperis artem:
> Ut cura ingenium, sic et manus adiuvat usum.[104]
>
> [Practise your lesson, even though you've learned your craft:
> As attention furthers talent so labour furthers skill.]

---

102 Boas, *Disticha Catonis*. There is an English translation by Wayland Johnson Chase, *The Distichs of Cato: A Famous Medieval Textbook*, University of Wisconsin Studies in the Social Sciences and History 7 (Madison: n.p., 1922), 1–43. On the manuscripts, glossing, and use of the *Disticha Catonis* in late Anglo-Saxon England see Filippa Alcamesi, 'Remigius's Commentary to the *Disticha Catonis* in Anglo-Saxon Manuscripts,' in *Form and Content of Instruction in Anglo-Saxon England*, 143–85; Richard Hazelton, 'The Christianization of "Cato": The *Disticha Catonis* in the Light of Late Mediaeval Commentaries,' *Mediaeval Studies* 19 (1957): 157–73 at 163–4, argues that this early school text was made acceptable to Christian orthodoxy by reading its 'wisdom' in terms of Ecclesiastes and the sapiential books of the Bible. For citations see Michael Lapidge, *The Anglo-Saxon Library*, 124, 190, 274.

103 Garmonsway, *Colloquy*, p. 41, lines 237–40: 'Et hoc consilium do omnibus operariis, ut unusquisque artem suam diligenter exerceat, quia qui artem suam dimiserit, ipse dimittatur ab arte' [And I give this advice to all workers, that each one should practise his craft diligently, because the man who abandons his craft will be abandoned by his craft]. For the *Disticha Catonis* on the importance of learning see Boas, *Disticha Catonis*, IV.19, 21, 23, 27, 29, 48 [OE Dicts 56, 58, 59].

104 Boas, *Disticha Catonis*, IV.21, p. 217. Alfred J. Wyatt, *An Anglo-Saxon Reader* (Cambridge: Cambridge University Press, 1919), 222, n. 67, suggests that Ælfric's *Colloquy*, line 238, is a 'reminiscence of Disticha IV.21.' Chase, *Distichs of Cato*, translates: 'Practice with zeal the skill thou'st learned. Thou'lt find, / Use trains the hand as study does the mind' (p. 39).

One wonders how often this pretty sentiment was repeated in monastic classrooms. It is hardly surprising that, apart from the Old English citation in the *Colloquy*, this distich, with its emphasis on practice, enjoyed a further, independent, translation into Old English: 'Gif ðu hwylcne cræft cunne, bega þone georne: swa swa sorga 7 embhogan geycan monnes mod, swa geycð se cræft his are'[105] [If you know a skill, practise it eagerly: just as cares and sorrows enlarge a man's mind, so a skill increases his worth]. The translator's Old English prose rendition of the first verse is tolerably faithful, emphasizing the importance of practising a skill. The translation of the second verse, however, reframes the sentiment for an early medieval monastic context. The Latin distich confines itself to the arena of skill – one continues to work at whatever one does simply to perfect the skill. Practice makes perfect, as our own proverb would have it. By contrast with the Latin, the Old English prose translation extends the field of reference by importing a moral. In this translation, one should practise a skill eagerly because one's skill is an index of one's worth.[106] Revealing the grammatical instruction at the root of studying the Distichs, the Old English translation identifies and attempts to parallel the rhetorical effect of the distributed 'adiuvat' in the second hexameter by using a form of 'geycan' in the two clauses. But the translation's turn to the moral overwhelms any sense of literal faithfulness when it fixes on the meaning of 'cura' as 'sorga,' translating the word as 'cares' rather than 'care' and reformulating 'usus' as 'worth' (or ?'profit').[107] Against both the Latin distich and the Old English prose translation, the *Colloquy*'s added preoccupation with the habitus of identity is apparent. Ælfric's version of Distich IV.21

105 R.S. Cox, 'The Old English Dicts of Cato,' *Anglia* 90 (1972): 1–42 at 12, distich 58. Cox believes an early variant, *virum* for *usum*, lies behind the Old English translation (25). He suggests that 'composition of the Dicts was begun between the mid-[t]enth century and the mid-eleventh' (34).

106 'Ar' is polysemous, and thus a difficult word to translate. The DOE assigns its first meaning to the semantic field, 'honour.' But 'ar' equally denotes 'property' (sense C), suggesting the double sense of 'worth.'

107 For *cura* as 'sorg' see 'cura: sorg,' in William Garlington Stryker, 'The Latin-Old English Glossary in MS Cotton Cleopatra A. III' (PhD diss., Stanford University, 1951), item 499, p 117. For 'cura' in the sense of care, see 'Cura .i. sollicitudo. cogitatio. studium ... siue dicitur quod cor agitat ... ' (Robert T. Oliphant, *The Harley Latin-Old English Glossary*, Janua linguarum, series practica 20 [The Hague: Mouton, 1966], p. 117, lines 2217–18). This entry is not affected by the lengthy list of corrections by Hans Schabram, review of *The Harley Latin-Old English Glossary*, by Robert T. Oliphant, *Anglia* 86 (1968): 495–500.

frames the proverbial wisdom in terms of the identity conferring property of proper labour. To be abandoned by one's *ars* means much more than becoming rusty: in the understanding of the *Colloquy*, the loss of *ars* entails the loss of the distinguishing characteristic of one's life.

It is striking how closely the first lines of the Latin distich and Old English Distich 58 align with the sentiment in the *Colloquy*. OE Distich 58 offers 'Gif ðu hwylcne cræft cunne, bega þone georne,' and the Consiliarius offers the same sage advice: 'þæt anra gehwylc cræft his geornlice begange' [that each one should go about his craft diligently].[108] The sentiments and lexicons align neatly in both languages. The language of the Latin hexameter 'Exerce studium, quamvis perceperis artem' finds echoes in the *Colloquy*'s 'ut unusquisque *artem* suam diligenter *exerceat*' (emphasis added). Beyond this, the Old English gloss to the *Colloquy* approximates the language of the Old English translation of the Distich with 'cræft,' 'geornlice' (for 'georne'), and 'begange' (for 'bega'). It is unnecessary to look for a source relationship in the standard sense or a deliberate citation across the Old English translations.[109] The nearness of the sentiment and of the language suggests the degree to which this distich (and the *Disticha* in general) was part of Ælfric's mental furniture and part of the curriculum that he assumed. It was certainly part of Ælfric Bata's educational arsenal. But the *Colloquy* extends the simple commonplace of practise your skill, embedding the statement of practice in a larger existential statement. It does so by making the moral advice '*exerce* temet ipsum in hoc, et esto quod es' follow and inflect what might otherwise be merely practical: 'unusquisque artem suam diligenter *exerceat*' (emphases added). In the cultural logic governing this coupling, 'doing' an occupation produces 'being' within an identity. You are what you do. The *Colloquy*'s further insistence, 'esto quod es,' shows the degree to which the stability of the relation between being and doing was seen to be disrupted by the desire to be other. Policing that stability within monastic identity and curbing that desire were understood to be the province of a good will and the habit of obedience. Articulations of this cultural logic governing the oblates' development abound in Prosper's *Epigrammata*.

The *Epigrammata* of Prosper of Aquitaine was a widely circulated school text central to a schoolboy's early study. As Michael Lapidge has

108 Garmonsway, *Colloquy*, p. 41, line 238: 'ut unusquisque artem suam diligenter exerceat.'

109 There is no sourcing given in *Fontes Anglo-Saxonici* for the *Colloquy*. http://fontes.english.ox.ac.uk/ (accessed 11 March 2010).

pointed out, 'every literate Anglo-Saxon appears to have studied Prosper's epigrams.'[110] Multiple citations by Aldhelm (24), Bede (20), Alcuin (21), and Byrhtferth (2), as well as Alcuin's testimony that the *Epigrammata* was in the library at York, speak to both that text's power and its hold on the memory.[111] The four surviving manuscripts of the *Epigrammata* and fragments of a fifth, dated to the period of the Benedictine Reform and after, suggest the continuing appeal of the *Epigrammata* in later Anglo-Saxon England.[112] The epigrams it offers are composed of selections from Prosper's *Liber sententiarum*, his prose collection of extracts taken from his own brief commentary on Psalms 100–50, the *Expositio psalmorum* (prompting the first thirty-seven *epigrammata*), as well as from a wide selection of the writings of St Augustine, among them the *Enarrationes in psalmos, De spiritu et littera, De natura et gratia, De civitate Dei, De trinitate, Confessiones, De doctrina Christiana, De Genesi ad litteram, Contra Iulianum, Tractatus in euangelium Ioannis,* and *De libero arbitrio*.[113] The *Epigrammata* pairs each prose extract with its verse elaboration, effectively offering readers a simple prose epitome of the topic before it tackles the verse. More advanced than the *Disticha Catonis* both in terms of grammar and sentiments, its added value as early schoolroom exercises lay in transmitting simplified and easily memorizable ideas gleaned from the great works of Augustine.[114] The *sententiae* from which the *epigrammata* are composed are not arranged by topic, but follow the order of Prosper's continuing reading of Augustine's works.[115] Given the breadth of references

---

110 Lapidge, 'The Study of Latin Texts,' 466.

111 Lapidge, *Anglo-Saxon Library*, 327 and 231–3.

112 On the manuscripts, see n. 101 above.

113 M. Gastaldo, ed., *Sancti Prosperi Aquitani Liber Sententiarum*, CCSL 68A (Turnhout: Brepols, 1972), sources the prose *Sententiae* from which the verse are taken.

114 On the role of Prosper of Aquitaine in the transmission of Augustine's ideas, especially from the *Confessions*, see Pierre Courcelle, *Les confessions de saint Augustin dans la tradition littéraire* (Paris: Études Augustiniennes, 1963), pp. 217–18. See also M. Cappuyns, 'Le premier représentant de l'Augustinisme médiéval, Prosper d'Aquitaine,' *Recherches de théologie ancienne et médiévale* 1 (1929): 309–37. It should be observed that the text of the *Epigrammata* in PL 51.497–532 is reprinted from the eighteenth-century edition of Luc Urbain Mangeant, and a reliable text would require a full collation. It is thus difficult to make confident assertions about the text, in the absence of a modern edition. As printed in the PL, the arrangement of the *Epigrammata* follows the order of the *Sententiae* exactly for the first fifty-eight *sententiae*. Thereafter, the order of the *Sententiae* is only loosely followed.

115 Rudolf Lorenz, 'Der Augustinismus Prospers von Aquitanien,' *Zeitschrift für Kirchengeschichte* 73 (1962): 217–52 at 218. Michael Lapidge, *The Anglo-Saxon*

in the *sententiae*, the work covers numerous spiritual topics.[116] Although the *Epigrammata* after *Epi.* 48 selects freely from the *Sententiae*, it is clear that the *Epigrammata* shares the overall spiritual interests of the prose extracts. Quite apart from the various themes of dying to the world, avoiding pride, and cultivating humility, the appeal of the text, in Rodolf Lorenz's view, is clearest in the agreement of individual *sententiae* with later monastic rules.[117] There is little wonder, therefore, that the schoolrooms of English monastic houses found Prosper's epigrams so congenial.

For a text so fundamental to early monastic education, it is mildly surprising to find only a modest level of glossing in the manuscripts surviving from England. The elementary nature of the text clearly did not warrant the level of glossing found in manuscripts of Aldhelm, say, or of Boethius. And the rudimentary Latin glossing that the English manuscripts of Prosper have in common, elucidating matters of lexicon and morphology, is redolent of the beginner's classroom. While these shared glosses can tell us nothing unique to Anglo-Saxon pedagogy – Michael Lapidge suspects that the common origin of those shared Latin glosses is ninth-century Francia[118] – they do show, fairly starkly, the elementary grammatical orientation of engagement with the text. The heavy Old English lexical glossing in the surviving leaves of Tiberius A. vii, similarly, are also not an early eleventh-century master's classroom notes.[119] Karl

---

Library, 252–4, lists some fourteen separate works of Augustine (not counting individual homilies) cited by Ælfric, the most heavily cited of which are *Enarrationes in psalmos* and *Tractatus in Euangelium Ioannis*. See also Godden, *CH* III, xlvii–xlix. Lynne Grundy, *Books and Grace: Ælfric's Theology* (London: King's College London, Centre for Late Antique & Medieval Studies, 1991), sees in Ælfric a 'profound affinity with the teaching of Augustine's later works' (86) and stresses the ways Ælfric adopts Augustine's later teaching on predestination and the absolute necessity of divine grace to any meritorious action.

116 Lorenz, 'Der Augustinismus,' 226, classifies them as suffering, 'temporalis severitas,' the adversities and temptations of life, the sadness of suffering injustice, the power and fortune of the wicked, the sense of evil and suffering, what is destined in the will of God, and the exhortation of the silent sufferer, among others.

117 'In den Sentenzen atmet man die Luft des Mönchtums,' ibid., 230. He finds particularly that the double command of love as *propria* and *specialis* is found in the so-called *Disciplina monasterii Augustini*, the Rule of St Basil, and the chapter in *RSB* on the *instrumenta bonorum operum*, ibid., 230–1.

118 Lapidge, 'Study of Latin Texts,' pp. 467–8, 469, n. 51.

119 For an edition of these glossed fragments see Karl Toth, 'Altenglische Interlinearglossen zu Prospers *Epigrammata* und *Versus ad coniugem*,' *Anglia* 102 (1984): 1–36. The order of the folios is reversed: fol. 166 contains *Epi.* 90, line 3 ('Sed

Toth points out that differences between the gloss in Tiberius A. vii and some of its lemmata make it likely that these Old English glosses were copied *en bloc* from another manuscript of the *Epigrammata*.[120]

There is, however, a set of somewhat fuller glosses to four of these epigrams (*Epigrammata* 6–9), peculiar to Harley 110, which offers some detail on the kind and direction of comment that may have accompanied instruction in the *Epigrammata*.[121] It is difficult to explain why these four *epigrammata* received such additional glossing in this manuscript. The sheer ordinariness of their topics, excerpted by Prosper from his own commentary on Psalms 102 and 103, shows us some fundamentals of monastic education and the way in which the glossator applied Prosper's late antique sentiments to tenth-century monastic life.[122] Their glosses explain unusual or figuratively used words with more common expressions (as, for example the phrase 'ore precantis' in *Epi.* 6.1 is glossed above the line 'id est uoce' above 'ore' and 'id est orantis alicuius' above 'precantis' [4v/6]); mark relative pronouns with their referent, inflected for context (for example, 'quarum' in *Epi.* 8.9 is glossed 'scilicet deliciarum,' referring to 'deliciis' in the previous line [5r/3]); or insert a personal pronoun to assist translation (as with 'scilicet ille' glossing 'qui' in *Epi.* 7.7 [4v/22]). In the same line, the glossator explicates 'istis geminis virtutum' as 'caritate scilicet dei ac proximi' in case the reader had not connected the 'twins of the virtues' to the subject of the prose *sententia*, the double love of God and neighbour.[123] But they also carefully embed the fundamentals of grammatical instruction in the basics of Christian monastic life.

One of the four *epigrammata* that receive extra glossing in Harley 110 (*Epi.* 8), entitled 'De doctrina apostolica,' illustrates how the learning to which the boys were put combined grammatical analysis and spiritual

dum mens...') through *Epi.* 93, and the title and prose description of *Epi.* 94; fol. 165v preserves a portion of the final epigram (=106). The *Versus Prosperi ad coniugem* follows. See Toth, 'Altenglische Interlinearglossen,' 6–8; Ker, *Catalogue*, no. 189; Gneuss, *Handlist*, no. 365.

120 Toth, 'Altenglische Interlinearglossen,' 20.

121 Neither CUL Gg. 5. 35, CCCC 448, nor Trinity College O. 2. 31 has anything other than sporadic glosses or construe marks for these poems. In my presentation of the glosses to Harley 110 I have silently expanded all abbreviations.

122 On the use of glosses as evidence for the teaching of reading and interpretation see M.B. Parkes, '*Rædan, areccan, smeagan*: How the Anglo-Saxons Read,' *ASE* 26 (1997): 1–22, esp. 3–4.

123 These are standard manoeuvers in glossing: see Parkes, '*Rædan, areccan, smeagan*,' 14–15.

doctrine, and how both learning and teaching assumed that what was learned was also lived.[124] 'Doctrina' in the *sententia* has its sense of body of teaching, but in the epigram the subject is extended to include both senses, body of teaching and learning.[125] The *sententia* to *Epi.* 8, taken from Prosper's commentary on Psalm 103:11, asserts the universal application of apostolic teaching to all, whether young or old. Its dominant metaphor, feeding, underlies the development of the following *epigramma*. For the second statement of the *sententia*, 'Quia siue paruuli siue magni. siue infirmi siue fortes habent in ea unde alantur et unde satientur' (4v), the glosses resolve the metaphor and apply the statement to the monastic community: for the pairing 'great and small,' 'paruuli' is glossed 'indocti pueruli' [ignorant little boys] while 'magni' is glossed 'eruditi senes' [learned elders]. 'Weak' and 'strong' are glossed 'id est inperfecti' and 'id est perfecti' respectively. With the inexperienced reader in mind, the gloss to 'unde alantur' [whence they are nourished] illustrates the function of *unde* as an adverb, simplifies the expression, and identifies an etymon by offering 'id est alimenta sumant.'[126] The further gloss builds on the previous grammatical analysis, explicating the parallel 'unde satientur' by explaining that the subject is 'cibum scilicet anime' [that is, the food of the soul]. The ten-line *epigramma* expands on its prose *sententia*: to banish the darkness of the world, God kindles the light of apostolic teaching that is suited to all ages. It suckles the young and feeds the strong with bread. Knowing no limits, it cares for, nurtures, justifies, and animates all. In the last four lines, the *epigramma* changes grammatical mood and addresses its readers directly:

> Sumite quae magnae apposuit sapientia mense
> Et uariis pasci discite diliciis
> Quarum pars totum est epulum et qui[cum]que iuuatur
> [for q<uod>cu<m>q<ue> in MS]
> Inde capit uitam quam parit una fides. (5r/1–4)

---

124 Harley 110, fols. 4v–5r (PL 51.501). Trinity O. 2. 31 offers 'id est conuenit' for 'congruit' in the text, 'omnibus' to explain the function of 'nullis,' and explains the import of 'ualidos' by supplying 'spirituali intelligentia.' In editing the glosses I have printed 'e' for 'e' caudata throughout and expanded all abbreviations.

125 The children of the *Colloquy*, when asked about their willingness to be beaten, answer that they prefer to be beaten 'pro doctrina' (glossed 'for lare' [i.e., for learning]) than not to learn (Garmonsway, *Colloquy*, pp. 18–19, lines 8–9.

126 See A. Walde and J.B. Hofmann, *Lateinisches etymologisches Wörterbuch*, 3rd ed., 3 vols. (Heidelberg: Carl Winter's Universitätsbuchhandlung, 1938–56), I.31–2, s.v. *alo*.

> [Eat what Wisdom sets out on her great table, and learn to be nourished by its various delights. Part of them is a whole feast, and everyone is delighted by it, whence they take the life that one faith brings forth.]

In glossing 'sumite' as 'invitatio poete' the glossator makes a grammatical point about the rhetoric of the final four lines, highlighting the change in person and grammatical mood. Along with further, fairly basic, syntactic glossing ('quarum' is glossed 'deliciarum' to connect it to its referent; 'capit' is glossed 'quisque' to link its subject to that of the previous clause), the glossing extends to spiritual significances: 'Sapientia' is explained as 'Christus deus noster,' and his table is glossed 'id est libris sacris' (in the dative as is the lemma, presumably to show that the 'quae' of the invitation to eat is found in books). The 'epulum' provided on Wisdom's table is glossed for lexicon as 'obsonium,'[127] but the further elaboration 'siue dulcedo doctrine' [or the sweetness of learning (or doctrine)] connects the comment back to resolving the theme. Above the last line of *Epi.* 8 and extending into the margin, the glossator has written a lengthy comment to explain how the learning of Christian doctrine gives life: 'quia ex illa doctrina qua fuerit quisque imbutus ad bona opera agenda incitatur. ac sic crescendo paulatim ad summam intellegentiae plerumque progreditur' [Because by this teaching by which everyone is instructed he will be encouraged to do good works, and so being strengthened gradually in such a way very often advances to the height of understanding].

The common theme of the glossing of this *epigramma* is the resolution of its major metaphor, the feast of apostolic teaching by which all are nourished. But the glosses also accommodate these verses to the monastic community, construing the contrasting pair of 'paruuli' and 'magni' as ignorant little boys and their learned seniors, and identifying the source of what is to be learned as holy books (as opposed to 'doctrina apostolica,' which might be orally conveyed). In this interpretive accommodation, the extended comment on the final line moves beyond simple grammar to interpret these verses within an institutional understanding of the *Epigrammata* and the context in which its tyro readers were educated. 'Doctrina' is life-giving, we learn, as both body of knowledge and process of learning, because it incites one instilled with it to the doing of good works. The reader is commanded 'pasci discite' (learn to be nourished), and such

127 See the *Dictionary of Medieval Latin from British Sources*, s.v. 'obsonium,' sense 2, 'feast.'

learning, if and only if brought to fruition in the doing of good works, draws everyone ('quicumque') along the path to the highest knowledge.

The integral connection of learning and doing, where the naturalizing of textual identity is also the naturalizing of monastic habitus, is a theme that runs strongly through the *Epigrammata*. The young reader learns, for example, that simply parroting a text by rote is of no use. Such a warning is explicitly developed in the Harley gloss to Prosper's *sententia* to *Epi.* 6: 'Bene autem loqui et male uiuere nihil aliud est quam sua se uoce dampnare'[128] [However, to speak well and to live badly is nothing other than to condemn oneself by one's own voice]. The Harley glossator adds above the line (4v/4): 'Sicut faciunt ypochrite. locuntur enim sancte et uiuunt peruerse' [So the hypocrites do: in fact, they speak religiously and live wickedly]. Such a comment indicates that the Latin learning that the boys are meant to absorb has as its goal a mastery of language (however rare an achievement that proved to be) in the service of communal religious life. We are brought back full circle to the boy's reply to the Consiliarius, when asked if the children wished to become 'bene loquentes et male cogitantes.'[129] It is not enough to speak the language of community; one must live what one has learned to speak. The praxis of that life, lived bodily in the regular cycles of eating, sleeping, working, and praying, understood and defined itself through texts.

The interconnection of work and study in the *Epigrammata* is carefully focused on the understanding of scripture, whose reading required all the skills of grammatical analysis. So *Epi.* 70 encourages the reader to work at understanding scripture even though its meaning is elusive:

Quamvis in sacris libris, quos nosce laboras,
Plurima sint, lector, clausa et opaca tibi,
Invigilare tamen studio ne desine sancto.
Exercent animum dona morata tuum.
Gratior est fructus quem spes productior edit:
Ultro objectorum vilius est pretium.
Oblectant adoperta etiam mysteria mentem:
Qui dedit ut quaeras, addet ut invenias.[130]

---

128 The *sententia* is taken from Prosper's commentary on Psalm 102:21. See Gastaldo, *Sancti Prosperi Aquitani Liber Sententiarum*, p. 258, *Sent.* 6, lines 2–3.

129 Garmonsway, *Colloquy*, p. 43, line 256.

130 *Epi.* 70, appears in Harley 110 at 16r/4–11. CCCC 448 gives only variant readings: line 2, clausa et opaca/ i. obscura. inuisa; line 6 edit / i. componit. Harley 110 provides

[Reader, although in the sacred books that you labour to know there are many things that are hidden and opaque to you, nonetheless do not cease to be vigilant about your holy study. Moral gifts train your mind. The fruit that hope brings forth at length is more welcome: for the reward of obvious things is small. The One who gives that you might seek, bestows that you might find.]

Sententia 67, which accompanies these verses – 'Bonae sunt in Scripturis sanctis mysteriorum profunditates, quae ob hoc teguntur, ne uilescant, ob hoc quaeruntur, ut exerceant, ob hoc aperiuntur, ut pascant'[131] [There are excellent depths of mysteries in the Holy Scriptures, which should not be disregarded because they are concealed; therefore are they sought that they may train, they are opened, that they may nurture] – is excerpted from Augustine's explication of Psalm 140.[132] We see in this *epigramma* one of the ways Prosper adapts Augustine's thought to a broader audience. Augustine's point is that the difficult meanings of scriptures are veiled for a purpose – that they may challenge the reader to meditate – and they are laid open that they may nourish the persistent. But Prosper's verses transform this observation into a more homely message easily claimed for the initiation of oblates into textual culture: that however hard it is to understand passages from scripture, continued effort is necessary. The combination of the verbs 'quaeruntur' and 'aperiuntur' in the *sententia* echo Christ's words in the Gospel, 'Seek and you shall find; knock and it shall be opened to you' (Matt. 7:7–8; Luke 11:9–10). In the epigram Prosper draws on the third verb from these Gospel verses, 'invenietis' as an encouragement to continued labour at study. In Prosper's redaction of Augustine's observation, continued study of holy books is a moral obligation that God himself both requires and makes possible.

The obligation to live what one learns drives Ælfric's insistence that Latin grammatical learning is the *cæg* that unlocks the meaning of books.

---

a number of lexical glosses. In the two instances of overlap (lines 2 and 6) Harley's glosses are different. Trinity O. 2. 31 provides two glosses specifying grammatical relationships.

131 In Harley 110, 15v/34–16r/3. Verse text from PL 51.519. The *epigrammata* are usually accompanied by prose extracts from Prosper's *Liber sententiarum*. I give the prose *sententiae* from Gastaldo, *Sancti Prosperi Aquitani Liber sententiarum*, *Sent.* 67, p. 273. Gastaldo has promised an edition of the *Epigrammata*.

132 Eligius Dekkers and J. Fraipont, eds., *Sancti Aurelii Augustini Enarrationes in Psalmos*, 3 vols., CCSL 38–40 (Turnhout: Brepols, 1956), III: 2026, lines 6–9.

One cannot love, as Augustine observes in *De trinitate*, X.1, what one does not know,[133] nor can one live it:

> Scriptorum Domini plene videt omne profundum,
> Implet qui factis cognita verba piis.
> Nam nimis a sensu doctrinae devius errat,
> Si quae curavit scire, fugit facere.[134]
>
> [He sees fully the whole depth of the Lord's scriptures who fulfils the words he has learned with pious deeds. For the foolish man wanders far from the meaning of doctrine if he runs from doing what he has laboured to know.]

The critical concept in this *epigramma* (*Epi.* 13) is the importance of pairing learning and doing. In this framing of the concept, fulfilling what one has learned by moral acts indexes the learner's comprehension of the scriptures studied. Because the labour of learning is useless without living the life being studied, the student who has worked at learning ('curavit scire') has learned nothing if his deeds do not match. *Sententia* 13 on which this epigram is fashioned – 'He has a good understanding who performs what he well knows ought to be done. Otherwise, understanding without works is just like wisdom without fear, since it is written "The beginning of wisdom is fear of the Lord"'[135] – comments on Psalm 110:10: 'Initium sapientiae timor Domini; / Intellectus bonus omnibus facientibus eum. / Laudatio eius manet in saeculum saeculi,' and the added citation of the psalm provides the *epigramma* with a memorial context, recited in the weekly round of the Divine Office.[136]

While the previous examples of the injunction to practise what you learn focused rather generally on the importance of learning scripture, *Epi.* 24 focuses particularly on the observance of divine law. The *sententia*

133 W.J. Mountain with Fr. Glorie, eds., *Sancti Aurelii Augustini de Trinitate Libri XV*, 2 vols., CCSL 50, 50a (Turnhout: Brepols, 1968), X.1.29–30 (I: 312).

134 PL 51.502–3.

135 *Sent.*13.1–4: 'Bonum intellectum habet qui quod faciendum, recte intellegit facit. Alioqui talis est sine opere intellegentia, qualis sine timore sapientia, cum scriptum sit: *Initium sapientiae timor Domini*' (Gastaldo, *Prosper Aquitani Liber Sententiarum*, 260).

136 For this *sententia*, CCCC 448 has only an explanatory gloss, 'Bonum intellectum / scilicet ille homo'; Harley 110 only glosses 'plane / apte' (PL reads 'plene'). Trinity College O. 2. 31 only adds the missing words 'initium' and 'est' missing from 'sapientiae timor domini' in the manuscript.

from which it was developed combined two separate observations from Prosper's commentary on Psalm 118, vv. 71 and 77. For this lengthy psalm, the *RSB* specified that its twenty-two sections should be divided for recital across the little hours on Sunday and Monday.[137] The psalm itself praises God for his law and begs God to teach 'iustificationes tuas' that the speaker might carry them out. On v. 71, 'Bonum mihi quia humiliasti me; / Ut discam iustificationes tuas,' Prosper comments, 'You have changed my punishment to instruction ('disciplinam') and my humiliation into learning ('eruditionem'), because I desire to know your laws that I might carry them out. There is no true knowledge of good, unless it is so known that it is done.'[138] The second comment became the foundation of *Sententia* 24.

The four-line epigram that follows concludes: 'Non satis est Domini praeceptum volvere lingua: / Is meminit legis, qui memor est operis' [It is not enough to roll the Lord's command around your tongue. He remembers the law who observes it by doing]. *Epi.* 24 develops the by now familiar observation that the mouthing of religious truths is of no value unless they are lived by interconnecting study, the law, and memory. Speaking ('volvere lingua') of the law is made a function of memory, but the measure of memory is action. Although the formulation is slightly different, the message remains that knowledge carefully committed to memory in the classroom required incorporation into one's behaviour. Beyond the practice of the classroom in learning and doing, however, the *epigrammata* transmit basic notions about will, obedience, and practice to those whose 'memor est operis.'

An oblate, whose life of service was his parents' gift, learned that the praiseworthy conduct of a monastic life – from dormitory to oratory to schoolroom – depended on a rightly formed will. While every action of every day was judged a matter of free choice (*liberum arbitrium*), the test of the right exercise of that choice was its conformity to the will of God. Will (*uoluntas*) was either good or bad. An individual of good will, responding to God's grace, would act in a manner that would move him toward an eternal reward. An individual of bad will, oriented only towards

137 See Robert Taft, *The Liturgy of the Hours in East and West* (Collegeville, MN: The Liturgical Press, 1986), 137.

138 P. Callens, ed., *Sancti Prosperi Aquitani Expositio Psalmorum a Centesimo usque ad Centesimum Quinquagesimum*, CCSL 68A (Turnhout: Brepols, 1972), p. 101, lines 513–16: 'Poenam conuertisti mihi ad disciplinam, et humiliationem ad eruditionem, quia iustificationes tuas ita cupio nosse ut faciam. Non enim est uera scientia boni, nisi ad hoc cognoscatur ut agatur.'

himself, was likely to be lost. Salvation, then, depended on the formation and maintenance of a good will. In *Epi.* 63, taken from Augustine's discussion of will in *De trinitate*, Prosper makes a number of distinctions about the will and its objects.[139] Augustine argues that all happy people have what they will, although not all those who have what they will are thereby happy.[140] Those who either don't have what they will or have what they have willed improperly are, however, thereby miserable. Prosper's development of Augustine's argument changes the focus by explaining that getting what you will does not always bring happiness, because the improper object of the will may be the result of 'mala vota' [bad intentions]. But anything proceeding from a good will is a source of virtue. For this reason, whoever persists in willing good, is good:

> Non semper vere est felix impleta voluntas:
> Cum saepe injustis sint mala vota animis.
> Recta igitur cupiens, etiam si non sit adeptus,
> Persistendo tamen velle bonum, bonus est.
> At pravus, quod fert animo, si non habet actu,
> Tam miser est quam si quod cupit obtineat.[141]

> [A desire fulfilled is not always truly happy, since there are often bad intentions in wicked minds. Hence, if one desires virtuous things, even if he hasn't reached his goal, by persisting in willing good, he is good. But the wicked man, if he doesn't have in actuality what he has in his mind, is as miserable as if he were to obtain what he desires.]

There are two types of mind and two types of desire: good and bad. The person with a good will wills good things. But even if these virtuous things are not realized, if he persists in his good will, he is, in fact, a good man. But the person with a bad will, because his intentions by definition are

---

139 Mountain and Glorie, *Sancti Aureli Augustini De Trinitate Libri XV*, XIII.5.33–7 (II: 392–3). Gastaldo, *Sancti Prosperi Aquitani Liber Sententiarum, Sent.* 62 (p. 272, lines 1–6): 'Omnes beati habent quod uolunt, quamuis non omnes qui habent quod uolunt, continuo sint beati. Continuo autem sunt miseri, qui uel non habent quod uolunt, uel id habent quod non recte uolunt. Propior ergo est beatitudini uoluntas recta, etiam non adepta quod cupit, quam praua, etiamsi quod cupit obtinuit.'

140 On the implications of this statement for the relation of happiness to having a good will see James Wetzel, *Augustine and the Limits of Virtue* (Cambridge: Cambridge University Press, 1992), 45–6.

141 PL 51.517.

bad, cannot be happy, whether he gets what he wants or not. At the most elementary moral level, this epigram would help the child to see that there are real goods and apparent goods. What one desires doesn't always bring happiness.

Prosper's *Epi.* 47 on the consequence of a bad will's achieving what it desires speaks clearly to the issues raised by Ælfric's story of the runaway *munuccild*:

> Cum datur injusto peccandi optata potestas,
> Ut mala mens prave quod cupit efficiat,
> Ira Dei magna est, qua multos sic quoque punit,
> Ut quibus exsultant criminibus pereant.
> Crescit enim occulte cum longo poena reatu,
> Ausibus illicitis si nihil obstiterit.
> Et magis erranti ne parcant flagra timendum est,
> Quam ne non fiat quod voluisse nocet.[142]

> [When the desired power of sinning is granted to an unrighteous man, so that his wicked mind may carry out what it wrongly desires, God's anger is great, by which he punishes many indeed, so that they may perish by those crimes in which they exult. For with long sinning their punishment grows though hidden, if nothing has hindered their unlawful doings. And a sinner ought to fear more being spared by the lash than that he doesn't get what is harmful to have wanted.]

This epigram deals with the way in which God permits a sinner to do evil and with the condign nature of the resulting punishment. The longer the sin is left unpunished – that is, the longer the sinner leaves his offence

142 PL 51.512–13. Gastaldo, *Sancti Prosperi Aquitani Liber Sententiarum, Sent.* 47 (pp. 268–9, lines 1–6): 'Cum uoluntas mala potestatem accipit ut efficiat quod cupit, ex iudicio Dei uenit, apud quem non est iniquitas. Punit enim etiam isto modo, nec ideo iniuste, quia occulte. Ceterum iniquus puniri se ignorat, nisi cum manifesto supplicio senserit nolens, quantum mali sit quod perpetrauit uolens' [When an evil will receives the power of doing what it desires, that comes from the judgment of God, in whom there is no wrong. Indeed He punishes him in this manner, and not unjustly because hidden. Still, the evil-doer does not understand that he is being punished, unless against his will he perceives from his obvious punishment how evil what he has willingly done is]. Prosper excerpts this from Augustine's *De spiritu et littera.* C.F. Urba and J. Zycha, eds., *Sancti Aureli Augustini, De Spiritu et Littera Liber Unus*, CSEL 60 (Vienna: F. Tempsky, 1913), XXXI.54, p. 211, line 25, to p. 212, line 3.

without amendment – the greater the punishment he can expect. My interest here, however, is less in the severity of the punishment than in the notion that the punishment is condign. God arranges that sinners perish by those sins in which they delight ('quibus exsultant criminibus pereant'). The evil that God punishes comes from an evil intention; in such a mind the will is not good, and so evil acts proceed from it.

This poem offers an apt commentary on Ælfric's adaptation of Gregory's story of the runaway oblate in the Life of St Benedict. Read through Prosper's Augustinian lens, the *munuccild* of the Old English homily accomplishes what he wills, though it is against the will of God. His moment of apparent freedom comes from the desired power to sin ('peccandi optata potestas') as well as his desire to do something harmful ('quod voluisse nocet'). The combination guarantees that the ultimate outcome will be unhappy. When the child exercises his freedom of choice badly through wilful disobedience, the result is that he dies exulting in that which he ought not to have done. The very day he returns to his family, having left without permission, he dies. Committing Prosper's epigram to memory did more for (and to) the learner in the monastic classroom than simply assisting him in learning grammatical and rhetorical forms. Rather, it was part of his textual formation, whereby the grammatical knowledge gained from learning (and having learning beaten into him) helped define him as one of the monastic *familia* by his knowledge, and the content formed him in how he was to conduct his life. God permits evil, that the evil doer may be punished condignly.

Three practices, outlined prominently in the early chapters of the *RSB*, are required of monks who follow the Rule – obedience, silence, and humility. Of these, humility is described in degrees of accomplishment, embracing thoughts and attitudes, postures and behaviours. The second degree of this virtue is the practice of turning away from one's own will: 'Secundus humilitatis gradus est, si propriam quis non amans uoluntatem desideria sua non delectetur implere, sed uocem illam domini factis imitetur dicentis: *Non ueni facere uoluntatem meam, sed eius, qui me misit*'[143] [This is the second degree of humility, if someone not loving his own will, does not delight in fulfilling his own desires: but let him imitate the word of the Lord in his deeds, saying: 'I came … not to do my own will, but the will of him that sent me']. The *epigrammata* that Prosper developed from Augustine's many writings on the will were particularly suited to develop and enhance this simple message of the Rule. The second degree of

143 Hanslik, *Benedicti Regula*, cap. 7.31–2 (p. 45).

humility (as it would be developed in the *RSB*) is twinned with the practice of obedience, where the first precept is obedience without delay.[144] If the *arcta uia* (Matt. 7:14) that the oblate was set to learn and live felt like servitude, he would learn to understand his service as true freedom:

Libertas nulla est melior, majorve potestas,
Quam servire Deo, cui bene servit amor.
Absque jugo posita est ditionis amica voluntas:
Quae viget affectu, non gemit imperio.[145]

[There is no better freedom, or no greater power than to serve God, whom love serves well. A well-disposed will is formed without the yoke of subjection; it thrives by love, and does not groan from command.]

In constructing *Epi.* 85, Prosper works from 'Libera semper est seruitus apud Deum, cui non necessitas seruit, sed caritas'[146] [Servitude is always free with God, whom necessity does not serve, but love]. Prosper's modifications to Augustine's observation (one repeated across Augustine's works) illustrate how adaptable the *epigrammata* were to a monastic environment. However much Augustine's observation was indebted to neo-Platonist ideas of spontaneous movement toward the Good, Prosper's simple version worked outward from the familiar paradox of free (Christian) service to God. To this Prosper adds a further scriptural reference, to Christ's light yoke ('iugum enim meum suave est, et onus meum leve,' Matt. 11:30). Service to God is easy if the will is properly inclined. Such a will is not the product of the necessity arising from worldly subjection, but rather is a gift. As the monk's will is turned in love to God, he prospers by that love.[147] The commands of God, in this disposition of the will, are easy.

144 Ibid., cap. 5.1 (p. 38): 'Primus humilitatis gradus est oboedientia sine mora.'

145 PL 51.524.

146 Gastaldo, *Liber Sententiarum, Sent.* 124 (p. 285), which he sources to Dekkers and Fraipont, eds., *Sancti Aurelii Augustini Enarrationes in Psalmos*, II: 1397.

147 See Hanslik, *Benedicti Regula*, prol. 45–8, on the outcome of founding a 'dominici scola seruitii': 'Constituenda est ergo nobis dominici scola seruitii. In qua institutione nihil asperum, nihil graue nos constituturos speramus. Sed et si quid paululum restrictius dictante aequitatis ratione propter emendationem uitiorum uel conseruationem caritatis processerit non ilico pauore perterritus refugias uiam salutis.' [Therefore we must establish a school of the Lord's service. We hope to establish in that school nothing harsh and nothing burdensome. But if some small strictness emerges for the sake of justice in order to amend sins or preserve charity, do not immediately run from the way of salvation, frightened and shaking.]

'Esto quod factus es'

The resistance of 'Esto quod es' and 'Esto quod factus es' to the idea of labile identity would appear to foreclose the route to the monastic life taken by adults, the *conuersi* who entered religious life after living in the world. And yet clearly this interpretation of the implications of the Consiliarius's command cannot be correct. As we have seen, the great founders of the Benedictine Reform in England – Dunstan, Æthelwold, and Oswald – all embraced the monastic life after some time in the world. Osbern approaches an adult's taking up of monastic life as a matter of will and freedom. Ælfric, by contrast, approaches it through the demands of conferred identity on a child. In what way, then, can monastic conversion, that paradigm of a change in identity understood as an exercise of will in obedience, be understood to fit within the rubrics of the Consiliarius's command?

Ælfric's explanation of St Paul's conversion in his homily for the feast of St Paul directly addresses this problem by illustrating the embracing of religious identity not as personal desire but as proper alignment of will ('Esto quod es'), and this equation explains the unspoken of the Consiliarus's command. For Paul the adult, countless unnamed oblates, and members of Benedictine reformed religious communities, identity is shown powerfully to be a matter of alignment of will in obedience and of belonging to a textual community:

> Paulus ehte cristenra manna. na mid niðe swa swa þa iudeiscan dydon; ac he wæs midspreca 7 bewerigend þære ealdan æ. mid micelre anrædnysse; wende þæt cristes geleafa wære wiðerwinna þære ealdan gesetnysse; Ac se hælend þe gesette þa ealdan æ. mid mislicum getacnungum. se ylca eft on his andwerdnysse hi awende to soðfæstnysse æfter gastlicere getacnunge; ða nyste paulus þa gastlican getacnunge. þære .æ. 7 wæs for þi hyre forespreca. 7 ehtere cristes geleafan; God ælmihtig þe ealle þing wat. geseah his geþanc þæt he ne ehte geleaffulra | manna þurh andan ac þurh ware þære ealdan. .æ. 7 hine ða gespræc of heofonum ðus cweþende. saule. hwi ehtst þu min Ic eom seo soðfæstnyss þe þu werast geswic þære ehtnysse derigendlic bið þæt þu spurne ongean þa gade; Gif se oxa spyrnð ongean þa gade; hit derað him sylfum; Swa eac hearmað ðe. þin gewinn togeanes me.[148]
>
> [Paul persecuted Christian men not with hostility as the Jews did, but he was an advocate and defender of the old law with great perseverance. He thought

148 *CH* I.27, pp. 402–3, lines 66–80.

that belief in Christ would be an enemy of the old law ['gesetnysse']. But the saviour had established ['gesette'] the old law with various senses. He himself ['se ylca' = Christ] in his presence changed them to truth [= fulfilled?] according to the spiritual sense; Paul didn't know the spiritual sense of the law then, and for that reason, he was its advocate and a persecutor of belief in Christ. God almighty, who knows all these things, saw his thought, that he did not persecute believing men through malice but for protection of the old law. And he spoke to him from heaven, saying thus: 'Saul, why do you persecute me? I am the truth which you protect. Stop this persecution. It is harmful that you kick against the goad. If the ox kicks against the goad it hurts him. So also your struggle against me hurts you.']

Malcolm Godden has pointed out that 'Ælfric's resolute defense of Saul' has no parallel in the multiple sources of this homily and believes that there is probably an unidentified source underlying Ælfric's treatment.[149] I suggest that we think in a complementary direction. When Ælfric maintains that Saul/Paul's persecution of Christians was not from malice but from a misguided understanding of the Old Testament, he locates Paul's persecution not in terms of ethnic identity ('swa swa þa iudeiscan dydon') but in terms of *textual* identity – that is, Paul was not yet within the community of those understanding the proper relation between the two testaments ('ða nyste paulus þa gastlican getacnunge. þære .æ. 7 wæs for þi hyre forespreca. 7 ehtere cristes geleafan'). For Paul to be folded into the new community of interpretation required realignment. Ælfric's account of Paul here contrasts strikingly with that of St Augustine, which he otherwise follows. Augustine presents Paul's conduct as savagery so as to highlight God's mercy in the saint's dramatic conversion.[150] For Ælfric, by contrast, Paul was only a persecutor through mistaken interpretation. Ælfric takes up Christ's message to Saul from on high (Acts 9:5: 'durum est tibi contra stimulum calcitrare'), but translating and elaborating so that Christ is made to say that when the ox kicks against the goad, he only hurts himself; similarly when Paul opposes Christ.[151] Here, kicking against

149 Godden, *CH* III, p. 224.

150 Godden, *CH* III, p. 222 (following Förster) suggests Augustine, *Sermo* 279 (PL 38.1275–80).

151 See Augustine, 'Hoc est, quod et Paulo adhuc Saulo de coelo Christus clamavit: Non tibi expedit contra stimulum calcitrare (Acts 9:5). Saeviat, saeviat quantum potest; qui calces adversus stimulum mittit, nonne in se ipsum saevit?' *Sermo* 158, cap. 1 (PL 38.863). Gregory comments in a different direction, applying the lesson to monastic life, that monks should seek to do God's will in all things. See Marc Adriaen, ed., *S.*

the goad is a form of disobedience, suggesting that the structure of Paul's life was already a given and that Paul's conversion meant ceasing to resist. (Ælfric pays no attention to the change of name Saul/Paul at this point.) Paul's actual and symbolic prostration, as Ælfric portrays it, reveals the accession of humility ('eadmodnyss') that allows him to receive 'his modes onlihtinge' [enlightenment of mind].[152]

The resonance of Paul's conversion for the monastic life of Ælfric's day appears more explicitly in the second part of the homily, which explores the monastic life and its rewards: 'þa ðe for heofonan rices myrhðe forlætað fæder 7 moder. 7 flæsclice siblingas hi underfoð manega gastlice fæderas. 7 gastlice gebroþru. for þan ðe ealle þæs hades menn þe regollice lybbað beoð him to fæderum 7 to gebroþrum getealde 7 þærtoeacan hi beoð mid edleane þæs ecan lifes gewelgode'[153] [Those who for the joy of the kingdom of heaven abandon father and mother and fleshly siblings receive many spiritual fathers and spiritual brothers, because all men of the monastic order who live the regular life are enriched with the reward of eternal life]. But it also explores the *earfoðhylde* in monastic life. This nonce word combines 'difficult' with 'hylde' (=*hield*, observance, fidelity) as an adjective. The DOE gives 'not easily inclined; reluctant to submit/comply; ?discontented.' Such a resolution of the word suggests the direction that Ælfric is going in closing his homily on the failure of the monastic ideal, and it makes a useful connection with the command 'Esto quod es' in the *Colloquy*.[154] For both the homily, 'Natale Sancte Pauli,' and the *Colloquy* the injunction to be what you are points to a problematic desire. By desiring from the world what he did not have in the monastery, the *munuccild* lost his spiritual brothers and his life by longing for his blood kin.

The image of Eadui Basan presenting the Arundel Psalter to St Benedict (London, BL, Arundel 155, fol. 133r) illustrates spectacularly the dynamics of textual identity launched in the English Benedictine Reform and the

---

Gregorii Magni Moralia in Iob, 3 vols., CCSL 143, 143a, 143b (Turnhout: Brepols, 1979), X.xiii.24 (I: 554, lines 25–33).

152 *CH* I.27, p. 403, lines 85, 87.

153 *CH* I.27, p. 407, lines 199–203.

154 Ælfric uses the examples of Judas, Giezi, and Ananias and Saphira to illustrate how the monastic ideal may fail. On the interpretation of the story of Ananias and Saphira in monastic rules for both the holding of private property and for disobedience, see Bruce C. Brasington, 'Remember Always Ananias and Sapphira' in *Oboedientia: Zu Formen und Grenzen von Macht und Unterordnung in Mittelalterlichen Religiosentum*, ed. Sébastien Barret and Gert Melville, Vita regularis 27 (Münster: Lit Verlag, 2005), 83–97, esp. p. 90 and n. 31.

crucial role of obedience in it (plate 1 and opposite p. 3). In a single image it offers the idealized, positive content of 'you are what you do.' The image shows us initiation into a culture of writing, the primary importance of the Psalter (whose memorial performance was the first step for the *munuccild*); it shows us the group organized around a text (here the *RSB*), the learning and performance of that text as marker of identity, and Eadui, himself, kneeling in a posture of obedience and humility.[155] It shows us 'you are what you do' in its dramatization of identity formation through practice, as well as 'be what you were made' in its insistence on alignment of the will in obedience. The miniature in Arundel 155 shows us not one but two books, the central text for perfecting the monastic life and primary liturgical text for performing it: a portion of the *RSB* was read in chapter every day; the Psalter sung in full each week. Both texts were internalized, committed to writing and to memory. The boys imagined by the *Colloquy* at the beginning of their education would first have learned the Psalter *memoriter*, but their education in Latin was designed to bring them more fully into the textual identity of the monastery. The figures in the Arundel miniature are grouped in two arcades within a larger arch. In the arcade on the left is a painted image of St Benedict, identified in his nimbus as 'S<an>c<tu>s Benedictus. pater monaco<rum> et dux' [father and commander of monks]. He wears a band on his head inscribed 'Timor Dei' [fear of God] and the clasp of his cloak is inscribed 'Iust<us>' [just man] above a cross. In the arcade to the right is a group of monks, whose

155 Elżbieta Temple, *Anglo-Saxon Manuscripts, 900–1066*, Survey of Manuscripts Illuminated in the British Isles 2 (London: Harvey Miller, 1976), item 66, fig. 213. For a colour image see Janet Backhouse, D.H. Turner, Leslie Webster, eds., *The Golden Age of Anglo-Saxon Art, 966–1066* (London: British Museum Publications, 1984), p. 72, item 57, and pl. XVIII. An enlargeable image of fol. 133r is available at http://www.bl.uk/catalogues/illuminatedmanuscripts/ILLUMIN.ASP?Size=mid&IllID=824 (accessed 21 February 2011). The manuscript, written at Christ Church, Canterbury, is dated to between 1012 and 1023 (Gneuss, *Handlist*, item 306). For discussions of the manuscript and image see Robert Deshman, '*Benedictus Monarcha et Monachus*: Early Medieval Ruler Theology and the Anglo-Saxon Reform,' *Frühmittelalterliche Studien* 22 (1988): 204–40 and pll. 49–73 at 211–16; Robert Deshman, *The Benedictional of Æthelwold* (Princeton: Princeton University Press, 1995), 117–21 and 172–3; Margaret Gibson, T.A. Heslop, Richard W. Pfaff, eds., *The Eadwine Psalter: Text, Image, and Monastic Culture in Twelfth-Century Canterbury* (University Park: The Pennsylvania State University Press, 1992), 181; Richard W. Pfaff, 'Eadui Basan: Scriptorum Princeps?' in *England in the Eleventh Century: Proceedings of the 1990 Harlaxton Symposium*, ed. Carola Hicks (Stamford: Paul Watkins, 1992), 267–83 at 279–80; and Michelle P. Brown and Patricia Lovett, *The Historical Source Book for Scribes* (Toronto: University of Toronto Press, 1999), 76–7.

figures are tinted but not painted. At the bottom of the miniature is a monk, generally identified as Eadui Basan, the scribe of the Arundel Psalter, whose prostrate figure extends across the two arcades.[156] He offers a book to St Benedict, whose feet rest on Eadui's shoulders (and to think about the image from the direction of production, whom Eadui's shoulders support) and whose right foot the monk is embracing. The letters 'lib ps' [the b is crossed] visible on the proffered book identify it as 'lib<er> ps<almorum>,' the Psalter (Arundel 155) Eadui had copied. Across his brown tunic, he has a white belt on which is written 'zona humilitatis' [belt of humility]. Unlike the monks in the right-hand arcade, Eadui, the producer of the book, is fully coloured, and his extended body connects the two arcades. The other monks are, by contrast, incomplete, and Benedict points to the way they can perfect themselves. The pale monks in the right-hand arcade crowd forward, eyes intent on the saint, the lead monk holding out with both hands an open book on which are written the first words of the prologue to the *RSB*. Their eyes are fixed on the saint; while the saint's eyes, Christ-like, look out of the frame into the distance, his left hand points with its index finger to the first words of the proferred *RSB*, 'Ausculta, o fili, precept[a]' [Listen, o son, to the precepts].[157] The hand of God reaching down from the clouds at the top of the arch extends a scroll whose two sides read in Benedict's arcade 'Qui uos audit me audit' (Luke 10:16) [who hears you hears me] and for the monks 'Obedientes estote prepositi u<est>ro' (echoing Hebr. 13:17) [be obedient to your abbot]. This passage from the Gospel of Luke is cited twice in *RSB* 5, the chapter on obedience.[158]

The group of nine monks in the right-hand arcade reveal monastic identity by their dress: all in habits, six of the monks in the background are cowled; the front three have their heads uncovered to reveal their tonsures. If the habit may function as a general and passive identifier of simple monastic status, distinguishing secular from religious by marked ecclesiastical dress,[159] the composition of the group, the men's posture, and their action in proffering the book to Benedict proclaim both their community

156 Deshman, '*Benedictus Monarcha et Monachus,*' 219, identifies the prostrate figure as Æthelwold.

157 Hanslik, *Benedicti Regula*, prol. 1 (p. 1). The spelling of the manuscript differs from that of the standard edition. Unfortunately for Eadui, he has written, in a *lapsus calami*, 'precepti' (compare the form of 'ti' in 'prepositi' in the scroll above).

158 Hanslik, *Benedicti Regula,* cap. 5.6 and 15 (pp. 38–41).

159 Gale R. Owen-Crocker, *Dress in Anglo-Saxon England*, rev. ed. (Woodbridge: The Boydell Press, 2004), 326, points out that the cowl, 'like the tonsure, is diagnostic of monasticism ... The contrast between secular and ecclesiastical figures in art is immediate and obvious.'

Plate 1. (c) The British Library Board. London, British Library, Arundel 155, fol. 133r.

and their identity within the reformed Benedictine movement, rooted as these are in its textual culture. The gesture of the lead monk, holding open a book before Benedict, presents a scene of reading and learning, where Benedict teaches the primary lesson of the Rule. The monks group themselves behind the book, looking up to Benedict, who points, with his index finger, to the first symbolic line of the Prologue 'Ausculta o fili precept[a]': 'Listen, my son, to the precepts of your master, and incline the ears of your heart, and receive cheerfully the admonition of your benevolent Father, and carry it out effectually: that you may return to him through the labour of your obedience from whom you departed through the idleness of disobedience. Whoever renounces his own will, to you, therefore is my message directed. Take up the most powerful and excellent arms of obedience, you who are about to serve the true king, the Lord Christ.'[160] The grouping and the monks' posture define them as a community expressed in their attitude to the book and in their reverent presentation of it to Benedict. At the same time, Eadui Basan shows us book production in the presentation of a liturgical book to Benedict. That book, Arundel 155, containing the *Romanum* Psalter and monastic canticles, along with prayers, a calendar, and computus materials, offers the central texts for the liturgical observance of a reformed Benedictine monastery. The scene thus shows obedience and humility in a community's self-definition in the perpetuation of the life of the text and the reading and observation of the Rule.

Benedict, in pointing to 'Ausculta, o fili' commands hearing with obedient attention; 'fili' figures the remade filial relationship in the Benedictine monastic *familia*, marked and performed by the wearing of the habit, daily communal liturgical practice in the Mass and Office, and the reading and hearing of texts. As schoolboys would have learned from their Donatus (or from Ælfric's *Grammar*), the noun 'filius' was a noun of relationship ('nomen ad aliquid dictum') signifying in and of itself relation to a father, and in the context of the illustration, brothers in the monastic *familia*.[161]

---

160 See Hanslik, *Benedicti Regula*, prol. 1–3: 'Obsculta, o fili, praecepta magistri et inclina aurem cordis tui et admonitionem pii patris libenter excipe et efficaciter comple, ut ad eum per oboedientiae laborem redeas, a quo per inoboedientiae desidiam recesseras. Ad te ergo nunc mihi sermo dirigitur, quisquis abrenuntians propriis uoluntatibus domino Christo uero regi militaturus oboedientiae fortissima atque praeclara arma sumis.'

161 See Zupitza, *Aelfrics Grammatik und Glossar*, p. 12, lines 16–18, whose illustration is '*filius*, sunu.' On the language of grammatical analysis see Edna Rees Williams, 'Ælfric's Grammatical Terminology,' *PMLA* 73 (1958): 453–62 at 461–2, 'Table of Grammatical Terminology.' On such kinds of nouns see David W. Porter, ed.,

The monks in the right-hand arcade thus present Benedict with the sign of who they are, the Rule that specifies their way of life. The scroll, connecting the two arcades, distributes the two messages appropriately. To the left, in Benedict's arcade, the quotation of Luke 10:16 evokes the precepts in *RSB* 5.6 that connect obedience to a superior with obedience to God. The other side of the scroll, extending into the monks' arcade, commands obedience to their superior.

This then is the passage that the words written on the monks' book cite and evoke. The command to pay careful attention, the address by Benedict to a 'son' (so making the nine monks of the right arcade 'brothers'), must be understood within the context of personal formation that the *RSB* calls for. The crucial precept, the action from which all monastic virtues will proceed, is the call to obedience. Its centrality as a foundation of Benedictine monastic identity is underscored by the behaviour of the detested Sarabaites, those monks, the *RSB* explains, who live in groups of two or three, but have no abbot or rule to direct them:[162] 'for them, the pleasure of their own desires is law.'

By contrast, in the community ordered by the *RSB*, the prime labour is obedience, and the son who will perform this labour is the one who renounces his own will. His former state is construed as disobedience, presumably that condition inherited through the sin of the first parents, but also that 'idleness' of not working toward salvation. The Latin imperative 'ausculta' then is a critical key to the formation of the textual identity that is the subject of this chapter.

The practice of oblation was well established in Anglo-Saxon England. Its outlines are clear: the parents' promise, formalized by the ritual of oblation (where the child placed his offering and petition of admission on the altar), was irrevocable. The irreversible transfer of the child to the monastery was scripted in the parents' ritual promise and carefully coded in church law. Oblation, understood as the virtuous accession to the will of God, a praiseworthy sacrifice in the manner of Hannah, brought spiritual gain to the parents. For the children it was also understood to bring spiritual gain – in the form of a spiritual family and the promise of a celestial, eternal inheritance. But that spiritual family and inheritance came at a price: willing for oneself what had been willed by others. 'Esto quod

Excerptiones de Prisciano, II.10, p. 64, 'Nam dicendo "filium" patrem et dicendo "seruum" dominum quoque intellego.'

162 Hanslik, *Benedicti Regula*, 1.8 (p. 20): 'Qui bini aut terni aut certe singuli sine pastore, non dominicis, sed suis inclusi obilibus pro lege eis est desideriorum uoluptas.'

es' places that obligation in a larger, and deeply conservative, social vision, where the members of the three estates are understood to be fixed in their places. What the *Colloquy* tells its pupils is that they are no different: even desiring to be other is a sin and a shame. And so the *Colloquy*, in its operation as a normative text, demands that those who voice it desire to be what they are. But in this demand, the *Colloquy* blinds itself to the unstable contradiction at the centre of oblation – the demand that a child exchanged as an object will that exchange as a subject. The whip and the rod that marked the body of the writhing child thus looked beyond impressing his memory to shaping his will. And yet at the very moment of articulating 'Esto quod es' the Latin imperative itself imagines and fears an alternative world for the object of its command. Only against its will (as it were) does the *Colloquy*'s anxiety over an oblate's identity emerge in the very stuff – the form of language – that the text is trying to teach. Such anxiety over oblation makes a surprising appearance more than a century before the practice is formally discontinued in the twelfth century. Its anxiety boils over at the mid-point of the text, between the dialogue on the occupations and the more traditional catechesis on the routine of the monastic day, emerging at this point, I suggest, precisely as counter to the unpredictable desire that the fantasy of voicing other lives awakened in the children. Thereafter, the only *cræft* the children voice is that of a *munuccild*.

The three-part engine of the narrative of which Ælfric's comment is part – you are what you do; be what you are; be what you were made – shows us the *Colloquy* at work naturalizing young oblates into the textual identity of a reformed Benedictine monastery. The *Colloquy*'s imperatives of identity expose its contradictory expectations: that the oblate's identity is always already given but always in need of constructing. Its casual reference to whipping reminds us of the part such learning played in the bodily assumption of identity: that the shaping of memory was never far from the marking of bodies; that the training of the will was understood to require a propaedeutic pain. Its central occupation, the teaching of Latin, was understood as the foundation of the community's textual identity, without which neither knowledge nor belief could be continued. For the pupil to learn Latin was to participate in the shaping of who he was. Beyond all these things, the *Colloquy*'s imperatives shows us the installation in its pupils of a particular form of agent action, inextricably linked to their monastic identity, that understood complete obedience as the condition of freedom.

3 Edith's Choice

The Rule of St Benedict frames monastic life as the work of obedience, and in that understanding the imperatives of Ælfric's *Colloquy* call for its children's obedience in working to put on the life of religion required of them by their oblation. The naturalization of such a life was, the *Colloquy* insists, the labour of the classroom, where the textual identity specific to the Benedictine Reform in England was meant to be acquired. But we have seen the child's textual work, accompanied by a moral praxis designed to produce an obedient agent, raised the troubling question of the possibility of being other. By contrast with the adult Dunstan's existential moment in Osbern's theatre of choice, 'Esto quod es' in the *Colloquy* locates the moment of choice in the child oblate's past and, though the commitment was made by others, requires obedient accession of the will to its demands. This chapter approaches the nexus of obedience, identity, and agency from a complementary set of problems attendant on how the community recognizes irreversible religious identity and how that identity is understood to be freely chosen. In this chapter we return to the late eleventh century, this time in the writing of Goscelin of Saint-Bertin, for a fantasy of identity, commitment, and choice.

Goscelin of Saint-Bertin's ambitious *Vita S. Edithae* (ca 1080), though requested by the community of Wilton and by Herman, bishop of Ramsbury and Sherborne (1062–78), to whom Goscelin had been attached, is dedicated as 'primicias' [first fruits] to Lanfranc, archbishop of Canterbury (1077–89).[1]

1 André Wilmart, ed., 'La légende de Ste Édith en prose et vers par le moine Goscelin,' *AB* 56 (1938): 5–101, 265–307, at 38. Citations of the *uita* are to this edition. For Goscelin's career as a commissioned hagiographer see Thomas J. Hamilton, 'Goscelin of Canterbury: A Critical Study of His Life, Works and Accomplishments,' 2 vols. (PhD dissertation,

While offered in a commendatory prologue laced with modesty topoi, the composition was clearly intended to impress, combining as it does ornate prose with a number of poems in various metrical forms.[2] The time around 1080 brought personal and professional dislocation for Goscelin, following close upon the death of Bishop Herman, whom he had accompanied from Saint-Bertin to Sherborne. His patron's replacement, Osmund, whom Lanfranc had consecrated in 1079, was hostile to Goscelin and was likely responsible for his departure from the area. In commending his efforts to Lanfranc, then, Goscelin must have hoped that his achievement in the *Vita S. Edithae* would give the archbishop reason to notice him and that preferment to some stable position would follow.[3] In this he was disappointed.[4]

Although the *Vita S. Edithae* is a remarkable composition in several dimensions, drawing on liturgy, scripture, and oral history, one of the most striking features of its narrative is a fantasy ritual of commitment in which the saint chooses her future life. When his composition condenses two separate rites, oblation and consecration, to confect a ritual whose doubling reinforces the vows explicit in each, I argue that Goscelin is reacting to a fault line emerging in the self-representation of eleventh-century religious women in England. As he scripts a ritual in which King Edgar's infant daughter, Edith, 'takes the veil,' he has her action draw its meaning from the potent metonymy of veiling and a public drama of choice. But his narrative of her commitment, at once cloying and uneasy, sentimental and anxious, points away from the veil itself to a fracture in the production of religious identity that was emerging in various registers and from differing pressures. Most obviously and acutely, the aftermath of the Conquest,

---

University of Virginia, 1973), and more recently Frank Barlow, ed. and trans., *The Life of King Edward Who Rests at Westminster*, 2nd ed. (Oxford: Clarendon Press, 1992), Appendix C. For a global assessment of Goscelin's career and works see now Michael Lapidge and Rosalind C. Love, *The Latin Hagiography of England and Wales (600–1550)*, vol. 3 of *Hagiographies*, ed. Guy Philippart (Turnhout: Brepols, 2001), 203–325 at 225–33.

2 On the verse form see Wilmart, 'La légende,' 31–4.

3 Barlow, *The Life of King Edward*, 139–40. Sally N. Vaughn, *St Anselm and the Handmaidens of God: A Study of Anselm's Correspondence with Women* (Turnhout: Brepols, 2002), 176, associates the dedication with Lanfranc's self-description as 'novus Anglus.' Her redating of the composition of the *uita* to the 1070s (at 178) is not convincing.

4 On his wanderings following his dismissal from Sherborne, see Rosalind C. Love, ed. and trans., *Goscelin of Saint-Bertin: The Hagiography of the Female Saints of Ely*, OMT (Oxford: Clarendon Press, 2004), xx–xxi.

especially in its redistribution of property into the hands of 'new men' associated with the Norman king,[5] had a catastrophic effect on Anglo-Saxon elite families. Entrusting a daughter (and heiress) to a convent would appear to have acquired, in these circumstances, additional tactical properties in blocking inheritance and playing, perhaps, for time.[6] But religious life for women, while obviously affected by the broad social changes following the Conquest, had itself been slowly changing in the century before the Conquest, as endowments for convents dried up, the number of convents diminished, and alternate practices of religious commitment (that is, religious withdrawal outside the structure of convents) developed.[7] The fracture in the stability of women's religious identity that Goscelin's composition points to, even as he struggles to conceal it, emerges precisely from a tension between the ancient transformative and defining power of the veil to produce religious identity and the role of choice in the same process. As his flattering prologue to Lanfranc addresses the disruption in his own circumstances,[8] his work reacts to a different, and more consequential, disruption.

Though dedicated to Lanfranc, Goscelin's *uita* of a Wilton saint addresses as well the aristocratic inmates of the wealthiest convent in England in the wake of the disruption of the Norman Conquest.[9] Godiva, the abbess, and

---

5 H.R. Loyn, *The Governance of Anglo-Saxon England, 500–1087* (Stanford: Stanford University Press, 1984), 179–80, estimates that by 1086 a quarter of the landed wealth in England was held by about a dozen men, all of whom were personally connected to William.

6 On the retreat to nunneries see Barbara Yorke, *Nunneries and the Anglo-Saxon Royal Houses* (London: Continuum, 2003), 90.

7 See Patricia Halpin, 'Women Religious in Late Anglo-Saxon England,' *Haskins Society Journal* 6 (1994): 97–110. Sarah Foot, *Veiled Women: The Disappearance of Nuns from Anglo-Saxon England*, 2 vols. (Aldershot: Ashgate, 2000), I: 206, identifies the convents of the tenth and eleventh centuries in England: 'the royal women's houses of Wessex, namely Amesbury, Horton, Romsey, Shaftesbury, Wherwell, Wilton, and the Nunnaminster at Winchester, the royally-patronised Essex house at Barking, together with the single aristocratic foundation at Chatteris in Cambridgeshire.' Against these, she places the less structured (and virtually undocumented) arrangements of women who lived lives of religious withdrawal on family estates, as solitaries or in small groups, or lived in some association with male communities.

8 'Deuotus tuus coactus est longius peregrinari' [Your devoted one (scil. Goscelin) was forced to wander far away]. C.H. Talbot, ed., *The Liber Confortatorius of Goscelin of Saint Bertin*, Studia Anselmiana 37, Analecta Monastica, 3rd ser. (Rome: Herder, 1955), p. 29, line 25.

9 See Julia Crick, 'The Wealth, Patronage, and Connections of Women's Houses in Late Anglo-Saxon England,' *Revue Bénédictine* 109 (1999): 154–85, Table 1, 162–3. For a survey of the evidence see Foot, *Veiled Women*, II: 221–31.

other senior nuns had invited Goscelin to compose the *uita*, and they are complimented in the prologue as being 'tam fideles quam generose' [as faithful as they are of noble birth].[10] But the saint of Wilton whose life he commemorates for them was not merely noble but a royal daughter, who has much work to do in the present of the text. In a strategic, rhetorical sleight of hand, Goscelin erases the distance between the present moment of the work and the time of the saint it commemorates:

> ... uirgo Domini Editha, que in regno nata, ut ciuitas supra montem posita, que ex temporis uicinia – hesternum quippe regem fratris sui filium habuimus Edwardum, qui hodierno Willelmo reliquit imperium – tanta hodietenus signorum fulget presentia, tanta et externis et indigenis prerogat beneficia, ut sine uite eius relatione hec ad fidem meritorum deberent sufficere.[11]
>
> [Edith, virgin of the Lord, who was born in the kingdom as a city set upon a mountain, who from the nearness of time – for yesterday we had as King Edward, son of her brother, who left the throne to the present King William – up to the present moment shines with such a presence of signs and gives such benefactions to both foreigners and natives, that these things should suffice for the truth of her merits without this account of her life.]

Just as the miracles Edith is shown to have performed within the memory of the nuns connect the present of the text with the past of Edith's own life, so too does the passing of the throne from Edward to William collapse time politically and religiously and connect the present reign to the illustrious line of King Edgar, Edith's father. The effects of this rhetorical strategy erase the Conquest by refiguring its violent breaks as a bequeathal and, at the same time, link Edith (as Edward's aunt) to William

---

10 Wilmart, 'La légende,' cap. 1, pp. 36–7. This edition is based on Oxford, Bodleian Library, Rawlinson C. 938, fols. 1–29, a thirteenth-century manuscript, but Wilmart supplements where pertinent with what appears to have been revisions in Cardiff, Public Library, I. 381, fols. 81–120 (early twelfth century). The Rawlinson MS has the preface to Lanfranc, which is missing from the version in Cardiff. Stephanie Hollis argues that the Cardiff version, representing Goscelin's final intentions, was meant particularly for the nuns of Wilton and that the shorter, earlier version (that with the prologue) was originally meant for Lanfranc. See Stephanie Hollis, ed., with W.R. Barnes, Rebecca Hayward, Kathleen Loncar, and Michael Wright, *Writing the Wilton Women: Goscelin's 'Legend of Edith' and 'Liber confortatorius,'* Medieval Women: Texts and Contexts 9 (Turnhout: Brepols, 2004), 238–44. Their translation of the *uita* (by Michael Wright and Kathleen Loncar) is made from the Cardiff version. I note material differences in the two versions as necessary.

11 Wilmart, 'La légende,' cap. 1, p. 36.

and William (through her) to Edgar. But the collapsing of time through Edith's royal blood makes a further link in the moment of Norman *imperium,* by connecting the nuns of Wilton, through their patron saint, to the glory of the Benedictine Reform.

Goscelin is careful to portray Edith as a saint in the midst of the great saints of the tenth-century English Benedictine Reform. Æthelwold and Dunstan's roles as her teachers and protectors place her at the centre of the accomplished Reform: 'Huius etiam aule sue splendidissime et intimi sacrarii rex glorie quo introiret precipuos Dunstanum et Adeluuoldum ediles et edituos habuit'[12] [She also had the distinguished Dunstan and Æthelwold as custodians and sacristans of her most splendid shrine and interior sanctuary into which the king of glory would enter]. And while acting as guardians and protectors of her virginity, Dunstan and Æthelwold served to increase her ardour for eternal nuptials. In the spiritual utopia in which Goscelin portrays Edith, the two reforming bishops are joined by other famous saints of the Reform: Oswald of York, Ælfheah (Elphege), the martyred archbishop of Canterbury (d. 1012), Ælfstan, bishop of Ramsbury, 'aliique eclesiarum duces et ministri religiosi, quorum copia tunc pollebat Anglia, Edgari regis Deo deuotissimi almique Dunstani instantia'[13] [and other princes of the church and those in holy orders, a wealth of whom then flourished in England, at the direction of Edgar – a king most devoted to God – and the holy Dunstan].[14] While erasing the interval of the Conquest and compressing the time between William and Edgar, Goscelin makes Edith a central focus of the Benedictine Reform, portrayed as a golden age of saints, to which the women of Wilton have access through their patron saint. In recasting the at times ambiguous evidence of Edith's religious vocation, Goscelin also crafts a powerful narrative of her identity as a product of choice. In so doing, he is careful to contain signs of what we might be tempted to identify as agency, expressed at various moments as transgression of the very Benedictine principles he so carefully attributes to her.

Wilton had had strong associations with the West-Saxon royal family and in the eleventh century had received considerable royal patronage.[15]

---

12 Ibid., cap. 9, p. 57.

13 Ibid., cap. 9, pp. 57–8.

14 In the longer version, Goscelin adds the detail that Ælfstan plunged his hand into the stewpot, proving his great obedience. Goscelin resolves the tension in the relation between abbot and monk in Wulfstan's earlier account by having Ælfstan act 'ad alludentem uocem preceptoris' [on the jesting word of his superior (cap. 9, p. 58)].

15 Foot, *Veiled Women*, II: 224–5.

From what we know of its immates at the time of Goscelin's writing, Wilton had girls and women placed within its walls for various reasons, religious and secular – education, safe-keeping, religious commitment, or control of inheritance. Eve, later to become a recluse at St Eutrope in Angers, was a nun at Wilton, having been entrusted to that convent by her parents.[16] Gunhild (daughter of King Harold II), whose departure in 1093 would be a cause célèbre, was still, perhaps, in 1080, an inmate of that house, although the circumstances of her entrance are unknown.[17] Her older sister, Gyða, having left England, possibly with three of her brothers, was later given in marriage by King Svein of Denmark to Vladimir Monomakh, Russian prince of Smolensk. But as we will see, Gunhild had been left behind in England.[18] In the social disorder attendant upon the Conquest, women, moved by either familial or personal strategic considerations, sought refuge in convents throughout England to protect themselves from acquisitive Norman invaders.[19] Taking the veil, apparently, was a final, tactical manoeuvre. Edith/Matilda, later queen of Henry I, gives fear of the Normans as the reason for her aunt's overeager (and unwelcome) veiling when she was under her supervision.[20] Recognizing the strategy, Lanfranc's letter to Gundulf, bishop of Rochester, in the matter of the status of certain *sanctimoniales*, pronounced *timor Francigenarum* a questionable motive for withdrawing to a convent.[21] Such political and religious pressures on convents in late eleventh-century England, pressures that would provoke episcopal decisions balancing the meaning of the veil against the question of choice, form the immediate backdrop to Goscelin's overdetermined scene of choice.

---

16 Goscelin describes his relationship with Eve in the *Liber confortatorius*. See Talbot, *Liber Confortatorius*. André Wilmart identifies Eve in 'Ève et Goscelin (I),' *Revue Bénédictine* 46 (1934): 414–38, and 'Ève et Goscelin (II),' *Revue Bénédictine* 50 (1938): 42–83. See below, chapter 5.

17 For Gunhild, see below, chapter 4. Edith/Matilda (?b. ca 1080), daughter of St Margaret and Malcolm III of Scotland and the future wife of Henry I, would later live for a time at Wilton. Richard Sharpe, 'King Harold's Daughter,' *The Haskins Society Journal* 19 (2007): 1–27, at 23–4, has suggested moving the date of Gunhild's departure forward to the 1070s. On these matters see below, pp. 173–6.

18 See Kelly DeVries, *The Norwegian Invasion of England in 1066* (Woodbridge: The Boydell Press, 1999), 159. See also Sharpe, 'King Harold's Daughter,' 25 and n. 109.

19 See Eleanor Searle, 'Women and the Legitimisation of Succession at the Norman Conquest,' *ANS* 3 (1981 [for 1980]): 159–70 and 226–9.

20 See below, pp. 173–6.

21 On the date of the letter see below, n. 66.

Choice and Necessity

The eleventh- and early twelfth-century accounts of King Edgar's youth do not always gratify by clarity, although they appear to share an interest in the challenges the king presented to young women's virtue. The entry for 964 in John of Worcester's *Chronicle* recording Edgar's marital history and offspring, after naming his legitimate sons (by his wives Æthelflæd Eneda and Ælfthryth), mentions his daughter by St Wulfthryth, Edith, 'a virgin most devoted to God.'[22] However discreet John of Worcester's account, it is doubtful that Edgar married Wulfthryth.[23] Using information from Osbern's *uita* of Dunstan, William of Malmesbury writes a confused account of two royal sexual adventures connected with the king's consort in which Edgar rapes an unnamed nun and abducts a young woman who had futilely veiled herself 'timore regis.'[24] In his *uita* of another saint associated with Wilton, Goscelin gives a sharper though hardly less lurid narrative of Edgar's adventures by making his original object St Wulfhild, a consecrated virgin of that house.[25] Though not successful in his plot to spoil Wulfhild, Edgar did not leave Wilton empty-handed, as Goscelin records the story, for the saint's cousin, Wulfthryth, a secular inmate of the same convent, left with Edgar and became the mother of his daughter

22 R.R. Darlington and P. McGurk, eds., Jennifer Bray and P. McGurk, trans., *The Chronicle of John of Worcester*, 3 vols., OMT (Oxford: Clarendon Press, 1995–), II: 416–17. See also R.C. Love, 'Eadgyth [Edith], St,' in *The Blackwell Encyclopaedia of Anglo-Saxon England*, ed. Michael Lapidge, John Blair, Simon Keynes, and Donald Scragg (Oxford: Blackwell, 1999), 150.

23 Barbara Yorke, 'The Legitimacy of St Edith,' *Haskins Society Journal* 11 (2003 for 1998): 97–113, has argued, on the basis of Goscelin's *uita*, that Edgar married Wulfthryth, however briefly. Her claim that the *uita* 'merely begins with the fact of the marriage' (100–1) requires taking Goscelin's rhetoric at face value. Yorke is surely correct, however, in believing that the *uita*'s 'preoccupation with Edith's status could be seen as suggesting a certain defensiveness in the community [scil. Wilton] on this subject' (107).

24 R.A.B. Mynors, R.M. Thomson, and M. Winterbottom, eds. and trans., *William of Malmesbury: Gesta Regum Anglorum*, 2 vols., OMT (Oxford: Clarendon Press, 1998), vol. 1, II.159.1. His subsequent account of Edith's mother (II.159.2) misnames Wulfthryth 'Wlfrida.' The unnamed nun would seem to have been Wulfhild. Osbern's *Vita S. Dunstani*, cap. 35 (William Stubbs, ed., *Memorials of Saint Dunstan Archbishop of Canterbury*, RS 63 [London, 1874], p. 111) records Dunstan's anger at Edgar's debauching a veiled virgin.

25 M. Esposito, 'La vie de sainte Vulfhilde par Goscelin de Cantorbéry,' *Analecta Bollandiana* 32 (1913): 10–26 at 17. St Wulfhild became, for a time, abbess of Barking, and for a while held three abbacies simultaneously. On St Wulfhild and Barking, see Crick, 'Wealth, Patronage, and Connections,' 173.

Edith. Within a short time of the birth, Wulfthryth returned to Wilton with her daughter and took the veil. She and Edith are remembered thereafter for lives of exemplary sanctity and eventual sainthood. By vivid contrast, Edgar's queen, Ælfthryth, whom he married after Wulfthryth's retirement to Wilton, was remembered as a wicked step-mother and evil queen.[26] This indecorous episode in Edgar's life, so unbecoming the royal pillar of the Benedictine Reform, is, nonetheless, grist for Goscelin's hagiographic mill, permitting him to dramatize a woman's entrance into the religious life as a sacrificial and heroic choice. And as the virgin's frantic veiling in William of Malmesbury's account makes clear, what choice there might have been would have been exercised within a very narrow range of options.

In the *Vita S. Edithae*, his extended account of the life of Edgar's daughter, Goscelin labours rhetorically to work around the question of marriage between Edgar and Wulfthryth. Had they actually been married, her retirement to the convent would have been awkward but not impossible.[27] Had she been veiled at the time of Edgar's visit, however, her removal from Wilton would have occasioned even greater scandal than it did. Goscelin negotiates both difficulties:

> Hanc rex, ut Iacob Rachel dilexerat; hanc, splendidius nobilium puellarum sidus, de ipsis scolis diuina dispensatione assumserat, et insolubilibus uotis regno sociauerat; sed sola Christi caritas hos nexus dissoluere poterat.[28]
>
> [The king had loved her as Jacob loved Rachel; he had taken her from that school by divine guidance, a brilliant star among noble girls, and united her to the throne by indissoluble vows; but the love of Christ alone was able to dissolve these bonds.]

26 See Barbara Yorke, 'The Women in Edgar's Life,' in *Edgar, King of the English 959–975*, ed. Donald Scragg (Woodbridge, Suffolk: Boydell Press, 2008), 143–57 at 153–54.

27 On the possibility of marital separation because of a decision to enter religious life see James A. Brundage, *Law, Sex, and Christian Society in Medieval Europe* (Chicago: University of Chicago Press, 1987), p. 202 and n. 133. For comment on the canonical background to Ælfric's late tenth-century observations on the necessity of the husband's consent for a wife to become a nun (*LS* II. 36, lines 387–9) see Peter Jackson, 'Ælfric and the Purpose of Christian Marriage: A Reconsideration of the *Life of Æthelthryth*, lines 120–30,' *ASE* 29 (2000): 235–60. Wulfstan recorded two canons on the separation of married parties when one partner embraces the religious life in his so-called 'Commonplace Book.' See J.E. Cross and Andrew Hamer, eds., *Wulfstan's Canon Law Collection*, Anglo-Saxon Texts 1 (Cambridge: D.S. Brewer, 1999), Recension A, item 93; Recension B, item 129.

28 Wilmart, 'La légende,' cap. 2, p. 41.

This sentence, so straightforward in its assertion of divine direction, operates by a theological sleight of hand. That divine guidance directed Edgar's removal of Wulfthryth from Wilton covers over the fact that Edgar's actions otherwise look very much like rape.[29] His love, sealed by indissoluble vows, proves to be something less than marriage: she is joined to the throne, rather than the king. Nonetheless, Goscelin manages simultaneously to suggest that the bonds were nuptial, by evoking 'caritas Christi' to imply that the only way to break them was by the canonical manoeuvre of permitting a wife to withdraw to the convent.[30] Wulfthryth, former virgin, not quite wife, had the additional, political disadvantage of bearing a daughter. And while Goscelin nowhere suggests that Wulfthryth had chosen to leave Wilton with Edgar, he gives her a powerful, if contextually alarming, ability to choose to leave him: she cuts off the young king's 'sweet feelings' as a Judith ('Adolescentula, adolescentis regis dulces affectus et florentissimum decorem ut fortis Iudith abscidit').[31] The actual separation of the two, Goscelin continues, was accomplished by Bishop Æthelwold, wielding the sword of Christ.[32] Evoking St Paul on the division of parent

29 In a general survey of Anglo-Saxon law on violence against women, Julie Coleman, 'Rape in Anglo-Saxon England,' in *Violence and Society in the Early Medieval West*, ed. Guy Halsall (Woodbridge: Boydell Press, 1998), 193–204 at 194, observes: '[a]cts which we would consider as abduction, elopement or adultery are often grouped with rape by the Anglo-Saxons, and so it is frequently impossible to determine from the context whether or not the woman was a consenting party.' Laws against removing nuns from convents appear repeatedly in the legislation of Anglo-Saxon kings. See, for example, Alfred 18, I Edmund 4, Ethelred at King's Enham 39, the Northumbrian Priests' Law 63, Cnut (Christmas 1020–2) 50.1. These are usefully printed with translations in Dorothy Whitelock, Martin Brett, and C.N.L. Brooke, eds., *Councils and Synods with Other Documents Relating to the English Church*, 2 vols. (Oxford: Clarendon Press, 1981), I: 28, 63, 372, 466, 497.

30 Had they actually been married, the canonical sword that Æthelwold wielded might have had to perform some delicate surgery. Regino of Prüm's early tenth-century compilation *Libri duo de synodalibus causis et disciplinis ecclesiasticis*, II.cviii, cx (PL 132.305–6), gives contradictory regulations on the ability of the spouse to remarry. Burchard's early eleventh-century *Decretum* (IX.45–7) specifies that the lay spouse might not remarry after the other's entry into religious life (PL 140.822).

31 Wilmart, 'La légende,' cap. 2, p. 42. See Judith 9:13–14: 'Capiatur laqueo oculorum suorum in me, et percuties eum ex labiis charitatis meae. Da mihi in animo constantiam, ut contemnam illum: et virtutem, ut evertam illum' [Let him be caught in the net of his own eyes in my regard, and do thou strike him by the graces of the words of my lips. Give me constancy in my mind, that I may despise him: and fortitude that I may overthrow him]. See also the beheading, Judith 13:10.

32 Hebr. 4:12. But see Ambrose, *De uirginitate, liber unus*, I.3 (ed. Ignazio Cazzaniga [Turin: In aedibus Io. Bapt. Paraviae, 1954], 2–3) (PL 16.266–7).

and child, bone and marrow, flesh and spirit, Æthelwold's intervention might cut either way: aimed to separate an illicit union as well as to enable Wulfthryth's retirement from the world. But as Goscelin labours to 'maken vertu of necessitee,' he makes Wulfthryth the courageous woman of Proverbs 31:10, and when her transformation is effected by assuming the habit of religion, she is further changed from a mother in the flesh to the spiritual mother of a virgin troop ('et uirgineo contubernio eiusdem monasterii mater preficeretur spiritualis').[33]

Goscelin's graceful rhetorical recasting of Wulfthryth's situation as cast-off narrates in positive fashion a woman's (forced?) retirement from the world. Considering the narrow range of time between the presumed date of the death of Edgar's first wife, Æthelflæd (ca 960), and his marriage to Ælfthryth (964–5), the joining of Wulfthryth 'to the throne' must have been fairly up-tempo, and her departure following the birth of Edith swift.[34] Given Goscelin's relations with the convent at Wilton it is reasonable to assume a didactic as well as accommodating interest in presenting his female audience with an account of the religious vocations of their saints that would speak as well to issues affecting their own lives.[35] And his dedication suggests that he hoped Lanfranc would approve. Goscelin's handling of the circumstances of Wulfthryth's vocation offers both background and counterpoint to his presentation of her virgin daughter's life. Edith, distinguished from birth by the appearance of a celestial light that illuminated her parents' bedchamber, would be distinguished yet again by divine favour that directs the future course of her life. The royal saint, who died at twenty-three (?961–84), was to spend her entire life at Wilton, and at each point in his narrative, Goscelin is at pains to illustrate that the direction of her life was by her choice. It is the nature of that choice and its implications for the question of agency and the identity of women religious in the eleventh century that Goscelin's fantasy scene in cap. 5 elaborates for us.

In commemorating the birth of the saint (cap. 3), Goscelin prepares the two themes that he will develop and fuse in the staging of Edith's choice.

33 Wilmart, 'La légende,' cap. 4, p. 43.

34 On the estimated dates see Yorke, 'The Women in Edgar's Life,' 144–5.

35 On Goscelin's Wilton audience and patronesses see Georges Whalen, 'Patronage Engendered: How Goscelin Allayed the Concerns of Nuns' Discriminatory Public,' in *Women, the Book and the Godly: Selected Proceedings of the St Hilda's Conference, 1993*, vol. 1, ed. Lesley Smith and Jane H.M. Taylor (Cambridge: D.S. Brewer, 1995), 123–35 esp. 128–9.

The 'solare iubar' that illuminates the royal bedchamber ('thalamum') to mark her birth, evokes for Goscelin all the imagery connected with the ritual of consecrating virgins. This sign of celestial light suggests proleptically both the candles a girl would carry during her consecration ('iam lampadem suam accendere, iam sponso uisa est occurrere uelle,' as the wise virgins of Matt. 25:1–13) and the sun of her divine spouse, coming out of his bedchamber ('ipse tanquam sponsus procedens de thalamo suo' [Ps. 18.6]). But the thematics of a consecrated virgin's ritual marriage to the divine spouse are inflected by a second discourse, that of child oblation, where the actors are primarily the parents. Here Edith's status as first born ('patris primogenita et matris ... unigenita') makes her a particularly pleasing offering to God as first fruits, and Goscelin reads Edgar's paternal role through Abraham's sacrifice. Both themes, of course, significantly interpret Wulfthryth's return to Wilton with her daughter as an active and praiseworthy choice rather than the default ending of an unfortunate liaison. In the narrative logic of the *Vita S. Edithae*, Edgar does not put an inconvenient concubine away; rather, he accedes to the higher calling of his would-be spouse and heroically sacrifices his first child as 'dulces primitias ... germinis sui.' Yet the *uita*'s emphasis on his virgin daughter requires her to make her own heroic sacrifice.

The Choice of a Veil

Chapter 5 of the *Vita* presents an extraordinary scene of election and decision, God's will and a saint's obedience, in which child, parents, convent, court, church, and heaven are imagined to work in untroubled harmony. This chapter, in prose with a following verse section, turns around an elaborate device of placing the two-year-old Edith before an array of objects and interpreting her selection:

> Pretenditur pauimento insigne pallium ad gradus autentici altaris summe Dei genitricis, quasi ante tronum et pedes diuine maiestatis. Diuersa infunditur opulentia, temporalis et eterna. Regalis dignitas et matronarum ambitus coronulas aureas, aurotextas clamides, gemmatas trabeas, armillas, anulos, monilia uarieque radiantia rerum ornamenta, – materna fides apponit nigrum sanctimonie uelum, calicem et patenam dominice passionis ferculum, celestis oraculi psalterium.[36]

36 Wilmart, 'La légende,' cap. 5, p. 44.

> [A splendid covering is spread on the pavement at the steps of the true altar of the most high mother of God, as if before the throne and feet of divine majesty. It is strewn with various riches, temporal and eternal. The king and the surrounding womenfolk [place there] little golden crowns, cloaks in cloth of gold, jewelled ceremonial robes, bracelets, rings, necklaces and ornaments of wealth shining in different colours – whereas the faithful mother places the black veil of the nun, a chalice and a paten, the dish of the lord's passion, and a psalter of divine prophecy.]

The objects placed before the baby Edith index the two lives presented to her by each of her parents. Her father offers her power and wealth, and Goscelin makes much of her royal birth ('uirgo Domini Editha ... in regno nata') and connection to her half-brothers, Kings Edward and Ethelred.[37] After Edward's untimely death, Goscelin has the leading men of England demand that Edith leave Wilton to assume the rule of England.[38] But the objects Edgar causes to be placed on the cloth are not merely signs of his wealth, power, and rule. Those costly, luxurious objects anchor the wearer to the transitory world. In vivid contrast to the splendid riot of colours, textures, and shapes on the cloth, Wulfthryth proffers the objects defining her own newly embraced identity. In withdrawing to Wilton, Wulfthryth put off the world and received the habit of religion: 'pro aurotexta purpura induitur nigra peregrinantis a Domino tunica, pro aureis monilibus ornatur pudore, pro regali diademate fusco uelatur flammeolo'[39] [Instead of purple and cloth of gold, she was clothed in the black tunic of one absent from the Lord (2 Cor. 5:6), instead of in golden necklaces she was adorned in modesty, instead of a royal diadem she was covered in a dark bridal veil]. If her father offers Edith the world her mother left behind, Wulfthryth offers her daughter her own life in the objects she lays before her.

With the stage set for Edith's choice, Goscelin surrounds the child with witnesses of various sorts, engaged together in a prayer for divine guidance. Edgar, with the crowd of bishops who had accompanied his royal progress to Wilton, and Wulfthryth, with a church full of her sisters in

37 Ibid., cap. 1, p. 36, and references to her royal birth are ubiquitous. References to her brothers are made in cap. 2 (p. 40), cap. 10 (p. 64), and cap. 18 (pp. 82–3).

38 Ibid., cap. 19, p. 85: 'Itaque circumdant, instant, implorant, increpitant, denique uim facere gestiunt.' In a gesture to address the canonical problem posed by secularizing a professed nun, the magnates propose to replace Edith in the convent with one of their daughters (p. 84).

39 Wilmart, 'La légende,' cap. 4, p. 43.

Christ, pray 'ut prescia omnium diuinitas declarare dignaretur quam uitam indocilis etas presenti electione sortiretur'[40] [that the divinity foreknowing all things would deign to reveal what life her untutored age would select in the present choice]. In praying to know her choice they pray to know what she will be. The preparatory prayer, use of divination to determine a vow of chastity, the outcome understood as God's will, and, crucially, the child functioning as the medium of the revelation are central components shared with the practice of biblical *sortilegium* found in various texts from the fourth through the ninth centuries.[41] In cases where an extremely young child is the medium of revelation in the casting of lots (an *infans* too young to speak or read), the child is shown miraculously speaking or reading the name of the one chosen.[42] Yet the differences between biblical sortilege and Edith's scene of choice are equally distinctive: in the former, the Bible or liturgical books are used to convey the will of God through the choice of a directing text (as in Augustine's famous scene of 'tolle, lege' in the *Confessions*), and the child is the medium of a decision affecting someone else.[43] In the latter, however, Edith selects not a text or a lot but an object whose choice is encoded in an overdetermined gesture revelatory by its seeming impossibility:

> Sistitur ergo bima infantula ut in florido prato hostia lactea, ut in diuina libra dragma aurea. Que, ut arca Dei a dextris et a sinistris inreflexa, recto impetu de medio splendencium colorum solum uelum excipit et pro corona capiti imponit. Sola sanctitatis pignera eripit, in sacris suis Christum eligit, in sacro habitu Christum induit; cetera rerum insignia fatuis seculi uirginibus intacta relinquit.[44]
>
> [Accordingly, the child of two is set as a milky-white sacrifice in a flowering field, as a golden drachma in the divine scales. Just as the ark of God

40 Ibid., cap. 5, p. 44.

41 Pierre Courcelle, 'L'enfant et les "sorts bibliques,"' *Vigiliae Christianae* 7 (1953): 194–220 at 210.

42 Ibid., 202.

43 See James J. O'Donnell, ed., *Augustine, Confessions,* 3 vols. (Oxford: Clarendon Press, 1992), VIII.12.29 (vol. 1, p. 101): 'Dicebam haec et flebam amarissima contritione cordis mei. et ecce audio vocem de vicina domo cum cantu dicentis et crebro repetentis, quasi pueri an puellae, nescio: "tolle lege, tolle lege"' [I was speaking of these things and weeping from the bitter affliction of my heart, and suddenly I hear a voice from a nearby house with the sing-song of one saying and repeating again and again, whether a boy or a girl, I don't know: 'take up and read, take up and read']. See also O'Donnell's comment on the ambiguities of this passage at vol. 3, pp. 61–5.

44 Wilmart, 'La légende,' cap. 5, pp. 44–5.

did not deviate from the left or the right, from the middle of the splendid colours by a right impulse she picked out only the veil and placed it on her head instead of a crown. She took up only the pledges of sanctity; chose Christ in his holy objects, put on Christ in the sacred habit, and left untouched the other signs of things for the foolish virgins of the world.]

Through 'hostia' and 'velum' Goscelin binds Edith again in the doubled strands of his themes. Through oblation, Edith is made the passive sacrifice of her parents, and through the veil she is portrayed as an agent uniting herself to Christ.[45] The imagined ritual of cap. 5 thus fantasizes an untroubled mapping of the two roads to religious life by representing choice simultaneously as identical individual, parental, communal, and divine acts.

Goscelin himself provides a set of glosses on the scene of Edith's choice, offering a number of biblical precedents where holy men consult God and receive an answer. In the first of his examples God himself reveals to Abraham the promise of a son, and Abraham negotiates with God on behalf of the just in Sodom (Gen. 18:1–14; 20–33). Goscelin next offers Abraham's servant, sent to find a wife for Isaac (Gen. 24:12–27). When Rebecca's replies match the script the servant had communicated to God, Abraham's servant adores God in recognition of the sign he had been given. Similarly, Gedeon (Judges 6:36–40) specifies the way in which he will know God's purpose and receives in the sign of the dewy fleece confirmation that he will save Israel. David asks God directly if he should fight the Philistines at Ceila (1 Kings 23:2) and receives an affirmative answer. Like Gedeon, Ezechias specifies the sign by which he will know that

45 By contrast, when Osbert of Clare borrows this device for his *Vita sancte Edburge uirginis*, to shore up the validity of parental oblation, he does not include the veil along with the liturgical furnishings Eadburga is offered. Susan J. Ridyard edits this *uita* in *The Royal Saints of Anglo-Saxon England: A Study of West Saxon and East Anglian Cults* (Cambridge: Cambridge University Press, 1988), Appendix 1, pp. 253–308 at 265. She would date the composition to the 1120s or perhaps after (p. 18 n. 19). Barbara Yorke, '"Sisters under the Skin"? Anglo-Saxon Nuns and Nunneries in Southern England,' *Reading Medieval Studies* 15 (1989): 95–117 at 102 and n. 47, states that 'it was a convention of saints' lives that the embryonic saints were presented with a choice between secular and ecclesiastical items and always chose the latter,' but her only examples are Edith and Eadburga. The miraculous appearance of a veil on St Austreberta's head when she looks at herself in a pool of water confirms the saint in her vocation, but does not give us Edith's choice (*BHL* 832) (*Acta SS*, 10 February [February II]), cap. 6, col. 420.

God will heal him of his illness, and he receives the sign of the sun moving backwards ten degrees (4 Kings 20:9–11). Finally, Goscelin cites Acts 1: 24–6, in which Matthias is selected to replace Judas by the casting of lots.

Of these several biblical examples in which God reveals his will, two contain signs of events to come (e.g., the promise of Isaac, the healing of Ezechias), and two confirm a course of action (David's or Gedeon's success in battle). In the two instances of a choice to be made by the individual praying for guidance (Abraham's servant and Peter), that 'choice' is actually the discovery of a third party (Rebecca or Matthias). These examples, meant to justify and naturalize by biblical precedent the commitment of Edith to the religious life, reveal instead how peculiar the scene of Edith's choice is.

'Edytha nubit paruo regi paruula'

By contrast with Eadburga's 'choice' (in Osbert of Clare's borrowed scene, in which the veil does not appear among the liturgical objects on display), Goscelin's tiny saint takes a further, potent action in veiling herself: 'solum uelum excipit et pro corona capiti imponit' [she picked out only the veil and placed it on her head instead of a crown]. 'Taking the veil' is the powerful metonym for a woman's entry into religious life, and wearing the veil sets her apart by defining her as *sponsa Christi.* As the *ordo* of consecration makes clear, the placing of the veil on the virgin's head is the climactic moment in this ritual of transition.[46] In a consecration, the virgin is given to the bishop by her parents along with their offering. In a gesture borrowed from the ritual of oblation, the virgin's hand is wrapped in the altar cloth when she is given to the bishop by her parents for consecration during the Mass.[47] When the virgin retires to change into her blessed habit, the bishop retains the veil for the climax of the consecration ceremony. As he places the veil on her head, the bishop charges her to wear it without stain before the tribunal of God. She then begins the antiphon 'Induit me Dominus cyclade auro texta,' to which the rest of the community of nuns

46 *Ordines* for consecrating virgins who will be cloistered are proper to pontificals in the eleventh century. For a full discussion of the rites of consecration and their implications see below, chapter 4.

47 Mayke de Jong notes the indebtedness of this ritual action to the ceremony of a boy's oblation in *In Samuel's Image: Child Oblation in the Early Medieval West* (Leiden: E.J. Brill, 1996), 184, although she is incorrect in believing that this form of consecration in the PRG applies to consecrated virgins who will remain in the world.

join in. If more than one girl is to be consecrated, this portion of the ceremony is repeated serially. Such consecrations were so solemn that they were canonically reserved to the bishop himself.[48]

The veil is the metonym for both the virgin's dedicated state and the process of consecration itself.[49] It is the performative sign by which one reads the identity of an otherwise unknown woman. The English monastic sign language, which Debby Banham dates to the Benedictine Reform, illustrates just such a function in its sign for 'nuns' – stroking down along the cheeks 'on þæs haligryftes tacnunge' [in the sign of the veil].[50] However, Edith's act, though accepted by those surrounding her as definitive, encodes the choice of a canonical adult, and required special legal definition. When Goscelin has Edith 'velum ... capiti imponit,' he writes his fantasy of consecration in the canonical language that defines and constrains dedicated virgins vis-à-vis the rights of parents and guardians: 'Virgines quae ante XII annos, insciis mundiburdis suis, sacrum velamen capiti suo imposuerint, et illi mundiburdi annum et diem hoc tacendo consenserint, in sancto proposito permaneant'[51] [Virgins under twelve years of age who have placed the holy veil on their head without the knowledge of their guardians must remain in their vow if their guardians have consented to it by their silence for a year and a day]. This widely cited canon, specifying

48 That this privilege was jealously guarded is illustrated by Burchard, *Decretum* VIII.17 (PL 140.795) forbidding abbesses to veil would-be nuns. Gneuss, *Handlist*, no. 317, London, BL, Cotton Claudius C. vi, fols. 8–169, is a continental copy of Burchard's *Decretum*. Gneuss dates the manuscript to s. xi med. (after 1049), and gives the provenance in England as 'Canterbury CC?'

49 Hence in the *ordines* of consecration 'puellae uelandae' describes those women about to be consecrated, and 'mittere' or 'imponere uelum' makes the bishop's gesture stand in for the act of consecration. On 'uelare' as a synonym of 'consecrare' see René Metz, 'Les conditions juridiques de la consécration des vierges dans la liturgie latine des origines à nos jours,' *Revue de droit canonique* 1 (1951): 261–80 at 266 n. 20.

50 London, BL, Cotton Tiberius A. iii [Ker, *Catalogue*, no. 186; Gneuss, *Handlist*, no. 363, s. xi med., Christ Church, Canterbury]. See Debbie Banham, ed., *Monasteriales Indicia: The Anglo-Saxon Monastic Sign Language* (Hockwold-cum-Wilton, Norfolk: Anglo-Saxon Books, 1991), item 122, pp. 46 and 81. I have closed the space between *halig* and *ryftes* in Banham's text.

51 Burchard, *Decretum* VIII.10 (PL 140.794). At VIII.98 (PL 140.812), Burchard offers a slightly different formulation, found in Regino of Prüm, *Libri duo de synodalibus causis*, II.xxxviii (PL 132.392), citing the Council of Tribur (Germany), 895, cap. 24. Gratian, *Decretum* (Pars II, C. 20 q. 2 c. 2), cites this canon on questions of parental and individual consent in oblation. See Emil Friedberg, ed., *Corpus Iuris Canonici*, vol. 1, *Decretum Magistri Gratiani* (Leipzig, 1879), pp. 847–8.

at times 'parentes' at times 'mundiburdi' [guardians] establishes the age of consent for a girl and recognizes the performative power of the veil by its ability to override a parent's or guardian's rights over an underage girl. The witnesses provided for Edith's ritual (proper to both oblations and to consecrations), there to guarantee the binding force of the commitment, suggest Goscelin's awareness of the relevant canons.

'Velum ... imponit' are also words that transform Edith's oblation into a consecration and prepare rhetorically for the epithalamium celebrating her solemn marriage to Christ. Goscelin's negotiation of her tender age within the traditional language of the virgin's epithalamium produces the wedding of nursing infants with the Virgin Mary as *pronuba.*

Centena uos hinc paruulorum milia,
Herodiana mactat quos uesania,
Dulces amici sponsi collactanei,
Fouete: lactens sponsam duxit lacteam.[52]

[You hundred thousand little ones here whom Herod's madness sacrificed, sweet friends, foster-brothers to the groom, protect them: nursling he has married a nursling spouse.]

Here, the Holy Innocents, slaughtered by Herod to get to Christ, become the witnesses to the divine marriage of baby Jesus to baby Edith, imagined to take place in the stable in Bethlehem ('Presepe regi celi thalamus ponitur' [line 10]). The repeated emphasis on their tender age – tiny ('Edytha nubit paruo regi paruula' [14]; 'Paruamque Christo ferte Editham paruulo'[24]) and unweaned ('lactens ... lacteam' [4]; 'quem ... uirgo lactat' [6]) – consonant with the age of their witnesses, points, of course, to Edith's unstained purity ('Fauete puris puritate nuptiis' [17]), but just as 'nubit' connects her spiritual marriage with her veiling, the scene, cloying in its sentimental sweetness, requires a significant apparatus to support its imagined choice.

'Virgo matris hostia est'

A child of two is canonically incapable of due discretion, as Goscelin was doubtless aware. The various collections of canons, capitula, and excerpts from the fathers circulating in the last quarter of the eleventh century

52 Wilmart, 'La légende,' cap. 5, p. 46, lines 1–4.

offered widely varying and conflicting statements pertaining to children in religious life, but the dividing line for some kind of personal consent was puberty at the earliest. The third Council of Carthage had ruled that a virgin might take the veil without a parent or guardian's permission at twenty-five, and this age is widely cited.[53] But in the eleventh century, the age of consent for a girl was generally understood to be twelve, the legal age of puberty for a girl and hence for marriage. There can be little doubt about contemporary understanding of Edith's legal condition at two years old.[54]

This is not to say that a minor might not enter upon a religious life. A minor child's commitment to the religious life is made for her by the oblation of her parents. The connection of sacrifice and virginity, and the parents' duty to offer a child to God is one of Ambrose's insistent themes:

> Audistis, parentes, quibus erudire virtutibus, quibus instituere disciplinis filias debeatis, ut habere possitis quarum meritis vestra delicta redimantur. Virgo dei donum est, munus parentis, sacerdotium castitatis. Virgo matris hostia est, cuius cotidiano sacrificio vis divina placatur.[55]

53 PL 84.189, item iv. See also Regino of Prüm, *Libri duo de synodalibus causis* II.li (PL 132.396); Burchard, *Decretum*, VIII.15, 18 (PL 140.794–5); it appears as well in Wulfstan's so-called Commonplace Book. See Cross and Hamer, *Wulfstan's Canon Law Collection*, pp. 72–73 and 93 = items 15 and 63 of Recension A, and item 101 of Recension B (p. 139). It is extremely difficult to know precisely what mix of councils, canons, and capitularies were being drawn on before Gratian's *Decretum*. Since this chapter deals primarily with the background to Goscelin's understanding of oblation and veiling, I cite canons that appear multiply in popular continental collections and in Wulfstan's own collection. The *Collectio Lanfranci*, which draws substantially on the pseudo-Isidore Decretals, became a potent source of canon law in England until the middle of the twelfth century. See Mark Philpott, 'Lanfranc's Canonical Collection and "the Law of the Church,"' in *Lanfranco di Pavia e l'Europa del secolo XI*, ed. Giulio d'Onofrio (Rome: Herder, 1993), 131–47. I have not been able to see Philpott, 'Archbishop Lanfranc and the Canon Law,' DPhil thesis, University of Oxford, 1993.

54 As Osbert of Clare observes, a child of tender years (St Eadburga's comparatively mature three years old) is not capable of choice: 'tenera per etatem discernere non ualebat infantia.' Ridyard, *Royal Saints*, Appendix I, p. 265.

55 Ignazio Cazzaniga, ed., *S. Ambrosii Mediolanensis Episcopi De Virginibus Libri Tres* (Turin: In aedibus Io. Bapt. Paraviae, 1948), I.vii.32, p. 16, lines 18–22 (PL 16.198). On the connection of 'hostia' with 'delictum' see Hebr. 7:27. Elsewhere, in the polemic (and defensive) tract *De uirginitate* (ed. Cazzaniga, *S. Ambrosii Mediolanensis Episcopi De Virginitate Liber Unus* (Turin: In aedibus Io. Bapt. Paraviae, 1954), cap. 2.7, p. 5, lines 2–4 [(PL 16.268]), Ambrose defends his advocacy of virginity through the Old Testament example of sacrifice. Contrasting Jephthe's bloody sacrifice of his daughter

[Hear, parents, by what virtues you ought to instruct, by which disciplines you ought to teach your daughters, that you can have the wherewithal through whose merits your sins may be forgiven. The virgin is a gift of God, a parent's tribute, the sacred ministry of chastity. A virgin is her mother's sacrificial victim, by whose daily sacrifice God's anger is appeased.]

Here Ambrose offers to parents a spiritual exchange: instead of expected progeny from a marriageable daughter, they might receive forgiveness of sins by a kind of proxy. Such child oblation was widely practised in the early Middle Ages,[56] and the parents' commitment on behalf of the child had the force of law. The *RSB*, cap. 59, in describing the process through which parents dedicate a child to God, stipulates that if the child is a minor, the parents make its petition.[57] Because oblation (with its attendant property implications) was irrevocable, a considerable body of regulation accreted to it. The Rule of Saint Basil specified that multiple witnesses were required for the ritual of oblation, presumably to defend the commitment against later changes of heart by parents who lost their other children, and this requirement was widely cited.[58] The irrevocability of oblation was reaffirmed with thunderous finality in councils and collections.[59] Modelled on Hannah's oblation of the boy Samuel, the principle of the permanence

with the acceptable sacrifice of Abraham he draws the lesson that 'docuit [=Dominus] filiorum salutem religionis obsequio posthabendam: offerri a parentibus Deo debere filios, non debere iugulari' [the Lord showed that the welfare of children is to be valued less than religious observance: that children ought to be offered to God by their parents, not slain by them].

56 For a broad survey of oblation see John Doran, 'Oblation or Obligation? A Canonical Ambiguity,' in *The Church and Childhood*, ed. Diana Wood, Studies in Church History 31 (Oxford: Blackwell, 1994), 127–41. See also John Boswell, *The Kindness of Strangers* (New York: Pantheon, 1988), chaps. 5 and 8. De Jong, *In Samuel's Image*, presents a superbly detailed argument on oblation in the Carolingian empire.

57 Rudolph Hanslik, ed., *Benedicti Regula*, 2nd rev. ed., CSEL 75 (Vienna: Hoelder-Pichler-Tempsky, 1972) , cap. 59.1 (p. 151): 'Si quis forte de nobilibus offerit filium suum deo in monasterio, si ipse puer minore aetate est, parentes eius faciant petitionem.'

58 Cited in Cross and Hamer, *Wulfstan's Canon Law Collection*, 64A, 102B, pp. 94, 139. Smaragdus cites this portion of the *Regula Basili* in his commentary on the Benedictine Rule. See Alfred Spannagel and Pius Engelbert, eds., *Smaragdi Abbatis Expositio in Regulam S. Benedicti*, CCM 8 (Siegburg: Franz Schmitt, 1974), 299–300.

59 See Paulus Hinschius, ed. *Decretales Pseudo-Isidorianae et Capitula Angilramni* (Leipzig, 1863; repr. Aalen: Scientia Verlag, 1963), 370, Concilium IV Toletanum, cap. 48: 'Monachum autem paterna devotio aut propria professio facit: quidquid horum fuerit alligatum tenebit: proinde eis ad mundum reverti intercludimus aditum et omnem ad saeculum interdicimus regressum' (=Burchard, *Decretum*, VIII.6 [PL 140.793]).

of this oblation was articulated in Smaragdus's *Expositio in regulam S. Benedicti*, defended in Hrabanus Maurus's *De institutione clericorum*, and cited as well in Wulfstan's *Collection*.[60] The following formula for parental oblation, found in London, British Library, Cotton Tiberius C. i, fol. 93, was in wide use:

> OBLATIO PARENTVM.
>
> Ego frater N. offero hunc puerum illum cum oblatione in manu atque peticione, altaris palla manu eius inuoluta, ad nomen sanctorum quorum hic reliquię continentur & domni N. episcopi presentis. Trado coram testibus regulariter permansurum, ita ut ab hac die non liceat illi collum desub iugo excutere regulę, sed magis eiusdem regulę fideliter se cognoscat instituta seruare & domino cum ceteris gratanti animo militare. Et ut hæc nostra traditio inconuulsa permaneat, promitto cum iure iurando coram eadem Sancta Maria quia nunquam per me, nunquam per suspectam personam, nec quolibet modo per rerum mearum facultates aliquando egrediendi ei de monasterio tribuam occasionem. Et ut hęc petitio firma permaneat, manu mea subter firmaui testibusque tradidi roboranda.[61]
>
> [I, brother N., offer this boy N. with the offering and petition in his hand, and his hand wrapped in the altar cloth, in the name of the saints whose relics are contained here and in the name of our lord bishop N. here present. Before witnesses I commit him to remain under the rule so that from this day he may not remove his neck from the yoke of the rule, but rather that he may know that he will observe the requirements of the rule faithfully and serve the Lord along with the others with a joyful mind. And that our gift may remain intact, I promise by oath before this same Saint Mary that never through me nor any

---

Boswell notes individual exceptions in the eleventh and twelfth centuries (*Kindness of Strangers*, 316).

60 On this point Smaragdus, cites 'Isidorus' at cap. 59. See Spannagel and Engelbert, *Smaragdi Abbatis Expositio in Regulam S. Benedicti*, p. 300, lines 4–8, 'Hinc Ysidorus ait "Quicumque a parentibus propriis in monasterio fuerit delegatus, noverit se ibi perpetuo permansurum. Nam Anna Samuel puerum natum et ablactatum deo pietate obtulit, quique et in ministerio templi quo a matre fuerat functus permansit, et ubi constitutus est deservivit."' See also Hrabanus Maurus, *Liber de oblatione puerorum* (PL 107.419–40); Cross and Hamer, *Wulfstan's Canon Law Collection*, items 65A and 103B (pp. 94 and 139).

61 See Ker, *Catalogue*, no. 197, p. 261; Gneuss, *Handlist*, no. 376. The profession following this formula locates Tiberius C. i at Sherborne. For further discussion of this manuscript see my 'Goscelin and the Consecration of Eve,' *ASE* 35 (2006): 251–70, at 260 n. 57.

respected person, nor in any way through the power of my possessions will I provide opportunity for him to leave the monastery. And that this petition remain firm, I have affirmed below with my hand and have handed over to witnesses what are to be confirmed.]

The elements of this formula are adapted from *RSB* 58, outlining the steps by which an adult would be formally received into a monastery. Formal reception followed a period of testing, after which the postulant would be invited to promise stability in the monastery, knowing that from that day forward he would not be able to leave (*RSB* 58.15), 'nec collum excutere desub iugo regulae' [nor remove his neck from the yoke of the rule (*RSB* 58.16)]. Similarly, the Rule specifies for the postulant: 'De qua promissione sua faciat petitionem ad nomen sanctorum, quorum reliquiae ibi sunt, et abbatis praesentis' (*RSB* 58.19) [Let him make a petition concerning his promise in the name of the saints whose relics are there and of the abbot there present]. The written petition, signed by the postulant, is placed on the altar (*RSB* 58.20). In the following chapter, concerning the donation of a child to the monastery, the Rule specifies 'Si quis forte de nobilibus offerit filium suum deo in monasterio, si ipse puer minore aetate est, parentes eius faciant petitionem, quam supra diximus' (*RSB* 59.1) [If perhaps someone from the nobility offers his son to God in the monastery, if that child is a minor, let the parents make his petition, as we described above].[62]

The formula of oblation transmitted in Tiberius C. i hews fairly closely to the directions contained in the *RSB*, copying its liturgical gestures of placing the petition on the altar and making the petition in the name of the saints whose relics the altar contains. It also borrows language from the Rule to articulate the commitment to stability. Striking in this formula is the legal tenor of its language, underscoring the parent's promise never to remove the child from the monastery or assist him in leaving. The activity undertaken by the adult in *RSB* 58 is now assumed by the parent in both *RSB* 59 and the formula of oblation. Not only is the child passive (conveyed with gift and hand wrapped), he is described as an object, 'nostra traditio' [our gift] conveyed from his birth family to the *familia* of the monastery.[63] Although the arguments on oblation generally referred

62 Hanslik, *Benedicti Regula*, pp. 146–51.

63 For the transfer of property without reservation of usufruct upon the oblation of a child in later Anglo-Saxon England see Mechthild Gretsch, 'The Benedictine Rule in Old English: A Document of Bishop Æthelwold's Reform Politics,' in *Words, Texts and Manuscripts: Studies in Anglo-Saxon Culture Presented to Helmut Gneuss on the*

to male children, oblation was irrevocable as well for girls, as Gregory II's letter to Boniface makes explicit.[64] But the parent's commitment on the part of a minor child, always in uneasy tension with the principle of consent, would eventually be the fault line along which the practice of oblation would come undone in the course of the twelfth century.[65]

The irrevocability of oblation was still operative in the eleventh century when Lanfranc wrote his famous letter to Gundulf, bishop of Rochester, on the canonical status of women in English convents.[66] Replying to the bishop's inquiry, Lanfranc makes a clear distinction between two categories of 'nuns' ('sanctimoniales') who reside in convents: the first comprising professed nuns and oblated girls even if not yet professed, and the second comprising other women residing in the convents. The same word used for both categories speaks to the effectiveness of families' and perhaps individual women's tactical deployment of religious identity. Regarding the second category – that is, women merely residing in convents – Lanfranc rules that they should leave the convents immediately until their status was determined, based on an assessment of their desire to be religious ['*uoluntates earum* de seruando ordine'(emphasis added)]. At issue is the basis on which these women chose to live in the convent, whether for legitimate religious motives ['amore religionis'] or fear of the invading Normans ['timore Francigenarum']. To decide the case, unambiguous testimony of nuns 'better' than themselves ['meliorum sanctimonialium'] was required.

At three points in the letter Lanfranc uses the word 'sanctimoniales,' though with differing force. In the first clause, defining the subject of the

---

Occasion of His Sixty-Fifth Birthday, ed. Michael Korhammer with the assistance of Karl Reichl and Hans Sauer (Cambridge: D.S. Brewer, 1992), 131–58 at 132 and n. 8.

64 Michael Tangl, ed., *Die Briefe des heiligen Bonifatius und Lullus*, MGH Epistolae Selectae 1 (Berlin: Weidmann, 1916), letter 26, p. 46, lines 12–17: 'Addidisti adhuc, quodsi pater vel mater filium filiamque intra septa monasterii in infantiae annis sub regulari tradiderint disciplinę, utrum liceat eis, postquam pubertatis inoleverint annos, egredi et matrimonio copulare. Hoc omnino devitamus, quia nefas est, ut oblatis a parentibus Deo filiis voluptatis frena laxentur.' This decision is also cited in Ivo of Chartres, *Decretum*, VII.15 (PL 161.548), and Gratian, *Decretum*, Pars II C. 20 q. 1 c. 2. See Friedberg, *Corpus Iuris Canonici*, I: 843–4.

65 See Nora Berend, 'La subversion invisible: la disparition de l'oblation irrévocable des enfants dans le droit canon,' *Médiévales* 26 (Spring 1994): 123–36 esp. 127.

66 Helen Clover and Margaret Gibson, eds. and trans., *The Letters of Lanfranc Archbishop of Canterbury* (Oxford: Clarendon Press, 1979), letter 53 (pp. 166–7). Clover and Gibson date this letter between 19 March 1077 and 28 May 1089. Searle, 'Women and the Legitimisation of Succession,' p. 165, would date the letter to 'the mid or late 1070s.'

letter, Lanfranc describes all women living in convents as 'sanctimoniales,' a word normally used to distinguish religious from laywomen.[67] The second time he uses the word, 'sanctimoniales' refers to nuns properly understood, that is, either professed or oblated (with the implication that the oblate was required to continue on to profession). The third usage, with the comparative, 'better nuns,' once again lumps together all the inmates of the convents in question. In the usage of Lanfranc's letter, the women living in these English convents (other than those professed or oblated) were considered 'sanctimoniales' until established otherwise. Yet Lanfranc's indication that many of these might have fled to the convents out of fear of the Normans makes clear that their true canonical status could only be determined by investigating the evidence for motive in entering the convent rather than simply reading their mode of dress. Fleeing to a convent for fear of rape or enforced marriage would indicate, in Lanfranc's letter, that true commitment was lacking.[68] While this inference may seem a matter of common sense to us, the situation is more complex than it might appear, since the problem was intimately connected to the meaning of the veil.

Eleanor Searle has written persuasively of the background to Lanfranc's decision – that a number of the women who had retreated to convents during the 1070s were heiresses, and that a means to distinguish true nuns from heiresses who were permissible targets of opportunity would advance the Norman project of intermarriage.[69] How had families protected their interests or these women protected themselves? The answer, apparently, is by tactical use of the veil. Although the pertinent events would occur more than a decade after Goscelin was writing, the circumstances of another Edith's veiling tell much about the function of the veil as a marker of identity and the pressure to keep it as such.

Edith/Matilda, daughter of Malcolm, king of Scots, and St Margaret, had been entrusted to the care of her aunt Christina in the convent of Romsey. Sometime before 1093 she moved to Wilton.[70] The history of

67 On the difficulties in determining the meaning of 'sanctimonialis' see Sarah Foot, *Veiled Women*, I: 27–30 and esp. 102–4.

68 But compare, e.g., Burchard, *Decretum* VIII.16 (PL 140.795), which empowers a bishop to consecrate a girl to protect her virginity from an importunate suitor or from rape.

69 Searle, 'Women and Succession,' 165–6. For a discussion of marriage as an essential tool of Norman governance see Eleanor Searle, *Predatory Kinship and the Creation of Norman Power, 840–1066* (Berkeley: University of California Press, 1988), 246–9.

70 There are a number of accounts of the marriage arrangements for Edith/Matilda. R.W. Southern, *Saint Anselm and His Biographer: A Study of Monastic Life and Thought 1059–c. 1130* (Cambridge: Cambridge University Press, 1963), 183–93, is

marriage arrangements proposed for the girl is a complex story of moves and checks revolving around the question of whether Edith/Matilda was, in fact, a nun. The crucial point in her eligibility for marriage was the matter of her identity and how that identity had been produced. After her father Malcolm removed her from Wilton in a rage, claiming the he had never intended her to be a nun, Anselm, then archbishop of Canterbury, wrote to Osmund, bishop of Salisbury (spring 1094). His letter urged him to do what he could to get Edith/Matilda back into the convent, because 'quam diabolus velamen religionis deponere fecit et in habitu saeculari inverecunde permanere facit'[71] [the devil had caused her to put off the veil of religion and causes her to live her life shamelessly in secular dress]. The 'veil of religion' is no simple metaphor, for the wearing of the veil was presumptive evidence that the woman beneath it was irrevocably committed to the religious life.[72] Eadmer claims to offer Edith/Matilda's own explanation of the situation, in which she admits to Anselm that she had worn a veil, but claims that the veil (which Eadmer has Edith/Matilda call a little black rag) was her aunt's idea:

> 'Attamen,' inquit, 'me velum portasse non abnego. Nam cum adolescentula essem, et sub amitae meae Cristinae quam tu bene novisti virga paverem, illa, servandi corporis mei causa contra furentem et cujusque pudori ea tempestate insidiantem Normannorum libidinem, nigrum panniculum capiti meo superponere, et me illum abjicientem acris verberibus et nimium obscenis verborum convitiis saepe cruciare simul et dehonestare solebat. Quem pannum

the foundational account. Eleanor Searle analyses the negotiations in terms of Edith/Matilda as an heiress in 'Women and the Legitimisation of Succession.' On Matilda's marriage to Henry I see now C. Warren Hollister, *Henry I*, edited and completed by Amanda Clark Frost (New Haven, CT: Yale University Press, 2001), 128–30. See also Lois L. Huneycutt, *Matilda of Scotland: A Study in Medieval Queenship* (Woodbridge: Boydell Press, 2003), 21–30.

71 F.S. Schmitt, ed., *S. Anselmi Cantuariensis Archiepiscopi Opera Omnia*, 6 vols. (Edinburgh: Thomas Nelson and Sons, 1946–61), IV: 60–1 (= Letter 177).

72 In his letter to Bishop Osmund, Anselm alludes to 'canonum peritia' [knowledge of canon law] (= Schmitt, IV: 60) on the question. On Anselm's understanding of canon law see Mark Philpott, '"In primis … omnis humanae prudentiae inscius et expers putaretur": St Anselm's Knowledge of Canon Law,' in *Anselm: Aosta, Bec and Canterbury: Papers in Commemoration of the Nine-Hundredth Anniversary of Anselm's Enthronement as Archbishop, 25 September 1093*, ed. D.E. Luscombe and G.R. Evans (Sheffield: Academic Press, 1996), 94–105 at 102 and n. 44. I consider the canonical collections and Anselm's deployment of canonical principles in further detail in chapter 4.

in ipsius quidem praesentia gemens ac tremebunda ferebam, sed mox ut me conspectui ejus subtrahere poteram arreptum in humum jacere, pedibus proterere, et ita quo in eum odio fervebam, quamvis insipienter consueveram desaevire. Isto non alio modo, teste conscientia mea, velata fui. Acsi me oblatam quisque dicet, et hoc quale sit ex eo subintelligi licet, quod, sicut plurimi qui adhuc supersunt noverunt, pater meus, cum me quemadmodum dixi velatam forte vidisset, furore succensus injecta manu velum arripuit, et dissipans illud odium Dei imprecatus est ei qui mihi illud imposuit, contestans se comiti Alano me potius in uxorem, quam in contubernium sanctimonialium praedestinasse. Haec est unde calumnior ratio mea, quam quaeso perpendat prudentia tua, et agat pro me sicut novit agendum paternitas tua.'[73]

['Nonetheless,' she says, 'I do not deny that I wore the veil. For when I was a young girl, and trembled under the rod of my aunt Christina, whom you knew well, she imposed a little black rag on my head in order to protect my body and its purity against the mad, scheming lust of the Normans at that time, and when I would thrust it off, she would often abuse me with sharp blows and at the same time insult me greatly with disgusting verbal abuse. I wore that rag in her presence weeping and trembling, but as soon as I could escape from her sight, I would throw it to the ground, stamp it underfoot, and so rage, though senselessly, against what I seethed in hatred at. As my conscience is my witness, in this way, and in no other, was I veiled. And if someone says I was oblated, what the situation is can be deduced from this (as many who are still living know) that when my father chanced to see me veiled, as I have said, overcome by rage and grabbing the veil, he snatched it off and destroying it called down the wrath of God on whoever had veiled me, declaring that he would rather have arranged for me to be wife to Count Alan, than to be in the company of nuns. This is the matter about which I have been falsely accused, which, I beg, your prudence weigh carefully, and your fatherly care act in my case as it knows ought to be done.']

There are two central and complementary claims in this argument, each marking a route to the life of a woman dedicated to religion. The first addresses the ritual significance of the veil, the second the question of oblation. It is clear from the concession in Edith/Matilda's plea to Anselm, that she had worn something that passed for a veil. But her veiling, if such it could be called, was tactical, driven by her aunt Christina's fear that the

73 Martin Rule, ed., *Eadmeri Historia Novorum in Anglia et Opuscula Duo de Vita Sancti Anselmi et Quibusdam Miraculis Ejus*, RS 81 (London, 1884), 122.

girl would be raped by some predatory Norman looking for an heiress. In taking this action, Christina, herself a nun, seems to have gone beyond the simple shift of elite families who entrusted their daughters to convents by taking the ritual step of changing Edith/Matilda's formal identity.[74] As John Van Engen has pointed out, still in the eleventh century, prelates did not look to a legal moment of making a *propositum* for determining someone's religious status. Rather they looked for 'constitutive ritual moments, such as taking the cowl or veil, donning and blessing the habit, or practice in a habit over a year and a day.'[75] Whether Christina's action was practically successful in warding off attacks on the girl's virtue, her tactic (and others like it) put into question the significance of the veil itself. Was this or that woman who wore a veil actually a nun? This was the question Lanfranc's letter meant to address, and this is the fracture in identity to which Goscelin's anxious fantasy responds.

To undercut the significance of Christina's action to her canonical state, Eadmer has Edith/Matilda call what she was forced to wear a 'nigrum panniculum' [a little black rag] rather than a *velum* or *velamen*, casting the nature of the object she wore in doubt. But beyond that, she asserts that wearing the veil was against her will, that she was beaten into obeying, and that she raged in hatred against the 'veil.' In short, she did not wish to be a nun. Here, Eadmer has her set the ritual significance of imposing and wearing the veil against the individual's own choice. But the second strand of her argument addresses an equally grave determiner of identity – oblation. Here the question is not *her* choice, but that of her father. Had she been formally given to a life of religion, the question of her hasty veiling would have been of lesser significance. Edith/Matilda disposes of the question of oblation by noting that her father, when he saw that she was wearing a veil, ripped it off her head in a rage, exclaiming that she had been destined to marry not to become a nun. Ultimately, though apparently against his better judgment, Anselm accepted the father's and child's intention and ruled that Edith/Matilda was free to marry Henry I.[76]

---

74 On the decretal forbidding abbesses (and by implication any other nun) from veiling women and girls see above, n. 48.

75 John Van Engen, 'Professing Religion: From Liturgy to Law,' *Viator* 29 (1998): 323–43 at 329.

76 Eadmer's account of Anselm's deliberation on this case (*Historia novorum*, s.a. 1100) offers as background to understanding Matilda's status the numbers of women and girls who had fled to convents during the upheaval of the Conquest. This account is conveniently printed in Whitelock, Brett, and Brooke, *Councils and Synods*, II: 661–5.

By contrast, however, Anselm was unmovable on the performative significance of the veil in the case of Gunhild, the daughter of King Harold Godwinson and longtime inmate of Wilton.[77] Although Gunhild had apparently protested that she had never been professed as a nun, as we will see in the next chapter, Anselm ruled in favour of the performative function of the habit: that even without consecration by a bishop, her wearing of the habit in public and private was the equivalent of a vow.[78]

Two complementary issues emerge from Lanfranc's letter and from Anselm's reluctance on the question of Edith/Matilda's marriageability. The first is that a parent's oblation, where the decision taken on behalf of the child was finalized in the ritual of conveyance, continued to be regarded as irrevocable in the late eleventh century. However, the effect of this understanding of the status of the child oblate rendered intention merely *pro forma* at the time of profession.[79] The second, by contrast, is that intention is explicitly used to raise questions about the canonical state of inmates of convents in the decade or so after the Conquest. Was this or that woman *really* a nun even though veiled? Both issues are implicated in the meaning and function of the veil, and both issues provoke questions about the ability to 'read' the veil as an index of either identity or intention. If Lanfranc's letter was written in the late 1070s, as Searle has stipulated, it is nonetheless

77 Schmitt, *Anselmi Opera Omnia*, IV: 43–50, Letters 168, 169.

78 Gratian, *Decretum*, Pars II. C. 20 q.1 c. 8. (Friedberg, *Corpus Iuris Canonici*, I: 845): 'Puellae, que non coactae parentum inperio, sed spontaneo iudicio uirginitatis propositum atque habitum susceperint, si postea nuptias elegerint, preuaricantur, etiam si nondum eis consecratio accessit, cuius utique non fraudarentur munere, si in proposito permanerent' [Girls who have not been forced by the command of their parents, but have undertaken the vow of virginity and the habit by their own decision, commit a sin if they choose to marry, even if they have not received their consecration, whose duty they would certainly not violate if they were to remain in their vow]. See also Burchard, *Decretum*, VIII.2 (PL 140.792), and Ivo of Chartres, *Decretum*, VII.20 (PL 161.549). Philpott, 'St Anselm's Knowledge of Canon Law,' suggests that Anselm was familiar with specific rulings, cited in the pseudo-Isidorian Decretals, that forbade the casting off of the habit: Concilium VI Toletanum c. vi; Concilium X Toletanum c. v; and *Epistola Innocenti ad Victoricum* c. xii–xiii. See Hinschius, *Decretales Pseudo-Isidorianae*, 378, 401, 531. The first of these makes the performative nature of the habit clear: 'quamobrem quiqui virorum vel mulierum habitum *semel* induerint ... in utroque sexu praevaricator ad propositum invitus reverti cogatur' [emphasis added].

79 By contrast, see the discussion of the relative importance of profession and blessing by the Anonymous of Bec (after 1136): *Three Treatises from Bec on the Nature of Monastic Life*, ed. Giles Constable, trans. Bernard S. Smith (Toronto: University of Toronto Press, 2008), 40–3.

unclear that Goscelin could have known its contents. What does seem clear, however, is that Goscelin, as chaplain at Wilton and after as an itinerant hagiographer, knew at first hand the stories of contemporary women's withdrawal from the world and produced an exemplary narrative to encourage stability in their choice.

Choice and Transgression

In the light of these concerns, Goscelin's portrayal of Edith as both a product and star of the Benedictine Reform shows what freight the Reform is made to bear in the *uita*. Wilton's connection to the fruits of the Reform through its royal patron serves to highlight the convent's status as a royal nunnery. And Goscelin's collapsing of time (reducing a century to 'yesterday') keeps the Reform alive, notionally, in the present of the text. But associating Edith with the Reform also provides Goscelin with further opportunity to burnish Edith's image as an important saint. His record of her accomplishments in learning (reading and writing, copying and composing) produces for her a Benedictine identity within the literate ideology of the Reform. Her entrance into Wilton is styled as entrance into school: the convent is at once 'uirginale collegium,' 'diuinum gymnasium,' and 'scolas uirtutum' (cap. 6, p. 47). In such a school her mother prepares her for her spiritual bridegroom 'pro uariis ornatibus litterarum ac uirtutum decore' [with various adornments of learning and virtues (cap. 7, p. 49)]. And Edgar, in his role as supporter of ecclesiastical learning, provided his daughter two tutors from the Continent, 'tam morum quam scientie philosophia uenerandi' [venerable for their wisdom in morals as much as in knowledge (cap. 7, p. 50)]. These men, Radbod, a monk from Saint-Rémi, and Benna, a canon from Trier, instructed her in a manner befitting her holiness: 'eruditor pudicus a foris per fenestram docebat et audiri magis quam uideri assueuerat, ut sancti pudoris uernulam decebat' [her modest teacher taught from outside through a window, and was accustomed to being heard rather than seen, as was fitting for the little servant of holy modesty (cap. 7, p. 51)].[80] But her love of the heavenly kingdom surpassed even her love of learning (cap. 7, pp. 51–2), and from the midst of her studies she strove toward Christ with all her affection (cap. 7, p. 52). Not only could she read and write, Goscelin records that she composed a book of

80 See below, chapter 5, for Goscelin's expectation that Eve will have books read to her through a window in her cell.

her own prayers, written in her own virginal hand ('uirginea eius manu' [cap. 8, p. 55]) and still kept at Wilton. Her accomplishments were many:

> Uox cignea, canor angelicus, mellita facundia, generosum et ad omnia capax ingenium, legendi intellectuosa flagrantia; manus pingendi, scriptitandi, dictitandi tam decentes, quam artificiose; digiti aurifices, gemmarii, citharedi, citharizantes Christi nuptias et angelorum organa.[81]
>
> [A voice like a swan, angelic singing, honeyed eloquence, and a noble intellect capable of learning everything, an ardour for reading that was full of comprehension, hands as skilful in painting, copying, and composing as they were comely, the fingers of a goldsmith, a jeweller, a player of the cithara, playing the nuptials of Christ and the church organ of angels.]

Amid all these brilliant accomplishments, Edith is shown repeatedly to be firm in her *propositum*. She is a model of religious obedience: 'Exerta lacertos ad obedientiam, ad seruitutem omnium primam, ad dignitatem reddidit postremam. Quicquid mater indixerat, obauditionem uelut brauium in stadio occupabat' [showing strength for obedience, showing herself first in the service of all, she put behind her her royal dignity. In whatever her mother (scil. the abbess) enjoined, she practised obedience, as if it were the prize in the race (1 Cor. 9:24) (cap. 10, p. 61)].[82]

And yet Edith's riot of accomplishments in these passages suggests a strategic layering of monastic virtues that Goscelin advances to counterbalance certain behaviours – remembered by the community of Wilton – that suggested something less than the obedient agent of God's will. Edith and her mother seem to have retained a considerable income, since they were able to purchase a fragment of one of Christ's nails for the princely sum of one hundred pounds (by weight) in silver coins.[83] Edith collected native and exotic animals in a menagerie, on which she lavished considerable attention, though she only attended to the animals after tending to the poor.[84] It is true that she is shown to decline the urging of the chief men of England, who wished to make her queen upon the murder of King

81 Wilmart, 'La légende,' cap. 11, pp. 68–9.

82 See also ibid., cap. 16, p. 76, where she accepts the abbacy of three monasteries 'non ad prelationem, sed ad obedienciam' [not for authority but for obedience].

83 Ibid., cap. 14, p. 73: 'centum libras argenteorum patriorum.'

84 Ibid., cap. 10, pp. 65–6. The account of the menagerie is found only in the Cardiff manuscript. The Rawlinson text simply mentions that wild beasts learned to eat from her hand.

Edward (d. 978). Edith refuses their solicitations so vigorously 'ut facilius estimarentur saxa in plumbum conuerti quam illam a proposito suo posse reuocari' [that rocks were thought easier to turn into lead than she could be recalled from her vow (cap. 19, p. 85)]. But Goscelin's repeated praise of Edith's humility and her repudiation of royal status must be balanced by her fondness for wearing the royal purple and for keeping a wardrobe of splendid garments of purple cloth and of fur. Goscelin's rhetorical management of two incidents in the *uita* suggests that he sensed an agency in these behaviours that he was eager to repackage and discount.

In the first of these incidents Æthelwold, seeing Edith wearing the royal purple, judged her dress to be unsuited to her identity as a nun. He warns her: 'non his itur ad talamum Christi induuiis, nec exteriori cultu delectatur sponsus celestis' [you do not go to Christ's marriage chamber in these clothes, nor is the heavenly spouse pleased by exterior elegance (cap. 12, p. 70)]. Unknown to Æthelwold, Goscelin reveals, Edith wore a hair shirt beneath her elegant garments, practising 'glorious humility' beneath her public display. His sources for this information – the senior nuns of Wilton – suggest that the community cultivated the story and that the added detail of the hair shirt refigured Edith's transgressive behaviour as saintly humility. Her reply to Æthelwold in this story turns back his admonition in the same terms with which the bishop reproved her: 'Crede, o pater reuerende, nequaquam deterior mens Deo aspirante sub hoc habitabit tegmine quam sub caprina melote. Habeo Dominum meum, qui non uestem, sed mentem attendit. Hic dedicatum est uerbum Domini: Secundum fidem tuam fiat tibi' [Matt. 9:29] [Reverend father, believe that the mind, when it desires to reach God, in no way lives any the worse in such a garment than in a monastic goat-skin. I have my Lord who considers not clothing but the mind. Here the word of the Lord is declared: 'According to your faith, be it done unto you']. Goscelin records that Æthelwold was deeply impressed by her speech and honoured the saint's holy purpose. In Goscelin's retelling of the nuns of Wilton's memory of Edith, the marker of royal status becomes a tool of humility when the egregious behaviour of a princess is contained in a hagiographic trope. If we look a little closer at Edith's reply, we see her retort improvising on the repertoire of episcopal admonition. Where Æthelwold's reproof appeals to the discourse of monastic identity and its intimate connection to habit and veil (carefully commemorated in cap. 4 for her mother Wulfthryth), Edith offers a counterdiscourse of surface and spiritual depth in which God is the judge of men's souls, and the reply is capped with a citation of scripture.

Just how contained Edith's behaviour is in Goscelin's scene is nicely pointed by William of Malmesbury's presentation of the same exchange between Æthelwold and Edith:

> Vnum a maioribus accepi, quo non mediocriter iuditium offendebat hominum, fallens uidelicet oculos eorum apparatu auratarum uestium, siquidem cultioribus indumentis ornata procederet quam illius professionis sanctitudo exposceret. Vnde a sancto Adelwoldo palam increpata, respondisse fertur nec inepte nec infacete: 'Verax,' inquit, 'et irrefragabile iuditium Dei, sola mortalium operitur conscientia; nam et in sordibus luctuosis, ut Augustinus ait, potest esse iactantia. Quocirca puto quod tam incorrupta mens potest esse sub istis auratis uestibus quam sub tuis discissis pellibus.'
>
> [I have learned from our forebears one point in which she disturbed men's judgment not a little: she misled their eyes by an array of apparel rich in gold thread, and would go about more elegantly clothed than her sacred profession called for. She was told off for this in public by Bishop Æthelwold, but (they say) replied wittily and to the point: 'The judgement of God is true and irrefutable, while man's conscience, alone, is hidden; for, as Augustine says, there may be display even in mourning clothes. So, I think, as unblemished a mind can lie beneath these golden clothes as under your tattered skins!][85]

William, clearly unfettered by either Goscelin's obligations to his Wilton patrons or hopes for preferment from Archbishop Lanfranc, shapes the account to maximize the delicious riposte from an Edith whose royal attire is shown to be transgressive. The hair shirt, generously supplied by Goscelin to gratify, perhaps, pious memory at Wilton, is nowhere to be found. Rather, William records that her performance 'disturbed' ('offendebat') by misleading ('fallens') people who saw her, and he makes the judgment that her fashion sense was inappropriate for her religious profession. In so doing he objects to such a display on the same basis that Anselm did in his disposition of the case of Gunhild – that habit and identity are mutually reinforcing.[86] William clearly enjoys Edith's witty and pointed remark, sharpening the barb by having her refer directly to Æthelwold's own, shabby sartorial performance. The account works, rhetorically, pre-

85 M. Winterbottom, ed. and trans., with the assistance of R.M. Thomson, *William of Malmesbury, Gesta Pontificum Anglorum: The History of the English Bishops*, 2 vols., OMT (Oxford: Clarendon Press, 2007), I: 296–9 (II.87.3).

86 See below, chapter 5.

cisely because the extent of Edith's transgression increases the pleasure of a reply that turns monastic discourse against itself.

If we compare this scene of Æthelwold's reproof with the story of Ælfstan's great obedience, we may discern in each a very different agency in operation. Ælfstan's negotiation of his abbot's demand shows agency in the obedient monk's feverish improvisation to accomplish his abbot's order. It is an agency supported by his monastic identity and working within it. But Edith's agency is the agency of transgression, where wearing the gown of a princess not only accomplishes her own will but derives its justification from the same discursive repertoire that the bishop draws upon. Stephanie Hollis takes Edith's royal wardrobe as an indication that she was 'a secular member of the Wilton community rather than a professed nun.'[87] It seems safer, however, to consider the range of Edith's behaviours in this text as a reflection of the possibilities of contemporary (that is, late eleventh-century) life at Wilton rather than the conditions at Wilton in the previous century. Certainly, when Goscelin supplements his narrative of Edith's choice of religion in cap. 5 by reference to a consecration, in order to underline her unbending dedication to God, he draws on a ritual that was only becoming popular in the late eleventh century.[88] The memory of Edith's royal robes (when black was the colour for the habit) must have been a strong one, and the story of the secret hair shirt that valorized the saint's sharp reply to the bishop especially appealing.

Immediately following the account of this exchange between Edith and the bishop, Goscelin reports a brilliant miracle confirming Edith's sanctity. It seems that a servant had carelessly let a candle fall into the wardrobe containing Edith's clothing and thoughtlessly walked away. Everyone feared that the resulting conflagration (in which the wardrobe was charred) would have destroyed all Edith's royal finery. Although Edith herself laughed at the loss of earthly things, the clothes are miraculously spared: 'Cumque uestimenta singula uel pellicea uel purpurea cautis luminibus explorant reuoluta, mira perpetui custodis gratia, ita omnia ab omni ustulatione inuenta sunt illesa, ut fuerant ante ipsa incendia, immo, ut fiducialius fateamur, ut ipsa uirgo corruptionis erat aliena' (cap. 13, pp. 71–2) [And when they carefully examined in the light the unfolded

87 Hollis, *Writing the Wilton Women*, 249–50.

88 Wilmart, 'La légende de Ste Édith,' cap. 9, p. 57: 'quam regi uirginum sempiterneque integritatis sponso consecrarant' [whom they (scil. Dunstan andÆthelwold) consecrated to the king of virgins and spouse of eternal purity]. This statement appears only in the Cardiff manuscript.

individual garments, either of skin or of purple cloth, by the marvellous grace of the perpetual guardian, all of them were discovered to be as safe from any harm as they had been before that fire, indeed, as we confess more confidently, as the virgin herself was separate from any corruption].

The placement of this miracle in the *uita* (immediately following Æthelwold's reproof) shows its importance in affirming Edith's behaviour. Each piece of Edith's clothing is spared from the fire by divine providence. The adjective 'pelliceus' describes an object made of animal skin, with wool attached to the skin, or made of skins like leather or similar.[89] As such, the word could include crude garments or exotic furs. If we take 'pellicea' literally, it looks very much like Goscelin filled Edith's wardrobe with contrasting garb: with garments of the purple cloth that offended Æthelwold's sensibilities and the *melote* associated with the dress of desert monks.[90] In this way the objects in the wardrobe could show the ascetic side (as with the hair shirt) and the luxurious side (her royal display). But the fire that endangered everything in the wardrobe miraculously spared *all* her clothing. Goscelin reads it as a sign of her virtue – that as her clothing was unharmed so too was Edith untouched by corruption. But the miracle of preservation speaks also to her performance as a nun in the royal purple, in a tacit, disturbing recognition of the unsettling of identity. For it is Edith's claim (which Goscelin in narrating is pressed to endorse) that surface display (that is, wearing the identity-conferring habit or veil) is of no account; that only the inner disposition (which can be read only by God) matters. To negotiate the dangers to identity posed by this claim, Gocelin binds veil and choice in the scene of Edith's free commitment.

Goscelin's imagined ritual for Edith's choice must thus be read within the context of the flight to convents in the wake of the Norman Conquest and the increasing tension in the late eleventh and twelfth centuries between the irrevocability of oblation and the insistence on affirming religious life as an act of will.[91] Although Goscelin's fantasized ritual reduces this tension by making Edith's choice at once personal and communal, he can only achieve this effect by denying her agency when he folds the

89 See *Dictionary of Medieval Latin from British Sources*, s.v. *pelliceus*, senses 1–3.

90 Hollis, *Reading the Wilton Women*, gives the contents of the chest as 'purple garments and her furs' (262), although Wright's translation earlier in the volume (43) gives 'made of skin or of purple.' On fur garments in Anglo-Saxon England see Gail R. Owen-Crocker, *Dress in Anglo-Saxon England*, rev. ed. (Woodbridge: Boydell Press, 2004), 181–3.

91 See particularly Van Engen, 'Professing Religion,' 329–32.

parents' choice onto the child's in combining the moment of oblation and consecration. Her parents' irrevocable oblation is matched by Edith's demonstrated choice, and both are supported by God's will. In the gestures of the ritual, he reinforces the performative sign of the veil by the still-irrevocable force of oblation, and he reinforces the correctness of oblation by a *sortilegium* to reveal God's will.[92]

In Goscelin's anxious fantasy of oblation, we see individual choice emerge for a moment as the shadow of a complementary form of conveyance. Lanfranc's resolution of the question of religious identity and eligibility for marriage produces an individual whose status becomes dependent not on the sign of her state (through both ritual and performance) but on the merits of her personal choice. And while such a resolution raises further problems of interpreting the original authenticity of that choice by demanding a clear-cut decision on identity, it removed the improvisatory possibilities of using the convent tactically. As a result, women who thought to escape ruin at the hands of invading Normans might find their status changed for them in the following decade and become eligible to be conveyed as brides to the rapidly developing Norman seigneurial class. If Æthelwold's episcopal sword effected Wulfthryth's return to the convent from the world, Lanfranc's sword produced a different sort of severing whose effect, if brief, was to unsettle the veil as the definitive sign of a woman's religious identity. Goscelin's resolution of this unsettling, that the child chooses exactly what God chooses for her, and that her parents agree, addresses the problem of intention and identity surfacing in the English convents of Lanfranc's time only to cover it over by a fantasy of simultaneous choice directed by God. Although the fault lines had begun to appear, the problem of oblation and choice remained to be addressed by the canonists of the twelfth century.

---

92 In cap. 26 Goscelin repeats the fantasy. Following Edith's death, as Bishop Elphege is baptizing the infant Brihtgyva, the baby grabs for the candle used in the ceremony. (On the liturgical implications see Wilmart, 'La légende de Ste Édith,' pp. 99–100, n. 7.) Elphege, recognizing this as a sign, demands the oblation of the child, and she eventually becomes the fifth abbess of Wilton.

4 Leaving Wilton: Gunhild and the Phantoms of Agency

'Amasti amantem te comitem Alanum Rufum.'[1]

'I stayed because I was scared, not because I liked him.'
(Gypara Bek, kidnapped Kyrgyz bride)[2]

Separated by time and place, the two epigraphs of this chapter speak to each other from the narratives of women's agency within which each finds its meaning. In the first, Anselm of Canterbury writes to Gunhild, a nun of Wilton who had been taken from the convent by a powerful Norman magnate. In two remarkable letters Anselm presents Gunhild to herself as a woman who has *chosen* an inappropriate love, having abandoned her true spouse, Christ, for a mortal lover. Anselm's emplotting of the abduction of Gunhild within two interlocking narratives of women's identity – marriage and the religious life – has framed contemporary understanding of this moment in Gunhild's life in terms of will and choice. Indeed, Anselm's letters have been so convincing that much contemporary scholarship has viewed her abduction in terms of romance rather than rape. In order to construct Gunhild as a willing agent, Anselm draws on the master narratives of will and consent within which religious women were embedded in the early Middle Ages, using language drawn from both canonical collections and religious ritual, in order to imagine a Gunhild responsible for her own abduction. In doing so, he ascribes to Gunhild what I will

1 F.S. Schmitt, ed., *S. Anselmi Cantuariensis Archiepiscopi Opera Omnia*, 6 vols. (Edinburgh: Thomas Nelson and Sons, 1946–61), IV: 47.

2 Craig S. Smith, 'Abduction, Often Violent, a Kyrgyz Wedding Rite,' *New York Times*, 30 April 2005, http://www.frif.com/new2005/brid2.html.

call a 'phantom agency,' an agency that has only a rhetorical existence and functions solely to indict her for collusion in her own rape. This chapter traces the cultural logic of Anselm's narrative by examining its sources in canonical and liturgical texts, showing how a 'master narrative' of *individual* agency came into being as a way of protecting group identity – here, a group of women bound to life in the convent at Wilton. We can imagine that Gunhild, like Gypara Bek, 'stayed because she was scared' – and if we cannot in the end uncover her motivations, we can at least expose the ideological interests at work in Anselm's version of her life.

We have no words of Gunhild, neither protest nor assent, to meet Anselm's carefully crafted charge. But the kidnapped Gypara Bek's assessment of her own predicament – that silence is not consent, that resignation is not choice – urges in Gunhild's place a careful reading of Anselm's proffered narrative. What follows examines the cultural logic of this narrative in its canonical and liturgical manifestations as well as its continuing power.

Archbishop Lanfranc's letter to Gundulf, bishop of Rochester, making a disposition concerning certain women whose status in the convent was ambiguous, in essence addressed a fallout of the social disruption following the Conquest.[3] In the face of enterprising Normans looking for heiresses to acquire, many Anglo-Saxon families had placed their daughters in convents for education and safekeeping. Living in convents, these women and girls, who preserved their chastity (and tried to keep their options open) by wearing the veil tactically without making a formal religious commitment, used the identity of a nun to protect themselves from unwanted marriage and block the conveyance of property. This improvisational shift to adapt convent life to the needs of the family provoked in turn serious questions about the identity of any individual woman in the convent: was this or that woman really a nun? In answer to Bishop Gundulf's query seeking guidance on this issue, Lanfranc directs the bishop to send home any woman who had not been oblated or was not professed. The status of these women was then to be determined on the basis of their earlier intention: if they had fled to a convent for fear of the Normans, they were to be free to leave; if they entered the convent from a love of religion,

3 Helen Clover and Margaret Gibson, eds. and trans., *The Letters of Lanfranc Archbishop of Canterbury* (Oxford: Clarendon Press, 1979), letter 53, pp. 166–7. Clover and Gibson date this letter between 19 March 1077 and 28 May 1089. Eleanor Searle, 'Women and the Legitimisation of Succession at the Norman Conquest,' *Anglo-Norman Studies* 3 (1981 [for 1980]): 159–70 and 226–9 at 165, would date the letter to 'the mid or late 1070s.'

they could be kept. This solution accomplished several ends at once. It provided a mechanism for resolving the apparently intolerable ambiguity over individual women's religious identity, but in so doing it removed from the women concerned (and their families) the flexible defence they had adapted against their acquisitive conquerors. Requiring a sharp-edged determination of identity reduced a woman's options to two: she and her family could thwart unwelcome marriage only by the woman's claiming that she had originally entered the convent from love of religious life (*amore religionis*) and thereafter re-entering the convent permanently. In the case of a woman claiming to have entered from the wrong motive (*timore Francigenarum*), it is unclear who would be bringing a case to have the woman returned to the world, she and her family, or an interested suitor.

On the face of it, Lanfranc's episcopal decision to use intention as the basis for this resolution at first appears to give the woman concerned a moment of agency in speaking to determine her fate, but such a moment is more apparent than real. Any claim to prior intention and hence the confirmation of 'true' identity had to be proved by the 'unambiguous witness of nuns better than they' ('firmo meliorum sanctimonialium testimonio'),[4] nuns, presumably, who had been long professed. The consequence of this resolution of liminal identity is that women who previously had contrived to maintain flexibility with respect to their futures by tactically adopting religious identity might find themselves conveyed unwillingly, one way or the other, by a process that claimed to recognize and thus establish their earlier will. This chapter examines another case of ambiguous status and the very different path that Lanfranc's successor, St Anselm, took in handling it. In using both the lexicons of canon law and liturgy, Anselm's arguments raise tantalizing questions about the operation of intention and agency in a woman's commitment to religious life.[5]

Between 1080 and 1093 we know of three women who left the convent of Wilton. The first of these is Eve of Wilton, who left sometime in the period 1080–2 for reclusion in Angers, either by her own request or at the order of her superiors.[6] Eve's departure for Angers entailed no canonical question, since she was removing to a religious life defined as more severe

4 Clover and Gibson, *Letters of Lanfranc*, pp. 166–7 (their translation).

5 Clare A. Lees and Gillian R. Overing, *Double Agents: Women and Clerical Culture in Anglo-Saxon England* (Philadelphia: University of Pennsylvania Press, 2001), examine women's agency in the sociocultural practices of Anglo-Saxon England.

6 On Eve see chapter 5 below.

than the regular life at Wilton. The other two, perhaps leaving within a short time of one another in 1093, are Edith/Matilda, daughter of King Malcolm and St Margaret of Scotland, eventually to be queen of Henry I, and Gunhild, daughter of Harold II of England. These removals are linked as well in terms of the canonical question they raised about the status of both women as nuns. While both were royal daughters, they differed in their ages: Edith/Matilda was thirteen at the time of her removal by her father; Gunhild was thirty or older when Count Alan Rufus took her. The women were different, as well, in terms of Anselm's ultimate disposition of the cases of their removal. Although he originally judged her a runaway nun, Anselm eventually permitted Edith/Matilda to marry, but he remained immovable in the case of Gunhild. Edith/Matilda's relative youth at the time, her aunt's peremptory act in veiling her, her return to the Scottish court of her parents, and perhaps royal politics all must have worked for a favourable resolution. By contrast, Gunhild had been abducted to the court of a Norman magnate; her age and her dubious position in the household of Alan Rufus, and later with his brother, Alan Niger, clearly created a scandal.[7]

There are a number of persistent difficulties in understanding Gunhild's unenviable situation. We do not know the particular circumstances under which she left Wilton beyond the sketchy outline in the two letters that Anselm writes to her following her removal from the convent of Wilton. The letters are not precisely datable, but would appear to postdate Anselm's consecration as archbishop (4 December 1093).[8] Richard

7 There are a number of accounts of the marriage arrangements for Edith/Matilda. R.W. Southern, *Saint Anselm and His Biographer: A Study of Monastic Life and Thought 1059–ca 1130* (Cambridge: Cambridge University Press, 1963), 183–93, is the foundational account, on which see below, pp. 189–90. Eleanor Searle analyses the negotiations in terms of Edith/Matilda as an heiress in 'Women and the Legitimisation of Succession'; On Edith/Matilda's marriage to Henry I, see now C. Warren Hollister, *Henry I*, edited and completed by Amanda Clark Frost (New Haven, CT: Yale University Press, 2001), 128–30. See also Lois L. Huneycutt, *Matilda of Scotland: A Study in Medieval Queenship* (Woodbridge: Boydell Press, 2003), 21–30. Richard Sharpe has challenged Southern's account on the basis of dating: 'King Harold's Daughter,' *Haskins Society Journal* 19 (2007): 1–27 at 19.

8 Walter Fröhlich, trans., *The Letters of Saint Anselm of Canterbury*, 3 vols., Cistercian Studies Series, 96–7, 142 (Kalamazoo, MI: Cistercian Publications, 1990–4), II: 68, dates the first letter to 'December 1093 or early 1094' and the second to 'early 1094' (II: 74). The two letters (= Letters 168, 169 in Schmitt, *Anselmi Opera Omnia*, IV: 43–50) are not part of Anselm's own letter book collections. See Frölich, *Letters*, I: 43–4, and Sally N. Vaughn, *St Anselm and the Handmaidens of God: A Study of Anselm's Correspondence*

Southern thought that the first of the two letters (Letter 168 in Schmitt's numbering) refers to a situation that arose around the time of the failed meeting at Gloucester between William Rufus and Malcolm, king of Scots, in August 1093. At that time, before returning to Scotland, Malcolm travelled south to Wilton and removed his daughter Edith/Matilda from the convent, ripping from her head the veil that her aunt Christina had imposed and declaring that he had intended her for marriage not for the convent. At around the same time as Edith/Matilda left Wilton, the standard account runs, Count Alan Rufus, lord of Richmond, the most powerful magnate in the North of England, removed Gunhild, although there is no date certain for that occurrence.[9] Shortly thereafter Alan Rufus died, though the date of his death, often given as 4 August 1093, is likewise uncertain.[10] There does not seem to have been a marriage. Upon the death of Count Alan Rufus, his brother, Alan Niger, succeeded, and Gunhild remained with him.[11] What happened to Gunhild thereafter is unknown.[12]

Richard Sharpe has contested a number of elements in this narrative in an effort to explain the bequeathal of certain properties (held by Alan Rufus before 1075) by one Matilda d'Aincourt of unknown descent.[13] Sharpe speculates that this Matilda was daughter of Gunhild, and to do so, he must date Gunhild's removal from Wilton considerably earlier than

---

with Women (Turnhout: Brepols, 2002), at 37 and 52. Vaughn considers the letters to have been written between August 1093 and Anselm's consecration in December 1093, when he was 'archbishop-elect' (190). Compare Southern, *Saint Anselm and His Biographer*, p. 186, n. 1, who assigns the formula in letter 169, 'servus servorum Christi Jesu, vocatus archiepiscopus,' to letters 'probably written after 4 December 1093 and before the end of 1094.' Southern, *Saint Anselm and His Biographer*, 183, dates the letter to Bishop Osmund of Salisbury to shortly after February 1094.

9 For a review of the motivations of the various players in these removals see Huneycutt, *Matilda of Scotland*, 22–4.

10 Southern, *Saint Anselm and His Biographer*, p. 187 n. 2. This dating is questioned by P. McGurk, ed. and trans., *The Chronicle of John of Worcester*, vol. 3, *The Annals from 1067 to 1140 with the Gloucester Interpolations and the Continuation to 1141* (Oxford: Clarendon Press, 1998), p. 314, n. 8, who regards the date of Alan Rufus's death as uncertain. More recently, Sharpe, 'King Harold's Daughter,' 9–10, has supported 4 August 1093 as Alan Rufus's death date.

11 Southern, *Saint Anselm and His Biographer*, 188, indicates that he was dead by 1098.

12 On the basis of an account of St Wulfstan healing Gunhild of an eye problem, Southern believed that she returned to Wilton, 'for she was later remembered there with honour' (*Saint Anselm and His Biographer*, 188). However, Emma Mason, *St Wulfstan of Worcester ca 1008–1095* (Oxford: Basil Blackwell, 1990), 225, dates the miracle to the 1080s or before, and seems not to think that Gunhild returned to Wilton.

13 Sharpe, 'King Harold's Daughter,' 5.

1093 (to make it possible for her to be this Matilda's mother), suggesting that she had 'thrown off the habit to live with Count Alan on her mother's estates' at around age sixteen.[14] An important difficulty here, however, is that this new chronology underestimates the fresh urgency of Anselm's letters. For his revision, Sharpe must also dispute as chronologically impossible Southern's scenario about the failure of marriage arrangements for Edith/Matilda in 1093 and Alan Rufus's abduction of Gunhild. For all this, however, he does not dispute some important facts – that Gunhild was removed from Wilton by Alan Rufus, that his death was recent when Anselm wrote his letters, and that Alan Rufus had never married Gunhild. But while Sharpe resists Southern's emplotment of Alan Rufus's actions as 'romance,' he takes at face value Anselm's characterization of Gunhild's predicament, accepting that 'she cast off her own veil and she loved Alan,' and that there was, between Gunhild and Alan Rufus, 'a wholly mutual relationship.'[15] As we will see, the question of Gunhild's will is precisely what is in play in Anselm's (and our) understanding of her case.

Although in the case of Edith/Matilda Anselm wrote to Osmund, bishop of Salisbury,[16] in whose diocese Wilton was located, to urge him to compel Edith/Matilda to return, Anselm wrote two letters directly to Gunhild in an effort to bring her back to Wilton. In both letters the argument is driven by the potent narrative of spiritual marriage to Christ, invoked with both affective and legal force. In maintaining that Gunhild is the spouse of Christ, Anselm claims that her salvation depends on honouring her commitment to him and returning to the convent of Wilton. At issue, however, was precisely the question of Gunhild's identity. While Anselm concedes that she had never made a profession and had never been consecrated by a bishop, he nonetheless insists that she is not free to marry and is espoused to Christ on the basis of her previous life at Wilton. What stands out in these letters, in the forest of Anselm's rhetorical bravura, are two instances of passivity that Anselm construes as acts of will and on the basis of which makes his claims. In the first, Anselm argues that Gunhild's wearing of the habit was a tacit profession,[17] whereby in lieu of a verbal performative, simply wearing the habit established identity as a nun; in the second, in the case of Gunhild's removal from Wilton, Anselm interprets

14 Ibid., 24.

15 Ibid., 18, 19.

16 Schmitt, *Anselmi Opera Omnia*, IV: 60–1 (Letter 177).

17 On the 'legal fiction' of tacit profession see Richard Yeo, *The Structure and Content of Monastic Profession*, Studia Anselmiana 83 (Rome: Pontificio Ateneo S. Anselmo, 1982), 177.

her forced abduction as yet another instance of her will. As different as these circumstances are, they are linked by the practice of assessing intent by reading externals (wearing a habit, living in someone's household). We may see that practice in action in the canons to which Anselm alludes, but it is the cultural logic driving the ritual of consecration that more clearly elucidates Anselm's construction of what I would call phantom agency for Gunhild. The following argument examine the ways in which Anselm uses the language of spiritual marriage in scripting for Gunhild a narrative of identity and choice, and how the logic of that narrative constructs for Harold's daughter a phantom agency through which she is assigned blame for her own abduction.

In commenting on Anselm's claim in Letter 168 that Gunhild was a nun obligated to return to Wilton and resume wearing the habit, Giles Constable argues that Anselm 'regarded the practice of profession and consecration as relatively recent and not essential to making a monk or nun.'[18] Certainly, as Constable points out, formal profession became increasingly popular in the twelfth century. This is not to say, however, that consecration was unusual at the end of the eleventh century. Although we lack records of profession ceremonies for women from the eleventh century,[19] surviving English pontificals from the late tenth through the eleventh century contain rituals of consecration, and the frequent glossings for plural forms in blessings in these pontificals suggest that consecrations must have been performed. Indeed, in the *Liber confortatorius* Goscelin of Saint-Bertin describes a consecration ceremony for fourteen Wilton inmates, antedating 1078, when Bishop Herman died.[20] Gunhild, who was probably in her early teens at the time, would have witnessed the ceremony as a resident of the community and understood the force of the ritual. In equating the daily wearing of the habit to a punctual act of formal profession, Anselm's letters raise questions about the conditions for a woman's agency at the end of the eleventh century. What follows attends first to Anselm's legal argument and the relationship between the canons he draws on and the modification he makes. The argument

18 Giles Constable, *The Reformation of the Twelfth Century* (Cambridge: Cambridge University Press, 1996), 17.

19 Odelia G. Harrison, OSB, 'The Formulas *Ad virgines sacras*: A Study of the Sources,' *Ephemerides Liturgicae* 66 (1952): 252–[273] and 352–66, imagines the constituent prayers of 'a possible first profession ceremony' at [273].

20 C.H. Talbot, ed., *The Liber Confortatorius of Goscelin of Saint Bertin*, Studia Anselmiana 37, Analecta Monastica, 3rd ser. (Rome: Herder, 1955), p. 28, lines 7–14.

thereafter examines the cultural logic of the ritual of consecration (whose force Anselm insists Gunhild had felt) and its implications for thinking women's agency.

Performance and Profession

The critical passage in Anselm's Letter 168 warns Gunhild that her salvation depends upon returning to Wilton and resuming her religious life. This is necessarily so, Anselm argues, because Gunhild is a nun by virtue of her having worn the habit of religion:

> Impossibile namque est te ullo modo posse salvari, nisi ad habitum et propositum abiectum redieris. Quamvis enim ab episcopo sacrata non fueris nec coram ipso professionem legeris, hoc solum tamen est manifesta et quae negari non potest professio, quia publice et secrete habitum sancti propositi portasti, per quod omnibus te videntibus deo dicatam te esse non minus quam professionem legendo affirmasti.[21]
>
> [For it is impossible for you to be saved in any way unless you return to the habit and religious life you have cast off. Indeed, although you were not consecrated by a bishop and did not read your profession before him, nevertheless, profession is clear and cannot be denied, seeing as in public and in private you wore the habit of holy commitment to religious life, through which, no less than by reading a profession, you affirmed to all who saw you that you were consecrated to God.]

In this statement of the case, Anselm anticipates an argument that Gunhild is free to marry because she had never been oblated nor formally made a profession to live her life as a nun. Such an argument would place Gunhild in a situation analogous to that of the women about whom Lanfranc wrote to Gundulf, though more than a decade later. The position Anselm takes at this point, however, is very different from Lanfranc's, since he chooses to draw his argument from the performative force of the habit itself. In this understanding, because the habit is read by those seeing it as a sign of religious life, wearing the habit constitutes profession and as such is as

21 Schmitt, *Anselmi Opera Omnia*, IV: 44–5. The word 'propositum' is not easily translated, and in rendering it I follow Constable, *Reformation of the Twelfth Century, p.* 7 and n. 24. See also Richard Yeo, *Structure and Content of Monastic Profession*, 84–5. All translations are mine, unless otherwise indicated.

binding as a formal vow. The fundamentals of this principle were widely available in canonical collections. Although Anselm's knowledge of canon law has been widely mooted, Mark Philpott has shown that Anselm was a canonist worthy of comparison to Ivo of Chartres or Lanfranc.[22] The principal canons pertinent to this case were available to him in pseudo-Isidorian canon law, though whether he availed himself of the *Collectio Lanfranci* or gained his knowledge of these canons elsewhere is unknown.[23] Two pseudo-Isidorian canons confirm that women who have once worn the habit may not put it off and are not free to marry.[24] The second of these is especially pertinent to the particulars of Anselm's argument, since it explains why women who have once worn the habit face excommunication and must be returned to their convents against their wills if necessary:

> Omnes foeminae quae iam in praeterito religionis veste fuisse probantur indutae, nihil ad excusationem valeat oppositionum quaelibet obiectio, quamvis diversis aut callidis adumbrare se velint fallaciae argumentis, sed ad sacratissimas sanctiones disciplina sanctior eas teneat religatas atque subnixas: commoneantur sane sacerdotis auctoritate ut sponte redeant; quae si redire noluerint impulsu sacerdotis, ad religionis habitum reducantur et in

22 Mark Philpott, '"In primis ... omnis humanae prudentiae inscius et expers putaretur": St Anselm's Knowledge of Canon Law,' in *Anselm, Aosta, Bec and Canterbury: Papers in Commemoration of the Nine-Hundredth Anniversary of Anselm's Enthronement as Archbishop, 25 September 1093*, ed. D.E. Luscombe and G.R. Evans (Sheffield: Sheffield Academic Press, 1996), pp. 94–105 at 102 and n. 44, observes apropos Anselm's use of canons forbidding a nun to put off her veil: 'Anselm's doctrine was correct in terms of the ancient canons of pseudo-Isidore or those of his own day.' This is, in effect, a corrective to R.W. Southern's sweeping portrait of Anselm in *Saint Anselm: A Portrait in a Landscape* (Cambridge: Cambridge University Press, 1990): 'Lanfranc's collection of Canon Law was in the library at Canterbury, but there is no evidence that Anselm ever used it while he was archbishop' (256) and 'We may infer from these two cases that Anselm set no great store by an extensive knowledge of Canon Law' (257).

23 On the *Collectio Lanfranci* see now Mark Philpott, 'Lanfranc's Canonical Collection and "the Law of the Church,"' in *Lanfranco di Pavia e l'Europa del secolo XI nel IX centenario della morte (1089–1989)*, ed. Giulio d'Onofrio, Italia Sacra: Studi e documenti di storia ecclesiastica 51 (Rome: Herder, 1993), 131–47 at 147.

24 Paulus Hinschius, ed., *Decretales Pseudo-Isidorianae et Capitula Angilramni* (Leipzig, 1863; repr. Aalen: Scientia Verlag, 1963), Concilium VI Toletanum cap. 6 and Concilium X Toletanum cap. 5 (pp. 378 and 401). See the important caution by Martin Brett, 'The *Collectio Lanfranci* and Its Competitors,' in *Intellectual Life in the Middle Ages: Essays Presented to Margaret Gibson*, ed. Lesley Smith and Benedicta Ward (London: Hambledon Press, 1992), 157–74 at 160, n. 10, on the problems of Hinschius's edition.

monasteriis redactae excommunicationis condignae sententia feriantur. Hic idem quoque ordo in illarum condemnatione manebit, quae quamlibet a sacerdote vel ministro sanctimoniae vestem non accepissent, ipsae tamen aut indutae sunt aut in illo indui habitu consenserunt, qui religionis esse cultus ab intuentibus crederetur, sic que coram ecclesia vel sacerdote aut etiam competentibus testibus quandoque indutae visae certis indiciis aut testimoniis approbantur.[25]

[(For) all women who are now determined to have been clothed with the garment of religion in the past, let no sort of opposing objections be admitted for excuse, although they might wish to misrepresent themselves with various shrewd and deceptive arguments, rather let holy discipline hold them bound and subject to the most sacred ordinances: let them be warned plainly by the authority of the priest that they should return of their own wills; if they do not wish to return by the influence of the priest, let them be led back to the habit of religion, and when returned to their monasteries let them be punished by the condign sentence of excommunication. This same rule will apply in condemnation of those who – even if they did not receive the habit of a nun from a priest or deacon – nevertheless, either were clothed or had agreed to be clothed in that habit understood by those seeing it as the garb of religion, and who are thus determined by clear evidence and testimony as having been clothed (in the habit) in the presence of the church or a priest or competent witnesses.]

This canon applies to women who have left conventual life after a period of having worn the habit, holding them bound by regarding the wearing of the habit equally as binding as the taking of a vow. In it we see the essentials of Anselm's argument to Gunhild: that the wearing of the habit of religion at any point is irrevocably binding; that returning *sua sponte* is the required course of action; that excommunication is the consequence of intransigence. What connects this canon so particularly to the argument of Anselm's letter, however, is its parenthetical understanding of the habit's force as sign. When it is worn, the canon explains, the habit is understood by those seeing it ('ab intuentibus crederetur') to be evidence of the wearer's religious life. Such an external resolves any question of the person's identity, and the understanding of the community is taken to be identical to the unreadable intention of the individual. In this sense, the habit does make the monk. This understanding of the action and

25 Hinschius, ed., *Decretales Pseudo-Isidorianae,* Concilium X Toletanum cap. 5 (p. 401).

force of wearing the habit in the pseudo-Isidorian collection is close to, but not exactly, Anselm's argument. In Letter 168, Anselm goes beyond the pseudo-Isidorian canon's collapsing of *signum* and *res*.[26] In the latter, the habit both marks and installs identity; Anselm's argument keeps the habit as a performative equal in force to a vow, but in addition makes that performative an act of will: when you wore the habit in public and in private, he tells Gunhild, by doing so you affirmed to all who saw you that you had been consecrated no less than by reading a profession. With 'per quod … affirmasti' [through which … you affirmed] Anselm materially shifts the emphasis of Concilium X Toletanum cap. 5, for *affirmasti* predicates will of an identity-conferring performance. While the inference of those who see her is still of utmost importance, Anselm makes a further claim that the habit is not just a sign of state but a sign of will. For the purposes of ascertaining Gunhild's identity in law, the wearing of the habit is here scripted as an instance of agent action, through which Gunhild is made culpable for any variance from her earlier performance.

The Logic of Consecration

The forms and prayers for a consecration, a ritual reserved to the bishop alone, are found in a pontifical, the book of *ordines* proper to a bishop.[27] The development and distribution of such liturgical books and the rites they transmitted have a complex history, not least because of the variations found in individual compilations. For the purposes of this discussion, where the circumstances are contained to the late eleventh century, I use the forms of Consecration found in the Pontificale Romano-Germanicum (PRG), widely disseminated on the Continent in the eleventh century (though in England only with the reign of Edward the Confessor [d. 1066]), as a way of examining the ritual of consecration in a form that was demonstrably influential.[28] My aim is to explore the cultural logic that

26 See Giles Constable, 'The Ceremonies and Symbolism of Entering Religious Life and Taking the Monastic Habit, From the Fourth to the Twelfth Century,' in *Segni e riti nella chiesa altomedievale occidentale, 11–17 aprile 1985*, 2 vols., Settimane di studio del centro italiano di studi sull'alto Medioevo 33 (Spoleto: Centro italiano di studi sull'alto Medioevo, 1987), II: 771–834 at 774–5.

27 Richard W. Pfaff, ed., *The Liturgical Books of Anglo-Saxon England*, Old English Newsletter Subsidia 23 (Kalamazoo, MI: Medieval Institute Publications, 1995), 87.

28 Cyrille Vogel and Reinhard Elze, eds., *Le Pontifical Romano-Germanique du dixième siècle*, 3 vols., Studi e Testi 226, 227, 269 (Vatican City: Bibliotheca Apostolica Vaticana, 1963–72), I: 38–46 (=PRG). Michael Lapidge has demonstrated the availability of the

underlies the ritual of consecration contained in this widely disseminated pontifical.[29] In what follows I explore how the ritual of consecration encodes social expectations about the contradictory status of a virgin. In constructing such a woman both as a gift to be exchanged between men of different families and as an agent of her own giving, the ritual of consecration, as it transfers a woman from her own family to the *familia* of the convent, dramatizes that contradiction in the demand for her to be at once object and agent.[30] My reading of the gestures, prayers, and antiphons of the ritual lays out the demand for her simultaneous passivity

---

PRG in the later eleventh century in England in 'The Origin of CCCC 163,' *TCBS* 8.1 (1981): 18–28 at 19: 'CCCC 163 was copied in England from a manuscript of the Romano-German Pontifical which originated in Cologne sometime after 1021.' See also his 'Ealdred of York and MS Cotton Vitellius E. xii,' in his *ALL* II, 453–67 and 492 at 462–3. On rituals of consecration surviving from Anglo-Saxon England see my 'Goscelin and the Consecration of Eve,' *ASE* 35 (2006): 251–70 at 'Appendix,' 265–70. Consecration is a ritual distinct from that for making a profession, but unfortunately, rituals of profession for women do not survive. For selected early rituals of profession for monks see Edmond Martène, *De antiquis ecclesiae ritibus libri*, 5 vols. (Antwerp, 1736; repr. Hildesheim: Georg Olms Verlagsbuchhandlung, 1967), II: 451–69, and Marquard Herrgott, *Vetus disciplina monastica: seu collectis auctorum Ordinis S. Benedicti maximam partem ineditorum, qui ante sexcentos fere annos per Italiam, Galliam atque Germaniam de monastica disciplina tractarunt* (Paris, 1726), 589–92. Stephanie Hollis believes an Old English fragment from Lambeth Palace to contain a description of a ritual admitting St Mildrith to the convent of her mother, Domne Eafe: 'The Old English "Ritual of the Admission of Mildrith" [London, Lambeth Palace 427, fol. 210],' *JEGP* 97.3 (1998): 311–21. Despite the interest of a possible vernacular account of admission, the ritual described would be quite distinct from profession.

29 Michael Gullick and Richard W. Pfaff, 'The Dublin Pontifical (TCD 98 [B.3.6]): St Anselm's?' *Scriptorium* 55.2 (2001): 284–94 at 292–4, argue that Dublin, Trinity College MS 98 (B.3.6) was compiled for the use of St Anselm. For a list of contents see Marvin L. Colker, *Trinity College Library Dublin: Descriptive Catalogue of the Mediaeval and Renaissance Latin Manuscripts*, 2 vols. (Dublin: Scolar Press, 1991), I: 195–98. I have not been able to see TCD 98, but the collation of that manuscript against the 'Magdalen Pontifical' reveals that among the prayers and blessings shared with the PRG, it contained the 'Deus castorum corporum.' H.A. Wilson, *The Pontifical of Magdalen College*, Henry Bradshaw Society 39 (London: Harrison and Sons, 1910), 270–2.

30 Jocelyn Wogan-Browne, *Saints' Lives and Women's Literary Culture ca 1150–1500: Virginity and Its Authorizations* (Oxford: Oxford University Press, 2001), 57–90, examines virginity and the gift. She points out that 'in the rhetoric of virgin sainthood and treasure, the principal tropes of nuptiality and dotality connote not just privatized sexual fantasy but a range of social meaning' (76). The classic feminist critique of the exchange of women is Gayle Rubin, 'The Traffic in Women: Notes on the "Political

and will that underlies the contradictory affirmations in Anselm's letters to Gunhild.[31]

The ritual of consecration is a form of marriage, where the woman, formally espoused to Christ, is given to her new *familia*, where she will wait perpetually a virgin for the fulfilment of her espousal to Christ. The consecration begins with a ritual action whose gestures draw upon ceremonies of oblation and on the nuptial exchange of women.[32] Although the woman to be consecrated will have already spent considerable time in a convent, 'Virginem episcopo parentes cum oblatione offerunt et ille involutam manum eius in palla altaris recipiat, dicendo cum astantibus: Antiphona: Ipsi sum desponsata cui angeli serviunt, cuius pulchritudinem sol et luna mirantur'[33] [The parents offer the virgin to the bishop along with their offertory gift, and let him receive her with her hand wrapped in the altar cloth, singing with those standing around her, 'I am espoused to him whom the angels serve, at whose beauty the sun and moon marvel']. The actions specified in this rubric, conveying the woman with the family's gift and wrapping her hand in the altar cloth, are citations of the ceremonies of child oblation,[34] where the giving of the child was understood to be an irrevocable gift.[35] Like the child, and like the offering, the woman given for consecration is herself a gift, whose conveyance is enacted by her parents before the witnesses of the ceremony. The antiphon at this point, sung alike on the feast of the virgin martyr St Agnes and on the common of virgins, inflects the gift in the lexicon of the exchange of women (she is 'desponsata'), even as it locates that gift in the register of sacrificial virginity. To be a virgin is to be given, and Jocelyn Wogan-Browne has

---

Economy" of Sex,' in *Toward an Anthropology of Women*, ed. Rayna R. Reiter (New York: Monthly Review Press, 1975), 157–210.

31 For a provocative reading of 'fictional' agency, 'produced only so that the novice may speak her own subjection,' see Sarah Salih's reading of the much later Vespasian Ritual in her *Versions of Virginity in Late Medieval England* (Cambridge: D.S. Brewer, 2001), 134.

32 It would be well to register the caution that Vogel and Elze offer, in effect, a composite edition of the PRG, and that the rubrics are not present in all the witnesses.

33 PRG, XX.1, p. 39. For the antiphon see René-Jean Hesbert, ed., *Corpus Antiphonalium Officii*, 6 vols., Rerum Ecclesiasticarum Documenta, series maior, fontes 7–12 (Rome: Herder, 1963–79), vol. 3, item 3407.

34 On the indebtedness of these actions to the ceremony of a boy's oblation see Mayke de Jong, *In Samuel's Image: Child Oblation in the Early Medieval West* (Leiden: Brill, 1996), 184.

35 For early canon law on the irrevocability of oblation see chapter 3 above, pp. 169–72.

highlighted the importance of understanding a virgin's 'dotality' in understanding the experience of medieval women.[36] The identity of a virgin as one to be exchanged was founded on her expectation of espousal in either the secular or religious world. Her conveyance from father to husband effected a change of identity, as she moved from the family of her birth to the family of her marriage or to the *familia* of her religious order. Among elites, the giving of a virgin in marriage also conveyed property, and her conveyance as *sponsa Christi* might well be used to block transference of property in marriage.

The parents' ritual action of presenting their daughter to the bishop could be complemented by a further gesture of presentation that spoke to the woman's incapable legal condition. In many strands of the PRG, an *adstipulator* accompanied the woman up to the altar, 'cuius licentia religionis habitum est susceptura'[37] [by whose permission she is about to receive the habit of religion]. As René Metz has pointed out, because the woman did not have the right to give herself, the ritual presence of the *adstipulator* was meant to demonstrate that the woman undertook the life of religion with the permission of those who exercised *mundiburdus* over her, that is, the parents or guardians whose right it was to give her.[38] Vesting and consecrating only proceed after the *adstipulator* has given ritual permission.[39]

The language of the various prayers for blessing the habit the woman is about to assume emphasizes its function as a sign of dedicated virginity as they ask for divine help in strengthening the woman in her resolve. As do the canons cited above, these prayers understand the habit as a sign by which her religious commitment is to be recognized, a sign that sets her apart 'that among other women she may be known as one dedicated to [God].'[40] When worn, the habit is also a sign of the chastity that she has vowed to preserve.[41] Identifying the garments in which she is to be

36 On 'freely willed choice [as] a saving gloss' in virgin exchange see Wogan-Browne, *Saints' Lives and Women's Literary Culture*, 86.

37 PRG, XX.4, p. 39.

38 René Metz, *La consécration des vierges dans l'église Romaine: étude d'histoire de la liturgie* (Paris: Presses Universitaires de France, 1954), 182–222 at 193–4.

39 PRG, XX.5, p. 39, 'dato eius assensu' [after his approval has been given].

40 PRG, XX.7, p. 40, lines 11–13, 'pro indicio cognoscendae religionis' and 'ut inter reliquas feminas tibi [i.e., to God] cognoscatur dicata.'

41 PRG, XX.8, p. 40, line 15, 'quam famula tua N. pro conservandae castitatis signo se adoperiandam exposcit' [which your servant, N., has requested to cover herself as a sign of consecrated chastity].

clothed as a sign of humility of heart and contempt of the world, the blessing 'Deus aeternorum bonorum' sees them as well as a connection to the next world. It begs God to 'make her to be clothed in blessed immortality, whom you clothe temporally in the garments of a promise to be held sacred.'[42] Each variant blessing in the consecration of the PRG shows how integral the habit is to the performance of dedicated virginity, particularly in emphasizing how the habit both transforms the person wearing it and produces for those seeing the nun a sign of her life and commitment. The habit is understood as the visible guarantor of a monk or nun's religious life, but in the case of a nun, one part of that habit, the veil, functions as a metonym for the habit and its significance.[43]

After the woman has put on the blessed habit (with the exception of the veil, which is held back for symbolic imposition), the consecration proper may begin. At this point the language of the consecration highlights the ritual's function as spiritual espousal to Christ. After the conferral of the veil (the ritual action that seals her identity as *sponsa Christi*) the woman and those around her sing three different antiphons, all emphasizing her status as *sponsa*.[44] But it is in the great prayer of consecration, 'Deus castorum corporum,' that we see the clearest articulation of the nuptiality of the woman's conveyance, in which she is perpetually espoused, perpetually received but not taken:

> etiam hoc donum in quasdam mentes de largitatis tuae fonte defluxit, ut … existerent … sublimiores animae, quae, in viri ac mulieris copula fastidirent conubium, concupiscerent sacramentum, nec imitarentur quod nuptiis agitur, sed diligerent quod nuptiis prenotatur. Agnovit auctorem suum beata virginitas et emula integritatis angelicae, illius thalamo, illius cubiculo se devovit, qui sic perpetuae virginitatis est filius, sponsus quemadmodum perpetue virginitatis est.[45]

42 PRG, XX.6, p. 40, lines 7–8, 'quam vestibus venerandae promissionis induis temporaliter, beata facias immortalitate vestiri.'

43 For a discussion of the range of significance of the monk's habit see Constable, 'Ceremonies and Symbolism,' 812–14.

44 'Induit me dominus ciclade auro texta et immensis monilibus ornavit me' (PRG, XX.17, p. 44); 'Ipsi sum desponsata' (PRG , XX.19, p. 44); 'Posuit signum in faciem meam ut nullum, praeter eum amatorem admittam' (PRG, XX.21, p. 44); and 'Annulo suo subarrhavit me Dominus meus Jesus Christus et tamquam sponsam decoravit me corona' (PRG, XX.26, p. 46). For these antiphons see Hesbert, *Corpus Antiphonalium Officii*, items 3328, 3407, 4346, and 1426.

45 PRG, XX.15, p. 43, lines 2–10.

[also this gift flowed into certain minds from the font of your generosity, so that there existed some higher souls, who, while disdaining marriage in the joining of man and woman, desired the mystery [scil., of *sanctum coniugium*], not that they might imitate what is done in marriage, but that they might desire what is foretold by marriage. Blessed virginity has acknowledged its author and emulating angelic integrity has devoted itself to the bedchamber and bridal bed of him who is as much the son of a perpetual virgin as he is the spouse of a perpetual virgin.]

The woman's consecration thus effects a permanent change in her identity, which like marriage is irrevocable. The model for her consecrated life is the wise virgins of Matt. 25:1–13, who with lamps trimmed and filled with oil watch against the coming of the Bridegroom. 'Deus castorum corporum' makes explicit that consecration is not marriage, but is *like* marriage in that the woman devotes herself not to a mortal man but to Christ, awaiting the day that she may enter his *thalamum*. The spiritual erotics of such a heightened state of awareness and of waiting is feelingly explored in Jerome's famous letter to Eustochium, where he imagines:

Semper te cubiculi tui secreta custodiant, semper tecum sponsus ludat intrinsecus. oras: loqueris ad sponsum; legis: ille tibi loquitur et, cum te somnus oppresserit, ueniet post parietem et mittet manum suam per foramen et tanget uentrem tuum, et tremefacta consurges et dices: uulnerata caritatis ego sum, et rursus ab eo audies: hortus conclusus soror mea sponsa; hortus conclusus, fons signatus.[46]

[Let the solitude of your bedchamber protect you; let the Bridegroom always dally with you within it. Pray, and you speak to the Bridegroom; read and he speaks to you, and, when sleep overcomes you, he will come behind the wall and he will put his hand through its opening and he will touch you within[47] and trembling you will arise and say 'I am wounded by love,' and immediately you will hear from him 'my sister, my spouse, you are a garden enclosed, a sealed fountain.']

---

46 Epistle XXII.25. See Isidore Hilberg, ed., *Sancti Eusebii Hieronymi Epistulae*, 3 vols. in 2, CSEL 54–6 (Vienna: F. Tempsky, 1910–18), I: 178–9.

47 On the translation of this word see Patricia Cox Miller, 'The Blazing Body: Ascetic Desire in Jerome's Letter to Eustochium,' *Journal of Early Christian Studies* 1.1 (1993): 21–45, at 28, n. 35, who translates as 'inner body,' arguing that Jerome uses *venter* to be closer to the sense of Greek *koilia* and Hebrew *ma'im*.

The intense erotics of this passage figures the dedicated virgin, Eustochium, enclosed within her bedchamber, protected from the (male) gaze of the world, and simultaneously open to the Spouse, whose spiritual desire for her is presented in metaphors of physical passion cued by citation of the Song of Songs.[48] But such moments of spiritual exaltation are far fewer than the ordinary events of life. The 'Deus castorum corporum' begs help that the woman may continue strong in her vow, in terms that reinforce the consecration's spiritual analogue to marriage. She requires divine help against the devil who 'may creep in through some carelessness of mind and ravish from the vow of virgins what likewise fittingly pertains to the customs of marriage,'[49] that is, preservation of her body intact for the one to whom she is espoused. The woman's reward for a life of perfect virginity will be to cross the threshold with the wise virgins and enter into the fellowship of the Lamb. The blessing 'Deus plasmator corporum' makes her reward 'insolubilem ... copulam,' an indissoluble bond with Christ.[50] In some, though not all, versions of the PRG the bishop then confers upon the woman a ring and a crown.[51]

If the consecration of the PRG begins with the enactment of the woman's being given by her family to another, that is, with a set of ritual gestures encoding the woman's passivity as an object of transfer, the liturgy of consecration insists at key moments, from the blessing of the habit to the imposition of the veil, that the woman receives her consecration by her free consent. In the prayers used for the bishop's blessing of the habit, the habit is not simply a sign of religious life, but a sign of her *desire* for it, since they are garments she is presumed to wish to put on: 'vestes quas ... induere vult.'[52] Similarly, in an alternative blessing for the habit, the woman's desire for the habit (by which read the life of religion) is part of the articulation of the clothing's significance and purpose.[53] But

48 Miller, 'The Blazing Body,' 42, points out the erotics of this passage.

49 PRG, XX.15, p. 43, lines 14–16: 'per aliquam mentis serpat incuriam et rapiat de proposito virginum, quod etiam moribus decet inesse nuptiarum.'

50 PRG, XX.22, p. 45, lines 9–10.

51 PRG, XX.23, 24, p. 45, lines 27–31.

52 PRG, XX.7, p. 40, lines 11–12.

53 PRG, XX.8, p. 40, lines 14–16, 'hanc vestem quam famula tua N. pro conservandae castitatis signo se adoperiandam exposcit' [this garment about to cover her which your servant N. begs as a sign of the chastity she is to preserve]. The opening of the great prayer of consecration, the 'Deus castorum corporum,' interprets the ritual of consecration as the woman's offering her vow to God: PRG, p. 42, lines 25–8: 'respice super hanc famulam tuam N., quae in manu tua continentiae suae propositum collocans,

the clearest articulation of the insistence that consecration is the will of the woman is in the prayer following the antiphon after veiling ('Ipsi sum desponsata'), where the bishop, asking God to confer the virtues of humility, chastity, obedience, and charity on the newly veiled nun, identifies the woman as God's servant who *desires* to be consecrated, 'ut haec famula tua que pro spe retributionis eternae tibi domino *desiderat* consecrari, plena fide animoque in sancto proposito permaneat'[54] [that this, your servant, who *desires* to be consecrated to you, Lord, in the hope of eternal reward, may remain in her holy way of life filled with faith and purpose (emphasis added)].

Before veiling the woman, the bishop pauses to ask a ritual question.[55] The language of the rubric describing the bishop's question 'de observatione sacri velaminis' [concerning reverence for (and the duty imposed by) the holy veil] is primarily directed to the woman's understanding of the significance and obligation of the veil, rather than to establishing her explicit consent. Questioning her on her understanding of the obligations she is taking on, rather than asking her if the consecration is by her will, assumes her consent in the gesture meant to establish it. Reading beyond the scripting of the rubric, René Metz's interpretation of the virgin's presumed reply, 'La vierge répondait en affirmant la volonté de rester fidèle à ses obligations et prenait l'assistance à témoin de la sincérité de sa promesse,' assumes that the primary interest of the question is the woman's willingness to take up the responsibilities of the veil.[56] But even if Metz's reading of this rubric is correct, the PRG's cueing of the question 'off-stage,' as it were, makes the ritual consent of the consecrated woman still far less explicit than that of a man making monastic profession in the same pontifical. In this ceremony, the monk making his profession is prompted to speak his consent explicitly to the abbot: 'Tunc exuatur ipse novitius propriis vestimentis et interroget eum si propria voluntate abrenuntiet mundo

---

tibi devotionem suam offert, a quo et ipsa idem votum assumpsit' [look upon your servant N., who placing her vow of chastity in your hand, offers her vow to you, from whom she likewise receives a vow]. Later in the prayer (PRG, p. 43, lines 11–12), she is described as one 'confirmari se benedictionis tuae consecratione cupien[s]' [desiring to be strengthened by the consecration of your blessing]. On the 'Deus castorum' in the rituals of consecration see Odelia G. Harrison, OSB, 'The Formulas *Ad virgines sacras*: A Study of the Sources.'

54 PRG, XX.20, p. 44, lines 15–17.

55 PRG, XX.16, p. 44, lines 1–2. Not all versions have the portion of the rubric which indicates that the bishop questions the candidate at this point.

56 See René Metz, *La consécration*, 202.

et omnibus quae sunt mundi'[57] [Then the novice is stripped of his own clothes and let (the abbot) ask him if he renounces of his own free will the world and everything having to do with the world]. The difference between the two responses elicited is instructive: the monk is prompted to reply explicitly that he undertakes this life of his own free will. The nun to be consecrated is expected to make a reply concerning the obligations attendant upon the veil (where the veil is the metonym for the religious life and its requirements) in which her consent is implicit and assumed.

The Phantoms of Agency

In a consecration, the woman who undergoes the ritual is inserted into the narrative of spiritual marriage with Christ. As that narrative plays out in the consecration, the woman is both the passive gift of her family conveyed to the church and the willing agent of her own dedication. This same combination, where the object that is conveyed wills the conveyance, underwrites Anselm's insistence on Gunhild's guilt and on the capacity of her will to effect her return to Wilton as he scripts her abduction within the narrative of spiritual marriage. In abducting her from Wilton, Count Alan Rufus takes Gunhild from her spouse, Christ. Applying the logic of the willing object, Anselm transforms her passive conveyance into an act of will, construing her presence in Alan's household as something she desires and endowing her with the capacity to return to Wilton if she so wills it. 'Si enim mihi acquiescere volueris, certa esto quia valde tibi in fine placebit, et erit super te gaudium magnum angelis dei. Si vero nolueris, scito quia nimis tibi displicebit, et inexcusabilis eris in districto iudicio dei'[58] [If you are willing to agree with me, be very certain that things will please you in the end, and there will be great joy over you among the angels of God. If however you are not willing, know that things will be exceedingly displeasing to you, and you will be without excuse before the severe judgment of God]. The language of willing that Anselm uses here (*velle* and *nolle*) is critical. Gunhild's salvation or damnation is in her own hands, and her fate depends on her returning to Wilton *sua sponte*, in the way that Concilium X Toletanum cap. 5 specifies. To persuade her, Anselm explains to her that Christ is her spouse, contrasting the spiritual marriage of consecration (whose effect he argues she has already felt) with

57 PRG, XXVIII.4, p. 71, lines 6–8.

58 Schmitt, *Anselmi Opera Omnia,* IV: 43 (Letter 168).

the impurity of carnal love. The choice between the purity of spiritual delight ('in spirituali delectatione munditia') and the embrace of carnal impurity ('in carnali immunditia')[59] is underscored by the hope, security, and imperishable dowry that Christ offers his spouse as compared to the corruptible and contemptible things that Count Alan can offer her.

Gunhild's spiritual danger is grounded in having violated the identity that she had previously assumed by wearing the habit. 'Quid dicam modo te esse?' [What shall I say you are now?] Anselm asks at various points to highlight her fall: 'De electa et signata sponsa dei quid facta es?'[60] [From the chosen and sealed spouse of God, what have you become?]. No longer a virgin, and having cast off the habit that both makes and confirms her identity as a nun, Gunhild has taken on an intolerable liminal status outside the roles of daughter to be given, wife to be kept, or nun to be enclosed. Anselm lays out for her the path to regain the only identity now open to her: she can return to Christ her spouse, if she agrees to a life of perpetual penitence in chastity at Wilton. In this way she can once again be pleasing to God. Her course of action is clear: 'Reice et conculca saecularem habitum quem assumpsisti, et resume habitum sponsae Christi quem proiecisti'[61] [Throw off and trample the secular dress which you have assumed, and put back on the habit of the spouse of Christ which you threw away']. If she will not, the consequences are grave: 'Si vero hoc facere contempseris, omnes tibi adversi erunt, et ego et ecclesia dei faciemus quod de tali re faciendum intelligimus'[62] [But if you disdain to do this, everyone will be against you, and the church of God and I will do what we know must be done in such a situation].

Anselm's letter, larded with both enticements and veiled threats, warns Gunhild of her perilous canonical situation as the Concilium X Toletanum cap. 5 directs. The letter expects her to leave Count Alan Rufus, return, and do penance. The following letter to her (Schmitt Letter 169) makes it clear that this outcome did not happen. Rather, upon the death of Alan Rufus, Gunhild was now with his brother and heir, Alan Niger. Anselm's second letter is accordingly less gentle and at times distressingly direct in demanding her return, as it imagines for her the obscenity of embracing the first Alan's rotting corpse. Anselm has been given to believe in this letter that Gunhild left the convent because she was disappointed in not

59 Ibid., 44.
60 Ibid.
61 Ibid., 46.
62 Ibid.

having been made abbess after the position was promised to her. In this version of the argument, he tells her that leaving because others had lied to her still does not change her identity. He imagines God's address to her:

> 'Immo paratus sum introducere te ut electam et dilectam sponsam meam in thalamum gloriae meae et constituere te super omnia bona mea. An voluisti me fallere, cum hoc mihi promisisti? Si voluisti, certa esto quia nullatenus satisfacies mihi de hac falsitate, nisi feceris per veritatem quod promisisti per falsitatem. Si noluisti, fac ergo quod non fallendo, sed vera voluntate promisisti.'[63]
>
> ['Indeed, I am prepared to bring you as my chosen and beloved spouse into the bridal chamber of my glory and to set you over all my goods. Or did you intend to deceive me, when you promised this to me? If you intended to, be certain that you will make no satisfaction to me for this deception, unless you do in truth what you promised in falsehood. If you did not intend that, do therefore what you promised not by lying but with a true will.']

In this part of Anselm's argument the question is less whether Gunhild is or is not a nun, but whether she could leave Wilton because she did not receive a promised abbacy. Once again, this is an anticipated argument: Anselm does not indicate that he ever received a reply from Gunhild, merely that her disappointment was something that he had heard from others. What is even clearer in this letter than the earlier one is the degree to which the present situation is attributed to Gunhild's will and made a matter of Gunhild's guilt. God's reproving address to her is cast in the language of will (*voluisti, noluisti, vera voluntate*), and Anselm now explains that if Gunhild remains with Alan Niger, 'non solum te et illum virum aeterna morte damnabis, sed magnum et detestabile scandalum in eccclesia dei generabis, et omnibus hoc audientibus exemplum odibile … dabis'[64] [You will damn not only yourself but him to eternal death, and will also create a great and detestable scandal in the church of God, and will give a hateful example to all who hear of it].

The great rhetorical energy of Anselm's two letters occludes the fact that Gunhild was abducted from Wilton. Although her abduction was explained by Richard Southern as 'a strange and passionate romance' which happened when Alan Rufus saw a woman (Gunhild) he preferred

63 Ibid., 49.

64 Ibid., 50. Scandal is also an issue in Letter 168; see ibid., 43.

to Edith/Matilda,[65] the explanation is likely far more mundane. If Eleanor Searle is correct, that Gunhild was heir to her mother, Edith Swan-Neck's, estates, the reason for the abduction of the thirty-or-so Gunhild was more the land she might claim than the looks she had left.[66] Any doubt over such motivation should have been laid to rest by Alan Niger's keeping her after his brother's demise. Clearly, she (with any power she might convey through the estates of her mother) was too valuable to let go. Yet nowhere in the letters does Anselm mention the fact of her abduction; quite the contrary, in both of them he writes to her that remaining in the world endangers her, and through her both Alans.[67] In both letters, her removal from Wilton is portrayed as a choice she made, and her presence in the household of each brother a choice she is capable of undoing. The letters persistently urge her to take an action (leaving) that was not in her power and persistently endow her with guilt for actions beyond her control. In taking this stance, they show the same cultural logic as the ritual of consecration in which the woman conveyed by her family was scripted as a willing object. In the abduction, as Anselm writes it, Gunhild taken is assumed to be well pleased. The Kyrgyz woman of the epigraph, who, surrounded by the four children from her forced marriage, explains that she had stayed with her kidnapper/bridegroom out of fear, lives the unpleasant logic of the Kyrgyz proverb, 'Every good marriage begins in tears.' The woman, it is assumed, will be pleased with the arrangement. So with Gunhild, Anselm reads her abduction in the same way as he reads her habit – as a sign of her will.

Even if, however, Anselm were to have conceded that her abduction was against her will, the dilemma in which Gunhild found herself would not, in Anselm's logic, excuse her from the necessity of choosing the right course. It is easy to imagine a Gunhild stung by the force of Anselm's letters, seeing herself in an impossible bind: I must leave (because my salvation depends on it), but I cannot leave (because my abductor will not permit it). In this dilemma, Gunhild remains against her will. Yet the force of necessity to subvert the free operation of the will is precisely what Anselm will not allow in *De libertate arbitrii.* In this dialogue, when the student suggests that a man who lies to save his life when he is under a

65 Southern, *Saint Anselm and His Biographer*, 185.

66 Searle, 'Women and the Legitimisation of Succession,' 168–9. See also Sharpe, 'King Harold's Daughter,' 23–4.

67 Removing a woman from the convent was an excommunicable offence for the man as well, but that does not work its way into Anselm's letters either.

threat of death acts against his will, the teacher explains that the man does not lie against his will, since:

> M[agister] … Non enim cogitur magis velle vitam quam veritatem, sed quoniam vi aliena prohibetur utramque servare simul, ipsa eligit quod mavult; sponte utique et non invita, quamvis in necessitate utramlibet deserendi posita sit non sponte sed invita. Non enim minus fortis est ad volendum veritatem quam ad volendum salutem, sed fortius vult salutem. Nam si praesentem videret gloriam aeternam quam statim post servatam veritatem assequeretur, et inferni tormenta quibus post mendacium sine mora traderetur: procul dubio mox virium sufficientiam ad servandum veritatem habere cerneretur. D[iscipulus]. Aperte hoc videtur, cum maiores vires exhiberet ad volendum salutem aeternam propter se et veritatem propter praemium, quam ad servandum salutem temporalem.[68]
>
> [[Teacher]: For it [scil. the will] is not compelled to will life more than truth; but since an external power prevents it from preserving both, it chooses what it wills more. And certainly the will does so spontaneously, and not against its will, although its being in a position where it must abandon one or the other is not spontaneous, but against its will. For it has no less strength for willing truth than for willing well-being, but it wills well-being more forcefully. For if it saw right before its eyes the eternal glory that it would immediately attain if it preserved the truth, and the torments of hell to which it would be given over without delay if it lied, there's no question that it would quickly be found to have strength enough to preserve the truth. [Student]: That's clearly true, since it would show greater strength for willing eternal well-being for its own sake, and truth for the sake of the reward, than for preserving temporal well-being.][69]

Setting aside the logical problems inherent in Anselm's notion that the will cannot be compelled, this passage helps to understand Anselm's position in insisting that Gunhild sins if she does not return (in that the will in every person is free to choose good). As is the man in the student's

68 *De libertate arbitrii*, cap. 9, in Schmitt, *Anselmi Opera Omnia*, I: 205–26 at 221.

69 Anselm, *Three Philosophical Dialogues*, trans. Thomas Williams (Indianapolis: Hackett, 2002), 46. Williams specifies (at 108) that his translation of *sponte* is meant to capture the technical sense of the Latin word: 'In this technical sense, an act is spontaneous (or an agent acts spontaneously) when the act can be fully explained only by reference to something that originates within the agent.'

example, Gunhild is understood to be free to choose the good and to be in no way compelled to choose to sin. By this reasoning, at every moment of her life in Count Alan's household, she is free to leave and is required to do so at whatever price. Yet the passage does not help us to understand Anselm's plotting of her abduction in the narrative of spiritual marriage. An alternative plot was available to him – the narrative of the virgin martyr, whose heroic acts of resistance were used to encourage women to preserve their chastity and resist unwanted marriage.[70] That Gunhild's chastity had undoubtedly been violated was not necessarily a bar to using so popular a narrative. Goscelin of Saint-Bertin (who shows considerable interest in holy harlots) offered one such account in his *Liber confortatorius*, pointedly adapted from St Ambrose. The virgin of the story, fearing that she is destined to be corrupted by her tormentors before she can be martyred, prays to God: '[T]uum est, Domine, et uirginitatem seruare et martyrium dare. Quod si nec sponsa nec martir tua esse merear, uel scortum tuum in tua confessione permanens ero'[71] [It is yours, Lord, to preserve virginity and to grant martyrdom. But if I deserve to be neither your spouse nor your martyr, confessing you, I will remain your whore]. But the agency of the speaking virgin martyr clearly did not fit Anselm's understanding of Gunhild's position. Rather, in deploying the narrative of spiritual marriage with its cultural logic of the willing object, Anselm ascribes to the bride conveyed (and to its inverse, the bride removed) a phantom agency by which silence is read as consent. Such phantom agency is the means by which Anselm could insert will into the canon's folding of *signum* and *res* in the performative of the habit. Phantom agency proclaims intention from silence and incurs guilt.

In the end, Anselm's insistence on Gunhild's canonical state as a nun in contradistinction to Lanfranc's form of disposition may well stem from the accident of Anselm's having once met Gunhild and thus having observed her performance as a nun.[72] Certainly, he takes a pleasantry of hers remembered from that occasion (a wish that she could always listen to

70 Jocelyn Wogan-Browne, 'The Virgin's Tale,' in *Feminist Readings in Middle English Literature: The Wife of Bath and All Her Sect*, ed. Ruth Evans and Lesley Johnson (London: Routledge, 1994), at 181, reads virgin heroines as models of resistance. But see Robert Mills, 'Can the Virgin Martyr Speak?' in *Medieval Virginities*, ed. Anke Bernau, Ruth Evans, and Sarah Salih (Toronto: University of Toronto Press, 2003), 187–213 at 207, who questions the valence of 'I' in the virgin martyr's discourse.

71 Talbot, *The Liber Confortatorius*, 98, lines 35–7.

72 Perhaps in 1086. See Southern, *Saint Anselm and His Biographer*, 186.

his conversation) as proof that she would not abandon her intention of religious life, whose habit she wore ('[te] non abnegaturam sanctum propositum, cuius tunc habitum gerebas, potui cognoscere').[73] As one of the number of 'all those who saw you' wearing the habit, Anselm seizes on Gunhild's trifling remark; his anxious twisting of its meaning is an index of his refusal to tolerate women with liminal status in the convent. Anselm had seen her as a nun; nothing else mattered.

73 Schmitt, *Anselmi Opera Omnia*, IV: 47 (Letter 169).

5 The Silence of Eve

Mors et uita in manibus linguae[1]

In his prologue to the *Liber confortatorius*, Goscelin of Saint-Bertin, imagining the book to have fallen into hands other than those of Eve, his one-time pupil for whom the work was intended, describes it as 'archanum duorum ... Christo medio signatum'[2] [the secret of two, sealed with Christ as mediator]. The book's characterization as a secret, the defensiveness of its brief prologue, warning off leering, finger-wagging gossips, and the high emotion of its first book, portraying a Goscelin tearfully prostrate at the abrupt departure of Eve, have provoked considerable attention by

1 *RSB* cap. 6.5; Proverbs 18:21 [Death and life are in the power of the tongue].

2 C.H. Talbot, ed. *The Liber Confortatorius of Goscelin of Saint Bertin*, Studia Anselmiana 37, Analecta Monastica, 3rd ser. (Rome: Herder, 1955), 1–117 (=*LC*), p. 26, line 12. Hilarius of Orléans wrote a poem on Eve, 'Veni, dator omnis boni,' after her death. See Walther Bulst and M.L. Bulst–Thiele, eds., *Hilarii Aurelianensis Versus et Ludi, Epistolae*, Mittellateinische Studien und Texte 16 (Leiden: E.J. Brill, 1989), 21–5 and 71. In two essays, 'Ève et Goscelin, I,' *Revue Bénédictine* 46 (1934): 414–38 and 'Eve et Goscelin, II,' *Revue Bénédictine* 50 (1938): 42–83, André Wilmart assembled the historical information that would bring Eve to modern attention. Two translations of the *Liber confortatorius* have appeared: Monika Otter, trans., *Goscelin of St Bertin: The Book of Encouragement and Consolation ('Liber Confortatorius')* (Cambridge: D.S. Brewer, 2004), and Stephanie Hollis, ed., with W.R. Barnes, Rebecca Hayward, Kathleen Loncar, and Michael Wright, *Writing the Wilton Women: Goscelin's 'Legend of Edith' and 'Liber confortatorius,'* Medieval Women: Texts and Contexts 9 (Turnhout: Brepols, 2004). I discuss other treatments in the notes below.

modern scholars.[3] Scholarship has focused on the nature of the intimacy between the two, mostly concluding that the relationship was not sexual.[4] But 'the secret of two,' whatever it might have been, has resisted investigation. Goscelin's figuring of the book (and indeed the relationship between its author and its addressee) as an 'archanum' figures as well its rhetorical strategy, which uses citation of communal texts (scripture, patristics, hagiography) to describe a *private* love. This chapter looks at the *LC*'s account of that intimacy from the perspective of Eve's formation as a Benedictine nun, her move to reclusion, and the question of her agency that haunts the text. Beyond the rhetorical screen of his volume of words, Goscelin's desire with respect to Eve nonetheless shows itself in forming her as a Benedictine nun and keeping her near for his teaching. But the secret of Eve's desire, and an answer to the question of her agency, is screened effectively by her silence and leads Goscelin to write his lengthy work of commemoration and instruction.

The *LC* is the main resource for what is known about Eve of Wilton, though in it Goscelin only records a few details of his relationship with Eve, the daughter of a Danish father and Lotharingian mother. They met at the royal foundation of Wilton some time after Goscelin arrived at Sherborne (ca 1062) in the retinue of Bishop Herman,[5] and the early

3 Rebecca Hayward, 'Spiritual Friendship and Gender Difference in the *Liber confortatorius*,' in *Writing the Wilton Women*, ed. Hollis, 341–53 at 341–7, reviews scholarly opinion on the relationship.

4 Wilmart, 'Ève et Goscelin, II,' p. 60, n. 3, discourages suspicion by pointing to Goscelin's rhetorical excess: 'Même s'il y a quelque excès dans l'expression … nous aurions grand tort d'y trouver scandale, songeons plutôt qu'un bras de mer séparait désormais ces deux âmes.' Frank Barlow, ed. and trans., *The Life of King Edward Who Rests at Winchester*, 2nd ed., OMT (Oxford: Clarendon Press, 1992), 139, accepts Wilmart's judgment but thought that the friendship 'although probably innocent, was nevertheless dangerous.' Daphne Stroud, 'Eve, Nun of Wilton and Anchoress of Angers,' *Hatcher Review* 4, no. 37 (Spring 1994): 3–13 at 3, believes that '[t]heir relationship was an innocent one.' Hayward, 'Spiritual Friendship and Gender Difference,' in *Writing the Wilton Women*, ed. Hollis, 341–53, reads the *LC* as an example of chaste, ennobling love. H.M. Canatella follows Hayward (and others) in reading the relationship as spiritual friendship in 'Long-Distance Love: The Ideology of Male-Female Spiritual Friendship in Goscelin of Saint Bertin's *Liber confortatorius*,' *Journal of the History of Sexuality* 19.1 (2010): 35–53.

5 Michael Lapidge has shown that the common dating of Herman's appointment as bishop of Sherborne to 1058 is an error, since his predecessor, Ælfwold, was still bishop in 1062. Goscelin accompanied Bishop Herman from Saint-Bertin to Sherborne. See Michael Lapidge, *The Cult of St Swithun*, Winchester Studies 4.ii (Oxford: Clarendon Press, 2003), 614, n. 14. Herman died 20 February 1078 and Osmund succeeded him.

pages of the *LC* are filled with tantalizing references to the years of their contact. Goscelin alludes to his persistent (if initially unwelcome) efforts to persuade Eve to adopt the religious life, her eventual consecration as a nun of Wilton, their continuing contact for her instruction, their meetings and letters, and her unexpected departure for reclusion in Angers (between 1080 and 1082).[6] André Wilmart's influential account of the lives of the two, apparently taking Goscelin's diminutives at face value, made Eve an oblate of about seven when Goscelin first knew her.[7] Given the social and political circumstances surrounding the Conquest, and given Eve's wealth (evidenced in the books she gave Goscelin) and her early unwillingness to be a nun, it is more likely that the Eve Goscelin first knew while he was chaplain to the community of Wilton was an heiress committed to that convent for her education and for the protection of her inheritance.[8] As we have seen in chapters 3 and 4, Wilton was a convent with long-standing royal connections: St Edith, daughter of King Edgar, and her mother, Wulfthryth, were inmates of that house in the tenth century.[9] Edith, widow of Edward the Confessor, had been educated at Wilton,

6 *LC* 28–9.25.

7 Wilmart, 'Ève et Goscelin, II,' p. 58, n. 2, reading Goscelin's description of the liturgy at *LC* 28.7–14 as an oblation. Wilmart seems to have revised his opinion from his earlier comment in 'Ève et Goscelin, I,' p. 424, n. 2, where he suggests that 'Goscelin nous dira expressément, ayant été présent, qu'elle reçut la consécration des vierges, selon le rituel le plus élaboré.' Other scholars have followed Wilmart's lead in regarding Eve as an oblated child. See Barlow, ed., *The Life of King Edward*, p. 138, n. 43; Therese Latzke, 'Robert von Arbrissel, Ermengard, und Eva,' *Mittellateinisches Jahrbuch* 19 (1984): 116–54 at 137; Stroud, 'Eve, Nun of Wilton and Anchoress of Angers,' 5, suggests that Goscelin first encountered Eve when she was a little girl (about seven) committed to Wilton, though not, perhaps, as an oblate. Otter, *Book of Encouragement*, pp. 23–4, n. 9, recognizes the chronological problems and describes the ritual as more likely 'profession.' Hollis, *Writing the Wilton Women*, 2 and 226, accepts without further consideration Wilmart's assessment of Eve's early youth.

8 'Libros optatos dedisti' (*LC* 28.4–5) [you gave me wished-for books]. Hollis, *Writing the Wilton Women*, 316, argues that Eve, as a child, 'obtain[ed]' the books for Goscelin from the Wilton library. However, Barnes and Haywood in the same volume (102) translate 'gave.' I argue that Eve was neither a young child nor an oblate when Goscelin first knew her. Rather, the liturgy that Goscelin refers to in *LC* 28.7–14 was evidence of her consecration as a nun. See my 'Goscelin and the Consecration of Eve,' *ASE* 35 (2006): 251–70. Daphne Stroud, 'Eve of Wilton and Goscelin of St Bertin at Old Sarum ca 1070–1080,' *Wiltshire Archaeological and Natural History Magazine* 99 (2006): 204–12 at 205, revises her earlier argument (n. 7 above) and suggests that Goscelin became Eve's teacher when she was about twelve years old.

9 For St Edith and her mother, Wulfthryth, see above, chapter 3. For Wilton's foundation and earlier endowments see Sarah Foot, *Veiled Women*, 2 vols. (Aldershot: Ashgate, 2000), II: 221–31.

had its church rebuilt in stone (dedicated 3 October 1065), and may have been a resident of Wilton after the Conquest.[10] And during the time that Eve spent at Wilton, Edith/Matilda, later wife of Henry I, and Gunhild, daughter of Harold Godwinson, were both inmates of that house.[11] It is thus reasonable to assume from their placement of Eve at Wilton that her parents were both wealthy and well connected.[12]

Although the *LC* only hints at the personal relationship between Goscelin and Eve, it is considerably more direct in its efforts to continue, even at a long distance, Goscelin's pedagogical relationship with his former pupil. And in this purpose, the book reveals a careful deployment of discursive forces aimed at the spiritual formation of a late eleventh-century religious woman. Its complement in this work of constructing identity was the institutional life of regular Benedictinism, with its textual and somatic rhythms of liturgical life. This chapter examines the work of these two forces in making Eve to enable the question: in what way can we see agency operating in her life?

In recalling to Eve how he came to love her, Goscelin explains to her that 'continuata quoque silentia tua, sollicita continentia, frequens psalmodia, pia magistre testimonia, magis accenderunt uota mea' (*LC* 28.14–16) [your continued silence, careful continence, frequent singing of the psalms, and the conscientious reports of your superior also kindled my desires more and more]. Goscelin's attraction to her silence, a practice listed first among her other virtues, asks our attention for what it can tell us about her. The silence of Eve is, of course, an exercise in monastic virtue. Chapter 6 of the *RSB* stresses the importance of silence 'that I sin not with my tongue' (Ps. 38:2). But the chapter further explains silence in the Benedictine context

---

10 On Edith at Wilton see Pauline Stafford, *Queens, Concubines, and Dowagers: The King's Wife in the Early Middle Ages* (Athens: University of Georgia Press, 1983), 54–5 and 179. Edith's interest in Wilton and her rebuilding of the convent church is recorded in Barlow, *The Life of King Edward*, 70–5 and 138. On the churches associated with each Edith see Catherine E. Karkov, 'Pictured in the Heart: The Ediths at Wilton,' in *Intertexts: Studies in Anglo-Saxon Culture Presented to Paul E. Szarmach*, ed. Virginia Blanton and Helene Scheck (Tempe, AZ: Arizona Center for Medieval and Renaissance Studies, 2008), 273–85.

11 On Edith/Matilda and Gunhild, see above, chapter 4.

12 On the wealth and status of Wilton see Julia Crick, 'The Wealth, Patronage, and Connections of Women's Houses in Late Anglo-Saxon England,' *Revue Bénédictine* 109 (1999): 154–85, Table 1, 162–3, and Foot, *Veiled Women*, II: 224–5. On the retreat of heiresses to convents in the wake of the Conquest see chapter 4, and Eleanor Searle, 'Women and the Legitimisation of Succession at the Norman Conquest,' *Anglo-Norman Studies* 3 (1981 [for 1980]): 159–70 and 226–9.

of the monastery as proper to the *scola*: speech should be rare, and then reserved for the master: 'Nam loqui et docere magistrum condecet, tacere et audire discipulum conuenit'[13] [For it is proper for the master to speak and teach; it is proper for the pupil to be silent and listen]. In this observation, the *RSB* offers context for the institutional relation between their roles: Goscelin as member of Bishop Herman's household, chaplain to the nuns at Wilton, and teacher of Eve; and Eve, at first a lay resident and then a professed nun in that royally endowed convent. And yet, in the *LC* Eve's silence assumes a more urgent, intimate role in her relationship with Goscelin. It was, in Goscelin's estimation, the index of her compliance with his teachings: 'In allocutione mutua, tu quod facundissima, pia monita bibebas muta' (*LC* 29.11–12) [In mutual consolation, though most eloquent, you drank in my pious admonitions mute]. But after her departure, Eve's silence across the distance between Wilton and Angers takes on a double valence – was her departure for reclusion obedience to a higher order or something else? was it assent or revolt? – and torments him, driving him to write a book of formation whose rhetorical purpose professes to continue that mutual *allocutio*. For him, consolation lay in imposing a meaning on the departed Eve's silence. The anguishing doubt that haunted him thus makes the *LC* a material extension of the admonitions he had used to shape her conduct and form her as a Benedictine nun of Wilton.

The silence of Eve presents its own scholarly problems for us as we struggle to understand something of the life of this late eleventh-century woman and her move to reclusion. The style and range of the *LC* tell us that she was a woman of considerable accomplishment, measured by the letters she is said to have written and by her ability to read Goscelin's complex Latin style and appreciate his wide-ranging allusions.[14] Yet her silence figures as well for us the larger silence of the historical record of late eleventh-century England: there are few details of the conventual life of Wilton in this period with which to understand her life and the lives of her sisters in religion much beyond the economic fact that Wilton was one of the two richest convents in England. The circumstances of Eve's departure for reclusion between 1080 and 1082 impose similar handicaps amid the silence of the historical record. In the pages of Goscelin's instructional tract to Eve – some ninety printed pages in Talbot's edition – we hear the words

13 Rudolph Hanslik, ed., *Benedicti Regula*, 2nd rev. ed., CSEL 75 (Vienna: Hoelder-Pichler-Tempsky, 1972), cap. 6.6, p. 39.

14 *LC* 29.5–6.

of Jerome and Ambrose, Origen and Augustine, we read epitomes of *uitae* and *passiones*, and excerpts from homiliaries; we wade through scriptural centos, and mark learned allusions to classical authors, but we never read Eve's words, nor can we hear her voice, other than through Goscelin's occasional ventriloquism.[15] As the silence of Eve that Goscelin says 'kindled his longings' (*LC* 28.16) imposes considerable obstacles in understanding the forces at work in forming Eve, it also complicates our ability to see agency in her actions. In representing itself as the force responsible for Eve's formation by first shaping for her a particular, recognizable religious identity as Christian woman and consecrated virgin and then providing a pattern for her life in the new context of her anchor-hold, the contrasting plenitude of Goscelin's speech casts Eve's silence as consent. But it would be a mistake to accept this representation uncritically.

What follows reads the *LC* as a particular articulation of textual and social forces brought to bear in shaping the life of an English religious woman of the late eleventh century. In writing to Eve, Goscelin hoped (among many tangled motives) to continue his earlier work of forming her as a Benedictine nun of Wilton. To read the text with this goal in mind is to analyse Goscelin's multivalent practice of citation, writing within and against the tradition of advice to a consecrated virgin established by Ambrose and Jerome, adapting the archive to the particular circumstances of Eve, who had left her convent and her country for reclusion in Angers. But it also requires reading the contradictions of the text through and past the rhetorical screens that shield Eve (and Goscelin) from the scrutiny of his readership. In interrogating these contradictions I would like to look at several moments in the *LC* that balance Goscelin's claims of mastery against his crushed pleas for her continued love. Such a reading sets Goscelin's claims for the textual formation of Eve against the daily life of Wilton as it forged communal association through the corporal shapings of time, and through modes of dress, postures, and practices of space. And between these two deployments of social force – the mediation claimed by Goscelin and the habitus developed in communal life – the making of Eve raises the question of her agency in her removal to Angers. As with everything left to us of Eve's life in England, it is Goscelin who frames that question.

15 For example, he imagines her complaining that her cell is so narrow ('Sed cella mea quam angusta est, dicas' [*LC* 77.8]), and imagines her thinking that she has been buried alive ('Quid si te hic sepultam cogites, aut hoc cubiculum sepulcrum estimes?' [*LC* 79.8]).

Making Eve

In addressing Eve in the beginning of the *LC*, Goscelin makes a highly emotional appeal to her that she not imagine that they are parted, despite the distance separating them: he is present in his very soul: 'adest tibi Goscelinus tuus, inseparabili anime presentia' (*LC* 27.1–2). While they are separated bodily, and while she endures what he figures as an earthly exile, they may hope to be joined in that *patria* 'ubi nunquam perpetuo possimus seiungi' (*LC* 27.6) [where for eternity we can never be separated]. Rather than his tongue, his pages now will speak to her. And to console her he urges:

> Et que meis debebantur sceleribus, hec separationis tormenta, alligare et refouere nos poterit intercurrens epistola. Loquetur etiam edificatius tenax pagina quam fluxa lingua; poterit et tua dilectio uidere lectione quem reliquit facie, et uocem et uerba nostra suspiriosa oculis pro auribus haurire. Ne ergo me putes abscisum a te, quotiens, in Christo nostri memor, dignaberis hec nostra monimenta respicere, estimato me tecum Wiltonie coram sancta domina nostra Eadgyda aut etiam in hac pudica serie residere, te alloqui, te exhortari, te consolari, anhelantibus uulnerose caritatis affectibus Christum tuo infundere pectori. (*LC* 27.13–21)
>
> [And a letter running between us will be able to bind up what is owing to my sins, these torments of separation, and to refresh us again. The steadfast page may speak more edifyingly than a flowing tongue; and your love, by reading, will be able to see the one whom you abandoned bodily, and to drink in my voice and sighing words with eyes for ears. Lest you think me separated from you, mindful of me in Christ, as often as you deign to regard these writings of mine think that I reside with you at Wilton under the eyes of our holy lady Edith, or more, in that chaste connection, that I speak to you, exhort you, console you, pour Christ into your breast with the panting desires of wounded love.]

However distressed Goscelin is at the unspecified transgressions that led to Eve's departure, at the miles separating him from her, and at the loneliness of his bereavement, his most palpable loss in this passage is access to her ears, that he might speak, exhort, console, and pour Christ into her. The consolation he offers himself is the prospect of a different speaking to her and a different presence, this time through written words. Neither able nor worthy to visit her in the flesh, he must make do with what he styles 'anxious letters and long complaints.'[16] Separated from Eve in the flesh, Goscelin proceeds to disembody her in the treatise, addressing her as his soul.[17] The realm of souls beyond the gendered body offers Goscelin consolation, for in this realm, by writing and sending his treatise he contrives to be present and continue his work of exhortation, to continue making Eve. As the emotional opening to the *LC* makes clear, while Christ is invoked as the *medius* between them, Goscelin desires above all else to perpetuate the (for him) crucial role of mediating between Eve and God.

The *LC* makes it clear that Goscelin's continuing objective in their long association was Eve's formation, as he tells her that even though his exhortations to her were initially unwelcome, he was 'securus me facile correcturum tam piam animam' (*LC* 28.2) [certain that I would easily correct so pious a soul]. Though she had at first refused the life of a nun ('Aliquando indignabaris uocari monacha,' *LC* 104.1–2) her consecration, the ritual production and confirmation of her identity as a Benedictine nun, became, in his portrayal of it, the moving consequence of his earlier instruction and a welcome opportunity to instruct her further.[18] Goscelin's various descriptions of his pedagogical relationship with Eve are deeply ambiguous in their suffusion with a language of a love that eludes ready classification as either tutelary or amatory. But a dream that he ascribes to her speaks clearly about his own desire in making Eve:

> Recolisne quod te a me cibatam pane candidissimo ante nostrum spiritum somniaueras, tibique inter edendum massas aureas in ore repertas, quas sensim in gremium colligebas? Respice panem uite et uerbum Domini super aurum desiderabile, ac de hoc auro eternum monile tibi labore confice, omnia uerba hec Domini cum Maria conseruando et conferendo in corde tuo. (*LC* 29.13–18)
>
> [Do you recall that you dreamt that you had been fed by me with the purest bread before our spirit,[19] and among the golden lumps found in your mouth that you were about to eat, what you were slowly collecting in your heart? Look to the bread of life and the word of the Lord, desirable beyond gold,

16 'quia nec potuit nec meruit unanimis tuus te accessibus uisitare corporeis, querit nunc anxiis litteris et longis querelis' (*LC* 27.10–11).

17 See below, pp. 226–7.

18 See *LC* 28.6–14. On the details of Goscelin's evocation of the liturgy see my 'Goscelin and the Consecration of Eve,' esp. 260–3.

19 Cf. Otter, *Goscelin of St Bertin*, 25–6; Hollis, *Writing the Wilton Women*, p. 104, n. 10.

and from this gold prepare an eternal necklace by preserving with Mary all these words of the Lord and gathering them in your heart.]

Whatever Eve may have thought of the dream (and, indeed, whether she actually dreamt it or not), what Goscelin lays out here is of crucial importance to him in fixing the terms of their relationship and the character of his actions toward her. Although he is careful to describe it as *her* dream, framing it as a matter of *her* memory, it is for all that *his* dream, in that *his* words are the fabric of the dream and give it meaning.

The dream that Goscelin asks her to remember contains a single core of images for which Goscelin offers interlocking interpretations. Though set in the past, the dream, understood through late antique and early medieval interpretive frames, is nonetheless both predictive of future action and freighted with direct commands.[20] Its vivid images of feeding and eating figure the relationship with Eve that Goscelin wishes to keep and develop. The core action of the dream – Goscelin fills Eve's mouth – restated with variation in a separate clause, displaces and condenses different possibilities for Goscelin's mastery. In the description of filling up Eve's mouth, words for feeding or eating ('cibatam,' 'edendum') dominate. The dream proper presents the objects placed in her mouth as 'purest bread,' and in the act of feeding Eve Goscelin portrays himself as nurturing parent: he is the spiritual father who sent her the 'piscis assus' at the feast following a church dedication. But the pure bread he gives her in the dream is understood by a parallel metaphor as the Eucharist, which he offers her in his role as chaplain to the nuns of Wilton.[21] Goscelin himself fosters this interpretation by his metaphoric gloss on 'pane candidissimo.' The word

20 On the authority and meaning of dreams in patristic writing see Patricia Cox Miller, '"A Dubious Twilight": Reflections on Dreams in Patristic Literature,' *Church History* 55.2 (1986): 153–64. For a discussion of dream theory available in Anglo-Saxon England see Malcolm R. Godden, 'Were It Not That I Have Bad Dreams: Gregory the Great and the Anglo-Saxons on the Dangers of Dreaming,' in *Rome and the North: The Early Reception of Gregory the Great in Germanic Europe*, ed. Rolf H. Bremmer, Jr, Kees Dekker, and David F. Johnson (Paris: Peeters, 2001), 93–113. St Monica, of course, made good use of dreams; see Augustine, *Confessions*, ed. James J. O'Donnell, 3 vols. (Oxford: Clarendon Press, 1992), III.11 (vol. I, p. 31). For a use of dreams to predict behaviour, roughly contemporary to the *LC*, see Guibert of Nogent, *Autobiographie*, ed. and trans., Edmond-René Labande (Paris: Les Belles Lettres, 1981), cap. 14, p. 98, where his mother reads her steward's dream as confirmation of her retirement to a monastery. In cap. 16 Guibert quotes Eccles. 5:2 ('multas curas sequuntur somnia' [Dreams follow many cares]) on the significance of dreams.

21 On his role as chaplain see Barlow, *Life of King Edward*, 135.

'candidus' covers a range of meanings from 'pure' to 'shining.'[22] In the second clause of the dream, 'candidus' in its other sense of 'shining' is refigured as gold, and the 'massas aureas' Eve discovers in her mouth are, in Goscelin's glossing, the Bread of Life ('panem uite'). But Goscelin's gloss is doubled when he tells Eve to see and attend not simply to the Bread of Life but to the word of the Lord, more desirable than gold (evoking the 'desiderabilia super aurum' of Ps. 18:11).

As Goscelin interprets Eve's dream for them both, 'the purest bread' is, finally, neither food nor Eucharist; by a potent displacement, he reads what he feeds her as the word of the Lord desirable beyond gold. Just as the Blessed Virgin, not understanding the words her son told her after his teaching in the temple, 'kept all these words in her heart' ['et mater eius conservabat omnia verba haec in corde suo' (Lk 2:51)], Eve is enjoined to gather up all those words of the Lord given to her by Goscelin. As Mary, Eve is to treasure the words of the Lord that Goscelin speaks. Beyond being the passive receptacle filled from Goscelin's mouth, the silent Eve is urged to a further task of internalizing his admonitions and shaping her life from Goscelin's words by making from them an 'eternum monile' [an eternal necklace]. The image is not innocent. Eve's community would have sung the antiphon 'Induit me Dominus' regularly as part of the Divine Office for the common of Virgins and also for the Office of St Agnes on the commemoration of her martyrdom.[23] But more personally, by these words Eve was meant to recall the antiphon she sang at the climactic moment of her consecration, when the bishop had veiled her: 'Induit me Dominus cyclade auro texta, et immensis monilibus ornavit me'[24] [The Lord has clothed me with a robe woven of gold, and adorned me with costly jewels]. In making for herself an eternal necklace from the words of the Lord and the words of the antiphon, Eve is urged to adorn herself

22 Lewis and Short, s.v. 'candidus,' senses I and II. See also *Thesaurus Linguae Latinae*, senses A and B.

23 For the full text of the antiphon, see René-Jean Hesbert, ed., *Corpus Antiphonalium Officii*, 6 vols., Rerum Ecclesiasticarum Documenta, series maior, fontes 7–12 (Rome: Herder, 1963–79), vol. 3, item 3328. See further my 'Goscelin and the Consecration of Eve,' 263.

24 See Cyrille Vogel and Reinhard Elze, eds., *Le Pontifical Romano-Germanique du Dixième Siècle*, 3 vols., Studi e Testi, 226, 227, 269 (Vatican City: Bibliotheca Apostolica Vaticana, 1963–72), I: 44 (=PRG, XX.17). The 'cyclas' was a garment associated with young married women; see Albert Blaise and Henri Chirat, *Dictionnaire latin-français des auteurs chrétiens* (Turnhout: Brepols, 1967), s.v. 'cyclas,' http://clt.brepolis.net/dld/pages/QuickSearch.aspx (accessed 2 March 2011).

as the virgin bride joyfully awaiting her divine Spouse, whose call to her comes from Goscelin's lips.

However much Goscelin congratulated himself on Eve's embrace of the monastic life, producing her as the child of his efforts, more forces were at work on Eve than Goscelin's busy invitations, pious exhortations, and theatrically staged roast fish.[25] The daily practices of the community at Wilton, operating diurnally and somatically, formed Eve as dependably as Goscelin's encouragements or commands, whatever textual richness his commentary on the significance of monastic life may have brought to her understanding of the life she came to embrace.

Identity, Ritual, and Practice

The quiet heroism of the *RSB* lies in the multi-dimensioned self-discipline and obedience that it demands of its adherents; followers of the Rule in the disciplinary rigour envisioned by the *Regularis concordia* were produced as monks and nuns by life-long practices of: '[u]ictum cum pondere, mensura et numero, uestitum, ieiunium, abstinentiam, uigiliam, taciturnitatem, oboedientiae bonum' [victuals according to weight, measure and number; clothing, fasting, abstinence, watchings, silence, [and] the virtue of obedience].[26] This enumeration of the penitential aspects of monastic life undertaken by the inhabitants of the newly reformed houses of men and of women in tenth-century England draws the Proem to the *Regularis concordia* to a close with a significant rescripting of Psalm 67:7, here, 'qui facit unanimes, id est unius moris, habitare in domo' [who maketh those of one mind, that is, of one way of life, to dwell in that house].[27] In this citation, 'unanimes,' which comes from the Old Latin and *Romanum* Psalters,[28] is inserted into the Septuagint version of this Psalm (which contains the reading 'moris').[29] The rescript's identification of 'unanimes' with 'unius moris,' illuminates the reflexive relationship between being of 'one mind'

25 At *LC* 28.33–5 Goscelin recalls to Eve a feast he had arranged for her to attend, where he presented to her a dish of fish simultaneously urging on her mortification of the flesh with this rhyming tag: 'piscis assus, Christus passus' [roast fish; Christ suffered].

26 Thomas Symons, ed. and trans., *Regularis Concordia Anglicae Nationis Monachorum Santimonialiumque* (London: Thomas Nelson and Sons, 1953), 8 (his translation).

27 Ibid., 9.

28 Ibid., p. 9, n. 1.

29 For the Septuagint version see Robert Weber, ed., *Biblia Sacra Iuxta Vulgatam Versionem*, 2 vols. (Stuttgart: Württembergische Bibelanstalt, 1969), I: 848.

and exercising 'one way of life.' That is, the inclination to follow the *RSB* brings individuals together in the monastic community, and following one Rule in community reproduces the 'one mind.' The *RSB* thus makes individuals 'unanimes' through practice.

Communal identity begins with the wearing of the habit (as is illustrated, for example, by its conferral in rituals of boys' oblation or of monastic profession).[30] The habit not only confers and supports identity in the members of the community, but it receives back its signification by their corporate practice; as signifying structures the habit and the monk or nun are inseparable.[31] Beyond the habit, daily practice of the injunctions of the *RSB* formed the individual in the ways of the community. The *RSB*'s specifications of times of eating, numbers of meals and amounts of food, periods of sleep, work, and prayer, times and manner of dressing, of attitudes and postures, committed its followers to corporate time, a rhythm of bell and prayer where bodily necessities ceded to communal activity. The tempos of liturgical performance in coenobitic life mediated the sharp contrast between lengths of summer and winter days and ensured that the passing of time was experienced as a corporate rhythm. Such rhythm marked the very space of the convent, as it moved its inmates back and forth through the buildings of the convent for prayer, work, food, and sleep. The discipline of meals, regular in type, amount, and schedule, meant that the follower of the Rule was intimately acquainted with hunger much of her life.[32] Yet the heroic starvations of St Germanus or, more notably, of St Genovefa commended to Eve by Goscelin (*LC* 63.18–22) contrasted with the ordinary requirements of the *RSB*, which prescribed either one meal or two meals daily, depending on the liturgical season, the day of the

30 The habit's role as a marker of identity thus explains its juridical significance in determining religious status. See Giles Constable, 'The Ceremonies and Symbolism of Entering Religious Life and Taking the Monastic Habit, From the Fourth to the Twelfth Century,' in *Segni e riti nella chiesa altomedievale occidentale, 11–17 aprile 1985*, 2 vols., Settimane di studio del centro italiano di studi sull'alto Medioevo 33 (Spoleto: Centro italiano di studi sull'alto Medioevo, 1987), II: 771–834 at 774–5, and chapter 4 in this volume.

31 Hence Lacan's playful inversion of the expression 'l'habit ne fait pas le moine' to 'the habit loves the monk, as they are but one thereby.' See Jacques Lacan, *The Seminar of Jacques Lacan, Book XX*, ed. Jacques-Alain Miller, trans. with notes by Bruce Fink (New York: W.W. Norton, 1998), 6.

32 On specifications for food intake see *RSB* 39; for drink see *RSB* 40; for the times of meals see *RSB* 41.

week, and later the rank of the feast day.[33] Still, and this is the point about the discipline, embracing and practising the restrictions on what and when one ate installed monastic identity at the visceral level.

Although we do not have records of the particulars of observance at Wilton in the last half of the eleventh century, its observance of the *RSB*, while certainly not heroic, must still have been within an acceptable range. Had there been no recognizably 'regular' life there, Goscelin's cry to Eve that he had expected her to live out her life as a nun at Wilton would have been ludicrous (*LC* 36.31–3). And Goscelin's repeated allusions to the *RSB* indicate that he assumed that she knew the Rule in detail.[34] Goscelin's approval of her silences, careful self-restraint, and frequent singing of the psalms ('continuata … silentia tua, sollicita continentia, frequens psalmodia' [*LC* 28.15]) after her consecration suggests a degree of personal practice internalized beyond the structure of the *RSB*, something that the Rule itself encouraged. Read in the register of identity formation, Eve's embrace of the monastic life she had earlier spurned joins her to the *familia* of Wilton, reproducing her in the model of the nuns of the community by wearing the habit, assuming the discipline, becoming one of the 'unanimes.' In another register, such actions constitute submission to the *doxa*, in Bourdieu's formulation, acknowledging the effects of the dominant classification and 'submitting to them in order to make use of them.'[35]

In contradistinction to the daily rhythm of liturgy and its slowly routinized cycle of scripture and lections, the liturgical moment of highest drama, when the woman's irrevocable commitment is enacted and confirmed, is

---

33 See Gerd Zimmermann, *Ordensleben und Lebensstandard: Die Cura Corporis in den Ordensvorschriften des abendländischen Hochmittelalters* (Münster Westfalen: Aschendorff, 1973), section I.3 (pp. 52–71), 'Arten der Speisen und Getränke,' and section I.5 (pp. 74–87), 'Quantität und Qualität.' For a survey of Anglo-Saxon foodstuffs see Debby Banham, *Food and Drink in Anglo-Saxon England* (Stroud, Gloucestershire: Tempus, 2004). See also Barbara Harvey, *Living and Dying in England 1100–1540: The Monastic Experience* (Oxford: Clarendon Press, 1993), 39–41 and 154–9.

34 For example, *LC* 50.40–51.1 (*RSB* 7.33); *LC* 93.2–4 (*RSB* 7); *LC* 94.22–23 (*RSB*, Prol. 18); *LC* 100.1–3 (*RSB* 7.51).

35 Pierre Bourdieu, *Outline of a Theory of Practice*, trans. Richard Nice (Cambridge: Cambridge University Press, 1977), 164–5: 'Social categories disadvantaged by the symbolic order, such as women and the young, cannot but recognize the legitimacy of the dominant classification in the very fact that their only chance of neutralizing those of its effects most contrary to their own interests lies in submitting to them in order to make use of them.' Although the *Outline* does not theorize agency as such, Bourdieu's observation is a useful articulation of the role of identity in any improvisation.

the ritual of consecration. As we have seen, its solemnity was such that its performance was canonically reserved to the bishop alone.[36] Goscelin describes Eve's moment:

> Adhuc tamen te tolerabiliter forinsecus tantum in spe bona Christi dilexi. Vbi uero inter quattuordecim uirgines, coruscantibus cereis tanquam syderibus et lampadibus supernis, ad dominicas nuptias trepida et penultima accessisti ac, populosa caterua sollemniter expectante, pignus fidei diuine cum sacrata ueste induisti, ille humilis habitus, ille tremebundus accessus, ille suffusus uultus, tanquam ab igneo throno Dei sedentis super cherubim, sapienter metuentis, altius uiscera me percussere cum hoc epithalamico carmine admirabilis gratie: *Ipsi sum desponsata, cui angeli seruiunt, et an(n)ulo suo subarrauit me.* Tactus sum rore celesti et feruore irriguo fleui.[37]
>
> [To that point, I loved you outwardly well enough, only in the good hope of Christ. But when among fourteen virgins, with wax tapers shining as if constellations and heavenly torches, trembling and the last but one you approached the Lord's nuptials and put on the pledge of divine faith with the sacred garment, while a large crowd solemnly looked on, that habit of humility, that trembling approach, that countenance of one fearing wisely, blushing as if from the fiery throne of God sitting above the cherubim, pierced me to the core along with this epithalamium of admirable grace: 'I am espoused to him whom the angels serve and he has pledged me with his ring.' I was touched by a celestial dew and I wept with overflowing ardour.]

In this passage Goscelin describes a liturgy of consecration that took place in the convent of Wilton.[38] As we have seen, consecration is a ritual of conveyance beyond oblation or profession, a spiritual marriage in which the woman to be given is transferred from her family to the *familia* of the convent, as the *sponsa Christi.* In liturgical gestures borrowed from oblation, the Romano-Germanic Pontifical (=PRG) has the virgin to be consecrated offered by her parents.[39] The bishop presiding receives her, taking her by

36 See above, chapter 4.

37 *LC* 28.6–14.

38 On the elements of the liturgy, see my 'Goscelin and the Consecration of Eve,' 258–64.

39 Although rituals pre-dating the PRG survive in sacramentaries and, afterwards, in early pontificals, they do not incorporate the detailed *ordines* characteristic of the PRG. For this reason I use the PRG in the following discussion. Michael Lapidge, 'The Origin of CCCC 163,' *TCBS* 8.1 (1981): 18–28 at 19 and n. 8, demonstrates the availability of the PRG in later eleventh-century England.

her hand, which is at this point wrapped in the altar cloth.[40] The ritual actions the woman herself performs in this liturgy include retiring to put on her newly blessed habit, holding lighted candles during the mass, reciting particular antiphons, and being veiled by the bishop.[41]

As the *ordo* of consecration is specified in the PRG, before the recitation of the Introit the woman retires to the *sacrarium* to put on the newly blessed habit, though her veil is kept aside for the bishop's later ritual action of consecration proper. Now wearing the habit, the woman (or women in the case of multiple consecrations) returns to the church with two lighted candles, which she continues to hold in her hands throughout the consecration.[42] These are the candles to which Goscelin refers in the passage above as 'coruscant[es] cere[i]' [shining tapers], and their particular liturgical function Goscelin identifies by comparing them to lamps. *Lampades*, particularly in the context of 'dominicas nuptias' [the Lord's nuptials], as he calls the ritual that Eve undergoes, draws on the parable of the wise and foolish virgins of Matt. 25:1, 'quae accipientes lampades suas exierunt obviam sponso et sponsae' [who taking their lamps went out to meet the bridegroom and the bride]. Beyond the biblical allusion, the word and the reference to these Gospel verses appear prominently in the conclusion of the formula of consecration proper 'Deus castorum corporum,' which the bishop pronounces over the woman, who is at this point prostrate before the altar.[43]

The part of the liturgy of consecration that Goscelin claims pierced him to the core is the sung antiphons in which each woman voices at key moments in the ritual the words of her spiritual betrothal. Typical

40 PRG, XX.1, p. 39.

41 PRG, XX.11 p. 42.

42 We see such a direction in Cambridge, Corpus Christi College 163, p. 264, line 25 to p. 265, line 1: 'post hęc relinquens puella cęreos. st<et> inclinata usq<ue> || dum missa finiatur' [after this (the reading of the banns), let the girl return her candles and stand with her head bowed until the mass is completed]. London, British Library Tiberius C. i, fol. 114r, specifies a single candle. The damaged London, BL Cotton Vitellius A. vii, guard page 169r, reads '[san]c<t>imoniales tenere debent cereos' [the nuns should hold candles].

43 'Deus castorum corporum' is found in a long and in abbreviated versions. For a preliminary study of this prayer of consecration see Odelia G. Harrison, OSB, 'The Formulas *Ad virgines sacras*: A Study of the Sources,' *Ephemerides Liturgicae* 66 (1952): 252–[273] and 352–66 at 270–3. The prayer is also treated in Jean Magne, 'La prière de consécration des vierges "Deus castorum corporum,"' *Ephemerides Liturgica* 72 (1958): 245–67. For a discussion of 'Deus castorum corporum' see chapter 4 in this volume, pp. 199–202.

of Goscelin, he steals Eve's lines. In its full form, 'Ipsi sum desponsata cui angeli serviunt, cujus pulchritudinem sol et luna mirantur' [I am betrothed to him whom the angels serve, at whose beauty the sun and moon marvel] is the first antiphon sung in a consecration, after the bishop has received the woman from her parents.[44] At the climactic moment of her consecration, her veiling, the newly veiled nun recites alone: 'Induit me Dominus ciclade auro texta et immensis monilibus ornavit me'[45] [The Lord has clothed me with a robe of gold, and adorned me with costly jewels]. The second part of the 'epithalamium' Goscelin claims for himself abbreviates 'Annulo suo subarrhavit me Dominus meus Jesus Christus, et tamquam sponsam decoravit me corona'[46] [My lord Jesus Christ has espoused me with his ring, and has adorned me with a crown]. This final antiphon in the ritual is sung between the conferral of the ring and crown on the newly consecrated nun and before the final benediction. Ring and crown are signs ('signaculum' and 'signum') marking her as 'sponsa Dei' and 'uxor eius [scil., Christi].'[47] Although Goscelin's 'epithalamium' in the *LC* telescopes and appropriates for himself Eve's words in the moment of her consecration, it would be well to consider the work of Eve's voice at that moment in the convent church of Wilton. With Bishop Herman officiating, Eve, as one among fourteen women, ritually assumes her identity as Benedictine nun. Consecration is a liturgical accomplishment, in a sense a finalization of the work performed by the ceremony of oblation and the daily performance of wearing the habit. In the moments before and after her veiling, Eve speaks to voice an ideological script that crosses the lived discipline of the monastic community with the discourse of sacrificial virginity. Her performance of these ritual actions and her speech are understood to confirm her as one of the *unanimes* of Wilton.

Christi bibliotheca

With this background to the institutional forces at work in forming Eve to be *unius moris*, I would like to return to Goscelin and his claims to the formation of Eve. In the argument of the *LC*, forming Eve is filling Eve, and Goscelin, as master, takes on this task. But the *LC* is rife

44 PRG, XX.1, p. 39. See Hesbert, ed. *Corpus Antiphonalium Officii*, vol. 3, item 3407.
45 PRG, XX.17, p. 44. See Hesbert, ed. *Corpus Antiphonalium Officii*, vol. 3, item 3328.
46 PRG, XX.25, p. 46. See Hesbert, ed. *Corpus Antiphonalium Officii*, vol. 3, item 1426.
47 PRG, XX.23, 24, p. 45.

with contradictions that run counter to the spiritual formation he claims. Against the *unanimes,* Goscelin presses on Eve an intimacy where he is 'unanimis tuus' (*LC* 27.10), difficult to translate, but something like 'of one mind with you.' This emergence of the intimate in Goscelin's discourse of identity (hers and his), by setting the *unanimis* against the *unanimes,* fractures the spiritual counsel he offers. Goscelin's desire to make Eve is accompanied by deep feelings of love expressed through biblical tropes, especially on the Song of Songs. The darts of love he claims to feel for her in his heart (following her consecration as bride of Christ), produce the wounds of the non-Vulgate version of Sg 5.8, uttered in the words of the *sponsa* about her beloved. But in adopting the language of the bride for the Bridegroom, Goscelin reverses the mastery of his role as teacher and assumes, instead, the position of suppliant: aching, longing, and waiting.[48]

Erupting in anger at Eve's cruelty in parting from him without a word, Goscelin writes in an extended passage explicitly figuring himself not as father but as 'illa mater anima que te anhelis uisceribus peperit' (*LC* 29.28–9) [that mother soul that gasping gave birth to you from her womb]. In part, this manoeuvre is made possible by his disembodying of Eve in addressing her as 'anima.'[49] In strategic terms, in the larger

48 For a reading of the Song of Songs' 'adducing of projects that bring the maternal into signification' see Theresa Krier, *Birth Passages: Maternity and Nostalgia, Antiquity to Shakespeare* (Ithaca, NY: Cornell University Press, 2001), 55–81 at 65.

49 Across all four books, Goscelin consistently addresses Eve as 'anima': She is 'specialis anima' (*LC* 91.9), 'desideriosa anima' (*LC* 61.35), 'anima mi dulcissima' (*LC* 28.2; 45.21); 'dulcissima anima,' (*LC* 106.10), 'anima mi carissima' (*LC* 28.21–2.); occasionally she is simply 'anima' ('anima mi,' *LC* 39.2; 40.35; 'anima mea,' *LC* 46.4; 'anima,' *LC* 46.1). She is as well 'pignus anime mee dulcissimum' [sweetest child of my soul] (*LC* 103.18) and 'dulcis partus anime mee' [sweet offspring of my soul] (*LC* 116.26). See below for the rhetorical effect of such language in disembodying her. On personal affection in the monasteries of early Anglo-Saxon England see Catherine Cubitt, 'Monastic Memory and Identity in Early Anglo-Saxon England,' in *Social Identity in Early Medieval Britain*, ed. William O. Frazer and Andrew Tyrrell (London: Leicester University Press, 2001), 253–76 at 265. Especially congruent to Goscelin's rhetoric is Alcuin's reproach to an inattentive former pupil in *Epistola* 294: 'olim te genui, nutrivi, alui, et ad perfectum virum usque Deo donante perduxi, artibus studiose eruditum, sapientiae sole inluminatum, moribus adprime ornatum' [Long ago I fathered you, raised you, nurtured you, and guided you to full manhood by God's grace, carefully educated in the arts, enlightened by the sun of wisdom, and especially adorned by virtue]. See also his *Epistola* 295: 'Quare dimisisti patrem, qui te ab infantia erudivit, qui te disciplinis liberalibus inbuit, moribus instruxit, perpetuae vitae praeceptis munivit?' [Why have you abandoned your father, who taught you from infancy, who filled you with

argument of the book, figuring Eve as 'anima' keeps at bay the pointing fingers and filthy sneerers, because it lifts Goscelin's discourse above the carnal. But its potent effect is to reveal the different gendered positions Goscelin assumes for himself in his roles as teacher and lover. The nurturing parent of the dream is now specifically gendered feminine in a striking personification that allows Goscelin to change the register of his theme 'caritatis uulnerata' and depart from scriptural citation to speak to Eve in something close to his own words. As Eve's mother soul, s/he gave up her own country for Eve and lived in England as an exile (*LC* 29.29–30). Left behind, although s/he was expecting a meeting with Eve, s/he rages at the cruelty of Eve's leaving at his/her most vulnerable moment as s/he waited in hope for a meeting and in ignorance of Eve's plans. In the voice of Eve's mother soul, Goscelin accuses her, finally, of offending against the whole Law (James 2:10) by sinning against love ('Vnde, estimaris in caritatem peccasse' [*LC* 30.4]). By her cruel thoughtlessness, 'Parricida ei facta es pro filia' (*LC* 30.6) [You became a parricide to her (=mother soul), instead of a daughter]. Goscelin offers Christ as the consummate example of filial love: taking pity on his mother, even in his agony on the cross, he arranged for her to be comforted in her bereavement by giving to her another son:

> Sed renuit consolari anima eius, et quanquam diligatur uirginalis filii uicarius, solus desideratur uirginitatis unicus. Vnde interim animaduerte quam sancte et pie conueniant in ecclesiis iuxta crucem tres uirgines, aut trina uirginitas: Dominus, mater, discipulus, item sponsus et sponsa, et amicus sponsi, quomodo saluator, qui est ipsa uirginis uirginitas, medius utrumque sexum uirginitatis utraque manu amplectatur. (*LC* 31.17–23)
>
> [But her soul refused to be consoled, and although the substitute for her virginal son was loved, the one unique in his virginity was alone desired. From this think in how holy and pious a manner they place in churches three virgins about the cross, or rather a triple virginity: Lord, mother, disciple, at once bridegroom, bride, and friend of the bridegroom. In this way the Saviour, who is the very virginity of a virgin, embraces each gender of virginity with each hand.]

---

noble doctrines, who instructed you in virtues, who protected you with the teachings of eternal life?]. See Ernest Dümmler, ed., *Epistolae Karolini Aevi*, vol. 2, MGH Epistolae, vol. 4 (Berlin: Weidmann, 1895), p. 451, lines 18–20, and p. 452, lines 31–2. See also C. Stephen Jaeger, *Ennobling Love: In Search of a Lost Sensibility* (Philadelphia: University of Pennsylvania Press, 1999), esp. 46.

Pointing explicitly to the genders of the weeping figures at the foot of the cross, Goscelin, now cast as mourning mother, places himself in the position of the Virgin: weeping, bereft, and loving Christ alone. As Eve's mother soul, s/he has berated Eve for leaving without goodbyes, but the lesson s/he offers her in imitating Christ puts Eve on the cross that Goscelin might worship and love her in the mother's agony of separation. Lord and mother are 'at once bridegroom [and] bride,' and just as Goscelin 'wounded by love' positions himself as the *sponsa* of Song of Songs, here too in a starkly explicit statement of his love of Eve through Christ, Goscelin as Mary loves Eve as Christ. Unable to express (or perhaps even admit) love for Eve in terms of a man's love for a woman, Goscelin can nonetheless love and even demand love from Eve in Christ, so long as his language remains in the figurative realm of souls: on the model of love Christ has given us, 'uideas quid debueris matri caritati' [see what you owe to your mother love (*LC* 31.34)].[50] In commending to her another mother and daughter pair, Paula and Eustochium, he refers to their message to Marcella, 'Mensuram caritatis non habet'[51] [Love has no measure]. But his comment on the letter, that it shows the friendly hand of St Jerome ('que tamen beati Ieronimi amicam redolet manum'), reveals how strongly Goscelin genders learning and teaching male.[52]

If Goscelin genders himself female to express his wounded love, the voice of instruction that he recovers in the subsequent books is emphatically male. Goscelin's predominant mode of writing in Book I of the *LC* is biblical citation, where he creates a text through biblical assemblage and then tropes off its language. While the cento, or more broadly, the adaptation of biblical verses, is a compositional technique that Goscelin uses in *Vita S. Edithae* and elsewhere, in the *LC*, Goscelin's compositional practice is a device for forming Eve spiritually as an anchoress and as his former pupil. Biblical citation is a practice of authority: as a rhetorical tactic that suffuses the work, with respect to Goscelin's potentially hostile

50 Compare Stroud, 'Eve of Wilton and Goscelin of St Bertin at Old Sarum ca 1070–1078,' 208: 'Goscelin makes no attempt to conceal the intensity of the emotional bond between himself and Eve – indeed he can almost be said to flaunt it in his determination to demonstrate the difference between Eve's sublimated, sacred love and his own profane and sinful passion.'

51 *LC* 31.6. See Isidore Hilberg, ed., *Sancti Eusebii Hieronymi Epistulae*, 3 vols., CSEL 54–6 (Vienna: F. Tempsky, 1910–18), I: 329 (*Ep.* XLVI.1).

52 *LC* 31.35–6. See also his story of St Gregorius Nazianzenus's indignant reaction to his dream of the twin girls in 'sapientie domicilium' (*LC* 81.9–15).

readers (the 'aliena[e] manus' into which he hopes his book will not fall [*LC* 26.9]), it is insurance against the suspicion that Goscelin's address to Eve is something it ought not to be. But the rhetoric of biblical citation has a more particular function with respect to Eve, where Goscelin, through his self-glossing, places himself in the rhetorical and didactic position of a Jerome or an Ambrose, or, indeed, a Paul. As we shall see, while Goscelin recommends first in his reading program for Eve the scriptural commentaries of Jerome, Augustine, Gregory, and 'the other teachers of virtue' [*LC* 80.27], before she reads these, she has heard, and then reads, Goscelin.

The explicitly pedagogical mode of book II finds Goscelin working from the library in Peterborough.[53] Citations of a broad range of sources pepper the early pages of this book, where Goscelin offers remembered snatches from the *Aeneid*, from Boethius's *De consolatione Philosophiae,* and from Prudentius's *Cathemerinon.* Gone is the emotion of the first book, replaced by a hard-edged display of knowledge. Having characterized the theme of book II as 'bella cupidinibus' (*LC* 26) [wars against desires], Goscelin draws on some familiar and some fairly rare texts to urge Eve to take up the spiritual combat characteristic of the anchoritic life.[54] As illustration of the challenges she faces, he also offers her models of exemplary women. He cites the *passio* of Perpetua and offers accounts of three women (Blandina, the 'mulier quaedam captiva,' and Potamiana) from Rufinus's translation of Eusebius's *Ecclesiastical History.* In the latter case, Goscelin doesn't bother to redact his material, simply copying at length from the book in front of him.[55] He also offers Eve an extended quotation on spiritual warfare from Origen (whom he misnames 'Jerome' following a particular recension of the text).[56] Here he adapts his text to focus on the tropological reading of physical battles.

From the textual display emerging from his time with the library at Peterborough, Goscelin moves in book III to form Eve by filling her with

53 For the evidence supporting this location see my 'Goscelin, the *Liber confortatorius*, and the Library of Peterborough,' in *Poetry, Place, and Gender: Studies in Medieval Culture in Honor of Helen Damico*, ed. Catherine E. Karkov (Kalamazoo, MI: Medieval Institute Publications, 2009), 151–70.

54 Talbot, at *LC* 26, prints the mistaken 'Pella cum demonibus' as the first words of the second line of the verses that begin the Prologue. The line should read 'Bella cupidinibus mouet euincitque secundus' [The second promotes battles against desires and conquers].

55 See my 'Goscelin, the *Liber confortatorius*, and the Library of Peterborough,' 158–64.

56 His extended quotation is from Origen's Homily 15 (and to a lesser extent from Homily 20) from his *Homiliae* .xxvi. in Iosue (Rufinus's translation). See my 'Goscelin, the *Liber confortatorius*, and the Library of Peterborough,' 165 and 169.

books. In the chapter 'Mensa scripturarum,' Goscelin's opening gambit speaks for Eve: 'Quid si te hic sepultam cogites, aut hoc cubiculum sepulcrum estimes?' (*LC* 79.8) [What if you think that you are buried here, or consider this cell a tomb?]. His consolation is that by bearing Christ's cross, she will rise from the tomb; as a vine that must be buried to bear fruit, so she will live again from her tomb. This chapter is the most direct of the entire book in imagining the life of prayer and work in the solitude of Eve's anchor-hold. 'By praying speak with the Lord, by reading, hear the Lord speaking with you' (*LC* 80:15–16). It produces Eve as a willing, sacrificial victim: 'Ipsa Deo sacerdos esto, te ipsam sacrificando, et ignis amoris diuini semper ardeat in altari cordis tui, quem nutries alimentis sanctorum documentorum et operum, unde uapores Domino sanctorum odoramenta desideriorum' (*LC* 80.6–9) [Be, yourself, a priest before God by sacrificing yourself, and let the fire of divine love always burn on the altar of your heart, which you should nourish with the food of holy lessons and works, whence may you give off the scent of holy desires]. Balancing delicately on a single point, the agency that Goscelin imagines for Eve emerges in the act of her undoing it: she becomes *sacerdos* only in the reflexive action of sacrificing herself. Moving beyond the sacrifice of self-will in the Benedictine practices of obedience and humility, Goscelin orders for her a world evacuated of all associations. As the following passage describes (*LC* 80.11–15), her sacrifice lies in a successive removal of any kind of companionship in order to be profoundly alone with the Lord. Goscelin prohibits her from keeping a cat, or little bird, or pet, or any irrational 'anima' to mitigate her solitude (*LC* 80.13–14). Thereafter he urges her: 'Sola sis cum Domino solitaria' [May you be a solitary alone with the Lord]. And so Goscelin, the self-described 'solitarius in mundo' (*LC* 26.1) comforts himself in restricting her life.

As Goscelin envisions her reclusion, the cell she inhabits becomes the enclosing body for her 'anima.' 'Celle, lingue et aurium fenestre a fabulis et uaniloquiis, immo maliloquiis, sint obserate' (*LC* 80.12–13) [Let the openings of your cell, your tongue, and your ears be shut against tales, and idle talk and by all means from wicked talk]. In this echo of Jerome's Letter to Eustochium on the dangers of an open door, Goscelin maps the openings of Eve's body onto the openings of her cell. In the place of Eve's mouth (which Goscelin filled in the dream of book I) there is now the window of her cell.[57] As with the dream of nourishing words that he

57 See André Wilmart, ed., 'La légende de Ste Édith en prose et vers par le moine Goscelin,' *AB* 56 (1938): 5–101, 265–307 at cap. 7, p. 51, where Goscelin imagines St

recalled earlier, here Goscelin urges Eve to be a glutton at the banquet of sacred scripture, echoing Matt. 4:4 that man lives not by bread alone but by the word of God. Such an idea is both a commonplace (found for example in Prosper's *Epigramma* 8, glossed in several Anglo-Saxon manuscripts) and consonant with Goscelin's theme of filling Eve.[58] He reminds her, too, of his continued role in teaching her: 'Hec tibi, si recolis, tanquam clauim dans intelligendi, frequentius et presens uerbis, et absens scriptis inculcaui' [If you recall, I impressed these things on you frequently as if giving you a key to understanding, in words when I was present, and in writing when absent].[59] He turns to stuffing her cell: he wishes it to be capable of admitting the book collection he wishes her to consume – either the size of the window should be sufficient to receive the books, or she should be able to read through the window if the book is supported from outside ('Ipsa quoque ut possit admittere bibliotecam tam capacem, in longum esse uelim huius celle fenestram, aut per fenestram te legere posse a foris ap(p)ositam' [*LC* 80.29–31]). So contained, Eve is set to exercise her 'ingeniolum'[60] [modest intellect] on an impressive list of writers. He would have her read the interpretations of Jerome, Augustine, Gregory, and other teachers of virtue in order to understand scripture. In terms of specific texts, he recommends that she read aloud ('recita') the life of Antony and the lives and writings of the desert fathers to learn how to fight against the devil;[61] Augustine's *Confessions* will instil divine love in her;[62] he recommends the *Historia tripartita* and Eusebius's *Historia ecclesiastica* as sources for the struggles of the saints.[63] That she might learn

Edith's teachers reading to her through a cell window. The thirteenth-century *Ancrene Riwle* imagines the anchoress's soul with two bodies, the body proper and the cell; see J.R.R. Tolkien, ed., *Ancrene Wisse, The English Text of the Ancrene Riwle,* with an introduction by N.R. Ker, EETS o.s. 249 (London: Oxford University Press, 1962), 193.10–12.

58 *LC* 80.20–2. On Prosper's *Epigramma* 8 ('De doctrina apostolica'), its function in a school text, and its glossing in London, BL Harley 110, see chapter 2 above, pp. 131–4.

59 *LC* 80.23–5. 'Inculcare' also has the sense of 'to stuff, press, or force in.' See Lewis and Short, s.v. 'inculco,' sense II a.

60 *LC* 80.19. Lewis and Short, s.v. 'ingeniolum,' 'a little genius, feeble intellect.'

61 The *Vitas patrum* (*BHL* 6524–7) is a collection of lives and sayings of the desert fathers. The Peterborough Booklist, item 30, indicates that Goscelin had access to it at Peterborough. See Michael Lapidge, *The Anglo-Saxon Library* (Oxford: Oxford University Press, 2006), 144.

62 O'Donnell, *Augustine, Confessions.*

63 The 'Historia tripartita' was a reworking and Latin translation of the ecclesiastical histories of Socrates, Sozomen, and Theodoret. See Walter Jacob and Rudolf Hanslik,

that nothing is more miserable than the abyss of this world, he wishes her to read Augustine, *De ciuitate Dei*, Orosius, *Historiae aduersum paganos*, and Boethius, *De consolatione Philosophiae* [*LC* 80.26–81.4].[64] He urges her to work at her reading: 'Nec uero refugias sicubi sensu hereas, sed occupa, reuolue, relege, donec affatim capias, quia nil tam difficile est quin possit querendo inueniri, et labor omnia uincit improbus, et querenti et pulsanti aperiet Dominus, et intrabit ad te benignus sapientie spiritus' (*LC* 81.6–9) [Nor indeed should you retreat if anywhere you have difficulty with the sense, but take it up, go through it again, reread it, until you may grasp it sufficiently, since nothing is so difficult but that it can be discovered by searching, and persistent labour overcomes everything]. In this way by reading continually she can emulate Blesilla, whom, he misremembers, Jerome called 'Christi bibliotecam' (*LC* 81.17–19) [library of Christ]. Goscelin's urging here, on the importance of labour in learning the contents of sacred books, offers the same homely exhortation as Prosper's *Epigramma* 70, with its evocation of 'seek and you shall find' (Matt. 7:7).[65] In calling on Eve to take the example of Blesilla as a 'library of Christ,' Goscelin is precisely attempting to build in Eve a textual identity. In such a process, as we have seen, one takes in writings, internalizes them, voices them, lives them, and finally is them. A library of Christ is full of sacred texts, and thus the scene that Goscelin imagines places Eve in the second body of her cell, receiving books through her window as (spiritual, textual) food from the table, and taking texts into herself to become the library. But Goscelin only imagines the text/food going in. He doesn't imagine for Eve the other function documented of later anchoresses, acting

---

eds., *Cassiodori-Epiphanii Historia Ecclesiastica Tripartita*, CSEL 71 (Vienna: Hoelder, Pinchler, Tempsky, 1952). What Goscelin calls 'historia Eusebii' is edited by Eduard Schwartz and Theodor Mommsen, eds., *Die Kirchengeschichte*, vol. 2, Eusebius Werke (Leipzig: J.C. Hinrichs'sche Buchhandlung, 1903–8). These are items 9 and 7 on the Peterborough Booklist (Lapidge, *The Anglo-Saxon Library*, 143).

64 *De ciuitate Dei* is item 1 on the Peterborough Booklist (Lapidge, *The Anglo-Saxon Library*, 143). See Bernard Dombart and Alphonsus Kalb, eds., *Sancti Aurelii Augustini De Civitate Dei Libri XXII*, 2 vols. (Stuttgart: Teubner, 1993). Goscelin calls Orosius's History 'De ormesta mundi'; on 'ormesta' see Patrick Sims-Williams, 'Some Functions of Origin Stories in Early Medieval Wales,' in *History and Heroic Tales: A Symposium*, ed. Tore Nyberg et al. (Odense: Odense University Press, 1985), pp. 97–132 at 116 and 132 nn. 65–6. For *De consolatione Philosophiae* see Ludwig Bieler, ed., *Anicii Manlii Severini Boethii Philosophiae Consolatio*, CCSL 94 (Turnhout: Brepols, 1957). Goscelin's single quotation from this work (*LC* 48.1–8) appears to be remembered bits.

65 See above, chapter 2, pp. 134–5.

prophetically and socially from the opening of her cell.[66] In short, the Eve he imagines does not speak.

Jerome and the Letter to Eustochium, present throughout the *LC*, haunt this chapter, though, significantly, the Letter is refused in its detail. Goscelin lifts a tag from the Letter to Eustochium without mentioning its source: 'Orando cum Domino loquere, legendo tecum loquentem Dominum attende' (*LC* 80.15–16) [In praying speak to the Lord, in reading be intent on the Lord speaking with you].[67] Only when we read the larger context of Jerome's comment in *Ep.* XXII.25 can we see both Goscelin's debt to Jerome and his careful avoidance of explicit reference to it: while Goscelin parallels, and indeed repeats, many of Jerome's prescriptions for Eustochium, he differs significantly from Jerome in his careful avoidance of issues having to do with the body and the flesh and in his own peculiar handling of the tropes of the dedicated virgin's rewards after death.

Jerome's Letter to Eustochium means not to praise her virginity but to teach her to fear those things that endanger it. Indeed, the letter insists, the consecrated virgin must ever fear the loss of her virginity: 'qui uiderit, inquit, mulierem ad concupiscendum, iam moechatus est eam in corde suo. perit ergo et mente uirginitas'[68] [(God) says, 'whosoever shall look on a woman to lust after her, hath already committed adultery with her in his heart.' Thus virginity is lost even in the mind]. Jerome urges that merely physical virginity is not sufficient for the life that Eustochium aspires to. And thus, because as a virgin she is different from other women, Eustochium should remain at home in her room [*cubiculum* = bedchamber]. Jerome uses the erotics of the Song of Songs powerfully to figure Eustochium as physically closed and simultaneously open to the Spouse whose spiritual desire for her is presented in metaphors of physical passion.[69] While Goscelin also cites the Song of Songs throughout the *LC*, and while *uulnerata caritatis*, the non-Vulgate version of 'amore langueo' (Sg 5.8), recurs again and again, gone are Jerome's explicit erotics of the

66 Anneke B. Mulder-Bakker, *Lives of the Anchoresses: The Rise of the Urban Recluse in Medieval Europe*, trans. Myra Heerspink Scholz (Philadelphia: University of Pennsylvania Press, 2005), esp. 176–7 and 191.

67 Jerome has 'oras: loqueris ad sponsum; legis: ille tibi loquitur.' See Hilberg, *Sancti Eusebii Hieronymi Epistulae, Ep.* XXII.25, p. 178, lines 16–17.

68 Ibid., *Ep.* XXII.5.3, p. 150, lines 9–10.

69 For a discussion of this passage see above, chapter 4, and Patricia Cox Miller, 'The Blazing Body: Ascetic Desire in Jerome's Letter to Eustochium,' *Journal of Early Christian Studies* 1.1 (1993): 21–45 at 42, on its erotics.

cubiculum; nowhere does Goscelin discuss the preservation of Eve's virginity, but more curious, he significantly reconfigures Jerome's presentation of Eustochium's reward after death. Jerome imagines for Eustochium a glorious reward for her dedicated virginity, when Mary, the mother of God, comes to welcome her with her virgin company. Then the Bridegroom himself will step forward and speak to Eustochium with words from Sg 2.10, 'Arise, make haste, my love, my dove, my beautiful one, and come,' and she will be transformed. And the chaste wives and widows will come to greet her, and in those bands will be her mother Paula and her spiritual mother Marcella (*Ep*. XX.41).

In stark contrast, Goscelin's reconfiguration of Eve's eternal reward is to watch St Edith's spiritual marriage to Christ:

> Huc quotiens uoluerit, descendet potens regina tua Edgytha, magni Christi thalamo superba. Huc dilectum sponsum inducet cum summis amicis suis angelis et archangelis, apostolis et martyribus, cum regibus et patribus Romanis et Angligenis, cum patre Edgaro et fratre Eduuardo, cum Thecla, Agnete, Cecilia, et Argina, Caterina, multaque uirginum turba, totaque sua VViltoniensis populi familia, quotquot dignos fecit Dominus in sorte sua.
>
> Nec dedignabitur interesse nuptiis filii maxima socrus Maria, et ibi diem festum aget cum nuru sua, omnesque qui diligunt Dominum cum ea, cantantes Domino in gaudio et letitia sempiterna, cum quibus et tu cantes canticum nouum in sanctorum ecclesia. (*LC* 115.16–26)
>
> [Here, as often as she desires, your powerful queen Edith will descend, magnificent, into the wedding chamber of the great Christ. Here she will lead her chosen bridegroom with her greatest friends, angels and archangels, apostles and martyrs, with Roman and English kings and bishops, with her father Edgar and brother Edward, with Thecla, Agnes, Cecilia, and Argina, Catherine, and a great crowd of virgins, and her whole family of the people of Wilton, as many as the Lord has made worthy in their lot.
>
> Nor will the great mother-in-law Mary disdain to take interest in the marriage of her son, and there she will prepare the festal day with her daughter-in-law, and all who love the Lord with her, singing to the Lord in joy and eternal gladness, and you will sing with them a new song in the church of the saints.]

This passage complements the epithalamium in the *Vita S. Edithae* (written around the same time as the *LC*), where Goscelin makes the Holy Innocents groomsmen and the Blessed Virgin the *pronuba* of the baby Edith's spiritual marriage to the infant Christ. The contrast between Goscelin's visions for

Edith and for Eve poses an intriguing, if unanswerable, question: Why, given Jerome's textual precedent and given the explicit script of the ritual of consecration, did Goscelin make Eve simply a bridesmaid?

'Non nocet sepultura resurrecturis'

In a work so insistent on citation as its mode of address, so self-conscious about quotation of boyhood school texts and the deployment of authorities, a lengthy narrative that claims no source but 'song and story' stands out starkly. If book I uses a dream to present Goscelin's relationship to Eve in the past at Wilton, the fantasy of book IV, in the dark narrative of Alexander – anchorite, molester, murderer, and saint – offers a story of redemption as a screen for desire.

In the story Goscelin offers to Eve, bizarre in context, Alexander, renowned for his ascetic sanctity, is tempted by the devil, who, disguised as a young monk, brings to him for fosterage a baby girl whom the devil had stolen from her royal cradle. Little time is wasted on the details of the girl's childhood – in fact virtually nothing is said about her. 'Quid multa?' Goscelin asks rhetorically and collapses the narrative of her sad young life into four verbs: 'Suscepit, educauit, iamque habilem corrupit, grauidauit.' [He received her, educated her, and then, when she was old enough, seduced her and made her pregnant (*LC* 104.17–18)]. Alexander is less concerned about the girl's pregnancy than about its effect: the visible sign of her swollen belly will be the occasion of intolerable scandal, which will bring Alexander and the whole monastic world into disrepute. The devil, returning again in disguise, persuades Alexander of the dire consequences of discovery:

> Hostis se fingens condolere tante calamitati, persuadet misero maius nefas illum esse preclarum sanctimonia, prouectum etate, nil turpius sene apostato, si in populum eruperit de priori odore tam feda infamia; protinus omnia turbis et scandalis misceri, totum mundum, non tam in eum quam in omnes sanctos uiros, odiis, detractionibus, maledictis, subsannationibus, conuitiis armari, omne sacrum ab omnibus execrari, illum perditionis multorum magis quam proprii criminis esse reum. (*LC* 104.22–8)
>
> [The enemy, pretending to condole over such a calamity, persuades the wretch that this notorious crime was the greater by his sanctity, increased by his age, that there was nothing more disgraceful than an old apostate, if from earlier sweet odour so revolting a scandal would emerge in public; that forthwith

everything would be embroiled in riots and scandals; that the whole world, not so much against him as against all holy men, would be roused to arms with hatreds, slanders, curses, mockeries, outcries; everything sacred would be cursed by all; that he would be accused of the ruin of many rather than of his own crime.]

Rather than incur responsibility for such prospective sins, Alexander allows himself to be tempted into killing and burying the pregnant girl, accepting the argument that one evil is better than many, and that by burying his crime it would be easier to repent and make amends for this one sin through divine mercy than risk human mobs (*LC* 104.30–2).

Alexander's fall is merely the prelude to his redemption, of course, but Goscelin's claims for the story, ostensibly to remind Eve not to rely on her 'constantia' [steadfastness], are at odds with what the story actually tells us. At first blush, it appears to have a prospective force: beware lest you become overconfident in your own ability to withstand temptation. If that were the case, however, Alexander's story could end with his horrific, self-regarding act of murder, an exemplum with the moral that not even the most ascetic of anchorites is immune to temptation. But the greatest portion of Alexander's story is not his temptation, but his repentance, forgiveness, and elevation to sainthood. In terms of the discourse of chastity, the hermit monk's sexual transgression hardly registers, meriting only two verbs. Rather, the *crimina* of this story are borne by the pregnant girl, whose scandalous belly threatens the status of all religious everywhere, and who must be put away, buried, to preserve (holy) order. Alexander asks to be forgiven for her death and her burial.

Although the overt logic of the story would place Eve in Alexander's shoes (in an injunction to avoid spiritual complacency), the momentum of the story always moves away from temptation and toward the opportunity for redemption. And the gendering of the passage places Eve in the position of the girl, entrusted to Alexander's spiritual direction. The destructive scandal that Goscelin deplores and attempts to fend off in the prologue to *LC* – the 'wicked eye, the sly finger, the inciter and the filthy sneerer' (*LC* 26.13–15) – appear in this fantasy as the evil precipitating the girl's death. Because her imagined desire threatens order and her body threatens to tell, she must be made to disappear: to die to this world, to be buried in the hope of rising again.

It would be a mistake to read the story of St Alexander as Goscelin's attempt to allegorize his relationship with Eve. Such an allegory would make Goscelin literally Eve's debaucher, and the evidence for this, if occasionally suggestive, is vanishingly slight. The tidiness of such a reading is too crude to capture the messy irruptions of desire and repression, law and transgression into the complex intertwining of tutelage and love that sped their correspondence and attended their meetings. Rather I am arguing that the fantasy of Alexander shows us that Goscelin's desire for Eve, here as an obscene filling, requires her death. It is a death he has imagined before in the *LC* by ventriloquizing her burial in her cell. Such a death fends off the wicked eye and sly finger and, in ensuring her silence, guarantees Goscelin's continuing desire for Eve. This fantasy, in imagining a punishment that keeps Eve with him and prevents her from speaking, also screens Goscelin from knowledge he will not have: the reason for her leaving.

In the moment of burying the girl, Alexander recognizes his crime, and weeps for forgiveness. Noticing the trunk of an oak that has marvellously opened, he inserts his hands to explore it and is imprisoned for fifteen years until King Gundoforus – the girl's father – happens onto the scene. Alexander confesses to him, and the king disinters his daughter, only to find that her body is incorrupt. But the unnamed, dead girl still has work to perform, for Alexander begs from her father permission to ask her forgiveness. The king puts a straw ('festucam remissoriam') into the girl's lifeless fingers, and her hand miraculously moves in the gesture of manumission.[70] Immediately, Alexander is released from his imprisonment. Goscelin explains this miracle in terms of Christ's parable of the paralytic (Luke 5:17–26) where the healing of the body follows upon the forgiveness of sin. But Alexander's redemption by the wordless gesture of the buried girl fantasizes a larger order, where transgression is not merely forgiven, but spiritually undone, by an act of interpreting silence. King, monk, and girl are all transformed into saints as Goscelin offers her death as the *felix culpa* that enables their salvation.

'Precipitata et ignorata fuga'

Eve's removal to Angers required planning on both sides of the Channel, both for the journey itself and for the arrangements for her reclusion at

70 *LC* 105:14–15. 'Pater orans festucam remissoriam incorruptis digitis nate imponit, illa susceptam more indulgentis proicit' [Praying, the father placed a straw in the incorrupt fingers of his daughter; she extended it in a gesture of remission]. 'Festuca' was also the name for the ceremonial rod used in the manumission of slaves. See Lewis and Short, s.v. 'festuca,' sense I.b.

St Laurent du Tertre.[71] As a professed nun of Wilton, Eve required the permission of her abbess to embark on a life of anchoresis. The Rule of St Benedict recognized 'anchorites or hermits' as a respected identity within monasticism, and allowed individuals to pursue that life only after a long period of spiritual training in the monastery (*RSB* 1.3–5). Grimlaic's mid-tenth-century *Regula solitariorum* describes a procedure for testing the resolve and worthiness of a candidate for reclusion that was to last four or five days, followed by a year of probation within the monastery. The procedure for enacting reclusion thereafter nonetheless drew on the procedure for receiving brothers in the monastery specified in *RSB* 58.[72] While Grimlaic's Rule specified active involvement of the bishop in the making of a recluse, the degree of actual episcopal participation in individual cases of reclusion cannot be determined.[73]

Beyond the structures of ecclesiastical permission, the journey from Wilton to Angers would have involved considerable time, hardship, expense, and planning. I know of no account of routes connecting the two places, but it is clear that such a journey would have been made in a group and required travel by road and river in England and on the Continent as well as the obvious Channel crossing.[74] Although travel by foot, by cart, or by riding on an ass was possible, travel on foot was quicker than oxcart, involved less jostling, and showed pious humility.[75] Goscelin alludes to a woman who made arrangements for Eve on the Angevin side of the Channel: 'hec benedicta domina, que tibi hunc locum parauit, que Christum secuta, nunc est uerius comitissima, te colit et affectat' [that

71 Hollis, *Writing the Wilton Women*, 229, cites Irene van Rossum, '*Adest meliori parte*: A Portrait of Monastic Friendship in Exile in Goscelin's *Liber confortatorius*' (DPhil, University of York, 1999), 47, 64, to the effect that there was a small group of recluses at St Laurent.

72 Grimlaicus, *Regula solitariorum*, cap. 15, PL 103.592–4. Phyllis G. Jestice, *Wayward Monks and the Religious Revolution of the Eleventh Century* (Leiden: Brill, 1997), p. 92 n. 4, dates the *Regula*, written perhaps in Lotharingia, to ca 950. I have found no evidence for the knowledge of this text in Anglo-Saxon England.

73 Tom Licence, 'Evidence of Recluses in Eleventh-Century England,' *ASE* 36 (2007): 221–34 at 224.

74 For a map of the roads and waterways available for travel to and from the convent of Wilton see David A.E. Pelteret, 'The Roads of Anglo-Saxon England,' *Wiltshire Archaeological and Natural History Magazine* 79 (1985): 155–63, fig. 1. For travel in groups see Patricia A. Halpin, 'Anglo-Saxon Women and Pilgrimage,' *ANS* 19 (1997): 97–122 at 99.

75 Albert C. Leighton, *Transport and Communication in Early Medieval Europe AD 500–1100* (New York: Barnes and Noble, 1972), 60–5, 172.

blessed lady who prepared this place for you, who followed Christ, is now the more truly your most obliging friend, cares for you and cherishes you] (*LC* 92.9–10). Beyond this, Goscelin offers (or knows) no particulars of her involvement in Eve's reclusion. It is tempting to speculate that she provided the endowment to support Eve in her life as an anchoress, since such an endowment had to be ensured before the person seeking reclusion could be established, but the fact remains that we do not have information on the economic arrangements underlying Eve's life in Angers.[76]

I have dwelt on the complications attending Eve's departure for Angers in part to counter the impression of impulsiveness left by Goscelin's characterization of Eve's departure as 'precipitata et ignorata fuga' (*LC* 29.36) [a flight hasty and unknown (to him)]. However rash her departure may have seemed to him, its accomplishment required significant time and organization to bring to fruition. It also required planning and persuasion, and it is in the latter, perhaps, that we may find evidence of Eve's agency in accomplishing her move to reclusion. As we will see, the move to Angers was sufficiently unusual in context to suggest improvisation in crossing and combining contradictory forms of religious life.

The age of the recluse begins (at least in terms of its documentation) in the twelfth century.[77] This is not to say that religious solitaries were unknown in England – the hagiographical literature from earliest Anglo-Saxon England knew solitaries, most famous among them Cuthbert and Guthlac, both of whom were already professed religious before embarking on eremitic life.[78] Bede mentions a number of solitaries in the *Historia ecclesiastica*, and the ninth-century Durham *Liber uitae* lists some twenty-eight 'anchorit[ae],' each of whom it describes as 'presbyter.'[79]

---

76 Licence, 'Evidence of Recluses,' 233.

77 Ann K. Warren, 'The Nun as Anchoress: England 1100–1500,' in *Distant Echoes: Medieval Religious Women*, vol. 1, ed. John A Nichols and Lillian Thomas Shank (Kalamazoo, MI: Cistercian Publications, 1984), 197–212 at 198. See also her *Anchorites and Their Patrons in Medieval England* (Berkeley: University of California Press, 1985), 280. See Mulder-Bakker, *Lives of the Anchoresses*, 21: 'For the period 1100 to 1300 I have the names of more than two hundred recluses. Only five of these were men – and they, in my view, were stragglers from the preceding monastic period. Until the thirteenth century recluses almost without exception lived south of the rivers Rhine and Meuse.'

78 Bertram Colgrave, ed. and trans., *Two Lives of Saint Cuthbert* (Cambridge: Cambridge University Press, 1940); Bertram Colgrave, ed., and trans., *Felix's Life of Saint Guthlac* (Cambridge: Cambridge University Press, 1956).

79 For a survey of early hermits in Anglo-Saxon England see Mary Clayton, 'Hermits and the Contemplative Life in Anglo-Saxon England,' in *Holy Men and Holy Women: Old*

Thereafter, evidence for solitaries is sparse, and in the later Anglo-Saxon period, following the Benedictine Reform, Mary Clayton notes that 'the individualism that allowed the anchoritic ideal to coexist with the cenobitic in the early period seems to have been less common.'[80] While early on 'anachoreta' and 'eremita' were synonymous, as reclusion developed in the twelfth-century 'hermit' kept the older sense of solitary and 'anachoreta' took on a more restricted sense of one enclosed without access to the outer world.[81] Tom Licence has recently argued that reclusion gained in popularity in the third quarter of the eleventh century in England, in connection with a developing ascetic movement (1075–1125), and these 'new' recluses were laypersons, not religious.[82] Licence assembles evidence of some eight of these 'new' recluses from eleventh-century England, arguing that their appearance in the record is a function of a developing terminology for the practice, 'a sign that a recognized vocation was emerging, albeit slowly and imperceptibly.'[83] And Goscelin is the first to use the continental term 'inclusus/a' in England.[84] For the present argument, however, it is important to note that the recluses that Goscelin offers to Eve as examples of the practice were laypersons, not professed religious.[85]

Looking at forms of religious life outside the walls of the monastery from a different viewpoint, there is evidence from the late tenth century in Anglo-Saxon England of religious women from elite families living outside of formal nunneries, either in their own homes or associated with male

---

English Prose Saints' Lives and Their Contexts, ed. Paul E. Szarmach (Albany: State University of New York Press, 1996), 147–75 at 153–6.

80 Ibid., 167.

81 See Warren, 'The Nun as Anchoress,' 198.

82 Licence, 'Evidence of Recluses,' 221.

83 Ibid., 233.

84 Ibid., 223.

85 At *LC* 67–8, Goscelin tells the story of a contemporary English anchorite which he says was related to him by one Eilsius. The anchorite, a simple man named Brihtric (Brithricus), burned alive in his anchor-hold rather than flee Viking pirates. Goscelin locates the anchor-hold in a 'certain village' about two miles ('XV fere stadiis distante') from Bury St Edmunds. However, the incident is not mentioned in either the Ramsey Chronicle or the *Miracula* of St Ivo (*BHL* 4622). John of Worcester repeates Marianus Scotus's entry s.a. 1080 (recte 1058) for the death of St Paternus at Paderborn under similar circumstances. See R.R. Darlington and P. McGurk, eds., Jennifer Bray and P. McGurk, trans., *The Chronicle of John of Worcester*, vol. 2, OMT (Oxford: Clarendon Press, 1995), 584. At *LC* 68.7–10 Goscelin also mentions a woman recluse who survived 'in hoc loco' [in this place] when the church in which she was enclosed burned down. Licence, 'Evidence of Recluses,' 226–7, suggests, correctly in my view, that Goscelin is referring to the burning of Peterborough in 1070.

foundations.[86] Such women lived lives of religion, individually or in small groups, taking vows of some sort and dressing distinctively, but without supervision of an abbess or the liturgical structure of a convent. These women were primarily widows, although some virgins were included in their numbers.[87] Such vowesses could live lives of relative ease on their own estates or lives of prayer and fasting.[88] Whichever course of life they pursued, it was not governed by obedience in the monastic sense of the practice. In this context, it would appear that Eve's move to reclusion in Angers, leaving behind the convent of her religious profession and the adopted country of her family, put her in the vanguard of a religious movement whose contours had not yet assumed a familiar shape. But it also means that her move was outside the repertoire of possibilities normally open to her. As a professed nun of Wilton, she did not fit the profile of the 'new' recluse: a layperson who was also uneducated. Nor did she fit the profile of those religious women, widows or devoted virgins, who retired to their own estates, singly or in small groups. If we look to the Continent, to Guibert of Nogent's mother, for example, we see a model of reclusion that is also strikingly different from Eve's case. Guibert's (unnamed) mother retired from the world circa 1067 (by another estimate 1077) by commissioning a cell for herself at the abbey church of St Germer-de-Fly.[89] The differences in their cases are greater than simply age and geography: Eve was a virgin, Guibert's mother was not. Eve was a consecrated nun, Guibert's mother a widow. Eve went into solitary reclusion, Guibert's mother took an elderly nun as a model and companion. Eve was highly educated, Guibert's mother was not. I suggest that in several combinations and crossings of scripts, Eve improvised her move to reclusion: by reclusion outside the walls of Wilton, by leaving England, by adopting a way of life ('new' or 'urban' recluse) that was only beginning to be defined. In persuading her abbess to permit her reclusion and to support her wish, Eve used her identity as

86 Patricia Halpin, 'Women Religious in Late Anglo-Saxon England,' *Haskins Society Journal* 6 (1994): 97–110, esp. 103. Foot, *Veiled Women*, I: 199–208.

87 Foot, *Veiled Women*, I: 104–10 and 120–6. Foot argues that the term 'nunnan' is often applied to these women, in contradistinction to women religious in convents (*mynecenu*). She prefers 'vowess' to the ambiguous 'nun.' For an argument that the addressee of Ælfric's *Judith* was a 'dedicated virgin living among a community of *nunnan*' see Mary Clayton, 'Ælfric's *Judith*: Manipulative or Manipulated?' *ASE* 23 (1994): 215–27 at 225–7.

88 See Stephanie Hollis and Jocelyn Wogan-Browne, 'St Albans and Women's Monasticism,' in *Christina of Markyate: A Twelfth-Century Holy Woman*, ed. Samuel Fanous and Henrietta Leyser (London: Routledge, 2005), 25–52 at 30.

89 Mulder-Bakker, *Lives of the Anchoresses*, 26.

a Benedictine nun to undo it, moving, improvisationally, 'from one set of socially and culturally formed subjectivities to another.'[90]

The foregoing discussions of Goscelin's deployment of discourse in forming Eve and the concomitant role of habitus in shaping her life bring us to this question: can we see agency in her departure for Angers? In posing this question by way of conclusion, I present Eve as a thought experiment in imagining the terms in which we might identify religious women's agency in the last quarter of the eleventh century in England. We have seen how in the rapidly changing social circumstances following the Conquest, Anglo-Saxon families placed daughters in English convents to protect them and their inheritance from unwelcome Norman intermarriage. The canonical status of these women was ambiguous – due to families' strategic use of the convent and perhaps even tactical, informal veiling – and Lanfranc's letter to Gundulf, bishop of Rochester,[91] sought to clarify their status on the basis of their intentions, whether legitimate, from a love of religion ('amore religionis'), or illegitimate, from fear of invading Normans ('timore Francigenarum'). His resolution of the ambiguity of their position, effected through the language of choice, produced a woman whose status became dependent not on the sign of her state (the veil) but on the merits of what was construed as her previous choice. Her subsequent mandatory choice of life forced her into one of two forms of conveyance – either as a bride of Christ or as a Norman bride.

In 1080 there was no ambiguity about Eve's canonical status. She was a consecrated Benedictine nun of the community of Wilton, whose commitment meant stability in that house. And yet she left. In imagining the possibility of agency in her leaving, do we read into Eve's silence the scruples of a Christina of Markyate? Should we imagine her stung by Jerome's pronouncement that virginity is lost merely by thinking, or perhaps impelled by the bilious misogyny of the *De lapsu Susannae*, which urged that loss of virginity required lifelong, self-abnegating penitence?[92] Perhaps we should look to Wilton itself: should we imagine that Eve left for Angers to undertake a

90 Dorothy Holland, William Lachicotte Jr., Debra Skinner, and Carole Cain, *Identity and Agency in Cultural Worlds* (Cambridge, MA: Harvard University Press, 1998), 7.

91 See above, chapter 3, pp. 172–3.

92 C.H. Talbot, ed. and trans., *The Life of Christina of Markyate: A Twelfth-Century Recluse*, rev. ed., Medieval Academy Reprints for Teaching 39 (Toronto: University of Toronto Press, 1997), cap. 44, pp. 114–16; Hilberg, *Sancti Eusebii Hieronymi Epistulae, Ep.* XXII.5.3; Ignazio Cazzaniga, ed., *De lapsu Susannae* (Turin: In aedibus Io. Bapt. Paraviae, 1948).

life of greater spiritual rigour during a 'crisis' of monastic life, disappointed in the easy familiarity of the regular life of that house?[93] All of these routes offer us ways to console ourselves by constructing stories of agency to fill the uncomfortable void of Eve's silence.

Whether we imagine Eve leaving because of Goscelin or because of Wilton itself, her departure presents itself as a negation. Goscelin, in his rage, called her a parricide – killing her 'mother/soul' and her spiritual father by her departure. As such her silent leaving looks like revolt,[94] in a symbolic act of purification, transgressing the law of stability, indeed the whole Law (James 2:10) in Goscelin's view. Her departure meant leaving behind the structures of identity that supported her in her life as a Benedictine nun and the geography that supported her identification as one of the *Angli (LC* 41.19–21). It is difficult to know if her embrace of the anchoritic life began with an early version of a ritual of inclusion. Such a ritual would make her the central actor in a rite of burial, paralleling in some ways her consecration, but ending not in a 'marriage' but in a funeral that pronounced her dead to the world. Grimlaic's Rule outlines such a ritual, but there is no evidence for knowledge of this Rule in Anglo-Saxon England, and the surviving rituals of inclusion date from well after the turn of the twelfth century.[95]

In a negation of the 'unanimes' for something less well defined, Eve left the regular identity of the *familia*, supported by the somatic rhythms of prayer and work, food and fast, for a singular life, the dimensions of whose definition were very much in process. In the void created by the anchoress's freedom from obedience, as Anne K. Warren phrases it, 'her day, her life, were of her own devising. Whatever her expression of her commitment to God, whatever her pattern of prayer, work and meditation,

93 On hypotheses about Eve's motives and speculations about the religious life at Wilton, see Hollis, *Writing the Wilton Women*, 230. For a salutary corrective to taking the reformers' critiques as accurate snapshots of Benedictine monasticism ca 1050–1150 see John Van Engen, 'The "Crisis of Cenobitism" Reconsidered: Benedictine Monasticism in the Years 1050–1150,' *Speculum* 61 (1986): 269–304, esp. 303.

94 Julia Kristeva, *Revolt, She Said*, trans. Brian O'Keeffe, ed. Sylvère Lotringer (Los Angeles: Semiotext(e): 2002) at 85: 'It's about re-rooting the self that takes us nearer to revolt in the Augustinian sense – *se quaerere*, i.e. put yourself on the line to reciprocally stimulate memory, thought and will. But there is also revolt in the psychoanalytic sense: Freud's insight means an invitation to revolt (anamnesis, desire, love and hatred) all the better to reveal oneself to create and re-create the self). Understood in these ways, revolt takes on forms that are themselves more complex, less immediately transgressive.'

95 Warren, *Anchorites and Their Patrons in Medieval England*, 76–7; 97–100.

whatever the clothes she wore, the silence she endured, the food she ate, all this was to be her own decision.'[96] This, then, is the ambiguous freedom of Eve's condition in Angers. With the props of her nun's identity removed in her removal from the convent of Wilton, how did she fill the time that Goscelin's devil describes for her: 'in tam longos dies, tam profundas noctes, in tam prolixos labores, tam iuges carceres, tam continuas desolationis mortes' (*LC* 70.13–15) [in such long days, such boundless nights, in such protracted hardships, in such a perpetual prison, such an ongoing death of desolation]?

While imagining the void of this freedom, the *LC* cannot offer Eve a rule for living. If it is backward-looking in its models (for example, its reliance on Jerome's *Ad Eustochium* and Ambrose on the virgin life), it is necessarily so, at a loss for ready narratives. The anchoritic life for women was considerably less 'theorized' in the last decades of the eleventh century than it would become in the twelfth. While anchoresis at the time of Eve's departure is clearly not freakishly new (as Goscelin knew stories of the anchorite of Ramsey and of an unnamed anchoress at Peterborough), nonetheless, Goscelin finds himself writing in, essentially, a new genre, considerably antedating Aelred's *De institutione inclusarum* and the *Ancrene Wisse*.[97] His lack of a narrative model for writing to and about an anchoress indexes the freedom available to Eve to reinvent herself, however difficult that might be.

And what of our limit case of agency? Eve's presence at Wilton was the effect of her parents' decision. Goscelin's determined indoctrination was directed to persuade her to a life against her will. Her integration into the Wilton community appears as the efficient crossing of an ideological script,[98] given particular form by Goscelin's suasions, with the somatic routinization of conventual life. And yet, if we attend to Goscelin's embarrassment for contemporary narratives of reclusion, we may find that the life that awaited Eve differed importantly from the silence of the cell that Goscelin attempted to fill. Recluses, enabled by the sanctity of their lives and the stability of their abode, were to play a profoundly social role in the communities of which they were a part. Tenth- and eleventh-century recluses were spiritual advisers, teachers, consolers of the poor and ill, and

---

96 Warren, 'The Nun as Anchoress,' 201.

97 See A. Hoste and C.H. Talbot, eds., *Aelred of Rievaulx, Opera Ascetica*, CCCM 1 (Turnhout: Brepols, 1971); Tolkien, *Ancrene Wisse*.

98 Paul Smith, *Discerning the Subject* (Minneapolis: University of Minnesota Press, 1988), 156.

intermediaries for the giving of alms.[99] Later recluses are remembered for similar functions.[100] If we assess Eve's removal from the props and signs of cenobitic life, we may imagine in her reclusion a terrifying silence of pure possibility. In this we may imagine for Eve the parricide the jouissance of a revolt – a freedom from obedience that trades convent for cell, radical aloneness in another country,[101] the severity of bodily practices designed to free soul from body, a life of living death, and the internalization of a rule ever more demanding because now found within.[102] Here is where we must look for agency, emerging in the interstices and contradictions among the discursive and social forces that formed her. But if the possibilities of her agency clearest to us lay in negating what came before, we may also imagine for Eve en route to reclusion a productive inadvertence, enabled by the crossing of scripts for the religious life, and allow her a sacrificial life she would regard as her own choice.

---

99 Jestice, *Wayward Monks*, 113–22.

100 On the axial social role of a recluse see for example Henry Mayr-Harting, 'Functions of a Twelfth-Century Recluse,' *History* 60 (1975): 337–52, who outlines the activities of the English recluse Wulfric of Haselbury as arbitrator, healer, agent for the relief of the poor, and, perhaps, banker. For the Continent see also Mulder-Bakker, *Lives of the Anchoresses*.

101 Sometime after 1102, Eve moved to St Eutrope, in a suburb of Angers called Lévière, for reclusion with St Hervé. By 1125 she was dead (Wilmart, 'Ève et Goscelin (I),' 438). Dyan Elliot, 'Alternative Intimacies: Men, Women and Spiritual Direction in the Twelfth Century,' in *Christina of Markyate: A Twelfth-Century Holy Woman*, ed. Samuel Fanous and Henrietta Leyser (London: Routledge, 2005), 160–83 at 167, mistakenly states that Eve left Wilton to live with Hervé in Angers. Some twenty years separated her departure for Angers and her removal to St Eutrope.

102 Julia Kristeva, *The Sense and Non-Sense of Revolt: The Powers and Limits of Psychoanalysis*, vol. 1, trans. Jeanine Herman (New York: Columbia University Press, 2000), 22–4.

Afterword

Over the course of this book, I have pursued a series of questions about agency (here to use the term in its most general meaning) that emerge from my study of the discourses of Anglo-Saxon monastic life during the Benedictine Reform. While concerns about will and obedience figure widely across the centuries of Christian thinking on individual responsibility, I have been interested to study agency and its interconnections with identity and obedience in the last hundred years of Anglo-Saxon England, marked as that time span was by two dissimilar but culturally transformative events – the Benedictine Reform and the Norman Conquest. My approach has been two-pronged. On the one hand, I have mapped some ways writers in late Anglo-Saxon England constructed, understood, and used particular notions of agency. On the other, I have sought to distinguish between past and present notions of agency as a way of highlighting what is historically distinctive from our own about the arguments and assumptions of their writings on this issue. To that end, I have deployed the terms 'agent action' and 'agency' when describing what can seem like deeply paradoxical representations of the role of choice in the assumption of Anglo-Saxon religious identities. Narratives of monastic life in Anglo-Saxon England understood individual men, women, and children as responsible agents in the assumption and performance of religious identities, even as – to modern eyes – they portray the circumstances in which those 'choices' are made as compulsory. Exploring this seemingly paradoxical Christian master narrative of choice and responsibility, (free) will and obedience, has allowed me to distinguish early medieval claims for individual agency (cast as the operation of free will, intention, and individual responsibility) from 'agency' as a current term of art in cultural critique. The early medieval claims for agency traced here, which I have labelled 'agent action,' inevitably seem merely formal, or even hollow, when measured by much modern thought that would insist on the existence of alternatives in order for there to be choice. The dominant cultural scripts at work in the Anglo-Saxon monastic context that define the boundaries of an individual's actions seem to twenty-first-century secular readers to be modes of compulsion or coercion. But I argue that even in this unpromising context, a modern understanding of agency as an individual's *improvisation* when faced with conflicting cultural scripts may assist our reading of Anglo-Saxon narratives of obedience in the taking up of religious identity. Attending to the cultural and institutional conflicts driving these narratives will make possible a more productive approach to the questions of choice and identity they present. From this perspective, attribution of 'agency' to an individual for a particular action requires an attentive reading of cultural norms and a careful disentangling of 'ideological scripts.' In particular, it demands carefully distinguishing between 'agent action' – an action understood to be free while nonetheless conforming to powerful cultural expectations (as when an individual assumes a religious identity) – and 'agency,' a term I reserve for an individual's improvisation when confronted with cultural norms at moments of ideological incoherence, contradiction, or conflict.

Within the assumptions of the early medieval religious narratives studied here, what I have labelled 'agent action' was attributed to individual actors from a master narrative of responsibility. Since the wills of individual Christians were understood to be free by definition, it was possible to attribute praise or blame, merit or guilt, on the basis of intentions inferred from observing those individuals' performances. It is in the light of this master narrative of intention and free will that I have framed my inquiry here, attending particularly to two concurrent questions. First I have asked how the narratives of religious men, women, and children who are the subjects of this book depict the relationship between individuals and responsibility of choice. Second, I have sought to map the specific qualities of that relationship and to parse its effects by reading narrative moments of contradiction and surprise, moments in which individuals respond to conflicting social and cultural demands with a kind of improvisation. That improvisation, I argue, marks a moment at which early medieval 'agent action' becomes something we can recognize as agency.

The story of Æthelwold and Ælfstan with which the Introduction begins epitomizes contradictions inherent in the narrative of obedience structuring the Rule of St Benedict and thereby dramatically shows how agency (in the modern, cultural sense) is possible even in the most rigorous relation of obedience. The potential for such agency can be found in the necessity for interpretation fundamental to the discursive relation between an authority figure and his subordinate, between abbot and subject. The subject must parse the order given to him by his abbot, and the abbot must interpret the resulting performance of that order, inevitably a product of the slippage intrinsic to the act of interpretation. Whatever the 'good will' of the subject or desire to obey, interpretation opens a space for slippage and thus for improvisation, however inadvertent. Indeed, it requires the abbot to reinterpret his own order in the light of his subject's performance. But the agon of Æthelwold and Ælfstan also points us to other dimensions of will and obedience in Christian life. As the monk must interpret the command of his abbot, so must the Christian interpret the will of God. This explicit derivation of monastic obedience to an abbot (or abbess) from the Christian's obedience to God ('qui vos audit, me audit') allows the operation of agency and obedience in monastic relations to function as a model for understanding broader early medieval claims about will, freedom, and obedience. Considered in social terms, Æthelwold's concern about Ælfstan's execution of his command shows how central the reading of performance was (as a process of discerning intention) for evaluating obedience, both in itself and as a marker of religious identity. Such reading was fundamental in canons and conciliar decrees that adjudged religious identity a function of performance, that is, where having been seen to wear the habit was itself the critical marker of identity.

As the preceding chapters have explored, the capacity for agent action, identified by thinkers from Augustine through Anselm as God's gift to rational beings, was re-scripted in practical terms by Anglo-Saxon writers as a demand for responsibility. Because choice was understood always to be possible (since the will, by definition, could not be compelled), men, women, and children, whatever the limitations to their capabilities suggested by their secular legal status, were considered responsible for acts of religious commitment even when made on their behalf by others. They were cast, in this respect, as agents of their own making. Since the choice of the religious life, as it was construed in later Anglo-Saxon England, was presumptively free, both choice itself and its putative freedom had to be defended vigorously and thereby reconciled to God's will and to the realities of contemporary life. In this light, Osbern's theatre of choice for Dunstan's entrance into monastic life in chapter 1 (structured as a drama of freedom and obedience in which Dunstan takes up an identity already adumbrated for the saint by providence) shows a 'modern' pressure to represent free choice of the will (*liberum arbitrium uoluntatis*) operating within the traditional understanding of God's predestination for his saints. As we have seen, the primary interest of early English hagiographers was showing the saint's praiseworthy accession to divine will as a reflexive obedience. Thus when Dunstan is made to object (in Osbern's theatre) that the vow of obedience made otherwise praiseworthy actions worthless because not free, he undercuts the entire monastic enterprise. While it is possible for us to view Osbern's narrative as a fairly daring attempt to combine Anselm's thinking on freedom of choice with standard hagiographical tropes, the scandalized reactions of Eadmer and William of Malmesbury show how very disturbing even a fictional critique of obedience could be.

In a different register, the injunction to oblated boys in Ælfric's *Colloquy* in chapter 2 to 'be what you are' shows fractures arising from contradictory presumptions about religious identity. On the one hand, religious identity was understood as always already given; on the other, the *Colloquy* also presents the assumption of religious identity as a necessary choice, that is, a process requiring agent action. The cautionary tale of the *munuccild*, whose life and identity disappeared in an act of wilful disobedience, illustrates the centrality of the obedient will in the taking up of monastic identity. As a text designed to further the Latin education of boys in a Benedictine monastery, the *Colloquy* also constituted an identity-conferring exercise, as the speaking of Latin by the children imagined in the *Colloquy* would have produced both training in Latin and acculturation in the life of the monastery. Chapter 2 explores the paradox created by the *Colloquy*'s command to 'be what you are': that the children's religious identity was always already given and always in need of constructing, that it required choice to accomplish providence.

If not surprising, it is nonetheless instructive to see how the notion of agent action was deployed in the cases of children and women, two classes of people under tutelage. Chapters 2 through 4 particularly illustrate the way in which agent action, although explained by early medieval writers as a form of choice, functioned instead as a demand for responsibility through which guilt was imposed. For children and women especially, who were legally subordinated in similar ways, religious identities were conferred by the pious ritual actions of others. Much as the *Colloquy*'s command to 'be what you are' reveals concerns about the action of the will in naturalizing religious identity, Goscelin's fantasy ritual in chapter 3 shows how necessary it was for Anglo-Saxon religious writers to defend that naturalization as an act of choice. Goscelin's account of St Edith's 'taking the veil' narrates an anxious fantasy in which divine, parental, and communal wills align simultaneously with the infant's 'free' choice of religious life – a fantasy that ultimately works to counter the unsettling of religious identity for nuns in the later eleventh century. If Goscelin portrays the infant Edith as the heroic agent of her own sacrifice in 'taking the veil,' his recording of Edith's other relation to clothing – the wearing of royal purple – reveals something else about her will. Goscelin's portrayal of Edith's sweet reply to Bishop Æthelwold's reproof – that God 'considers not the clothing but the mind' – together with her citation of scripture might also be read as an improvisational counter-discourse in which Edith gets to wear the identity she wants. Goscelin's recording of the story suggests that the community of Wilton nuns cherished the memory of their royal saint in an act of pious transgression.

Chapters 2 and 3 trace fractures appearing in the representation of agent action in these accounts of the assumption and naturalization of monastic identity as acts of obedience to God's will. But the very nature of such narrative representations militates against our being able to see in them a modern notion of agency, that is, improvisation within an identity in conflicting social structures. By contrast, in the correspondence of Anselm with Gunhild discussed in chapter 4, the question of agency forcefully obtrudes itself. I demonstrate that the letters are positioned in a master narrative that demands agency be assigned to Gunhild by insisting that she was responsibility for her own abduction and rape. Anselm grounds his understanding of Gunhild's departure from Wilton in the complementary discourses of canonical regulation and philosophical speculation. First, the canons lying behind Anselm's judgment on Gunhild's situation insist on the traditional understanding of the identity-conferring powers of the habit. In this canonical model, when an individual's wearing of the habit is witnessed by another, his or her performance of religious identity as a monk or nun becomes real: when the habit is seen to be worn, religious identity is confirmed. And second, Anselm's philosophical analysis of free choice maintained rigorously that the will could not be compelled. These two modes of understanding, canonical and philosophical, combined in Gunhild's case to produce a judgment whose two parts were mutually reinforcing: that her wearing of the habit was in itself a choice to become a nun and that as a nun (identified by the habit) she was guilty of her own rape by violating her identity and improperly using her will. I argue that the rhetorical bravura of Anselm's letters, which desperately attempts to demonstrate Gunhild's agency, in fact reveals what I call 'phantom agency,' a spectre of free choice designed to assign responsibility to the subject of compulsion by insisting that she willingly chose her fate.

Chapter 5, working from the fraught relationship between Goscelin of Saint-Bertin and his one-time pupil Eve of Wilton, pursues the question of agency in her departure for reclusion in Angers. In many ways, it is a limit case of what we can know about individual agency: between Goscelin's labour to form her textual identity and Wilton's communal work in forming her as a nun, can we see agency in Eve's move to reclusion? I have suggested that we look for the possibility of Eve's agency in the opportunities created by the rise of the 'new' recluse. If Eve's commitment to Wilton was her parents' doing, her acculturation in Wilton the work of the community, and her textual formation owing to Goscelin, Eve's move to reclusion may yet be seen as her own. Reclusion in Angers meant abandoning her identity as a Benedictine nun of Wilton for a religious life not yet formally theorized. Whether we look for the possibility of agency in the silence of pure possibility or in the jouissance of revolt, the move to reclusion meant crossing contradictory structures (coenobitic and eremitic) and scripts of religious performance (the practices of consecrated nuns and those of 'urban' recluses). As a result, the new life she would lead was substantially a matter of her own interpretation of the demands of heroic obedience to the will of God, both improvised from stories of past and present eremitic life and inflected by the practices of a Rule internalized in long observance.

Æthelwold's extraordinary recourse to ordeal in order to assess the monk Ælfstan's obedience to his command stands as testament to the difficulty, then as now, of assessing agency in individual action. While the saint could appeal to divine judgment to assist him in interpreting his subject's performance, our own acts of reading agency, identity, and obedience are considerably more contingent. My exploration of the difference between agent action and agency as such has made it possible to read narratives of the adoption and naturalization of religious identity for what they tell us about early English understandings of choice and obedience. The situations of children and women, especially, are revelatory for the ways in which attributions of freedom and choice to the legally incompetent show not agency but its phantoms. In its broadest sense, the early medieval location of freedom precisely within obedience to the will of God (because disobedience meant enslavement to sin) may strike a present-day, secular reader as paradoxical, or worse. But as I hope to have shown, even the most rigorous relation of obedience (as seen in Ælfstan's performance of Æthelwold's order) opens a space for agency through interpretation and improvisation. It would be pleasant to think that both Ælfstan and Æthelwold were surprised.

Bibliography

Primary Sources

Adriaen, Marc, ed. *S. Gregorii Magni Moralia in Iob*. 3 vols. CCSL 143, 143a, 143b. Turnhout: Brepols, 1979.

Ambrose. *De uirginibus ad Marcellinam*. PL 16.187–232.

Anselm. *Three Philosophical Dialogues*. Translated by Thomas Williams. Indianapolis: Hackett, 2002.

Archambault, Paul J., ed. *A Monk's Confession: The Memoirs of Guibert of Nogent*. University Park: Pennsylvania State University Press, 1996.

Assmann, Bruno, ed. *Angelsächsische Homilien und Heiligenleben*. Bibiothek der angelsächsischen Prosa 3. Kassel, 1889. Reprinted with an introduction by Peter Clemoes. Darmstadt: Wissenschaftliche Buchgesellschaft, 1964.

Attenborough, F.L., ed. and trans. *The Laws of the Earliest English Kings*. Cambridge: Cambridge University Press, 1922. Facsimile reprint, Fenlinfach: Llanerch Publishers, 2000.

Banham, Debbie, ed. *Monasteriales Indicia: The Anglo-Saxon Monastic Sign Language*. Hockwold-cum-Wilton, Norfolk: Anglo-Saxon Books, 1991.

Barlow, Frank, ed. and trans. *The Life of King Edward Who Rests at Westminster*. 2nd ed. Oxford: Clarendon Press, 1992.

Barry, David, trans. *Smaragdus of Saint-Mihiel: Commentary on the Rule of Saint Benedict*. Kalamazoo, MI: Cistercian Publications, 2007.

Bethurum, Dorothy, ed. *The Homilies of Wulfstan*. Oxford: Clarendon Press, 1957.

Bieler, Ludwig, ed. *Anicii Manlii Severini Boethii Philosophiae Consolatio*. CCSL 94. Turnhout: Brepols, 1957.

Boas, Marcus, ed. *Disticha Catonis*. Revised by H.J. Botschuyver. Amsterdam: North-Holland Publishing, 1952.

Bulst, Walther, and M.L. Bulst-Thiele, eds. *Hilarii Aurelianensis Versus et Ludi, Epistolae*. Mittellateinische Studien und Texte 16. Leiden: E. J. Brill, 1989.

Burchard. *Decretum*. PL 140.537–1058.

Callens, P. ed. *Sancti Prosperi Aquitani Expositio Psalmorum a Centesimo usque ad Centesimum Quinquagesimum*. CCSL 68A. Turnhout: Brepols, 1972.

Cazzaniga, Ignazio, ed., *De lapsu Susannae.* Turin: In aedibus Io. Bapt. Paraviae, 1948.

– ed. *S. Ambrosii Mediolanensis Episcopi De Virginibus Libri Tres.* Turin: In aedibus Io. Bapt. Paraviae, 1948.

– ed. *S. Ambrosii Mediolanensis Episcopi De Virginitate Liber Unus.* Turin: In aedibus Io. Bapt. Paraviae, 1954.

Chase, Wayland Johnson. *The Distichs of Cato: A Famous Medieval Textbook.* University of Wisconsin Studies in the Social Sciences and History 7. Madison, WI: n.p., 1922.

Clemoes, Peter, ed. *Ælfric's Catholic Homilies: The First Series, Text.* EETS s.s. 17. Oxford: Oxford University Press, 1997.

Clover, Helen, and Margaret Gibson, eds. and trans. *The Letters of Lanfranc Archbishop of Canterbury.* Oxford: Clarendon Press, 1979.

Cockayne, [Thomas] Oswald, ed. *Leechdoms, Wortcunning, and Starcraft of Early England.* Vol. 3. RS 35. London, 1866.

Colgrave, Bertram, ed. and trans. *The Life of Bishop Wilfrid by Eddius Stephanus.* Cambridge: Cambridge University Press, 1927. Reprint, Cambridge: Cambridge University Press, 2007.

– ed. and trans. *Two Lives of Saint Cuthbert.* Cambridge: Cambridge University Press, 1940. Reprint, Cambridge: Cambridge University Press, 1985.

– ed. and trans. *Felix's Life of Saint Guthlac.* Cambridge: Cambridge University Press, 1956.

– ed. and trans. *The Life of Christina of Markyate, A Twelfth-Century Recluse.* Oxford: Clarendon Press, 1959.

Colgrave, Bertram, and R.A.B. Mynors, eds. *Bede's Ecclesiastical History of the English People.* OMT. Oxford: Clarendon Press, 1969.

Colker, Marvin L. 'Texts of Jocelyn of Canterbury Which Relate to the History of Barking Abbey,' *Studia Monastica* 7 (1965): 383–460.

Constable, Giles, ed., and Bernard S. Smith, trans. *Three Treatises from Bec on the Nature of Monastic Life.* Toronto: University of Toronto Press, 2008.

Cox, R.S. 'The Old English Dicts of Cato.' *Anglia* 90 (1972): 1–42.

Crawford, S.J., ed. *The Old English Version of the Heptateuch, Aelfric's Treatise on the Old and New Testament and His Preface to Genesis.* EETS o.s. 160. London: Oxford University Press, 1922.

Cross, J.E., and Andrew Hamer, eds. *Wulfstan's Canon Law Collection.* Anglo-Saxon Texts 1. Cambridge: D.S. Brewer, 1999.

Darlington, R.R., and P. McGurk, eds., Jennifer Bray and P. McGurk, trans. *The Chronicle of John of Worcester*. 3 vols. Oxford: Clarendon Press, 1995–.
Dekkers, Eligius, and J. Fraipont, eds. *Sancti Aurelii Augustini Enarrationes in Psalmos*. 3 vols. CCSL 38–40. Turnhout: Brepols, 1956.
Dombart, Bernhard, and Alfonsus Kalb, eds. *Sancti Aurelii Augustini De Ciuitate Dei Libri XXII*. 2 vols. CCSL 47–8. Turnhout: Brepols, 1955.
Du Cange, Charles. *Glossarium ad scriptores mediæ et infimæ Latinitatis*. Basil, 1762.
Dümmler, Ernest, ed. *Epistolae Karolini Aevi*. Vol. 2. MGH, Epistolae 4. Berlin: Weidmann, 1895.
Ehwald, Rudolf, ed. *Aldhelmi Opera Omnia*. MGH, AA 15. Berlin: Weidmann, 1919.
Esposito, M. 'La vie de sainte Vulfhilde par Goscelin de Cantorbéry.' *Analecta Bollandiana* 32 (1913): 10–26.
Evans, E., ed. *Enchiridion ad Laurentium de Fide et Spe et Caritate*. Aurelii Augustini Opera, part 13.2. CCSL 46. Turnhout: Brepols, 1969. 21–114.
Folcard. *Vita Sancti Johannis Episcopi Eboracensis*. In *The Historians of the Church of York and Its Archbishops*, edited by James Raine. RS 71. London, 1879. 239–60.
Fontaine, Jacques, and Nicole Dupré, eds. *Gallus, Dialogues sur les 'Vertus' de Saint Martin*, Sources chrétiennes 510. Paris: Éditions du Cerf, 2006.
Fowler, Roger, ed. *Wulfstan's Canons of Edgar*. EETS o.s. 266. London: Oxford University Press, 1972.
Friedberg, Emil. *Corpus Iuris Canonici*. Vol. 1, *Decretum Magistri Gratiani*. Leipzig, 1879.
Fröhlich, Walter, trans. *The Letters of Saint Anselm of Canterbury*. 3 vols. Cistercian Studies Series 96–7 and 142. Kalamazoo, MI: Cistercian Publications, 1990–4.
Garmonsway, G.N., ed. *Ælfric's Colloquy*. Rev. ed. Exeter: University of Exeter Press, 1978.
Gastaldo, M., ed. *Sancti Prosperi Aquitani Liber Sententiarum*. CCSL 68A. Turnhout: Brepols, 1972.
Godden, Malcolm, ed. *Ælfric's Catholic Homilies: The Second Series, Text*. EETS s.s. 5. Oxford: Oxford University Press, 1979.
– *Ælfric's Catholic Homilies: Introduction, Commentary and Gloss*. EETS s.s. 18. Oxford: Oxford University Press, 2000.
Godden, Malcolm, and Susan Irvine, eds. *The Old English Boethius: An Edition of the Old English Versions of Boethius's 'De Consolatione Philosophiae.'* 2 vols. Oxford: Oxford University Press, 2009.
Godman, Peter. *Alcuin, The Bishops, Kings and Saints of York*, OMT. Oxford: Clarendon Press, 1982.

Green, W.M., ed. *Sancti Aurelii Augustini, De Libero Arbitrio*. CCSL 29. Turnhout: Brepols, 1970.

Gwara, Scott, ed. *Latin Colloquies from Pre-Conquest Britain*, Toronto Medieval Latin Texts 22. Toronto: Pontifical Institute of Mediaeval Studies, 1996.

Gwara, Scott, and David W. Porter, trans. *Anglo-Saxon Conversations: The Colloquies of Ælfric Bata*. Woodbridge: Boydell Press, 1997.

Hanslik, Rudolf, ed. *Benedicti Regula*. 2nd rev. ed. CSEL 75. Vienna: Hoelder-Pichler-Tempsky, 1977.

Hecht, Hans, ed. *Bischofs Waerferth von Worcester Übersetzung der Dialoge Gregors des Grossen*. Bibliothek der angelsächsischen Prosa 5. Leipzig: G.H. Wigland, 1900–7.

Herrgott, Marquard. *Vetus disciplina monastica: seu collectio auctorum Ordinis S. Benedicti maximam partem ineditorum, qui ante sexcentos fere annos per Italiam, Galliam atque Germaniam de monastica disciplina tractarunt*. Paris, 1726.

Hesbert, René-Jean, ed. *Corpus Antiphonalium Officii*. 6 vols. Rerum Ecclesiasticarum Documenta, series maior, fontes 7–12. Rome: Herder, 1963–79.

Hilberg, Isidore, ed. *Sancti Eusebii Hieronymi Epistulae*. 3 vols. CSEL 54–6. Vienna: F. Tempsky, 1910–18.

Hill, Joyce. 'Ælfric's *Colloquy*: The Antwerp/London Version.' In *Latin Learning and English Lore: Studies in Anglo-Saxon Literature for Michael Lapidge*, edited by Katherine O'Brien O'Keeffe and Andy Orchard, 2 vols., II: 331–48. Toronto: University of Toronto Press, 2005.

Hinschius, Paulus, ed. *Decretales Pseudo-Isidorianae et Capitula Angilramni*. Leipzig, 1863. Reprint, Aalen: Scientia Verlag, 1963.

Holder-Egger, O., ed. *Vitae Willibaldi et Wynnebaldi Auctore Sanctimoniali Heidenheimensi*. MGH, Scriptores 15.1. Hannover, 1887.

Hoste, A., and C.H. Talbot, eds. *Aelred of Rievaulx, Opera ascetica*. CCCM 1. Turnhout: Brepols, 1971.

Hrabanus Maurus. *Liber de oblatione puerorum*. PL 107.419–40.

Hurst, D. ed. *Bedae Venerabilis Opera: In Lucae Evangelium Expositio*. CCSL 120. Turnhout: Brepols, 1960.

Isidore of Seville. *Quaestiones in Vetus Testamentum*. PL 83.207–424.

– *Synonyma de lamentatione animae peccatricis*. PL 83.827–68.

Jaager, Werner, ed. *Bedas metrische Vita Sancti Cuthberti*. Palaestra 198. Leipzig: Mayer and Müller, 1935.

Jacob, W., and R. Hanslik, eds. *Cassiodori-Epiphanii Historia Ecclesiastica Tripartita*. CSEL 71. Vienna: Hoelder, Pichler, Tempsky, 1952.

Jones, Charles W., ed. *Libri Quatuor in Pricipium Genesis. Bedae Venerabilis Opera*, part 2.1: *Opera Exegetica*. CCSL 118A. Turnhout: Brepols, 1967.

Knowles, David, ed. and trans. *The Monastic Constitutions of Lanfranc*. Revised edition by Christopher N.L. Brooke. Oxford: Clarendon Press, 2002.

Krusch, Bruno, ed. *Gregorii Episcopi Turonensis Libri Octo Miraculorum*. MGH, SRM 1.2. Hannover, 1885. Reprint, Hannover: Hahn, 1969.

Labande, Edmond-René, ed. *Guibert de Nogent, Autobiographie*. Paris: Belles Lettres, 1981.

Lapidge, Michael, ed. *The Cult of St Swithun*. Winchester Studies 4.ii. Oxford: Clarendon Press, 2003.

– ed. and trans. *Byrhtferth of Ramsey, The Lives of St Oswald and St Ecgwine*. Oxford: Clarendon Press, 2009.

Lapidge, Michael, and Michael Winterbottom, eds. *Wulfstan of Winchester, The Life of St Æthelwold*. Oxford: Clarendon Press, 1991.

Levison, Wilhelm, ed. *Vita Willibrordi Archiepiscopi Traiectensis Auctore Alcuino*. MGH, SRM 7. Hannover, 1920.

– ed. *Vitae Sancti Bonifatii Archiepiscopi Moguntini*. MGH, SRG 57. Hannover: Hahn, 1905.

Liebermann, F., ed. *Die Gesetze der Angelsachsen*. 3 vols. Halle: Max Niemeyer, 1903–16.

Love, Rosalind C., ed. and trans. *Three Eleventh-Century Anglo-Latin Saints' Lives*. OMT. Oxford: Clarendon Press, 1996.

– ed. and trans. *Goscelin of Saint-Bertin: The Hagiography of the Female Saints of Ely*. OMT. Oxford: Clarendon Press, 2004.

MacLean, George E., ed. 'Ælfric's Version of *Alcuini Interrogationes Sigeuulfi in Genesin*.' *Anglia* 7 (1884): 1–59.

Martène, Edmond. *De antiquis ecclesiae ritibus libri*. 4 vols. Antwerp, 1736. Reprint, Hildesheim: Georg Olms Verlagsbuchhandlung, 1967.

McGurk, P., ed. *The Chronicle of John of Worcester*. Vol. 3, *The Annals from 1067 to 1140 with the Gloucester Interpolations and the Continuation to 1141* Oxford: Clarendon Press, 1998.

Miller, Thomas, ed. and trans. *The Old English Version of Bede's Ecclesiastical History of the English People*. EETS o.s. 95, 96, 110, 111. London, 1890–8. Reprint, London: Oxford University Press, 1959.

Millett, Bella, ed. *Ancrene Wisse*. With a glossary and additional notes by Richard Dance. 2 vols. EETS 325, 326. Oxford: Oxford University Press, 2005–6.

Mittermüller, Rupert, ed. *Vita et Regula SS. P. Benedicti*. Vol. 3, *Expositio Regulae ab Hildemaro Tradita*. Regensburg, 1880.

Mountain, W.J., and Fr. Glorie, eds. *Sancti Aurelii Augustini de Trinitate libri XV*. 2 vols. CCSL 50, 50a. Turnhout: Brepols, 1968.

Mynors, R.A.B., R.M. Thomson, and M. Winterbottom, eds. and trans. *William of Malmesbury: Gesta Regum Anglorum*. 2 vols. OMT. Oxford: Clarendon Press, 1998–9.

O'Donnell, James J., ed. *Augustine, Confessions*. 3 vols. Oxford: Clarendon Press, 1992.

Oliphant, Robert T. *The Harley Latin-Old English Glossary.* Janua linguarum. Series practica 20. The Hague: Mouton, 1966.

Otter, Monika C., trans. *Goscelin of St Bertin, The Book of Encouragement and Consolation ('Liber Confortatorius')*. Cambridge: D.S. Brewer, 2004.

Pauli Warnefridi Diaconi Casinensis in Sanctam Regulam Commentarium. Monte Cassino, 1880.

Petschenig, Michael, ed. *Iohannis Cassiani Opera: De Institutis Coenobiorum et de Octo Principalium Vitiorum Remediis Libri XII*. CSEL 17. Vienna, 1888.

Pope, John C., ed. *Homilies of Ælfric: A Supplementary Collection*. 2 vols. EETS 259, 260. London: Oxford University Press, 1967–8.

Porter, David W., ed. *Excerptiones de Prisciano: The Sources for Ælfric's Latin-Old English Grammar*. Anglo-Saxon Texts 4. Cambridge: D.S. Brewer, 2002.

Prosper of Aquitaine. *Epigrammata*. PL 51. 497–532.

Regino of Prüm. *Libri duo de synodalibus causis et disciplinis ecclesiasticis*. PL 132. 185–370.

Rule, Martin, ed. *Eadmeri Historia Novorum in Anglia et Opuscula Duo de Vita Sancti Anselmi et Quibusdam Miraculis Ejus*. RS 81. London, 1884.

Salu, M.B., trans. *The Ancrene Riwle*. 2nd ed. Exeter Medieval English Texts and Studies. Exeter: University of Exeter Press, 1990. Reprint, 2001.

Schmitt, F.S., ed. *S. Anselmi Cantuariensis Archiepiscopi Opera Omnia*. 6 vols. Edinburgh: Thomas Nelson and Sons, 1946–61. Electronic Edition. Charlottesville, VA: InteLex Corp., 2002.

Schröer, Arnold, ed. *Die angelsächsischen Prosabearbeitungen der Benedictinerregel*. 2nd ed., with supplement by Helmut Gneuss. Bibliothek der angelsächsischen Prosa 2. Kassel, 1885–8; Darmstadt: Wissenschaftliche Buchgesellschaft, 1964.

Schwartz, Eduard, and Theodor Mommsen, eds. *Die Kirchengeschichte*. Vol. 2. Eusebius Werke. Leipzig: J.C. Hinrichs'sche Buchhandlung, 1903–8.

Scragg, D.G., ed. *The Vercelli Homilies and Related Texts*. EETS o.s. 300. Oxford: Oxford University Press, 1992.

Skeat, Walter W., ed. *Ælfric's Lives of Saints*. EETS o.s. 76, 82, 94, 114. Oxford, 1881–1900. Reprinted as two volumes, Oxford: Oxford University Press, 1966.

Smaragdus of Saint-Mihiel. *Diadema monachorum*. PL 102.593–690.

Spannagel, Alfred, and Pius Engelbert, eds. *Smaragdi Abbatis Expositio in Regulam S. Benedicti*. Corpus Consuetudinum Monasticarum 8. Siegburg: F. Schmitt, 1974.

Stevenson, W.H., ed. *Early Scholastic Colloquies*. Oxford: Clarendon Press, 1929.

– ed. *Asser's Life of King Alfred*, with an introductory article by Dorothy Whitelock. Oxford: Clarendon Press, 1959.

Stubbs, William, ed. *Memorials of Saint Dunstan, Archbishop of Canterbury*. RS 63. London, 1874.

Sweet, Henry, ed. *King Alfred's West-Saxon Version of Gregory's Pastoral Care*. EETS o.s. 45, 50. London, 1871–2. Reprint, with corrections by N.R. Ker. London: Oxford University Press, 1958.

Symons, Thomas, ed. and trans. *Regularis Concordia Anglicae Nationis Monachorum Santimonialiumque*. London: Thomas Nelson and Sons, 1953.

Talbot, C.H., ed. and trans. *The Anglo-Saxon Missionaries in Germany*. London: Sheed and Ward, 1954.

– ed. *The Liber Confortatorius of Goscelin of Saint Bertin*. Studia Anselmiana 37, Analecta Monastica, 3rd ser. Rome: Herder, 1955.

– ed. *The Life of Christina of Markyate: A Twelfth-Century Recluse*. Revised edition, Medieval Academy Reprints for Teaching 39. Toronto: University of Toronto Press, 1997.

Tangl, Michael, ed. *Die Briefe des heiligen Bonifatius und Lullus*. Vol. 1. MGH, Epistolae Selectae. Berlin: Weidmann, 1916.

Tolkien, J.R.R., ed. *Ancrene Wisse: The English Text of the Ancrene Riwle*, with an introduction by N.R. Ker. EETS o.s. 249. London, Oxford University Press, 1962.

Turner, Andrew J., and Bernard J. Muir, eds. *Eadmer of Canterbury: Lives and Miracles of Saints Oda, Dunstan, and Oswald*. OMT. Oxford: Clarendon Press, 2006.

Urba, C.F., and J. Zycha, eds. *Sancti Aureli Augustini, De Spiritu et Littera Liber Unus*. CSEL 60. Vienna: F. Tempsky, 1913.

Verba seniorum. PL 73.855–1022.

Verheijen, Lucas, ed. *Sancti Augustini Confessionum Libri XIII*. CCSL 27. Turnhout: Brepols, 1981.

Vitas patrum. PL 73.

Vogel, Cyrille, and Reinhard Elze, eds. *Le Pontifical Romano-Germanique du dixième siècle*. 3 vols. Studi e Testi, 226, 227, 269. Vatican City: Bibliotheca Apostolica Vaticana, 1963–72.

Vogüé, Adalbert de, ed. and trans. *La Règle du Maître*. 3 vols. SC 105–7. Paris: Les Éditions du Cerf, 1964–5.

Vogüé, Adalbert de, ed., and Paul Antin, trans. *Grégoire le Grand, Dialogues*. Vol. 2. Sources chrétiennes 260. Paris: Éditions du Cerf, 1979.

Vogüé, Adalbert de, and Jean Neufville, eds. *La Règle de Saint Benoît*. 6 vols. Sources chrétiennes 181–6. Paris: Éditions du Cerf, 1971–7.

Waitz, G., ed. *Vita Leobae Abbatissae Biscofesheimensis, Auctore Rudolfo Fuldensi*. MGH, Scriptores 15.1. Hannover, 1887.

Weber, Robert, ed. *Biblia Sacra Iuxta VulgatamVersionem*. 2 vols. Stuttgart: Württembergische Bibelanstalt, 1969.

Whitelock, Dorothy, Martin Brett, and C.N.L. Brooke, eds. *Councils and Synods with Other Documents Relating to the English Church*. 2 vols. Oxford: Clarendon Press, 1964–81.

Wilcox, Jonathan, ed. *Ælfric's Prefaces*. Durham Medieval Texts 9. Durham: Durham Medieval Texts, 1994.

Willems, Radbod, ed. *Sancti Aurelii Augustini in Iohannis Evangelium Tractatus CXXIV*. CCSL 36. Turnhout: Brepols, 1954.

Williams, Thomas, trans. *Anselm: Three Philosophical Dialogues*. Indianapolis, IN: Hackett, 2002.

Wilmart, André, ed. 'La légende de Ste Édith en prose et vers par le moine Goscelin.' *AB* 56 (1938): 5–101, 265–307.

Wilson, H.A., ed. *The Pontifical of Magdalen College*. Henry Bradshaw Society 39. London: Harrison and Sons, 1910.

Winterbottom, Michael, and Michael Lapidge, eds. *The Early Lives of St Dunstan*. OMT. Oxford: Clarendon Press, 2011.

Winterbottom, Michael, and R.M. Thomson, eds. *William of Malmesbury, Saints' Lives: Lives of SS. Wulfstan, Dunstan, Patrick, Benignus and Indract*. OMT. Oxford: Clarendon Press, 2002.

Winterbottom, Michael, ed. and trans., with the assistance of R.M. Thomson. *William of Malmesbury, Gesta Pontificum Anglorum: The History of the English Bishops*. 2 vols. OMT. Oxford: Clarendon Press, 2007.

Zupitza, Julius, ed. *Aelfrics Grammatik und Glossar: Text und Varianten*. 4th ed. With an introduction by Helmut Gneuss. Hildesheim: Weidmann, 2003.

Zycha, Joseph, ed. *Sancti Aureli Augustini De Genesi ad Litteram Libri Duodecim*. CSEL 28.1. Vienna, 1894.

Secondary Sources

Alcamesi, Filippa. 'Remigius's Commentary to the *Disticha Catonis* in Anglo-Saxon Manuscripts.' In *Form and Content of Instruction in Anglo-Saxon England in the Light of Contemporary Manuscript Evidence*, edited by Patrizia Lendinara, Loredana Lazzari, and Maria Amalia D'Aronco, 143–86. Turnhout: Brepols, 2008.

Althusser, Louis. 'Ideology and Ideological State Apparatuses.' In his *Lenin and Philosophy and Other Essays*. Translated by Ben Brewster, with an introduction by Frederic Jameson, 85–126. New York: Monthly Review Press, 2001.

Anderson, Earl R. 'Social Idealism in Ælfric's *Colloquy*.' *ASE* 3 (1974): 153–62.

Appiah, Anthony. 'Tolerable Falsehoods: Agency and the Interests of Theory.' In *Consequences of Theory*, edited by Jonathan Arac and Barbara Johnson, 63–90.

Selected Papers from the English Institute, 1987–88, n.s. 14. Baltimore: Johns Hopkins University Press, 1991.

Asad, Talal. *Genealogies of Religion: Discipline and Reasons of Power in Christianity and Islam.* Baltimore: Johns Hopkins University Press, 1993.

– *Formations of the Secular: Christianity, Islam, Modernity.* Stanford, CA: Stanford University Press, 2003.

Backhouse, Janet, D.H. Turner, and Leslie Webster. *The Golden Age of Anglo-Saxon Art, 966–1066.* London: British Museum Publications, 1984.

Banham, Debby. *Food and Drink in Anglo-Saxon England.* Stroud, Gloucestershire: Tempus, 2004.

Barrow, Julia. 'Wulfstan and Worcester: Bishop and Clergy in the Early Eleventh Century.' In *Wulfstan, Archbishop of York*, edited by Matthew Townend, 141–59. Turnhout: Brepols, 2004.

Bartlett, Robert. *Trial by Fire and Water: The Medieval Judicial Ordeal.* Oxford: Clarendon Press, 1986.

Baumeister, Roy F. *Identity: Cultural Change and the Struggle for Self.* Oxford: Oxford University Press, 1986.

Berend, Nora. 'La subversion invisible: la disparition de l'oblation irrévocable des enfants dans le droit canon.' *Médiévales* 26 (Spring 1994): 123–36.

Berschin, Walter. *Biographie und Epochenstil im lateinischen Mittelalter.* Vol. 2, *Merowingische Biographie. Italien, Spanien und die Inseln im frühen Mittelalter.* Stuttgart: A. Hiersemann, 1988.

Blair, John. *The Church in Anglo-Saxon Society.* Oxford: Oxford University Press, 2005.

Blokhuis, B.A. 'Bede and Ælfric: The Sources of the Homily on St Cuthbert.' In *Beda Venerabilis: Historian, Monk, and Northumbrian*, edited by L.A.J.R. Houwen and A.A. MacDonald, 107–38. Groningen: Egbert Forsten, 1996.

Boswell, John. *The Kindness of Strangers.* New York: Pantheon, 1988.

Bosworth, Joseph. *An Anglo-Saxon Dictionary.* Edited and enlarged by T. Northcote Toller. Oxford, 1898; Oxford: Oxford University Press, 1973.

Bourdieu, Pierre. *Outline of a Theory of Practice.* Translated by Richard Nice. Cambridge: Cambridge University Press, 1977.

Brasington, Bruce. 'Remember Always Ananias and Sapphira.' In *Oboedientia: Zu Formen und Grenzen von Macht und Unterordnung in Mittelalterlichen Religiosentum*, edited by Sébastien Barret and Gert Melville, 83–97. Vita regularis 27. Münster: Lit Verlag, 2005.

Brett, Martin. 'The *Collectio Lanfranci* and its Competitors.' In *Intellectual Life in the Middle Ages: Essays Presented to Margaret Gibson*, edited by Lesley Smith and Benedicta Ward, 157–74. London: Hambledon Press, 1992.

Brooks, Nicholas. 'The Career of St Dunstan.' In *St Dunstan: His Life, Times and Cult*, edited by Nigel Ramsay, Margaret Sparks, and Tim Tatton-Brown, 1–23. Woodbridge: The Boydell Press, 1992.

– 'The Anglo-Saxon Cathedral Community, 597–1070.' In *A History of Canterbury Cathedral*, edited by Patrick Collinson, Nigel Ramsay, and Margaret Sparks, 1–37. Oxford: Oxford University Press, 1995.

Brooks, Nicholas, and Catherine Cubitt, eds. *St Oswald of Worcester: His Life and Influence*. London: Leicester University Press, 1996.

Brown, George H. 'The Dynamics of Literacy in Anglo-Saxon England.' In *Textual and Material Culture in Anglo-Saxon England*, edited by Donald Scragg, 183–212. Cambridge: D.S. Brewer, 2003. First published in the *Bulletin of the John Rylands University Library of Manchester* 77 (1995): 109–42.

Brown, Michelle P. 'The Role of the Wax Tablet in Medieval Literacy: A Reconsideration in Light of a Recent Find from York.' *British Library Journal* 20 (1994): 1–16.

Brown, Michelle P., and Patricia Lovett. *The Historical Source Book for Scribes*. Toronto: University of Toronto Press, 1999.

Brundage, A. *Law, Sex, and Christian Society in Medieval Europe*. Chicago: University of Chicago Press, 1987.

Bullough, D.A. 'The Educational Tradition in England from Alfred to Ælfric: Teaching *utriusque linguae*.' In *Carolingian Renewal: Sources and Heritage*, edited by D.A. Bullough, 297–334. Manchester: Manchester University Press, 1991.

Busse, Wilhelm G. '"Sua gað ða lareowas beforan ðæm folce, & ðæt folc æfter": The Self-Understanding of the Reformers as Teachers in Late Tenth-Century England.' In *Schriftlichkeit im frühen Mittelalter*, edited by Ursula Schaefer, 58–106. ScriptOralia 53. Tübingen: Gunter Narr Verlag, 1993.

Butler, Judith. *The Psychic Life of Power: Theories in Subjection*. Stanford, CA: Stanford University Press, 1997.

Canatella, H.M. 'Long-Distance Love: The Ideology of Male-Female Spiritual Friendship in Goscelin of Saint Bertin's *Liber confortatorius*.' *Journal of the History of Sexuality* 19.1 (2010): 35–53.

Capelle, Catherine. *Le voeu d'obéissance des origines au XIIe siècle: étude juridique*. Bibliothèque d'histoire du droit et droit romain 2. Paris: R. Pichon et R. Durand-Auzias, 1959.

Cappuyns, M. 'Le premier représéntant de l'Augustinisme médiéval, Prosper d'Aquitaine.' *Recherches de théologie ancienne et médiévale* 1 (1929): 309–37.

Carruthers, Mary J. 'Reading with Attitude: Remembering the Book.' In *The Book and the Body*, edited by Dolores W. Frese and Katherine O'Brien O'Keeffe, 1–33. Notre Dame, IN: University of Notre Dame Press, 1997.

– *The Book of Memory: A Study of Memory in Medieval Culture*. 2nd ed. Cambridge: Cambridge University Press, 2008.

Clayton, Mary. 'Ælfric's *Judith*: Manipulative or Manipulated?' *ASE* 23 (1994): 215–27.

– 'Hermits and the Contemplative Life in Anglo-Saxon England.' In *Holy Men and Holy Women: Old English Prose Saints' Lives and Their Contexts*, ed. Paul E. Szarmach, 147–75. Albany: State University of New York Press, 1996.

– 'Ælfric's *De auguriis* and Cambridge, Corpus Christi College 178.' In *Latin Learning and English Lore*, ed. Katherine O'Brien O'Keeffe and Andy Orchard, 2 vols., II: 376-94. Toronto: University of Toronto Press, 2005.

Clemoes, P.A.M. 'The Chronology of Ælfric's Works.' In *The Anglo-Saxons: Studies in Some Aspects of Their History and Culture Presented to Bruce Dickins*, edited by Peter Clemoes, 212–47. London: Bowes and Bowes, 1959.

Cochelin, Isabelle. 'Besides the Book: Using the Body to Mould the Mind – Cluny in the Tenth and Eleventh Centuries.' In *Medieval Monastic Education*, edited by George Ferzoco and Carolyn Muessig, 21–34. Leicester: Leicester University Press, 2000.

Coleman, Janet. *Ancient and Medieval Memories: Studies in the Reconstruction of the Past*. Cambridge: Cambridge University Press, 1992.

Coleman, Julie. 'Rape in Anglo-Saxon England.' In *Violence and Society in the Early Medieval West*, edited by Guy Halsall, 193–204. Woodbridge: Boydell Press, 1998.

Colgrave, Bertram.'The Earliest Saints' Lives Written in England.' *Proceedings of the British Academy* 44 (1958): 35–60.

Colker, Marvin L. *Trinity College Library Dublin: Descriptive Catalogue of the Mediaeval and Renaissance Latin Manuscripts*. 2 vols. Dublin: Scolar Press, 1991.

Constable, Giles. 'The Ceremonies and Symbolism of Entering Religious Life and Taking the Monastic Habit, from the Fourth to the Twelfth Century.' In *Segni e riti nella chiesa altomedievale occidentale, 11–17 aprile 1985*, 2 vols., II: 771–834. Settimane di studio del centro italiano di studi sull'alto Medioevo 33. Spoleto: Centro italiano di studi sull'alto Medioevo, 1987.

– 'Liberty and Free Choice in Monastic Thought and Life, Especially in the Eleventh and Twelfth Centuries.' In his *Monks, Hermits and Crusaders in Medieval Europe*, IV.99–118. London: Variorum Reprints, 1988.

– *The Reformation of the Twelfth Century*. Cambridge: Cambridge University Press, 1996.

Coon, Lynda L. *Dark Age Bodies: Gender and Monastic Practice in the Early Medieval West*. Philadelphia: University of Pennsylvania Press, 2011.

Courcelle, Pierre. 'L'enfant et les "sorts bibliques."' *Vigiliae Christianae* 7 (1953): 194–220.

– *Les confessions de saint Augustin dans la tradition littéraire*. Paris: Études Augustiniennes, 1963.

Crick, Julia. 'The Wealth, Patronage, and Connections of Women's Houses in Late Anglo-Saxon England.' *Revue Bénédictine* 109 (1999): 154–85.

Cubitt, Catherine. 'Memory and Narrative in the Cult of Early Anglo-Saxon Saints.' In *The Uses of the Past in the Early Middle Ages*, edited by Yitzhak Hen and Matthew Innes, 29–66. Cambridge: Cambridge University Press, 2000.

– 'Monastic Memory and Identity in Early Anglo-Saxon England.' In *Social Identity in Early Medieval Britain*, edited by William O. Frazer and Andrew Tyrrell, 253–76. London: Leicester University Press, 2000.

– 'The Tenth-Century Benedictine Reform in England.' *Early Medieval Europe* 6 (1997): 77–94.

Curtius, Ernst Robert. *European Literature and the Latin Middle Ages*. Translated by Willard R. Trask. Princeton, NJ: Princeton University Press, 1953.

Dennett, Daniel C. *Elbow Room: The Varieties of Free Will Worth Wanting*. Oxford: Clarendon Press, 1984.

Deshman, Robert. '*Benedictus Monarcha et Monachus*: Early Medieval Ruler Theology and the Anglo-Saxon Reform.' *Frühmittelalterliche Studien* 22 (1988): 204–40.

– *The Benedictional of Æthelwold*. Princeton: Princeton University Press, 1995.

DeVries, Kelly. *The Norwegian Invasion of England in 1066*. Woodbridge: The Boydell Press, 1999.

Dictionary of Old English: A to G. Edited by Angus Cameron, Ashley Crandell Amos, and Antonette di Paolo Healey. Toronto: University of Toronto Press, 2007.

Dihle, Albrecht. *The Theory of Will in Classical Antiquity*. Berkeley: University of California Press, 1982.

Di Sciacca, Claudia. *Finding the Right Words: Isidore's 'Synonyma' in Anglo-Saxon England.* Toronto: University of Toronto Press, 2008.

Doran, John. 'Oblation or Obligation? A Canonical Ambiguity.' In *The Church and Childhood*, edited by Diana Wood, 127–41. Studies in Church History 31. Oxford: Blackwell, 1994.

Dunn, Marilyn. *The Emergence of Monasticism: From the Desert Fathers to the Early Middle Ages*. Oxford: Blackwell, 2000.

Elliot, Dyan. 'Alternative Intimacies: Men, Women and Spiritual Direction in the Twelfth Century.' In *Christina of Markyate: A Twelfth-Century Holy Woman*, edited by Samuel Fanous and Henrietta Leyser, 160–83. London: Routledge, 2005.

Evans, Gillian R. 'Two Aspects of *Memoria* in Eleventh and Twelfth Century Writings.' *Classica et Mediaevalia* (Copenhagen) 32 (1971–80): 263–78.

– 'The Grammar of Predestination in the Ninth Century.' *Journal of Theological Studies*, n.s., 33 (1982): 134–45.

Fanous, Samuel, and Henrietta Leyser, eds. *Christina of Markyate: A Twelfth-Century Holy Woman*. London: Routledge, 2005.

Fontes Anglo-Saxonici Project. 'Fontes Anglo-Saxonici: World Wide Web Register.' http://fontes.english.ox.ac.uk/.

Foot, Sarah. *Veiled Women: The Disappearance of Nuns from Anglo-Saxon England*. 2 vols. Aldershot: Ashgate, 2000.

Foucault, Michel. 'About the Beginning of the Hermeneutics of the Self.' In *Religion and Culture by Michel Foucault*, edited by Jeremy R. Carrette, 158–81. Manchester: Manchester University Press, 1999.

– *Security, Territory, Population: Lectures at the Collège de France, 1977–1978*. Translated by Graham Burchell. Edited by Michel Senellart. London: Palgrave, 2007.

Fox, Michael. 'Ælfric on the Creation and Fall of the Angels.' *ASE* 31 (2002): 175–200.

Frank, Karl Suso. 'Gehorsam.' In *Reallexikon für Antike und Cristentum*. Stuttgart: Anton Hiersemann, 1976.

Frankfurt, Harry. 'Freedom of the Will and the Concept of a Person.' *Journal of Philosophy* 68.1 (1971): 5–20.

Gibson, Margaret, T.A. Heslop, and Richard W. Pfaff, eds. *The Eadwine Psalter: Text, Image, and Monastic Culture in Twelfth-Century Canterbury*. University Park: The Pennsylvania State University Press, 1992.

Giddens, Anthony. *Central Problems in Social Theory*. Berkeley: University of California Press, 1979.

Gilson, Étienne. *The Christian Philosophy of Saint Augustine*. Translated by L.E.M. Lynch. New York: Random House, 1960.

Gneuss, Helmut. 'The Origin of Standard Old English and Æthelwold's School at Winchester.' *Anglo-Saxon England* 1 (1972): 63–83.

– 'The Study of Language in Anglo-Saxon England.' *Bulletin of the John Rylands Library of Manchester* 72 (1990): 3–32. Reprinted with a postscript in *Textual and Material Culture in Anglo-Saxon England: Thomas Northcote Toller and the Toller Memorial Lectures*, edited by Donald Scragg, 75–105. Cambridge: D.S. Brewer, 2003.

– *Handlist of Anglo-Saxon Manuscripts: A List of Manuscripts and Manuscript Fragments Written or Owned in England up to 1100*. Tempe, AZ: Arizona Center for Medieval and Renaissance Studies, 2001.

Godden, Malcolm R. 'Anglo-Saxons on the Mind.' In *Learning and Literature in Anglo-Saxon England: Studies Presented to Peter Clemoes on the Occasion *of His Sixty-Fifth Birthday*, edited by Michael Lapidge and Helmut Gneuss, 271–98. Cambridge: Cambridge University Press, 1985.

– 'Were It Not That I Have Bad Dreams: Gregory the Great and the Anglo-Saxons on the Dangers of Dreaming.' In *Rome and the North: The Early Reception of Gregory the Great in Germanic Europe*, edited by Rolf H. Bremmer, Jr., Kees Dekker, and David F. Johnson, 93–113. Paris: Peeters, 2001.

– 'Ælfric and the Alfredian Precedents.' In *A Companion to Ælfric*, edited by Hugh Magennis and Mary Swan, 139–63. Leiden: Brill, 2009.

– 'The Sources of Ælfric's *Lives of Saints* 17 (On Auguries) (C.B.1.3.18).' Fontes Anglo-Saxonici: World Wide Web Register. http://fontes.english.ox.ac.uk/.

Goffart, Walter. 'Bede's *uera lex historiae* Explained.' *ASE* 34 (2005): 111–16.

Green, Dennis Howard. *Women Readers in the Middle Ages*. Cambridge: Cambridge University Press, 2007.

Gretsch, Mechthild. 'Æthelwold's Translation of the *Regula Sancti Benedicti* and Its Latin Exemplar.' *ASE* 3 (1974): 125–51.

– 'The Benedictine Rule in Old English: A Document of Bishop Æthelwold's Reform Politics.' In *Words, Texts and Manuscripts: Studies in Anglo-Saxon Culture Presented to Helmut Gneuss on the Occasion of His Sixty-Fifth Birthday*, edited by Michael Korhammer with the assistance of Karl Reichl and Hans Sauer, 131–58. Cambridge: D.S. Brewer, 1992.

– *The Intellectual Foundations of the English Benedictine Reform*. Cambridge: Cambridge University Press, 1999.

– *Ælfric and the Cult of Saints in Late Anglo-Saxon England*. Cambridge Studies in Anglo-Saxon England 34. Cambridge: Cambridge University Press, 2005.

Griffith, Mark. 'How Much Latin Did Ælfric's *Magister* Know?' *Notes and Queries*, n.s., 46.2 (1999): 176–81.

Grotans, Anna A. *Reading in Medieval St Gall*. Cambridge: Cambridge University Press, 2006.

Grundy, Lynne. *Books and Grace: Ælfric's Theology*. London: King's College London, Centre for Late Antique & Medieval Studies, 1991.

– 'Ælfric's Grammatical Theology and Theological Grammar.' In *Essays on Anglo-Saxon and Related Themes in Memory of Lynne Grundy*, edited by Jane Roberts and Janet Nelson, 1–14. London: King's College London, Centre for Late Antique & Medieval Studies, 2000.

Gullick, Michael and Richard W. Pfaff. 'The Dublin Pontifical (TCD 98 [B.3.6]): St Anselm's?' *Scriptorium* 55.2 (2001): 284–94.

Gwara, Scott. 'The *Hermeneumata pseudodositheana*, Latin Oral Fluency, and the Social Function of the Cambro-Latin Dialogues Called *De raris fabulis*.' In

Grammar and Rhetoric: From Classical Theory to Medieval Practice, edited by Carol Dana Lanham, 109–38. London: Continuum, 2002.

Hafner, P. Wolfgang. *Der Basiliuskommentar zur Regula S. Benedicti*. Beiträge zur Geschichte des alten Mönchtums und des Benediktinerordens 23. Münster Westfalen: Aschendorffsche Verlagsbuchhandlung, 1959.

Hall, Thomas N. 'Ælfric as Pedagogue.' In *A Companion to Ælfric*, edited by Hugh Magennis and Mary Swan, 193–216. Brill's Companions to the Christian Tradition 18. Leiden: Brill, 2009.

Halpin, Patricia A. 'Women Religious in Late Anglo-Saxon England.' *Haskins Society Journal* 6 (1994): 97–110.

– 'Anglo-Saxon Women and Pilgrimage.' *ANS* 19 (1997): 97–122.

Hamilton, Thomas J. 'Goscelin of Canterbury: A Critical Study of His Life, Works and Accomplishments.' 2 vols. PhD dissertation, University of Virginia, 1973.

Harrison, Odelia G., OSB. 'The Formulas *Ad virgines sacras*: A Study of the Sources.' *Ephemerides Liturgicae* 66 (1952): 252–[73] and 352–66.

Harvey, Barbara. *Living and Dying in England 1100–1540: The Monastic Experience.* Oxford: Clarendon Press, 1993.

Harwood, Britton J., and Gillian R. Overing, eds. *Class and Gender in Early English Literature: Intersections*. Bloomington: Indiana University Press, 1994.

Hayward, Rebecca. 'Spiritual Friendship and Gender Difference in the *Liber confortatorius*.' In *Writing the Wilton Women: Goscelin's 'Legend of Edith' and 'Liber confortatorius,'* edited by Stephanie Hollis, et al., 341–53. Medieval Women: Texts and Contexts 9. Turnhout: Brepols, 2004.

Hazelton, Richard. 'The Christianization of "Cato": The *Disticha Catonis* in the Light of Late Mediaeval Commentaries.' *Mediaeval Studies* 19 (1957): 157–73.

Hildebrand, Stephen M. '*Oboedientia* and *Oboedire* in the Rule of St Benedict: A Study of Their Theological and Monastic Meanings.' *American Benedictine Review* 52.4 (2001): 421–36.

Hill, Joyce. 'Winchester Pedagogy and the *Colloquy* of Ælfric.' *Leeds Studies in English*, n.s., 29 (1998): 137–52.

– 'Learning Latin in Anglo-Saxon England: Traditions, Texts and Techniques.' In *Learning and Literacy in Medieval England and Abroad*, edited by Sarah Rees Jones, 7–29. Utrecht Studies in Medieval Literacy 3. Turnhout: Brepols, 2003.

– 'Ælfric's Grammatical Triad.' In *Form and Content of Instruction in Anglo-Saxon England in the Light of Contemporary Manuscript Evidence*, edited by Patrizia Lendinara, Loredana Lazzari, and Maria Amalia D'Aronco, 285–307. Turnhout: Brepols, 2007.

Hofstetter, Walter. 'Winchester and the Standardization of Old English Vocabulary.' *ASE* 17 (1988): 139–61.

– *Winchester und der spätaltenglische Sprachgebrauch: Untersuchungen zur geographischen und zeitlichen Verbreitung altenglischer Synonyme.* Texte und Untersuchungen zur Englischen Philologie 14. Munich: Wilhelm Fink, 1987.

Holland, Dorothy, William Lachicotte Jr., Debra Skinner, and Carole Cain. *Identity and Agency in Cultural Worlds.* Cambridge, MA: Harvard University Press, 1998.

Hollis, Stephanie. 'The Old English "Ritual of the Admission of Mildrith" (London, Lambeth Palace 427, fol. 210).' *JEGP* 97.3 (1998): 311–21.

Hollis, Stephanie, ed., with W.R. Barnes, Rebecca Hayward, Kathleen Loncar, and Michael Wright. *Writing the Wilton Women: Goscelin's 'Legend of Edith' and 'Liber confortatorius.'* Medieval Women: Texts and Contexts 9. Turnhout: Brepols, 2004.

Hollis, Stephanie, and Jocelyn Wogan-Browne, 'St Albans and Women's Monasticism: Lives and Their Foundations in Christina's World.' In *Christina of Markyate: A Twelfth-Century Holy Woman*, edited by Samuel Fanous and Henrietta Leyser, 25–52. London: Routledge, 2005.

Hollister, C. Warren. *Henry I.* Edited and completed by Amanda Clark Frost. New Haven, CT: Yale University Press, 2001.

Huneycutt, Lois L. *Matilda of Scotland: A Study in Medieval Queenship.* Woodbridge: Boydell Press, 2003.

Hyams, Paul R. 'Trial by Ordeal.' In *On the Laws and Customs of England: Essays in Honor of Samuel E. Thorne*, edited by Morris S. Arnold, et al., 90–126. Chapel Hill: University of North Carolina Press, 1981.

Jackson, Peter. 'Vitae Patrum.' In *Sources of Anglo-Saxon Culture: A Trial Version*, edited by Frederick M. Biggs, Thomas D. Hill, and Paul E. Szarmach, with the assistance of Karen Hammond, 162–5. Medieval and Renaissance Texts and Studies 74. Binghamton: State University of New York at Binghamton, 1992.

– 'The *Vitas Patrum* in Eleventh-Century Worcester.' In *England in the Eleventh Century: Proceedings of the 1990 Harlaxton Symposium,* edited by Carola Hicks, 119–34. Harlaxton Medieval Studies 2. Stamford: Paul Watkins, 1992.

– 'Ælfric and the Purpose of Christian Marriage: A Reconsideration of the *Life of Æthelthryth*, lines 120–30.' *ASE* 29 (2000): 235–60.

– 'Ælfric and the "Uita Patrum" in Catholic Homily I.36.' In *Essays on Anglo-Saxon and Related Themes in Memory of Lynne Grundy,* edited by Jane Roberts and Janet Nelson, 259–72. King's College London Medieval Studies 17. London: King's College London, Centre for Late Antique & Medieval Studies, 2000.

Jaeger, C. Stephen. *Ennobling Love: In Search of a Lost Sensibility*. Philadelphia: University of Pennsylvania Press, 1999.

Jayatilaka, Rohini. 'The *Regula Sancti Benedicti* in Late Anglo-Saxon England: The Manuscripts and Their Readers.' PhD thesis, University of Oxford, 1996.

Jestice, Phyllis G. *Wayward Monks and the Religious Revolution of the Eleventh Century*. Leiden: Brill, 1997.

Johnson, Penelope D. *Prayer, Patronage, and Power: The Abbey of la Trinité, Vendôme, 1032–1187*. New York: New York University Press, 1981.

Jones, Alex I. 'Ælfric's Life of Saint Cuthbert.' *Parergon* 10.1 (1992): 35–43.

Jones, Christopher A. '*Meatim sed et rustica*: Ælfric of Eynsham as a Medieval Latin Author.' *JML* 8 (1998): 1–57.

– 'The Irregular Life in Ælfric Bata's *Colloquies*.' *Leeds Studies in English*, n.s., 37 (2006): 241–60.

– 'Ælfric and the Limits of "Benedictine Reform."' In *A Companion to Ælfric*, edited by Hugh Magennis and Mary Swan, 67–108. Brill's Companions to the Christian Tradition 18. Leiden: Brill, 2009.

Jong, Mayke de. 'Growing Up in a Carolingian Monastery: Magister Hildemar and His Oblates.' *Journal of Medieval History* 9 (1983): 99–128.

– *In Samuel's Image: Child Oblation in the Early Medieval West*. Leiden: E.J. Brill, 1996.

Kane, Robert Kane. *The Significance of Free Will*. New York: Oxford University Press, 1999.

– *A Contemporary Introduction to Free Will*. Oxford: Oxford University Press, 2005.

Kardong, Terrence G. 'The Earliest Commentator on RB: Smaragdus on Benedict's Prologue.' *American Benedictine Review* 55.2 (June 2004): 171–93.

Karkov, Catherine E. 'Pictured in the Heart: The Ediths at Wilton.' In *Intertexts: Studies in Anglo-Saxon Culture Presented to Paul E. Szarmach*, edited by Virginia Blanton and Helene Scheck, 273–85. Tempe, AZ: Arizona Center for Medieval and Renaissance Studies, 2008.

Kehnel, Annette. 'Das Gehorsamsparadox: Vorüberlegungen zu einer Kulturhistorischen Interpretation der evangelischen Räte.' In *Oboedientia: Zu Formen und Grenzen von Macht und Unterordnung im mittelalterlichen Religiosentum*, edited by Sébastien Barret and Gert Melville, 69–82. Vita regularis 27. Münster: Lit Verlag, 2005.

Kelly, J.N.D. *Jerome, His Life, Writings, and Controversies*. 2nd ed. New York: Harper and Row, 1998.

– *Early Christian Doctrines*. 5th rev ed. London: Continuum, 2000.

Ker, N.R. *Catalogue of Manuscripts Containing Anglo-Saxon*. Oxford: Clarendon Press, 1957. Reissued with supplement, 1990.

Keynes, Simon. 'Regenbald the Chancellor [*sic*].' *ANS* 10 (1988): 185–222.

Kittredge, Cynthia Briggs. *Community and Authority: The Rhetoric of Obedience in the Pauline Tradition*. Harrisburg, PA: Trinity Press International, 1998.

Kleist, Aaron J. *Striving with Grace: Views of Free Will in Anglo-Saxon England*. Toronto: University of Toronto Press, 2008.

Knappe, Gabriele. 'Classical Rhetoric in Anglo-Saxon England.' *ASE* 27 (1998): 5–29.

Knowles, David, C.N.L. Brooke, and Vera C.M. London, eds. *The Heads of Religious Houses, England and Wales*. Vol. 1, *940–1216*. 2nd ed., with new material by C.N.L. Brooke. Cambridge: Cambridge University Press, 2001.

Knowles, Dom David. *The Monastic Order in England*. 2nd ed. Cambridge: Cambridge University Press, 1963. Reprint, 1966.

Krier, Theresa. *Birth Passages: Maternity and Nostalgia, Antiquity to Shakespeare*. Ithaca, NY: Cornell University Press, 2001.

Kristeva, Julia. *The Sense and Non-sense of Revolt: The Powers and Limits of Psychoanalysis*. Vol. 1. Translated by Jeanine Herman. New York: Columbia University Press, 2000.

– *Revolt, She Said*. Translated by Brian O'Keeffe. Edited by Sylvère Lotringer. Los Angeles: Semiotext(e): 2002.

Lacan, Jacques. *The Seminar of Jacques Lacan, Book XX*. Edited by Jacques-Alain Miller. Translated with notes by Bruce Fink. New York: W.W. Norton, 1998.

Lahaye-Geusen, Maria. *Das Opfer der Kinder: Ein Beitrag zur Liturgie- und Sozialgeschichte des Mönachtums im Hohen Mittelalter*. Münsteraner theologische Abhandlungen 13. Altenberge: Oros Verlag, 1991.

Lapidge, Michael. 'The Origin of CCCC 163.' *TCBS* 81.1 (1981): 18–28.

– 'Bede's Metrical *Vita S. Cuthberti*.' In *St. Cuthbert: His Cult and His Community to AD 1200*, edited by Gerald Bonner, David Rollason, and Clare Stancliffe, 77–93. Woodbridge: Boydell Press, 1989.

– *Anglo-Latin Literature 900–1066*. London: Hambledon Press, 1993.

– 'Abbot Germanus, Winchcombe, Ramsey and the Cambridge Psalter.' In his *Anglo-Latin Literature 900–1066*, 387–417 and 490 at 405–14.

– 'Æthelwold as Scholar and Teacher.' In his *Anglo-Latin Literature 900–1066*, 183–211.

– 'B. and the *Vita S. Dunstani*.' In his *Anglo-Latin Literature 900–1066*, 280–92 and 487.

– 'Ealdred of York and MS Cotton Vitellius E. xii.' In his *Anglo-Latin Literature 900–1066*, 453–67 and 492.

– 'The Hermeneutic Style in Tenth-Century Anglo-Latin Literature.' In his *Anglo-Latin Literature 900–1066*, 105–49 and 474–79.

– 'Schools, Learning and Literature in Tenth-Century England.' In his *Anglo-Latin Literature 900–1066*, 1–48 and 469.
– *Anglo-Latin Literature 600–899*. London: Hambledon Press, 1996.
– 'The Study of Latin Texts in Late Anglo-Saxon England.' In his *Anglo-Latin Literature 600–899*, 455–98 and 516.
– 'Byrhtferth and Oswald.' In *St Oswald of Worcester: His Life and Influence*, edited by Nicholas Brooks and Catherine Cubitt, 64–83. London: Leicester University Press, 1996.
– *The Anglo-Saxon Library*. Oxford: Oxford University Press, 2006.
Lapidge, Michael, and Rosalind C. Love. 'The Latin Hagiography of England and Wales (600–1550).' In vol. 3 of *Hagiographies*, edited by Guy Philippart, 203–325. Turnhout: Brepols, 2001.
Latham, R.E., and D.R. Howlett. *Dictionary of Medieval Latin from British Sources*. London: Oxford University Press, 1975.
Latzke, Therese. 'Robert von Arbrissel, Ermengard, und Eva.' *Mittellateinisches Jahrbuch* 19 (1984): 116–54.
Law, Vivien. 'The Study of Grammar.' In *Carolingian Culture: Emulation and Innovation*, edited by Rosamond McKitterick, 88–110. Cambridge: Cambridge University Press, 1994.
– *Grammar and Grammarians in the Early Middle Ages*. London: Longmans, 1997.
Lees, Clare A., and Gillian R. Overing. *Double Agents: Women and Clerical Culture in Anglo-Saxon England*. Philadelphia: University of Pennsylvania Press, 2001.
Leighton, Albert C. *Transport and Communication in Early Medieval Europe AD 500–1100*. New York: Barnes and Noble, 1972.
Lendinara, Patrizia. 'The World of Anglo-Saxon Learning.' In *The Cambridge Companion to Old English Literature*, edited by Malcolm Godden and Michael Lapidge, 264–81. Cambridge: Cambridge University Press, 1991.
'The *Colloquy* of Ælfric and the *Colloquy* of Ælfric Bata.' In *Anglo-Saxon Glosses and Glossaries*, edited by Patrizia Lendinara, 207–87. Aldershot: Ashgate, 1999.
– 'Instructional Manuscripts in England: The Tenth- and Eleventh-Century Codices and the Early Norman Ones.' In *Form and Content of Instruction in Anglo-Saxon England in the Light of Contemporary Manuscript Evidence*, edited by Patrizia Lendinara, Loredana Lazzari, and Maria Amalia D'Aronco, 59–113. Turnhout: Brepols, 2008.
Lewis, Charlton Thomas, and Charles Short. *A Latin Dictionary*. Oxford: Clarendon Press, 1966.
Licence, Tom. *Hermits and Recluses in English Society 950–1200*. Oxford: Oxford University Press, 2011.

– 'Evidence of Recluses in Eleventh-Century England.' *ASE* 36 (2007): 221–34.

Lorenz, Rudolf. 'Der Augustinismus Prospers von Aquitanien.' *Zeitschrift für Kirchengeschichte* 73 (1962): 217–52.

Love, Rosalind C. 'Eadgyth [Edith], St.' In *The Blackwell Encyclopaedia of Anglo-Saxon England*, edited by Michael Lapidge, John Blair, Simon Keynes, and Donald Scragg, 150. Oxford: Blackwell, 1999.

– 'Goscelin of Saint–Bertin and the Life of St Amelberga.' In *Latin Learning and English Lore: Studies in Anglo-Saxon Literature for Michael Lapidge*, edited by Katherine O'Brien O'Keeffe and Andy Orchard, 2 vols., II: 232–52. Toronto: University of Toronto Press, 2005.

– ed. and trans. *Three Eleventh-Century Anglo-Latin Saints' Lives*. OMT. Oxford: Clarendon Press, 1996.

Loyn, H.R. 'Kinship in Anglo-Saxon England.' *ASE* 3 (1974): 197–209.

– 'The Scholarship of Monasticism.' *History Today* (November 1980): 48–9.

– *The Governance of Anglo-Saxon England, 500–1087.* Stanford: Stanford University Press, 1984.

MacDonald, Scott. 'Primal Sin.' In *The Augustinian Tradition*, edited by Gareth B. Matthews, 110–39. Berkeley: University of California Press, 1999.

MacKendrick, Karmen. *Fragmentation and Memory: Meditations on Christian Doctrine.* New York: Fordham University Press, 2008.

Magennis, Hugh, and Mary Swan, eds. *A Companion to Ælfric*. Leiden: Brill, 2009.

Magne, Jean. 'La prière de consécration des vierges "Deus castorum corporum,"' *Ephemerides Liturgica* 72 (1958): 245–67.

Manning, Eug[ène]. 'La signification de 'militare-militia-miles' dans la Règle de saint Benoît.' *Revue Bénédictine* 72 (1962): 137–8.

Marsden, Richard. *The Cambridge Old English Reader*. Cambridge: Cambridge University Press, 2004.

Mason, Emma. *St Wulfstan of Worcester ca 1008–1095*. Oxford: Basil Blackwell, 1990.

Mayr-Harting, Henry. 'Functions of a Twelfth-Century Recluse,' *History* 60 (1975): 337–52.

Menzer, Melinda. 'Ælfric's *Grammar*: Solving the Problem of the English-Language Text.' *Neophilologus* 83.4 (1999): 637–52.

– 'Ælfric's English *Grammar.*' *JEGP* 103.1 (2004): 106–24.

Metz, René. 'Les conditions juridiques de la consécration des vierges dans la liturgie latine des origines à nos jours.' *Revue de droit canonique* 1 (1951): 261–80.

– *La consécration des vierges dans l'église Romaine: étude d'histoire de la liturgie*. Paris: Presses Universitaires de France, 1954.

Miller, Patricia Cox. '"A Dubious Twilight": Reflections on Dreams in Patristic Literature.' *Church History* 55.2 (1986): 153–64.
– 'The Blazing Body: Ascetic Desire in Jerome's Letter to Eustochium.' *Journal of Early Christian Studies* 1.1 (1993): 21–45.
Mills, Robert. 'Can the Virgin Martyr Speak?' In *Medieval Virginities*, edited by Anke Bernau, Ruth Evans, and Sarah Salih, 187–213. Toronto: University of Toronto Press, 2003.
Mitchell, Bruce. *Old English Syntax*. 2 vols. New York: Oxford University Press, 1985.
Morrison, Karl F. *Understanding Conversion.* Charlottesville: University of Virginia Press, 1992.
– *Conversion and Text: The Cases of Augustine of Hippo, Herman-Judah, and Constantine Tsatsos.* Charlottesville: University Press of Virginia, 1992.
Mulder-Bakker, Anneke B. *Lives of the Anchoresses: The Rise of the Urban Recluse in Medieval Europe*. Translated by Myra Heerspink Scholz. Philadelphia: University of Pennsylvania Press, 2005.
Nelson, Janet. 'The Wary Widow.' In *Property and Power in the Early Middle Ages*, edited by Wendy Davies and Paul Fouracre, 82–113. Cambridge: Cambridge University Press, 1995.
O'Brien O'Keeffe, Katherine. 'Body and Law in Late Anglo-Saxon England.' *ASE* 27 (1998): 209–32.
– 'Guthlac's Crossings.' *Quaestio* 2 (2001): 1–26.
– 'Goscelin and the Consecration of Eve.' *ASE* 35 (2006): 251–70.
– 'Goscelin, the *Liber confortatorius*, and the Library of Peterborough.' In *Poetry, Place and Gender: Studies in Medieval Culture in Honor of Helen Damico*, edited by Catherine Karkov, 151–70. Kalamazoo, MI: Medieval Institute Publications, 2009.
O'Brien O'Keeffe, Katherine, and Andy Orchard, eds. *Latin Learning and English Lore: Studies in Anglo-Saxon Literature for Michael Lapidge*. 2 vols. Toronto: University of Toronto Press, 2005.
O'Daly, Gerard. 'Predestination and Freedom in Augustine's Ethics.' In *The Philosophy in Christianity*, edited by Godfrey Vesey, 85–97. Royal Institute of Philosophy Lecture Series 25. Cambridge: Cambridge University Press, 1989.
Omont, H. *Catalogue général des manuscrits des bibliothèques publiques de France*. Vol. 3. Paris, 1885.
Ortner, Sherry B. 'Subjectivity and Cultural Critique.' *Anthropological Theory* 5.1 (2005): 31–52.
Owen-Crocker, Gale R. *Dress in Anglo-Saxon England*. Rev. ed. Woodbridge: Boydell Press, 2004.

Parkes, M.B. '*Rædan, areccan, smeagan*: How the Anglo-Saxons Read.' *ASE* 26 (1997): 1–22.

Pelteret, David A.E. 'The Roads of Anglo-Saxon England.' *Wiltshire Archaeological and Natural History Magazine* 79 (1985): 155–63.

Pfaff, Richard W. 'Eadui Basan: Scriptorum Princeps?' In *England in the Eleventh Century: Proceedings of the 1990 Harlaxton Symposium*, edited by Carola Hicks, 267–83. Stamford: Paul Watkins, 1992.

– ed. *The Liturgical Books of Anglo-Saxon England.* Old English Newsletter Subsidia 23. Kalamazoo, MI: Medieval Institute Publications, 1995.

Philpott, Mark. 'Lanfranc's Canonical Collection and "the Law of the Church,"' In *Lanfranco di Pavia e l'Europa del secolo XI nel IX centenario della morte (1089–1989)*, edited by Giulio d'Onofrio, 131–47. Italia Sacra: Studi e documenti di storia ecclesiastica 51. Rome: Herder, 1993.

– '"In primis … omnis humanae prudentiae inscius et expers putaretur": St Anselm's Knowledge of Canon Law.' In *Anselm: Aosta, Bec and Canterbury: Papers in Commemoration of the Nine-Hundreth Anniversary of Anselm's Enthronement as Archbishop, 25 September 1093*, edited by D.E. Luscombe and G.R. Evans. Sheffield: Academic Press, 1996.

Ponesse, Matthew D. 'Editorial Practice in Smaragdus of St Mihiel's Commentary on the Rule of St Benedict.' *Early Medieval Europe* 18.1 (2010): 61–91.

Porter, David W. 'The Latin Syllabus in Anglo-Saxon Monastic Schools.' *Neophilologus* 78.3 (1994): 463–82.

– 'Ælfric's *Colloquy* and Ælfric Bata.' *Neophilologus* 80 (1996): 639–60.

Powell, Timothy E. 'The "Three Orders" of Society in Anglo-Saxon England.' *ASE* 23 (1994): 103–32.

Quinn, Patricia A. *Better Than the Sons of Kings: Boys and Monks in the Early Middle Ages.* New York: Peter Lang, 1989.

Rabin, Andrew. 'Female Advocacy and Royal Protection in Tenth-Century England: The Legal Career of Queen Ælfthryth.' *Speculum* 84.2 (2009): 261–88.

Radding, Charles M. *A World Made by Men: Cognition and Society, 400–1200.* Chapel Hill: University of North Carolina Press, 1985.

Raine, James. *The Historians of the Church of York and its Archbishops.* 3 vols. RS 71. London, 1879–94. Reprint, Wiesbaden: Kraus, 1965.

Riché, Pierre. 'L'étude du vocabulaire latin dans les écoles Anglo-saxonnes au début du Xe siècle.' In *La lexicographie du latin médiéval et ses rapports avec les recherches actuelles sur la civilisation du moyen-âge*, 115–24. Paris: Centre National de la Recherche Scientifique, 1981.

– 'La vie quotidienne dans les écoles monastiques d'après les colloques scolaires.' In *Sous la règle de saint Benoît: structures monastiques et société en France du Moyen Âge à l'époque moderne*. Geneva: Librairie Droz, 1982.
– *Écoles et enseignement dans le Haut Moyen Âge*. Paris: Picard, 1989. Reprint, with additional bibliography of *Les écoles et l'enseignement dans l'occident chrétien*, Paris, 1979.
– *Éducation et culture dans l'occident barbare VIe–VIIIe siècle*. 4th ed. Paris: Éditions du Seuil, 1995.
Ridyard, Susan J. *The Royal Saints of Anglo-Saxon England: A Study of West Saxon and East Anglian Cults*. Cambridge: Cambridge University Press, 1988.
Rist, John M. 'Augustine on Free Will and Predestination.' *Journal of Theological Studies*, n.s., 20.2 (1969): 420–47.
– *Augustine: Ancient Thought Baptized*. Cambridge: Cambridge University Press, 1994.
Rogers, Katherin. *Anselm on Freedom*. Oxford: Oxford University Press, 2008.
Rollason, David W. *The Mildreth Legend: A Study in Early Medieval Hagiography in England*. Leicester: Leicester University Press, 1982.
– 'The Concept of Sanctity in the Early Lifes of St Dunstan.' In *St Dunstan: His Life, Times and Cult*, edited by Nigel Ramsay, Margaret Sparks, and Tim Tatton-Brown, 261–72. Woodbridge: Boydell Press, 1992.
Rubin, Gayle. 'The Traffic in Women: Notes on the "Political Economy" of Sex.' In *Toward an Anthropology of Women*, edited by Rayna R. Reiter, 157–210. New York: Monthly Review Press, 1975.
Rubenstein, Jay. 'The Life and Writings of Osbern of Canterbury.' In *Canterbury and the Norman Conquest: Churches, Saints and Scholars 1066–1109*, edited by Richard Eales and Richard Sharpe, 27–40. London: Hambledon Press, 1995.
Ruffing, John. 'The Labor Structure of Ælfric's *Colloquy*.' In *The Work of Work: Servitude, Slavery, and Labor in Medieval England*, edited by Allen J. Frantzen and Douglas Moffat, 55–70. Glasgow: Cruithne Press, 1994.
Salih, Sarah. *Versions of Virginity in Late Medieval England*. Cambridge: D.S. Brewer, 2001.
Schabram, Hans. Review of *The Harley Latin-Old English Glossary*, by Robert T. Oliphant. *Anglia* 86 (1968): 495–500.
Searle, Eleanor. *Predatory Kinship and the Creation of Norman Power, 840–1066*. Berkeley: University of California Press, 1988.
– 'Women and the Legitimisation of Succession at the Norman Conquest.' *ANS* 3 (1981 [for 1980]): 159–70 and 226–9.
Sewell, Jr., William H. *Logics of History: Social Theory and Social Transformation*. Chicago: University of Chicago Press, 2005.

Sharpe, Richard. 'Words and Music by Goscelin of Canterbury.' *Early Music* 19, no. 1 (1991): 94–7.

– 'King Harold's Daughter.' *Haskins Society Journal* 19 (2007): 1–27.

– 'Anselm as Author: Publishing in the Late Eleventh Century.' *JML* 19 (2009): 1–87.

Sharpe, Richard, and Teresa Webber. 'Four Early Booklets of Anselm's Works from Salisbury Cathedral.' *Scriptorium* 63 (2009): 58–72.

Sims-Williams, Patrick. 'Some Functions of Origin Stories in Early Medieval Wales.' In *History and Heroic Tales: A Symposium*, edited by Tore Nyberg et al., 97–132. Odense: Odense University Press, 1985.

Smith, Craig S. 'Abduction, Often Violent, a Kyrgyz Wedding Rite.' *New York Times*, 30 April 2005.

Smith, Julia M.H. 'The Problem of Female Sanctity in Carolingian Europe, ca 780–920.' *Past and Present* 146 (1995): 3–37.

Smith, Paul. *Discerning the Subject*. Minneapolis: University of Minnesota Press, 1988.

Southern, R.W. *Saint Anselm and His Biographer: A Study of Monastic Life and Thought 1059–ca 1130*. Cambridge: Cambridge University Press, 1963.

– *Saint Anselm: A Portrait in a Landscape*. Cambridge: Cambridge University Press, 1990.

Špidlík, Tomáš. *The Spirituality of the Christian East: A Systematic Handbook*. Translated by Anthony P. Gythiel. Kalamazoo, MI: Cistercian Publications, 1986.

Stafford, Pauline. *Queens, Concubines, and Dowagers: The King's Wife in the Early Middle Ages.* Athens: University of Georgia Press, 1983.

– 'Queens, Nunneries, and Reforming Churchmen: Gender, Religious Status, and Reform in Tenth- and Eleventh-Century England.' *Past and Present* 163 (1999): 3–35.

Stancliffe, Clare. 'Cuthbert and the Polarity between Pastor and Solitary.' In *St Cuthbert: His Cult and His Community to AD 1200*, edited by Gerald Bonner, David Rollason, and Clare Stancliffe, 21–44. Woodbridge: Boydell Press, 1989.

Stanton, Robert. *The Culture of Translation in Anglo-Saxon England*. Cambridge: D.S. Brewer, 2002.

Steidle, Basilius. '"Per oboedientiae laborem … per inoboedientiae desidiam" (I): Zu Prolog 2 der Regel St. Benedikts.' *Erbe und Auftrag* 53 (1977): 428–35.

– '"Per oboedientiae laborem … per inoboedientiae desidiam" (II): Zu Prolog 2 der Regel St. Benedikts.' *Erbe und Auftrag* 54 (1978): 200–16.

Stephenson, Rebecca. 'Ælfric of Eynsham and Hermeneutic Latin: *Meatim sed et rustica* Reconsidered.' *JML* 16 (2006): 111–41.

– 'Scapegoating the Secular Clergy: The Hermeneutic Style as a Form of Monastic Self-Definition.' *ASE* 38 (2010): 101–35.

Stock, Brian. *The Implications of Literacy: Written Language and Models of Interpretation in the Eleventh and Twelfth Centuries.* Princeton: Princeton University Press, 1983.

Straw, Carole. *Gregory the Great: Perfection in Imperfection.* Berkeley: University of California Press, 1988.

Stroud, Daphne. 'Eve, Nun of Wilton and Anchoress of Angers.' *Hatcher Review* 4, no. 37 (Spring 1994): 3–13.

– 'Eve of Wilton and Goscelin of St Bertin at Old Sarum ca 1070–1078.' *Wiltshire Archaeological and Natural History Magazine* 99 (2006): 204–12.

Stryker, William Garlington. 'The Latin-Old English Glossary in MS. Cotton Cleopatra A.III.' PhD dissertation, Stanford University, 1951.

Stump, Eleonore. 'Augustine on Free Will.' In *The Cambridge Companion to Augustine*, edited by Eleonore Stump and Norman Kretzmann, 124–47. Cambridge: Cambridge University Press, 2001.

Swan, Mary. 'Identity and Ideology in Ælfric's Prefaces.' In *A Companion to Ælfric*, edited by Hugh Magennis and Mary Swan, 249–69. Leiden: Brill, 2009.

Taft, Robert. *The Liturgy of the Hours in East and West.* Collegeville, MN: Liturgical Press, 1986.

Temple, Elżbieta. *Anglo-Saxon Manuscripts, 900–1066.* Survey of Manuscripts Illuminated in the British Isles 2. London: Harvey Miller, 1976.

Thacker, Alan. 'Æthelwold and Abingdon.' In *Bishop Æthelwold: His Career and Influence*, edited by Barbara Yorke, 43–64. Woodbridge: Boydell Press, 1988.

Toth, Karl. 'Altenglische Interlinearglossen zu Prospers *Epigrammata* und *Versus ad coniugem.*' *Anglia* 102 (1984): 1–36.

Townsend, David. 'Anglo-Latin Hagiography and the Norman Transition.' *Exemplaria* 3.2 (1991): 385–433.

Vaughn, Sally N. *St Anselm and the Handmaidens of God: A Study of Anselm's Correspondence with Women.* Turnhout: Brepols, 2002.

Visser, Sandra, and Thomas Williams. 'Anselm's Account of Freedom.' In *The Cambridge Companion to Anselm*, edited by Brian Davies and Brian Leftow, 179–203. Cambridge: Cambridge University Press, 2004.

Van Engen, John. 'The "Crisis of Cenobitism" Reconsidered: Benedictine Monasticism in the Years 1050–1150.' *Speculum* 61 (1986): 269–304.

– 'Professing Religion: From Liturgy to Law.' *Viator* 29 (1998): 323–43.

Vanderputten, Steven. '*Oboedientia.* Réformes et discipline monastique au début du XIe siècle.' *Cahiers de civilisation médiévale* 53 (2010): 255–66.

Vogüé, Adalbert de. 'Persévérer au monastère jusqu'à la mort. La stabilité chez saint Benoît et autour de lui.' *Collectanea Cisterciensia* 43 (1981): 337–65.

– *The Rule of Saint Benedict: A Doctrinal and Spiritual Commentary*. Translated by John Baptist Hasbrouck. Kalamazoo, MI: Cistercian Publications, 1983. First published as *La Règle de saint Benoît, VII, commentaire doctrinal et spirituel*. Paris, 1977.

– *Les règles monastiques anciennes 400–700*. Typologie des sources du moyen âge occidental 46. Turnhout: Brepols, 1985.

– 'Obéissance et autorité dans le monachisme ancien jusqu'á Saint Benoît.' In *'Imaginer la théologie catholique': permanence et transformations de la foi en attendant Jésus-Christ: mélanges offerts à Ghislain Lafont*, edited by Jeremy Driscoll, 565–600. Rome: Centro Studi S. Anselmo, 2000.

Voss, Manfred. 'Strykers Edition des alphabetischen Cleopatraglossars: Corrigenda und Addenda.' *Arbeiten aus Anglistik und Amerikanistik* 13 (1988): 123–38.

Walde, A., and J.B. Hofmann. *Lateinisches etymologisches Wörterbuch*. 3rd ed. 3 vols. Heidelberg: Carl Winter's Universitätsbuchhandlung, 1938–56.

Warren, Ann K. 'The Nun as Anchoress: England 1100–1500.' In *Distant Echoes: Medieval Religious Women*, edited by John A. Nichols and Lillian Thomas Shank, I: 197–212. Kalamazoo, MI: Cistercian Publications, 1984.

– *Anchorites and Their Patrons in Medieval England*. Berkeley: University of California Press, 1985.

Watson, Gary, ed., *Free Will*, 2nd ed. Oxford: Oxford University Press, 2003.

Wetzel, James. 'The Recovery of Free Agency in the Theology of St Augustine.' *Harvard Theological Review* 80 (1987): 101–25.

– *Augustine and the Limits of Virtue*. Cambridge: Cambridge University Press, 1992.

Whalen, Georges. 'Patronage Engendered: How Goscelin Allayed the Concerns of Nuns' Discriminatory Public.' In *Women, the Book and the Godly: Selected Proceedings of the St Hilda's Conference, 1993*. Vol. 1, edited by Lesley Smith and Jane H.M. Taylor, 123–35. Cambridge: D.S. Brewer, 1995.

Whatley, E. Gordon. 'Acta Sanctorum.' In *Sources of Anglo-Saxon Literary Culture I: Abbo of Fleury, Abbo of Saint-Germain-des-Prés, and Acta Sanctorum*, edited by Frederick M. Biggs, Thomas D. Hill, Paul E. Szarmach, and E. Gordon Whatley, 22–486. Kalamazoo: Medieval Institute Publications, Western Michigan University, 2001.

Widerker, David and Michael McKenna, eds., *Moral Responsibility and Alternative Possibilities: Essays on the Importance of Alternative Possibilities*. Burlington, VT: Ashgate, 2003.

Williams, Edna Rees. 'Ælfric's Grammatical Terminology.' *PMLA* 73 (1958): 453–62.

Wilmart, André. 'Ève et Goscelin (I).' *Revue Bénédictine* 46 (1934): 414–38.
– 'Ève et Goscelin (II).' *Revue Bénédictine* 50 (1938): 42–83.
Wilson, Susan E. *The Life and After-Life of St John of Beverly: The Evolution of the Cult of an Anglo-Saxon Saint.* Aldershot: Ashgate, 2006.
Winterbottom, Michael, and Michael Lapidge, eds. *The Early Lives of St Dunstan.* OMT. Oxford: Oxford University Press, 2011.
Winterbottom, Michael, and R.M. Thompson, eds. *William of Malmesbury, Saints' Lives: Lives of SS Wulfstan, Dunstan, Patrick, Benignus and Indract.* OMT. Oxford: Clarendon Press, 2002.
Wogan-Browne, Jocelyn. 'The Virgin's Tale.' In *Feminist Readings in Middle English Literature: The Wife of Bath and All Her Sect*, edited by Ruth Evans and Lesley Johnson, 165–94. London: Routledge, 1994.
– *Saints' Lives and Women's Literary Culture ca 1150–1500: Virginity and Its Authorizations.* Oxford: Oxford University Press, 2001.
Wormald, Patrick. 'Æthelwold and His Continental Counterparts: Contact, Comparison, Contrast.' In *Bishop Æthelwold: His Career and Influence*, edited by Barbara Yorke, 13–42. Woodbridge: Boydell Press, 1988. Reprint, 1997.
– *The Making of English Law: King Alfred to the Twelfth Century.* Vol. 1. Oxford: Blackwell, 1999.
Wright, Roger. 'Foreigners' Latin and Romance: Boniface and Pope Gregory II.' In *A Sociophilological Study of Late Latin*, edited by Roger Wright, 95–109. Utrecht Studies in Medieval Literacy 10. Turnhout: Brepols, 2002.
Wyatt, Alfred J. *An Anglo-Saxon Reader.* Cambridge: Cambridge University Press, 1919.
Yeo, Richard. *The Structure and Content of Monastic Profession.* Studia Anselmiana 83. Rome: Pontificio Ateneo S. Anselmo, 1982.
Yerkes, David. *The Two Versions of Waerferth's Translation of Gregory's Dialogues: An Old English Thesaurus.* Toronto: University of Toronto Press, 1979.
Yorke, Barbara. '"Sisters under the Skin"? Anglo-Saxon Nuns and Nunneries in Southern England.' *Reading Medieval Studies* 15 (1989): 95–117.
– *Nunneries and the Anglo-Saxon Royal Houses.* London: Continuum, 2003.
– 'The Legitimacy of St Edith.' *Haskins Society Journal* 11 (2003 for 1998): 97–113.
– 'The Women in Edgar's Life.' In *Edgar, King of the English 959–975*, edited by Donald Scragg, 143–57. Woodbridge, Suffolk: Boydell Press, 2008.
Zimmermann, Gerd. *Ordensleben und Lebensstandard: Die Cura Corporis in den Ordensvorschriften des abendländischen Hochmittelalters.* Münster Westfalen: Aschendorff, 1973.

Index

Toronto Anglo-Saxon Series

1 *Preaching the Converted: The Style and Rhetoric of the Vercelli Book Homilies*, Samantha Zacher
2 *Say What I Am Called: The Old English Riddles of the Exeter Book and the Anglo-Latin Riddle Tradition*, Dieter Bitterli
3 *The Aesthetics of Nostalgia: Historical Representation in Anglo-Saxon Verse*, Renée Trilling
4 *New Readings in the Vercelli Book*, edited by Samantha Zacher and Andy Orchard
5 *Authors, Audiences, and Old English Verse*, Thomas A. Bredehoft
6 *On Aesthetics in* Beowulf *and Other Old English Poems*, edited by John M. Hill
7 *Old English Metre: An Introduction*, Jun Terasawa
8 *Anglo-Saxon Psychologies in the Vernacular and Latin Traditions*, Leslie Lockett
9 *The Body Legal in Barbarian Law*, Lisi Oliver
10 *Old English Literature and the Old Testament*, edited by Michael Fox and Manish Sharma
11 *Stealing Obedience: Narratives of Agency and Identity in Later Anglo-Saxon England*, Katherine O'Brien O'Keeffe
12 *Traditional Subjectivities: The Old English Poetics of Mentality*, Britt Mize
13 *Land and Book: Literature and Land Tenure in Anglo-Saxon England*, Scott T. Smith
14 *Writing Women Saints in Anglo-Saxon England*, edited by Paul E. Szarmach
15 *Anglo-Saxon Manuscripts: A Bibliographical Handlist of Manuscripts and Manuscript Fragments Written or Owned in England up to 1100*, Helmut Gneuss and Michael Lapidge

16 *The King's Body: Burial and Succession in Anglo-Saxon England*, Nicole Marafioti

17 *From Lawmen to Plowmen: Anglo-Saxon Legal Tradition and the School of Langland*, Stephen Yeager

18 *The Politics of Language: Byrthferth, Aelfric, and the Multilingual Identity of the Benedictine Reform*, Rebecca Stephenson

www.ingramcontent.com/pod-product-compliance
Lightning Source LLC
Chambersburg PA
CBHW030841030326
40538CB00001B/19
* 9 7 8 1 4 8 7 5 2 0 6 2 5 *